Early Praise for *Programming Kotlin*

Venkat is someone that can take any topic and make it pleasurable and easy to understand. In this book he will take you on an adventure of learning Kotlin in a clear and pragmatic way, providing real-world usages, while at the same time showing you the benefits of the language.

➤ **Hadi Hariri**
  Developer Advocate, JetBrains

This book will open the door to the amazing world of Kotlin. You'll be guided along this journey by one of the most famous public speakers and educators of our day. Have a nice Kotlin!

➤ **Eugene Petrenko, PhD**
  Developer, Speaker, JetBrains

Enter the cave of Kotlin using this excellent book as your headlight. Gain confidence in this beautiful language as a cave explorer gains self-assurance in finding his way in a newly explored cave never seen by the human eyes before. Explore pragmatically deeper and deeper into this modern JVM language using the knowledge, hints, and guidelines provided by an extraordinary, experienced programming-language enthusiast: Venkat.

➤ **Tom Adam**
  Senior Consultant, CEO, Lambda Consulting AS

The engaging and humorous way of explaining things, as Venkat does in his talks, is also displayed in this book. It is a very well-structured and easy-to-read guide for everyone who is—or wants to begin—programming in Kotlin.

➤ **Brian Vermeer**
  Developer Advocate, Snyk

Really a perfect book to get up and running, and not just hear about the hype of Kotlin. It actually explained what's the buzz about Kotlin. Venkat did it once more! A must-read book, not just to get up and running with Kotlin but also to compare what we are missing in Java.

➤ **Zulfikar Dharmawan**
  Software Engineer, ING Bank NV

Kotlin is a very promising new language, and Venkat uses his knowledge, humor, and clear admiration for Kotlin to create a very readable and educational book. Venkat explains things very well, provides helpful advice, and even gives an occasional laugh.

➤ **Tory Zundel**
  Software Architect

The book is well-crafted with good, succinct examples—highly recommended for Java developers looking to transition into Kotlin.

➤ **Ashish Bhatia**
  Software Enginner and Blogger, ashishb.net

If you're content with Java and see no need for null-safe traversal or first-class delegation then put this book down; you're not ready. Otherwise, read this book. You will be entertained and educated simultaneously.

➤ **Daniel DeGroff**
  CTO, FusionAuth

Programming Kotlin

Creating Elegant, Expressive, and
Performant JVM and Android Applications

Venkat Subramaniam

The Pragmatic Bookshelf

Raleigh, North Carolina

Many of the designations used by manufacturers and sellers to distinguish their products are claimed as trademarks. Where those designations appear in this book, and The Pragmatic Programmers, LLC was aware of a trademark claim, the designations have been printed in initial capital letters or in all capitals. The Pragmatic Starter Kit, The Pragmatic Programmer, Pragmatic Programming, Pragmatic Bookshelf, PragProg and the linking *g* device are trademarks of The Pragmatic Programmers, LLC.

Every precaution was taken in the preparation of this book. However, the publisher assumes no responsibility for errors or omissions, or for damages that may result from the use of information (including program listings) contained herein.

Our Pragmatic books, screencasts, and audio books can help you and your team create better software and have more fun. Visit us at *https://pragprog.com*.

The team that produced this book includes:

Publisher: Andy Hunt
VP of Operations: Janet Furlow
Managing Editor: Susan Conant
Development Editor: Jacquelyn Carter
Copy Editor: Sakhi MacMillan
Indexing: Potomac Indexing, LLC
Layout: Gilson Graphics

For sales, volume licensing, and support, please contact *support@pragprog.com*.

For international rights, please contact *rights@pragprog.com*.

ISBN-13: 978-1-68050-635-8
Book version: P1.0—September 2019

Contents

Foreword xi

Acknowledgments xiii

Introduction xv

1. Hello Kotlin 1
   Reasons to Love Kotlin 3
   Why Should You Choose Kotlin? 6
   Taking Kotlin for a Ride 7
   Compile to Bytecode and Run 8
   Compiling to Other Targets 13
   Which Option to Choose? 14
   Wrapping Up 14

Part I — Scripting with Kotlin

2. Kotlin Essentials for the Java Eyes 19
   Less Typing 20
   Sensible Warnings 24
   Prefer val over var 26
   Improved Equality Check 28
   String Templates 29
   Raw Strings 30
   More Expressions, Fewer Statements 33
   Wrapping Up 35

3. Working with Functions 37
   Creating Functions 38
   Default and Named Arguments 43
   vararg and Spread 46

Destructuring   49
Wrapping Up   51

4. **External Iteration and Argument Matching** 53
Range and Iteration   54
Iterating over Arrays and Lists   57
When It's Time to Use when   58
Wrapping Up   62

5. **Using Collections** 63
Flavors of Collections   63
Using Pair and Triple   66
Arrays of Objects and Primitives   68
Using List   70
Using Set   72
Using Map   73
Wrapping Up   75

6. **Type Safety to Save the Day** 77
Any and Nothing Classes   78
Nullable References   80
Type Checking and Casting   87
Explicit Type Casting   91
Generics: Variance and Constraints of Parametric Types   93
Reified Type Parameters   101
Wrapping Up   104

Part II — Object-Oriented Kotlin

7. **Objects and Classes** 107
Objects and Singletons   107
Creating Classes   113
Companion Objects and Class Members   124
Creating Generics Classes   127
Data Classes   129
Wrapping Up   132

8. **Class Hierarchies and Inheritance** 133
Creating Interfaces and Abstract Classes   134
Nested and Inner Classes   138
Inheritance   140

Sealed Classes   144
Creating and Using Enums   145
Wrapping Up   148

9. **Extension Through Delegation** **149**
When to Choose Delegation over Inheritance?   150
Designing with Delegates   151
Delegating to a Parameter   156
Dealing with Method Collisions   157
Caveats of Kotlin Delegation   160
Delegating Variables and Properties   162
Built-in Standard Delegates   166
Wrapping Up   170

Part III — Functional Kotlin

10. **Functional Programming with Lambdas** **175**
The Functional Style   176
Lambda Expressions   179
Lambdas and Anonymous Functions   186
Closures and Lexical Scoping   188
Non-Local and Labeled return   190
Inlining Functions with Lambdas   194
Wrapping Up   201

11. **Internal Iteration and Lazy Evaluation** **203**
External vs. Internal Iterators   204
Internal Iterators   206
Sequences for Lazy Evaluation   213
Wrapping Up   218

Part IV — Elegant and Efficient Kotlin

12. **Fluency in Kotlin** **221**
Overloading Operators   222
Injecting Using Extension Functions and Properties   226
Extending Functions   234
Function Fluency with infix   235
Fluency with Any Object   236

Implicit Receivers   243
Wrapping Up   247

13. Creating Internal DSLs   249
Types and Characteristics of DSLs   250
Kotlin for Internal DSLs   251
Challenges in Building for Fluency   254
Type-Safe Builders   260
Narrowing Access with Scope Control   265
Wrapping Up   268

14. Programming Recursion and Memoization   269
The Power and Perils of Recursion   269
Tail Call Optimization   271
Memoization   274
Applying Memoization to Dynamic Programming   279
Wrapping Up   281

Part V — Programming Asynchronous Applications

15. Exploring Coroutines   285
Coroutines and Concurrency   285
Running Concurrently Using Coroutines   287
Coroutine Context and Threads   293
Debugging Coroutines   298
async and await   300
A Peek at Continuations   301
Creating Infinite Sequences   303
Wrapping Up   307

16. Asynchronous Programming   309
Programming Asynchronously   309
Exception Handling   314
Cancellations and Timeouts   318
Wrapping Up   326

Part VI — Interop and Testing

17. Intermixing Java and Kotlin   329
Joint Compilation   330
Calling Java from Kotlin   333

Calling Kotlin from Java   336
Wrapping Up   346

18. **Unit Testing with Kotlin** **347**
The Code Under Test   348
Getting the Project Files   349
Starting with a Canary Test   352
Writing Empirical Tests   353
Writing Data-Driven Tests   356
Mocking Out Dependencies   357
Testing Top-Level Functions   363
Testing Coroutines and Asynchronous Calls   366
Integrating with the Service   370
Viewing the Code Coverage   371
Taking the App for a Drive   372
Wrapping Up   373

19. **Programming Spring Applications with Kotlin** **375**
Creating a Starter Project   376
Creating a Controller   378
Creating an Entity Class   380
Creating a Repository Interface   381
Creating a Service   381
Integrating the Service with Controller   383
Taking It for a Ride   385
Wrapping Up   386

20. **Writing Android Applications with Kotlin** **387**
Creating a Project   388
Defining Domain Objects   390
Creating Layouts   391
Implementing the Activity   395
Updating the RecyclerView   399
Seeing the App in Action   401
Wrapping Up   402

A1. **Transpiling to JavaScript** **405**
A2. **Kotlin/Native** **409**
A3. **Kotlin to WebAssembly** **413**

Bibliography **417**
Index **419**

Foreword

With this book, you are going to learn Kotlin. On behalf of the Kotlin team I say: welcome!

Back in 2010, when we started Kotlin, we thought of it as a tool for Java developers to let them build what they want with ease and pleasure. We bet on type safety for excellent tooling and early detection of programming errors. We bet on interoperability with Java to give all Kotlin developers access to the vast Java ecosystem. Nowadays, Kotlin is a multiplatform language that can run on a server running JVM, on an Android device, in a web browser, on an iOS device or a Linux machine or even a microcontroller. Yet, our principles stayed the same: we let people build software with ease and pleasure, and we bet on tooling, interoperability with every platform, and on catching errors early.

Language development has multiple stages. First, you just have an idea, and at that stage I was full of doubt and at the same time was very eager to try. One can call this faith, maybe. Then you have your first program compile and run. It's starting to take some shape. Then it grows. Then you fix a lot of problems. And more problems. Then if you are lucky somebody outside your team gets excited about your language, and you are in heaven. Early adopters come and give you feedback. Then more problems, and a lot of doubt: are we ready to release? Then you just can't wait any longer, you double down on it and release 1.0. You celebrate briefly and rush to fix all the issues that the new users reported. Some time goes by, the ecosystem grows, the team grows, more users, some new features, new releases, more bugs, people write bigger projects... Then an author who was well known before you even started writes a book about your language. I am here. It's a good feeling :).

As this book assumes some knowledge of Java, you'll start where we started, and when you get to the end of the book you'll have a very good picture of the language and its practical applications within the JVM world and Android. You'll know how to do what you want with Kotlin and how it can help you.

My goal as the language designer is to make Kotlin useful to you, and Venkat has done a great job of making it enjoyable to learn.

I wish you a good time with this book. Have a nice Kotlin!

Andrey Breslav

Lead Designer of Kotlin

July, 2019

Acknowledgments

I'd like to express my deepest respect and gratitude to the Kotlin team, the developers at JetBrains who are working tirelessly on different parts of the language and related tools. I always knew they were very smart, but a short visit with them showed me also how receptive, keen, and meticulous they are in learning about the usage of the language out in the wild, so they can improve the language. Thank you, team, keep up your hard work; what you do is sincerely appreciated.

Several developers who reviewed this book showed me so many ways in which I should improve. They taught me about the edge cases that I had missed, shared their experiences, and gave me useful pointers. This book is better because of the excellent review by Tom Adam, Ashish Bhatia, Andrey Breslav, Daniel DeGroff, Zulfikar Dharmawan, Roman Elizarov, Hadi Hariri, Steven Hicks, Rod Hilton, Ragunath Jawahar, Manuel Jordan, Dave Klein, Josh Long, Ted Neward, Eugene Petrenko, Owen Rumney, Nate Schutta, Brian Vermeer, Brian Sletten, Craig Walls, and Tory Zundel. In particular I would like to make special mention of the extensive and thorough reviews by Tom Adam and Eugene Petrenko—I am so glad I invited you to review this book, and I am thankful that you both accepted.

One of the nice benefits of bringing a book out in beta releases, making the contents available for readers while it's still being written, is the feedback from the early readers through the book's errata webpage. I would like to thank Cassian Braconnier, Pere Casafont, Freek de Bruijn, Nicholas Erasmus, Bill Judd, Daniel Kay, Jacques Ledoux, Michiel Leegwater, Adekunle Lukman, Ioannis Mavroukakis, Kin Pi, Paolo Pilloni, N. Raghavendra, Mark Rotteveel, Felipe Sultani, and Jeroen Wenting. The feedback you provided helped me to improve this book through each beta release.

Every page in this book benefited from extensive, multiple, and highly patient reviews of my editor Jackie Carter. She has set a very high standard for what to expect from an editor. Thank you, Jackie, for all that you do, both on the reviews and in terms of the moral support and encouragements you provided, especially when things were not going smoothly. I have so much to learn from you.

I'd like to thank the good folks at the Pragmatic Bookshelf, Andy Hunt, Brian MacDonald, Janet Furlow, and many others who worked behind the scenes to make this book a reality. The fast responses and assistance from each one of you made this such a pleasurable journey. Thank you for accepting this book for publication.

None of this would have been possible without the support, encouragement, and patience of my family. I am thankful to my wife Kavitha and my sons Karthik and Krupa. Now that I am done with this book, I should have more time for dad jokes.

Introduction

You can tell that programming languages fascinate me. As a language enthusiast, I code in about fifteen different languages and have written books on a few of them. I love languages, all of them.

Learning a language is like visiting a city. You come across new things but you also see things that are common. What's familiar brings comfort and the differences intrigue. To succeed in learning a language we need a good balance of the two.

Several of us aspire to be polyglot programmers. Kotlin is in itself a polyglot language. It brings together the powerful capabilities from many different languages. The creators of Kotlin took the good parts from various languages and combined them into one highly approachable and pragmatic language.

When I started learning Kotlin my mind was on fire, seeing the features I've enjoyed in different languages such as Java, Groovy, Scala, C++, C#, Ruby, Python, JavaScript, Erlang, Haskell... At the same time, there are so many nuances in Kotlin that made me so much more productive in programming than any one of those languages.

Some languages tell you how you should write code. Kotlin isn't one of those. With Kotlin, you decide which paradigm works best for the application at hand. For example, you may find that the imperative style is better in a large application because you have to deal with inherent side effects and exceptions, and Kotlin makes it easy to program in that style. But, in another part of the application, you may need to deal with big data transformations, so you decide the functional style is better for that, and Kotlin will transform into a charming functional programming language instantaneously. When you write object-oriented code, you'll see that the compiler works for you instead of you working for the compiler.

You'll see my excitement for the language throughout this book. It's been fun learning and applying Kotlin. I hope this book will make your journey to learn the language an enjoyable one. Thank you for picking it up.

Who Is This Book For?

This book is for programmers, lead developers, architects, and technical managers. The book assumes familiarity with the basics of programming and also assumes moderate knowledge of Java and the JDK. The book doesn't assume any knowledge of Kotlin. If you're an Android programmer, this book lays the good foundation you'll need to program those devices with Kotlin, though this book doesn't focus exclusively on the Android platform.

If you're new to Kotlin, this book will help you get started and quickly move forward with the application of the language for your projects. If you're already using Kotlin, you may use this book to gain deeper understanding of some of the advanced features of the language.

You may also use this book to train your developers to get proficient with Kotlin, to use it to create highly fluent and expressive code, and to solve intricate problems.

What's in This Book?

Kotlin is a multi-paradigm programming language. You may write plain scripts in Kotlin, write object-oriented code, functional style code, program asynchronously, and more. To provide reasonable coverage to this broad spectrum of topics, this book is divided into multiple parts.

Part I focuses on scripting with Kotlin. Part II is all about object-oriented programming. In Part III, you'll learn to use the functional-style capabilities of the language. Part IV will tie what you've learned so far together to make your code more fluent and teach you how to create internal domain-specific languages (DSLs). In Part V, you'll learn about the new coroutines and programming asynchronously. The final Part VI deals with Java interop, testing, using Kotlin with Spring, and programming Android applications with Kotlin.

Here's what's covered in each chapter:

In Chapter 1, Hello Kotlin, on page 1, we look at the reasons to use Kotlin, download the necessary tools, and get started with writing code.

Programmers coming to Kotlin from Java have a few practices and syntax to unlearn before they can jump into learning what's new and different in Kotlin. We'll cover those in Chapter 2, Kotlin Essentials for the Java Eyes, on page 19.

Functions are first-class citizens in Kotlin, and the language has so much to offer, like default and named arguments, and varargs. Explore these function-related capabilities in Chapter 3, Working with Functions, on page 37.

When programming in the imperative style, we often use external iterators. You'll see in Chapter 4, External Iteration and Argument Matching, on page 53, how Kotlin's iterators make that task bearable and how the argument matching syntax removes a lot of noise from conditional statements.

We work with collections extensively when programming. Chapter 5, Using Collections, on page 63, will show you how to use view interfaces to work with the JDK collections from Kotlin.

Kotlin has a sound type system, and its compile-time type checking goes beyond what we have come to expect from statically typed languages. In Chapter 6, Type Safety to Save the Day, on page 77, we'll look at Kotlin's fundamental types, nullable and non-nullable references, smart casts, generics variance, and more.

Though semantically equivalent, creating classes in Kotlin is quite different than in Java. In Chapter 7, Objects and Classes, on page 107, you'll learn to create singletons, classes, companion objects, and the reasons to use data classes.

Kotlin's treatment of inheritance is a lot different from the way it's used in Java. Classes are final by default, and the language places some rules to improve type safety and compile-time checks. We'll explore this topic in depth in Chapter 8, Class Hierarchies and Inheritance, on page 133.

As one of the languages that has direct support for delegation, Kotlin provides a few built-in delegates and also makes it easier to create custom delegates. We'll start with a discussion of when and why to use delegation and then dive into using delegates in Chapter 9, Extension Through Delegation, on page 149.

In Chapter 10, Functional Programming with Lambdas, on page 175, you'll learn how to create lambda expressions and how to write higher-order functions. We'll also cover the facilities offered in Kotlin to eliminate function call overhead and improve performance.

The internal iterators offer fluency, and sequences give us efficiency. We'll apply the functional style to iterate and process collections of objects in Chapter 11, Internal Iteration and Lazy Evaluation, on page 203.

Chapter 12, Fluency in Kotlin, on page 221, will show many of the capabilities of Kotlin to create concise, fluent, elegant, and expressive code.

Chapter 13, Creating Internal DSLs, on page 249, builds on the topic of fluency to create internal DSLs, to define your own syntax for your specialized language, but with full compile-time type safety.

Kotlin is one of the few languages on the JVM that provides tail call optimization. We'll see that in action in Chapter 14, Programming Recursion and Memoization, on page 269, along with using memoization to reduce computational complexity.

Coroutines are a stable feature in Kotlin 1.3 and, along with continuations, provide the fundamental infrastructure for programming asynchronously. The basics of coroutines and continuations are covered in Chapter 15, Exploring Coroutines, on page 285.

In Chapter 16, Asynchronous Programming, on page 309, you'll apply coroutines to create practical applications that can benefit from asynchronous program execution.

Kotlin can run on different platforms, including the Java Virtual Machine. In Chapter 17, Intermixing Java and Kotlin, on page 329, you'll learn how to intermix Kotlin with Java; how to use Kotlin in modern versions of Java—that is, with Java modules; how to use it with Maven and Gradle; and also how to smoothly work with both Java and Kotlin within the same application.

Even though the Kotlin compiler will catch several errors, automated testing is an essential practice for sustainable agile development. You'll learn about creating unit tests and measuring code coverage in Chapter 18, Unit Testing with Kotlin, on page 347.

In Chapter 19, Programming Spring Applications with Kotlin, on page 375, we'll explore the Spring libraries geared toward Kotlin programmers and the unique capabilities these offer.

Finally, in Chapter 20, Writing Android Applications with Kotlin, on page 387, we'll use Kotlin to create an Android application that talks to a back-end service.

Kotlin and Java Versions Used in This Book

To run the examples in this book you should have Kotlin 1.3 and Java 1.6 or higher. Although most examples will also work in earlier versions of Kotlin, some examples will require Kotlin 1.3. The examples in the Java Interop chapter will require Java 9 or later. Instructions for downloading the necessary tools are provided in the next chapter.

How to Read the Code Examples

Most examples in this book are written as Kotlin script so you can easily run them as a single file without explicit compilation. Where compilation and other steps are necessary, instructions are provided alongside the code.

To save space, the output from a piece of code is shown as a comment line on the same line as the println() command where possible or on the next line. Occasionally, a line of comment says something about the code instead of showing the expected output.

Online Resources

This book has an official page[1] at the Pragmatic Bookshelf website. From there you can download all the example source code for the book. You can also provide feedback by submitting errata entries.

If you're reading the book in PDF form, you can click on the link above a code listing to view or download the specific examples.

Now for some fun with Kotlin...

---

1. http://www.pragprog.com/titles/vskotlin

CHAPTER 1

Hello Kotlin

Ah, Kotlin—that's an island off St. Petersburg, Russia, but this book is about its namesake programming language. Programmers who use Kotlin don't just like the language—they say they love it. What are the reasons for such affection? That's the question we'll quickly start with. Then we'll be on our way to install the Kotlin Software Developer Kit (SDK), write some code, and compile and execute it so we can see it working.

Imagine taking the best of many different languages—C++, C#, Erlang, Groovy, Java, JavaScript, Python, Ruby, Scala, Smalltalk—throwing them into a blender and turning it on; the resulting cocktail is Kotlin. The strength of Kotlin is in its diversity.

Andrey Breslav[1] and the team of developers behind the language at JetBrains[2] set out to create a fluent, expressive, pragmatic, and easy to use language that is less verbose than many mainstream languages. As programmers pick up Kotlin, they quickly recognize good parts of their familiar languages and, at the same time, are intrigued by other awesome capabilities they've not been exposed to before. The familiar ideas in Kotlin makes programmers feel at home as they learn and adopt the language, yet the ideas that are new to them make them more productive compared to the languages they're used to. That's part of the reason why programmers are passionate about Kotlin.

The biggest uptick in interest for Kotlin came right after Google's announcement that Kotlin is an official language for Android development.[3] An endorsement from Google is certainly significant, but there are more reasons to be excited about Kotlin.

---

1.   https://twitter.com/abreslav

2.   https://www.jetbrains.com/

3.   https://developer.android.com/kotlin

Kotlin is one of the few languages that can be used for server-side, mobile/Android, and front-end development. Code, written appropriately, can compile down to Java bytecode or may be transpiled (compiled from the source code of one language to the source code of another language) to JavaScript. Kotlin/Native supports targeting platforms, including iOS, macOS, Linux, Windows, and WebAssembly, to compile your source code to native binaries. That makes Kotlin one of the few languages you can use for full-stack development.

As you journey through Kotlin, you may recognize a number of these features and trace their roots:

- Though syntactically different, Kotlin is semantically similar to Java, making it easy for Java programmers to adapt.

- Without inheriting from a class, you may add your own domain-specific convenience methods to classes. These methods, called extension functions, may be used just like methods that are part of the original class, with full integrated development environment (IDE) support. That's like C#-style extension methods in Kotlin, although Kotlin has much richer capabilities.

- Delegation is often a better design tool than inheritance to reuse code. Kotlin, inspired by languages like Groovy and Ruby, is versatile in the ways you can delegate method calls from one object to another, without compromising type safety.

- You can use the concise and elegant argument-matching syntax in Kotlin, which is similar to Erlang and Scala syntax, instead of the more verbose series of nested if-else statements.

- Extending existing functions and methods is easy in Kotlin (though it requires recompilation due to binary incompatibility), thanks to its default parameters' capabilities, similar to JavaScript, Scala, Ruby, and Python.

- Named arguments, like in Groovy, Scala, and Ruby, make the code highly expressive, easier to read, and less error prone.

- Where it makes sense, you may overload operators on your own classes or on third-party classes, much like in languages like C++ and Groovy.

- The elegance, fluency, and concise nature of Kotlin comes together to support creating internal DSLs, similar to languages like Groovy and Ruby, but with full support for static type checking.

- You can write C-style procedures, Scala-style scripts, Java-like OO code, and Smalltalk/Erlang-like functional-style code in Kotlin.

- Kotlin is leading innovation in the area of asynchronous programming with coroutines and continuations.

These are just a few of the significant features that are prominent in Kotlin.

Reasons to Love Kotlin

Once you dig in, Kotlin feels more like a Swiss Army knife than a cocktail—you can do so much with this language with so little code. The language supports multiple paradigms. It's statically typed with a healthy dose of strong type inference. It may be compiled to Java bytecode, transpiled to JavaScript, or it may target native binaries using Kotlin/Native. It is highly fluent and elegant, and it's a charm to work with. Let's further explore the reasons to adopt Kotlin.

Multi-Paradigm Programming

Kotlin treats us like an adult, it offers choices and lets us pick the approach that's best suited for the problem at hand. The language has few ceremonies; you're not required to write everything in classes nor are you required to compile every piece of code. The language is largely unopinionated and offers different programming paradigms for you to choose or even intermix.

You can see the different programming paradigms supported in Kotlin in the following figure.

Object-Oriented Programming

Elegant and Asynchronous Programming

Functional Programming

Scripting

You can write procedural code—that is, code and functions directly in a file—like in JavaScript or C, and you can run it as a script, without any extra compilation steps, but with the exceptional type safety you expect from a statically typed language. The benefit is that you can do rapid prototyping of your ideas or illustrate how a particular design pattern may be used, but without being drowned in the ceremonies that other languages often impose. That gives you the shortest time from idea to demo.

Much like in Java, you can create classes and write object-oriented code in Kotlin, but without much boilerplate code. Thus, it takes less code to achieve the same results as in Java. Kotlin guides you along to create your hierarchy of classes intentionally rather than accidentally. Classes are final by default, and if you intend a class to serve as a base class, you must specify that explicitly. Also, delegation has a language-level syntax, so we can select prudently between inheritance and delegation.

Though the mainstream world has predominantly used the imperative style of programming, code written using the functional style is less complex, more expressive, concise, elegant, and fluent. Kotlin provides exceptional support for both the imperative and functional style of programming. You can readily benefit from the key functional capabilities you're used to from other languages that support the paradigm.

You can make immediate use of the elegance and low ceremony of Kotlin syntax to create internal domain-specific languages (DSLs). In addition to creating your own fluent APIs, you can also benefit from fluency in a number of different libraries, for example the Kotlin API for the Spring framework.[4]

In addition to programming concurrency using the Java Development Kit (JDK), you may also write asynchronous programs using Kotlin's coroutines. This feature is critical for applications that make use of cloud services or are deployed as microservices; it allows you to interact efficiently with other services to exchange data asynchronously.

Statically Typed with Type Inference

Statically typed languages offer compile-time type safety, but Kotlin walks a few extra miles to prevent common errors that are likely in other statically typed languages. For instance, the Kotlin type system distinguishes nullable types from non-nullable types. It also has very strong type inference, in the same vein of languages like Scala, F#, and Haskell. You don't have to spend your time keying in type details that are obvious to everyone looking at the code. At the same time, when the type may not be 100 percent clear, Kotlin requires that you specify it. It's not overly zealous—it supports type inference to the right measure, so we can be productive and at the same time the code can be type safe.

---

4.   https://spring.io/blog/2017/08/01/spring-framework-5-kotlin-apis-the-functional-way

One Language for Full-Stack Development

Just like javac compiles Java source code to bytecode to run on the Java Virtual Machine (JVM), kotlinc-jvm compiles the Kotlin code to bytecode to run on virtual machines. You can write your server-side code and Android applications using Kotlin, and target the specific version of the virtual machine that you'd like to use for deployment. Thus your Spring code on the back end and your Android or iOS native code on the devices all may be written using the same language. Where necessary, you may also intermix Kotlin code with Java code—no legacy code has to be left behind.

Kotlin also transpiles to JavaScript. You can write Kotlin code that may transform to JavaScript and run in Node.js on the server side, or in browsers on the web front end.

Using Kotlin/Native, you can compile code to native binary to run on targeted platforms and to WebAssembly to run within browsers.

Fluent and Elegant

Some languages impose high ceremony and force you to create boilerplate code. Some developers argue that IDEs remove the burden of having to write that code manually. True, but even if the IDEs were to vomit that boilerplate code, your team has to spend the time and effort maintaining that code each day. Languages like Scala, Groovy, and Ruby synthesize code that programmers will have to otherwise write. Likewise, Kotlin creates a few things for you, like fields, getters, and setters, implicitly following the JavaBean convention. Less effort, better results.

Kotlin makes a few things optional. For example, a semicolon is optional. Not having to place the ; symbol leads to a more fluent syntax—a must for creating easy-to-read internal DSLs. Kotlin also provides an infix annotation that we can use, making the dot and parenthesis optional. With these capabilities you can write fluent and elegant code like this:

```
operate robot {
  turn left
  turn right
  move forward
}
```

Yes, it's not some fiction—that's real Kotlin code; you'll learn to create your own fluent code like this later in the book, without the need for any parsers or external tools.

Why Should You Choose Kotlin?

Kotlin may be the right choice for your current project, or the next one, for many reasons:

- Kotlin delivers on the "less is more" promise—you write less boilerplate code. The less code you write, the less your team has to maintain, resulting in fewer errors to deal with.

- Kotlin gives you the freedom to mix the imperative and functional styles of programming; you pick what's best for the problem at hand. Also, you may write it in one way and refactor it later as you desire—make it work, then make it better real soon.

- Kotlin offers lots more compile-time safety when compared to a lot of other statically typed languages. The code you write will fail less and fail fast—during compilation rather than runtime. This is one of the reasons why the Spring[5] team decided to embrace Kotlin.

- Kotlin coroutines makes it a lot easier to create high-performance asynchronous code, compared to what's available in the Java Development Kit.

- Some of the features that are scheduled to appear in future versions of Java are already in Kotlin—you can experience and benefit from future Java right now by using Kotlin.

- You may intermix Kotlin and Java code in your projects—using Kotlin is not an all-or-nothing proposition.

- You can not only use fluent DSL-like syntax to interact with APIs, like in the Spring Kotlin API, but also design your own APIs to be fluent and expressive for programmers who use your code.

- You can reduce duplication among parts of your system with Kotlin. For example, the same business rules that check users' input may be compiled to Java bytecode for back-end validations, transpiled to JavaScript for front-end validation, compiled to native binaries to run on targeted platforms like iOS and Android, or to WebAssembly to run within browsers.

- Finally, Kotlin is a great choice for Android development since it's an official language for that platform.

---

5. https://spring.io/blog/2017/01/04/introducing-kotlin-support-in-spring-framework-5-0

You'll see more about why Kotlin is exciting in the many pages of this book. Buckle up—it's going to be a fun ride. Let's start by getting the SDK installed so we can start writing Kotlin.

Taking Kotlin for a Ride

The rest of the book will focus on the syntax and the semantics of the Kotlin language. To thoroughly learn the concepts, you'll want to practice the examples. This section will show you how to set up and verify the necessary environment on your system.

Once you key in your code, Kotlin offers a variety of choices to execute code. Unlike Java, you don't have to compile every single line of code. You can run the code as is, directly from the source code in a file if you like. Alternatively, you may create class files and then reuse the binary to execute other classes or Kotlin files. While in the middle of writing code, you can fire up the Kotlin shell to experiment with the behavior of a little code snippet. You may run your code within the JVM, execute it on a JavaScript engine within Node.js or the browser, or run it on Android devices, and you can also run it on native targets like iOS and WebAssembly.

That's a lot of choices, but before we can exercise any of them, we need the SDK, so let's get that installed first.

Install Kotlin SDK

If you're using a recent version of IntelliJ IDEA,[6] then Kotlin comes bundled with the IDE. If you plan to compile and run code only from within that IDE, you're all set.

But even though we all use IDEs, it's good to start by learning how to compile and run on the command line, as it gives you full exposure to building the code. Install the standalone compiler from the Download Compiler link from the Kotlin website. This will take you to the Working with the Command-Line Compiler page.[7] You may download and unzip the zip files to install, using Homebrew or one of the other options, depending on your operating system. You'll also need JDK 1.6[8] or later on your system.

If you'd like to compile the code using build tools like Maven or Gradle, then refer to the instructions on the Kotlin website.[9] Later in the book, when we're

---

6.   https://www.jetbrains.com/idea/download
7.   https://kotlinlang.org/docs/tutorials/command-line.html
8.   http://openjdk.java.net/
9.   https://kotlinlang.org/

ready to write tests and intermix Kotlin with Java, we'll make use of Maven and Gradle project files.

Verify the Installation

Once you install and set the path to where Kotlin is installed, verify all is set by running the following command:

```
$ kotlinc-jvm -version
```

The output from that command, if Kotlin has been installed properly, will show the version number, like so:

```
info: kotlinc-jvm 1.3.41 (JRE 12.0.2+10)
```

Don't worry about the specific JRE version in the output. The output you'll see on your system will reflect the version of Java you have already installed.

Once you've verified the installation, move to the next step to write a small piece of Kotlin code and execute it.

Compile to Bytecode and Run

Let's first create a small *Hello World* program in Kotlin. Using your favorite text editor create a file named Hello.kt, like so:

```
running/Hello.kt
fun main() = println("Hello World")
```

Don't worry about the syntax in the code at this time; let's keep our focus on getting the code to run. We'll discuss the language syntax and semantics in following chapters. You may specify the parameter for the main() function if you like, but starting with Kotlin 1.3, it's optional. If you're using a version prior to 1.3, then you'll need to add the parameter, like so: fun main(args: Array<String>).

Running on the Command Line

To compile and run the code from the command line, first execute the following command:

```
$ kotlinc-jvm Hello.kt -d Hello.jar
```

This command will compile the code in the file Hello.kt into Java bytecode and place that into the Hello.jar file.

Once the jar file is created, run the program using the java tool, like so:

```
$ java -classpath Hello.jar HelloKt
```

Since the file Hello.kt contains only the main function and not a class, the Kotlin compiler, kotlinc-jvm, automatically creates a class named after the file name, without the .kt extension, but adds a Kt suffix.

Here's the output of running the code:

```
Hello World
```

Instead of specifying the classpath command-line option, you may also use the jar option to run the code. That's because, upon finding the main() function, the Kotlin compiler decided to add the Main-Class manifest attribute to the jar file. Go ahead and try out the following command on the Hello.jar file:

```
$ java -jar Hello.jar
```

The output of this command will be the same as the output produced when the classpath option was used instead of the jar option.

In this example we didn't use anything from the Kotlin standard library. However, any nontrivial program will make use of classes and functions from the Kotlin standard library and, in that case, the above execution using the java tool will fail with a java.lang.NoClassDefFoundError exception. To avoid this, include the kotlin-stdlib.jar file to the classpath, like so:

```
$ kotlinc-jvm Hello.kt -d Hello.jar
$ java -classpath Hello.jar:$KOTLIN_PATH/lib/kotlin-stdlib.jar HelloKt
```

The environment variable $KOTLIN_PATH on Unix-like systems, or %KOTLIN_PATH% on Windows, refers to the directory where Kotlin is installed. On Windows, instead of :, use ; to separate the paths in the classpath.

Instead of using the java tool, you may also use the kotlin tool. In this case, you don't have to refer to the kotlin-stdlib.jar. Let's run the code using kotlin. Here are the steps, but you may skip the first step; it's the same compilation command as before:

```
$ kotlinc-jvm Hello.kt -d Hello.jar
$ kotlin -classpath Hello.jar HelloKt
```

The output of the code will be the same whether we run the code using the java tool or kotlin tool.

Use the java tool if you're predominantly programming in Java and mixing Kotlin on your project. Otherwise, use the kotlin tool as that needs fewer configuration options.

Running in IDEs

It should be no surprise that IntelliJ IDEA from JetBrains, which is also the company behind Kotlin, has excellent support for programming with the language. Some developers think they need that IDE to use Kotlin, but that's not true. Kotlin doesn't require you to use a particular IDE, or any IDE for that matter.

Kotlin is bundled with the newer versions of IntelliJ IDEA and also with the free and open source IntelliJ IDEA Community edition. To use IntelliJ IDEA for development with Kotlin, start by creating a Kotlin project. Once you create a project, you can quickly create Kotlin files and execute with a few mouse clicks or keyboard shortcuts. The short tutorial[10] on the official website for the language will give you a quick jump start if you get stuck with any steps.

If you're an Eclipse aficionado, then you may use Eclipse Neon or later to program with Kotlin. The official Kotlin language website has a tutorial for Eclipse,[11] as well, to help get you started with Kotlin on Eclipse.

NetBeans fans can benefit from a NetBeans Kotlin Plugin[12] to program Kotlin applications.

Check to make sure you're using the right version of IDE and the correct version of Kotlin supported in that version.

Experiment with REPL

Several languages provide a read-evaluate-print loop (REPL) command-line shell to run small snippets of code. I like to call them micro-prototyping tools. When you're in the middle of coding or making your current automated test pass, instead of wondering what a particular function does, you can quickly take it for a ride in the REPL. Once you verify that a small piece of code is what you're looking for, you can use the best tool humans have invented—*copy-and-paste*—to bring that over from the REPL to your editor or IDE. The interactive tool is also very useful to show a colleague how a small piece of code works, without having to create a project in an IDE, for instance.

The Kotlin compiler that we used previously, kotlinc-jvm, turns into a REPL shell when run without any options or file names. Let's run an interactive session. From the command line, type the command kotlinc-jvm and the REPL

---

10. https://kotlinlang.org/docs/tutorials/getting-started.html

11. https://kotlinlang.org/docs/tutorials/getting-started-eclipse.html

12. http://plugins.netbeans.org/plugin/68590/kotlin

will respond with a prompt for you to key in some code. Type in some code, like in the following interactive session, and observe the response:

```
$ kotlinc-jvm
Welcome to Kotlin ...
Type :help for help, :quit for quit
>>> 7 + 5
res0: kotlin.Int = 12
>>> val list = listOf(1, 2, 3)
>>> list.map { it * 2 }
res2: kotlin.collections.List<kotlin.Int> = [2, 4, 6]
>>>
$
```

As soon as you key in a snippet of code and hit the enter key, the REPL will evaluate that piece of code, display the response, and prompt you for the next snippet. When you're done, hit ctrl+d (ctrl+c on Windows) or key in :quit to terminate the REPL session.

From within the REPL, you may also load existing files to execute code in them. For example, let's load the Hello.kt file we created earlier and run it within the REPL, without going through an explicit compilation step.

```
$ kotlinc-jvm
Welcome to Kotlin ...
Type :help for help, :quit for quit
>>> :load Hello.kt
>>> main()
Hello World
>>>
$
```

You may also specify the classpath to your own jar files, or third-party jar files, when firing up the REPL. Then you can interactively use instances of your classes or third-party classes from the REPL as well.

Run as Script

You saw earlier how to compile Kotlin code into bytecode, create a jar file, and then run the code using either the java or the kotlin commands. This two-step process is useful when you have multiple files in a large application. But not everything we write is large or enterprise scale—shell scripts and batch files have their places.

To perform some back-end tasks, parse some files, copy files around based on some configuration—in other words, for things you'd typically use shell scripts—you may write a script using Kotlin. The benefit in doing so is that you don't have to remember the shell commands between sh, zsh, bash, Windows

CMD, PowerShell, and so on. And you can use a powerful and fluent language to perform the tasks. Once you implement the desired task in Kotlin, you may run it as script, in a single step, instead of explicitly compiling the code to create bytecode.

If code has a syntax error, then the execution of the script will fail without actually running any part of the script; so it's pretty much as safe to run as script as it is to compile and execute.

Let's write a Kotlin script to list all files with a kts extension in the current directory. Here's the code for that:

```
running/listktsfiles.kts
java.io.File(".")
  .walk()
  .filter { file -> file.extension == "kts" }
  .forEach { println(it) }
```

The content of the file is not any different from a regular Kotlin file you'd write. The only difference is in the file name, the kts extension—to signify the intent to run as a script—instead of the kt extension.

The code uses the File class from the JDK java.io package, and also uses the extension functions that Kotlin has added to that class. It walks through all the files in the current (.) directory, filters or picks only files that end with the kts extension, and prints the file object—that is, the full path and name of each file picked.

To run this file, we'll use the kotlinc-jvm command, but this time instead of compiling, we'll ask the tool to run the code as script immediately. For this, use the -script option, like so:

```
$ kotlinc-jvm -script listktsfiles.kts
```

Here's the output from this code:

```
./listktsfiles.kts
```

On Unix-like systems, if you like to run the script without prefixing with kotlinc-jvm -script, then you may use the shebang facility, like this:

```
running/greet.kts
#!/usr/bin/env kotlinc-jvm -script

println("hi")
```

Make sure to run chmod +x greet.kts to give execution permission for the file.

Then, run the file directly from command line, like so:

```
$ ./greet.kts
```

This will produce the output:

```
hi
```

On some systems you have to provide the full path to the location of kotlinc-jvm instead of /usr/bin/env for the shebang facility to work properly.

If you intend to use scripts in production, you may find kscript[13] useful. It's a library that provides several capabilities to work with Kotlin scripts, including compiled script caching.

Kotlin code can not only be compiled to Java bytecode, it can also be compiled down to several other formats, as we'll see next.

Compiling to Other Targets

In addition to all the capabilities that Kotlin offers, it's one of the few languages that can be compiled to different targets.

- On Android devices: Kotlin is considered a first-class language for Android development. We'll explore using Kotlin to create Android applications in Chapter 20, Writing Android Applications with Kotlin, on page 387.

- To JavaScript: transpilation is compiling from the source code of one language to the source code of another language. You can see how to transpile Kotlin to JavaScript in Appendix 1, Transpiling to JavaScript, on page 405.

- To native targets: when compiling down to a virtual machine isn't an option, Kotlin/Native can be used to compile your source code to different native targets like iOS, Linux, MacOS, Windows, and others, and can be executed without a virtual machine. See Appendix 2, Kotlin/Native, on page 409, for an introduction to using Kotlin/Native.

- To WebAssembly to run in browsers: using Kotlin/Native, you may also compile Kotlin source code to WebAssembly or Wasm,[14] which is a binary format for virtual machines that run within modern browsers. In Appendix 3, Kotlin to WebAssembly, on page 413, we'll explore this capability to create Kotlin code that runs within browsers.

---

13. https://github.com/holgerbrandl/kscript
14. https://webassembly.org/

Which Option to Choose?

Kotlin doesn't dictate which option you choose to run the code; it's entirely up to you, depending on your needs and liking. Here are a few things to consider when choosing your option:

- To intermix Kotlin code with Java or other languages on the JVM, compile the code using kotlinc-jvm. Then, simply throw the jar file into the classpath or modulepath along with a reference to the kotlin-stdlib.jar file, and use it like you'd use any jar created from Java source code using javac.

- If you have multiple Kotlin files and intend to run the program as a Kotlin program, then use the kotlin tool to run the code.

- To implement system-level or back-end tasks using Kotlin, create a single Kotlin file and run it as script using the -script option. Alternatively, use the shebang to directly run the file from the command line or a cron task.

- To enjoy static typing and compile-time verification that comes with Kotlin for creating web applications, use the option to compile Kotlin to Java-Script.

- To run Kotlin code on different native platforms, like iOS and WebAssembly, use Kotlin/Native to compile the code to the desired targets.

- During active development, run the code from within the IDE for ease of development and the convenience offered by the IDEs.

- To experiment with small snippets of code, run kotlinc-jvm as REPL.

Wrapping Up

Kotlin is a language of choices, and that spirit shines from the beginning with support for multiple programming paradigms and a number of options for executing Kotlin code. Kotlin doesn't dictate how you should write applications. You can start small, with just a few lines to build scripts, and you can ask the language to take you all the way to build highly complex applications with classes and dependencies. You can use Kotlin to build server-side applications, optionally with Spring. You can create Android applications, transpile Kotlin to JavaScript, and also using Kotlin/Native to compile to targeted native platforms like iOS and WebAssembly. Kotlin's versatile nature makes it one of the few full-stack programming languages.

You may compile to Java bytecode and run within the JVM. Alternatively, you can run it as a script, skipping the extra compilation step. If you're into front-end development, you may get compile-time safety along with all the benefits of Kotlin to transpile the code into JavaScript. And to explore small snippets of code, you can use the Kotlin REPL.

In this chapter, you gained some high-level insights into the capabilities of Kotlin and got up and running with it. Next, you'll learn the fundamentals of the language that you'll use every day when programming with Kotlin.

Part I

Scripting with Kotlin

Kotlin is a language that scales—you can create scripts with a few lines, or an entire enterprise application with many classes and libraries. Our objective is to deliver value, not to write a lot of code. From that point of view, the conciseness and effectiveness of every line of code matters.

In this part, you'll learn about type inference, defining variables, using string templates, and creating multiline strings. Then we'll look at how to create functions to elegantly iterate over ranges of values and to process data using the argument-matching capabilities of Kotlin.

You'll learn to create scripts, but that knowledge will carry you forward to creating OO code, writing functional code...all the way to creating enterprise and Android applications.

CHAPTER 2

Kotlin Essentials for the Java Eyes

Simple things should be easy to create, and complicated things should be affordable. Quick, how many lines of code do you need to programmatically find the number of cores on a machine? How about the following:

```
println(Runtime.getRuntime().availableProcessors())
```

That's the entire program in Kotlin—with only half a line of code, no need for a semicolon, no imports, and using the Java JDK but with far less code and ceremony. That's Kotlin.

Kotlin is about getting your work done; it doesn't impose ceremony on you. You can start small and scale up. Programming is a series of mini experiments; you often prototype solutions to see if things make sense, and write code to get a feel and to tease out design ideas. Kotlin scripts are a great way to achieve that quickly without writing wasteful code.

In this chapter, you'll learn a few essentials—the building blocks that typically go into the body of functions and methods but which you can drop directly into scripts, as well, in Kotlin. These include defining variables of numbers and strings, creating constants, specifying the type information, creating a string expression with embedded values, creating multiline strings—a hodgepodge of features that we'll use often when programming with Kotlin, whether it's writing scripts, creating classes, or writing functional-style code.

Experienced Java programmers who begin to program in Kotlin have to unlearn a few of their Java practices while they learn the nuances of Kotlin. In this chapter, we'll look at things that eyes very familiar with Java have to adjust to when transitioning to Kotlin. Just like wearing a new pair of glasses or contacts, it takes some getting used to, but Kotlin's elegance will make you feel comfortable in no time.

We'll start with an appreciation for conciseness in Kotlin. Every line of code matters —you can't make an entire application concise when the most fundamental operations are verbose. Whether you write imperative-style, functional-style, or object-oriented code, expressions and statements are the building blocks. Kotlin removes ceremony, noise, and clutter from every single line of code, so your overall program can be shorter, more expressive, and easier to maintain.

Kotlin makes optional a number of things that are required in other languages—semicolons, explicit type specifications, and classes, to mention a few. Kotlin requires you to make a conscious decision at the time of creating a variable if it should be mutable or immutable. It provides string templates to ease the pain of creating string expressions and multiline strings. And it favors expressions over statements, to reduce the need for mutating variables.

Let's dive in and see the root of Kotlin's design philosophy at the most rudimentary part of code, a single line of statement or expression. Along the way, we'll look at how Kotlin reduces noise in code and how you can define variables, use type inference, rely on sensible warnings, easily embed expressions in strings, and create multiline strings. Learning these fundamental and essential concepts first will help to influence every line of code you write in Kotlin.

Less Typing

You'll do less typing—that act of hammering keys on the keyboard—to create applications with Kotlin. That's because a lot of things we've come to take for granted as required are optional in Kotlin.

Semicolon Is Optional

When you start programming in Kotlin, your right pinky immediately gets relief from repetitive stress injury that it may have endured for most of your programming career. Though you could, you don't have to end every single statement or expression with a semicolon. Use the semicolon sparingly—only on occasions when you want to place two or more expressions or statements on a single line.

The following example, is valid syntax in Kotlin, and can be written standalone:

```
6 * 2
```

At first thought it may not appear to be a big deal, but, as you'll see later in the book, not having to place semicolons makes the code fluent, especially when creating internal DSLs.

If you're transitioning into Kotlin from languages like Java and JavaScript, chances are that hitting the semicolon key is an involuntary action by now. That's understandable, but make it a habit to leave out semicolons when writing in Kotlin.

Variable Type Specification Is Optional

Kotlin is statically typed, but that doesn't mean you have to specify the details of variables' types. Static typing means that the type of variables is verified and type sanity is guaranteed at compile time.

Kotlin has the smarts—*type inference*—to determine the type of variables based on the context. Let's define a variable without specifying the type and then ask for the type of that variable.

essence/typeinference.kts
```
val greet = "hello"

println(greet)
println(greet::class)
println(greet.javaClass)
```

The ::class call is asking for the Kotlin class of the object referenced by the variable. The .javaClass call, however, is asking for the underlying Java class. It's rare for Kotlin and Java classes to be different—only classes that are intimately known to the Kotlin compiler will display such differences.

In the previous example, Kotlin's type-inference capability determines that the type of greet is String based on the value assigned to it. The output shows these details:

```
hello
class kotlin.String
class java.lang.String
```

Some developers fear type inference; they wonder if it's a runtime thing and if it somehow lowers the effectiveness of type checking at compile time. The short answer is no.

To be fair, the above code revealed the type of the referenced object at runtime, but what's the type of the variable greet at compile time? We can find that by making a mistake in code, like so:

essence/typechecking.kts
```
val greet = "hello"

println(greet)

greet = 0
```

Kotlin determined that the type of greet is String at compile time and, as a result, knew that assigning an integer to it isn't valid. In addition, reassigning a val isn't permitted. So the code didn't execute and resulted in compilation errors, even though it was run as script. The resulting compilation errors are:

```
typechecking.kts:5:1: error: val cannot be reassigned
greet = 0
^
typechecking.kts:5:9: error: the integer literal does not conform
  to the expected type String
greet = 0
        ^
```

Kotlin doesn't take type inference to the extreme—it permits leaving out the type details only in places where the type is obvious. When defining functions and methods, you're required to specify the type of the parameters, although you may leave out the type of the return. In general, specify the return type for APIs that aren't internal to your libraries but are visible to the outside user. We'll discuss this further when we explore creating functions.

For your part, encourage your colleagues to give meaningful names for variables so it becomes easier to identify the type and the intent of variables. For example, val taxRate = 0.08 is better than val t = 0.08.

Also, when using type inference, resist the urge to embed the type information into variable names—such efforts are the programmers' desire to overly compensate for not specifying the type that they're so used to providing. For example, avoid the following:

```
val taxRateDouble = 0.08   //Don't do this
//or
val dTaxRate = 0.08 //Also, don't do this
```

Local variables are internal and aren't seen by the users of your code. So the use of type inference doesn't take away any details from the users of your functions. Leave out the type details where possible and instead use type inference with descriptive, but not necessarily long, names for variables.

Classes and Functions Are Optional

Unlike languages like Java, Kotlin doesn't require a statement or expression to belong to a method and a method to belong to a class, at least not in the source code we write. When the code is compiled, or executed as script, Kotlin will create wrapper classes and methods as necessary to satisfy the JVM expectations.

In the following source code, the function doesn't belong to a class, and the code below the function is standalone and isn't part of any function. Nevertheless, Kotlin takes care of wrapping these, when necessary, into classes to satisfy the JVM.

Let's create a script with a function that doesn't belong to any class and some standalone code that's not part of any function.

essence/standalone.kts
```
fun nofluff() {
  println("nofluff called...")

  throw RuntimeException("oops")
}

println("not in a function, calling nofluff()")

try {
  nofluff()
} catch(ex: Exception) {
  val stackTrace = ex.getStackTrace()
  println(stackTrace[0])
  println(stackTrace[1])
}
```

The standalone body of code below the function calls the function nofluff(), which doesn't belong to any class. The function blows up with an exception, and the calling code prints the top two frames of the stack from the exception. The output from this code shows that, first, Kotlin doesn't force us to write classes and methods, and, second, it wraps the code into a class automatically.

```
not in a function, calling nofluff()
nofluff called...
Standalone.nofluff(standalone.kts:4)
Standalone.<init>(standalone.kts:10)
```

Kotlin quietly turned the function nofluff() into a method of a synthesized class named Standalone—a name inferred from the file name—and the standalone code into the constructor of the class, as indicated by <init> in the output.

When writing small pieces of code, place the code directly in a file and run it as a script—no need for the ceremony to create classes and methods. But when working on larger applications, you may create classes and methods. Simple code can be simple, and more complex code can have better rigor and structure.

try-catch Is Optional

The Java compiler forces us to either explicitly catch or propagate checked exceptions. The debate about whether checked exceptions are good or bad may never be settled—some developers love it while others hate it. We don't need to get dragged into that brawl; instead let's focus on what Kotlin provides.

Kotlin doesn't force you to catch any exceptions—checked or unchecked. If you don't place a try-catch around a function call and if that function blows up, the exception is automatically propagated to the caller of your function or code. If an exception is unhandled, it'll result in a fateful termination of your program.

In Java, for example, the sleep() method of the Thread class throws a checked exception, and the compiler forces us to deal with it. As a result, any call to sleep() has to be surrounded by a try and followed by a sleepless night wondering what to do with that stinking InterruptedException that may potentially be thrown from that call. No need to lose sleep over such issues in Kotlin:

essence/nocatch.kts
```
println("Lemme take a nap")
Thread.sleep(1000)
println("ah that feels good")
```

The code doesn't have any try and catch, but when executed it will print the two lines of output with a one-second delay after the first line is printed.

It's a good practice to program defensively to handle exceptions. At the same time, since Kotlin doesn't force a try-catch on us, we're not tempted to place those gnarly empty catch blocks that many Java programmers seem to write simply to quiet the Java compiler. Remember, what you don't handle is automatically propagated to the caller.

You've seen how the Kotlin compiler gives you a lot of flexibility by placing fewer demands. At the same time, the compiler looks out for potential errors in code, to make the code safer, as we'll see next.

Sensible Warnings

Even if a piece of code is valid syntactically, some potential problems may be lurking. Getting an early warning, during compilation time, can help us to proactively fix such possible issues. The Kotlin compiler looks out for quite a few potential issues in code.

For example, if a parameter that's received in a function or a method isn't used, then the compiler will give a warning. In the following script, the parameter passed to compute() isn't used.

essence/unused.kts
```kotlin
fun compute(n: Int) = 0

println(compute(4))
```

When you run this script, in addition to displaying the result, Kotlin will also report any warnings for unused parameters:

```
0
unused.kts:1:13: warning: parameter 'n' is never used
fun compute(n: Int) = 0
            ^
```

It's a good software development practice to *treat warnings as errors*—an agile practice emphasized in *Practices of an Agile Developer [SH06]*. Kotlin makes that easy with the -Werror option. To use this option, place it on the command line when you compile the code or run it as a script, like so:

```
$ kotlinc-jvm -Werror -script unused.kts
```

This option will fail the build or execution. Unlike the previous run without that option, there will be no output when the script is run; instead an error is reported:

```
error: warnings found and -Werror specified
unused.kts:1:13: warning: parameter 'n' is never used
fun compute(n: Int) = 0
            ^
```

The Kotlin compiler is sensible when giving warnings. For example, it's not uncommon for programs to ignore command-line arguments. Forcing us to use parameters given to main() is considered draconian, so Kotlin doesn't complain about unused parameters for main(), as we see in the next example. But if you have an unused parameter in main() within a script (a .kts file instead of a .kt file), then Kotlin will give you a warning—it decides based on the context.

essence/UnusedInMain.kt
```kotlin
fun compute(n: Int) = 0

fun main(args: Array<String>) = println(compute(4))
```

When you compile the code using kotlinc-jvm and then run it using either java or kotlin, you'll get the following output. The warning is from kotlinc and the output is from the execution of the generated jar file:

```
UnusedInMain.kt:1:13: warning: parameter 'n' is never used
fun compute(n: Int) = 0
            ^

0
```

Starting from Kotlin 1.3, you may leave out the parameters to main() if you don't need them.

We saw how Kotlin tries to make a preemptive strike against potential errors. Along those lines, the language wants you to be decisive about immutability. Let's explore that choice next.

Prefer val over var

To define an immutable variable–that is, a constant or a *value*—use val, like so:

```
val pi: Double = 3.14
```

Unlike Java, where you'd place the type before the name of the variable, in Kotlin you place the name of the variable first, then a colon, followed by the type. Kotlin considers the sequence Java requires as "placing the cart before the horse" and places a greater emphasis on variable names than variable types.

Since the type of the variable is obvious in this context, we may omit the type specification and ask Kotlin to use type inference:

```
val pi = 3.14
```

Either way, the value of pi can't be modified; val is like final in Java. Any attempt to change or reassign a value to variables defined using val will result in a compilation error. For example, the following code isn't valid:

```
val pi = 3.14
pi = 3.14 //ERROR: val cannot be reassigned
```

What if we want to be able to change the value of a variable? For that, Kotlin has var—also known as "keyword of shame." Variables defined using var may be mutated at will.

Here's a script that creates a mutable variable and then modifies its value:

```
var score = 10
//or var score: Int = 10
```

```
println(score) //10
```

```
score = 11
println(score) //11
```

Mutating variables is a way of life in imperative style of programming. But that's a taboo in functional programming. In general, it's better to prefer immutability—that is, val over var. Here's an example to illustrate why that's better:

```
essence/mutate.kts
var factor = 2

fun doubleIt(n: Int) = n * factor

factor = 0

println(doubleIt(2))
```

Don't run the code; instead eyeball it, show it to a few of your colleagues and ask what the output of the code will be. Take a poll. The output will be equal to what most people said it will be—just kidding. Program correctness is not a democratic process; thankfully, I guess.

You probably got three responses to your polling:

- The output is 4.
- The output is 0, I think.
- *WHAT*—the response the code evoked on someone recently.

The output of the above code is 0—maybe you guessed that right, but guessing is not a pleasant activity when coding.

Mutability makes code hard to reason. Code with mutability also has a higher chance of errors. And code with mutable variables is harder to parallelize. In general, try really hard to use val as much as possible instead of var. You'll see later on that Kotlin defaults toward val and immutability, as well, in different instances.

Whereas val in Kotlin is much like Java's final, Kotlin—unlike Java—insists on marking mutable variables with var. That makes it easier to search for the presence of var in Kotlin than to search for the absence of final in Java. So in Kotlin, it's easier to scrutinize code for potential errors that may arise from mutability.

A word of caution with val, however—it only makes the variable or reference a constant, not the object referenced. So val only guarantees immutability of the reference and doesn't prevent the object from changing. For example, String is immutable but StringBuilder is not. Whether you use val or var, an instance of String is safe from change, but an instance of StringBuilder isn't. In the following code, the variable message is immutable, but the object it refers to is modified using that variable.

```
val message = StringBuilder("hello ")

//message = StringBuilder("another") //ERROR

message.append("there")
```

In short, val only focuses on the variable or reference at hand, not what it refers to. Nevertheless, prefer val over var where possible.

Improved Equality Check

Just like Java, Kotlin also has two types of equality checks:

- equals() method in Java, or == operator in Kotlin, is a comparison of values, called *structural equality.*

- == operator in Java, or === in Kotlin, is a comparison of references, called *referential equality.* Referential equality compares references and returns true if the two references are identical—that is, they refer to the same exact instance. The operator === in Kotlin is a direct equivalent of the == operator in Java.

But the structural equality operator == in Kotlin is more than the equals() method in Java. If you perform str1.equals(str2); in Java, you may run into a NullPointerException if the reference str1 is null. Not so when you use == in Kotlin.

Kotlin's structural equality operator safely handles null references. Let's examine that with an example:

```
essence/equality.kts
println("hi" == "hi")
println("hi" == "Hi")
println(null == "hi")
println("hi" == null)
println(null == null)
```

If these comparisons were done with equals() in Java, the net result would have been a runtime NullPointerException, but Kotlin handles the nulls safely. If the values held in the two references are equal then the result is true, and false otherwise. If one or the other reference is null, but not both, then the result is false. If both the references are null, then the result of the comparison is true. We can see this in the output, but you'll also see an added bonus in there:

```
true
false
```

```
false
false
true
equality.kts:3:9: warning: condition 'null == "hi"' is always 'false'
println(null == "hi")
        ^

equality.kts:4:9: warning: condition '"hi" == null' is always 'false'
println("hi" == null)
        ^

equality.kts:5:9: warning: condition 'null == null' is always 'true'
println(null == null)
           ^
```

The output confirms the behavior of == operator like mentioned. The output
also shows yet another example of Kotlin's sensible warnings—if the result
of comparison will always be an expected value, it prompts a warning suggest-
ing we fix the code to remove the redundant conditional check.

When == is used in Kotlin, it performs the null checks and then calls equals()
method on the object.

You've learned the difference between using equals() in Java and == in Kotlin.
Next let's look at the ease with which we can create strings with embedded
expressions.

String Templates

In programs, we often create strings with embedded values of expressions.
Concatenating values to create strings using the + operator makes the code
verbose and hard to maintain. String templates solve that problem by providing
an elegant solution.

Within a double-quoted string, the $ symbol can prefix any variable to turn
that into an expression. If the expression is more complex than a simple
variable, then wrap the expression with ${}.

A $ symbol that's not followed by a variable name or expression is treated as
a literal. You may also escape the $ symbol with a backslash to use it as a
literal.

Here's an example with a string template. Also, it contains a plain string with
embedded $ symbols that are used as literals.

essence/stringtemplate.kts
```
val price = 12.25
val taxRate = 0.08

val output = "The amount $price after tax comes to $${price * (1 + taxRate)}"
val disclaimer = "The amount is in US$, that's right in \$only"
```

```
println(output)
println(disclaimer)
```

In the string template assigned to output, the first $ symbol is used as a delimiter for the expression, the variable name, that follows it. The second $ symbol is a literal since it's followed by another $, which isn't a variable or expression. The third $ symbol prefixes an expression that's wrapped in {}. The other $ symbols in the code are used as literals. Let's take a peek at the output of the code:

```
The amount 12.25 after tax comes to $13.23
The amount is in US$, that's right in $only
```

The earlier caution to prefer val over var applies here too. Let's take the code with var we saw previously and modify it slightly to use a string template.

essence/mutateconfusion.kts
```
var factor = 2

fun doubleIt(n: Int) = n * factor
var message = "The factor is $factor"

factor = 0

println(doubleIt(2))
println(message)
```

Once again, don't run the code, but eyeball it and figure out the output of this code. Does it correspond with the following output?

```
0
The factor is 2
```

The variable factor within the function doubleIt() binds to the variable outside its immediate scope—that is, in its lexical scope. The value of factor at the time of the function call is used. The string template, on the other hand, is evaluated when the variable message is created, not when its value is printed out. These kinds of differences increase cognitive load and makes the code hard to maintain and also error prone. No need to torture fellow programmers with code like this. It's inhumane. Again, as much as possible prefer val over var.

Next, let's look at using raw strings to remove some clutter and to create multiple lines of strings.

Raw Strings

Dealing with escape characters makes the code messy. Instead of using escaped strings, in Kotlin we may use raw strings which start and end with three double quotes. We may use raw strings to place any character, without the need to use escapes, and may also use them to create multiline strings.

No Escape

In an escaped string which starts and ends with a single double quote, we can't place a variety of characters, like new line or a double quote, for example, without using the escape character \. Even a simple case can be unpleasant to read, like this one:

```
val escaped = "The kid asked, \"How's it going, $name?\""
```

We had to escape the double quotes that were needed within the string. The more we use escaped strings, the messier it becomes. Instead of using escaped strings, in Kotlin we use raw strings. Just like escaped strings, raw strings can also be used as string templates, but without the mess of escaping characters. Here's the above escaped string changed to raw string—less clutter, more readable:

```
val raw = """The kid asked, "How's it going, $name?""""
```

Use escaped string, ironically, when you don't need to escape anything—for small, simple, plain vanilla strings. If you need anything more complex or multiple lines of string, then reach over to raw strings.

Multiline Strings

The infamous + operator is often used to create multiple lines of strings, and that leads to nasty code that's hard to maintain. Kotlin removes that ceremony with a multiline string, which is a raw string that contains line breaks. Multiline strings can also act as string templates.

Let's create a string that runs across several lines, but without the + operator.

```
essence/memo.kts
val name = "Eve"

val memo = """Dear $name, a quick reminder about the
party we have scheduled next Tuesday at
the 'Low Ceremony Cafe' at Noon. | Please plan to..."""

println(memo)
```

The multiline string starts with three double quotes, contains the string template expression to evaluate the variable name, and ends with three double quotes. The output of this code is multiple lines of string with the embedded expression evaluated.

```
Dear Eve, a quick reminder about the
party we have scheduled next Tuesday at
the 'Low Ceremony Cafe' at Noon. | Please plan to...
```

That worked beautifully, but—there always is a *but*—what if the multiline string were within a function, maybe within an if? Would the nesting mess things up? Let's find out.

essence/nestedmemo.kts
```
fun createMemoFor(name: String): String {
  if (name == "Eve") {
    val memo = """Dear $name, a quick reminder about the
        party we have scheduled next Tuesday at
        the 'Low Ceremony Cafe' at Noon. | Please plan to..."""

    return memo
  }

  return ""
}

println(createMemoFor("Eve"))
```

The createMemoFor() function returns a multiline string if the parameter passed is equal to Eve. Let's see what the output beholds:

```
Dear Eve, a quick reminder about the
        party we have scheduled next Tuesday at
        the 'Low Ceremony Cafe' at Noon. | Please plan to...
```

The resulting string has preserved the indentation—yikes. Thankfully, it's not too hard to get rid of. Let's rework the example:

```
fun createMemoFor(name: String): String {
  if (name == "Eve") {
    val memo = """Dear $name, a quick reminder about the
        |party we have scheduled next Tuesday at
        |the 'Low Ceremony Cafe' at Noon. | Please plan to..."""

    return memo.trimMargin()
  }

  return ""
}

println(createMemoFor("Eve"))
```

We made two changes. First, we placed a | on each line of the multiline string, starting with the second line. Second, we used the trimMargin() method, an extension function (we discuss these in Chapter 12, Fluency in Kotlin, on page 221), to strip the margin out of the string. With no arguments, the trimMargin() method removes the spaces until the leading | character. The | character that's not in the leading position doesn't have any impact. Here's the output that shows the fix worked.

```
Dear Eve, a quick reminder about the
party we have scheduled next Tuesday at
the 'Low Ceremony Cafe' at Noon. | Please plan to...
```

If you do not want to use | as the leading delimiter, because maybe your text contains that character in arbitrary places, including the first character of a new line, then you may choose some other character—for example, let's go ahead and choose ~:

```
val memo = """"Dear $name, a quick reminder about the
    ~party we have scheduled next Tuesday at
    ~the 'Low Ceremony Cafe' at Noon. | Please plan to..."""

return memo.trimMargin("~")
```

In the multiline string we use ~ as the delimiter instead of the default |, and in the call to trimMargin() we pass that specially chosen delimiter as argument. The output of this version is the same as the one where we used the default delimiter.

So far in this chapter, we've looked at the improvements to expressions and statements in Kotlin when compared to languages like Java. But Kotlin prefers expressions over statements. Let's discuss that next.

More Expressions, Fewer Statements

Languages like Java, C#, and JavaScript have more statements than expressions—if statement, for statement, try, and so on. On the other hand, languages like Ruby, F#, Groovy, Haskell, and many others have more expressions than statements. Let's discuss which is better before we discuss Kotlin's preference.

While statements are prevalent, they have a dark side—they don't return anything and have side effects. A side effect is a change of state: mutating a variable, writing to a file, updating to a database, sending data to a remote web service, corrupting the hard drive... Expressions are much nicer—they return a result and don't have to modify any state in order to be useful.

Let's look at an example to see the difference. Let's write a piece of Kotlin code as we would in languages like Java and C#:

```
fun canVote(name: String, age: Int): String {
  var status: String

  if (age > 17) {
    status = "yes, please vote"
```

```
  } else {
    status = "nope, please come back"
  }

  return "$name, $status"
}
println(canVote("Eve", 12))
```

The canVote() method uses if like a statement. Since statements don't return anything, the only way we can get any useful result out of it for further processing is to set up a mutable variable and modify its value within the branches.

In Kotlin, however, if is an expression. We can use the result of the call to if for further processing. Let's rework the previous code, to use if as an expression instead of a statement:

```
val status = if (age > 17) "yes, please vote" else "nope, please come back"

return "$name, $status"
```

We were able to use val instead of var since we're not mutating a variable. And we were able to use type inference for status, since the value is known from the if expression. The code is less noisy and less error prone as well.

Kotlin also treats try-catch as an expression. The last expression within the try part becomes the result if there was no exception; otherwise, the last statement within the catch becomes the result.

Here's an example of try-catch-finally being used as an expression.

```
fun tryExpr(blowup: Boolean): Int {
  return try {
    if (blowup) {
      throw RuntimeException("fail")
    }

    2
  } catch(ex: Exception) {
    4
  } finally {
    //...
  }
}

println(tryExpr(false)) //2
println(tryExpr(true))  //4
```

There's one surprise, though. While Java treats assignment as an expression, Kotlin doesn't. If variables a, b, and c are defined using var with some integer values, like, 1, 2, and 3 respectively, the following code will fail compilation in Kotlin:

```
a = b = c //ERROR
```

One reason for this behavior, of not treating = as an expression, is that Kotlin allows you to intercept both gets and sets on variables with delegates, as we'll see later in the book. If = were treated as an expression, then chaining of assignments may lead to unexpected and complex behavior that may be confusing and turn into a source of errors.

Wrapping Up

Kotlin removes a lot of ceremony from the most fundamental programming tasks. For the same task, you'll often find that you type a lot less in Kotlin than you would in a number of mainstream languages. The semicolon is optional, variable declarations enjoy type inference, you're not forced to place everything into a class or even a function, exception handling is not forced on you—these things ease the burden on programming. At the same time, Kotlin has sensible warnings to save you from common errors. It also improves safety by asking you to choose between immutability and mutability early on. Additionally, equality check is null safe. String templates and multiline strings reduce the effort to create strings with expressions. And, Kotlin provides more expressions than statements when compared to languages like Java, C#, and JavaScript.

We've focused on expressions and statements in this chapter. Next, we'll step up to working with functions.

CHAPTER 3

Working with Functions

Kotlin doesn't insist that you create classes for everything. No one gets praise for duplicating code, but to reuse doesn't mean building a class hierarchy. Unlike Java where a class is the smallest reusable piece, in Kotlin both standalone functions and classes can be reused.

Kotlin takes a highly pragmatic approach to creating good quality code—create small simple standalone functions where they suffice and roll your code into methods of classes only when necessary. In this chapter, we'll focus on standalone functions for two reasons. First, because we can—that is, in Kotlin we can create top-level standalone functions to reuse code and don't have to waste our time and effort with classes if there's little value. Second, all the capabilities of functions directly carry over to creating methods of classes—after all, methods are simply functions that run in the context of classes or objects. So what you learn here is useful when working with scripts, procedural code, and functional code, as well as when building complex object-oriented code.

With Kotlin you don't have to masquerade standalone functions as static methods of a class—that is, you don't have to pretend to do OO to please the language. You can create global top-level functions, as in languages like C and C++, if that's right for your application. Functions may reside at the top level or directly within packages—you decide where to place them.

Kotlin requires that you specify the types of the parameters to functions, but you can ask it to infer the return type for single-expression functions. When calling functions, you're not required to pass an argument for every parameter; instead you may choose to use default arguments. You can use this feature to easily evolve functions and methods. To make the call to methods expressive, Kotlin gives you the power to name your arguments. This greatly increases the readability of the code. In addition, you may pass a variable number of arguments to functions without losing compile-time safety. Kotlin also has the capability for destructuring, which provides a highly concise way to extract properties from objects into standalone variables.

In this chapter you'll learn how to work with global or standalone functions. We'll start with Kotlin's rules for defining functions, look at how it treats functions as expressions, and then examine many useful features, including default arguments, named arguments, defining variable number of arguments, the spread operator, and using destructuring. Using these features, you can create highly expressive code that's easy to read and also more flexible to maintain. If you're more interested in writing object-oriented code, be assured that the concepts you learn here apply to methods of classes as well.

Let's have some fun with functions.

Creating Functions

Creating functions, and methods, in Kotlin is refreshingly different from creating methods in Java. The greater flexiblity that Kotlin offers removes unnecessary ceremony when creating functions. Let's start with short functions, explore type inference, and then look at defining parameters and multiline functions.

KISS Functions

Kotlin follows the mantra "Keep it simple, stupid"—the KISS principle—to function definitions. Small functions should be simple to write, no noise, no fluff. Here's one of the shortest functions you can write in Kotlin, followed by a call to it.

functions/kiss.kts
```
fun greet() = "Hello"

println(greet())
```

Function declarations start with the keyword fun—Kotlin wants you to remember to have fun every time you look at a function or a method. The function name is followed by a parameter list, which may be empty. If the function is a *single-expression function*, which is very short, then separate the body from the declaration using the = operator instead of using the {} block syntax. For short functions, the return type can be inferred. Also, the return keyword isn't allowed for single-expression functions, which are functions without a block body.

Run this script to see Kotlin greet you:

```
Hello
```

Let's examine what the above function actually returns.

Return Type and Type Inference

The greet() function returns a String, but we didn't explicitly specify that. That's because Kotlin can infer the return type of functions with a non-block body—that is, functions without {}. The return type inference happens at compile time. Let's verify this by making a mistake in code:

```
fun greet() = "Hello"

val message: Int = greet() //ERROR
//type mismatch: inferred type is String but Int was expected
```

Based on the context, Kotlin determines that greet() is returning a String. We're assigning that to a variable message of type Int, which is a no-no, and the code will fail to compile.

Type inference is safe to use and the type checking happens at compile time; use it for internal APIs and where the functions are a single expression separated by =. But if the function is for external use or the function is more complex, specify the return type explicitly. This will help both you and the users of your functions clearly see the return type. It will also prevent surprises that could arise if the return type is inferred and the implementation is changed to return a different type.

Kotlin will infer the return type of functions only when the function body is a single expression and not a block.

Let's modify the greet() function to explicitly specify the return type.

```
fun greet(): String = "Hello"
```

The return type is prefixed with a : and goes right after the parameter list. The return keyword is still not permitted since the body of the function is a single expression and not a block.

Leave out the return type if it's obvious, specify it otherwise.

What if the function isn't returning anything? Let's visit those pesky void functions next.

All Functions Are Expressions

As you saw in More Expressions, Fewer Statements, on page 33, Kotlin favors expressions over statements. Based on that principle, functions must be treated as expressions instead of statements, and we can nicely compose a sequence of calls to invoke a method on the return value of each one.

Kotlin uses a special type called Unit that corresponds to the void type of Java. The name Unit comes from type theory and represents a singleton that contains no information. You can consistently use Unit to specify that you're not returning anything useful. Also, Kotlin will infer the type as Unit if the function isn't returning anything. Let's take a look at this inference first.

functions/inferunit.kts
```
fun sayHello() = println("Well, hello")

val message: String = sayHello() //ERROR
//type mismatch: inferred type is Unit but String was expected
```

The sayHello() function prints out a message on the standard output using println(), which we know is a void function in Java, but it returns Unit in Kotlin. We use type inference for the return type of sayHello(), but be assured that it's inferred as Unit. We verify the inferred type by assigning the result of sayHello() to a variable of type String, and that will fail to compile due to type mismatch.

Instead of using type inference, we may explicitly specify Unit as the return type as well. Let's change sayHello() to specify the return type and then assign the result to a variable of type Unit:

functions/specifyunit.kts
```
fun sayHello(): Unit = println("Well, hello")

val message: Unit = sayHello()

println("The result of sayHello is $message")
```

Since even void functions return Unit in Kotlin, all functions can be treated as expressions and we may invoke methods on the results from any function. For its part, the Unit type has toString(), equals(), and hashCode() methods. Though not highly useful, you may invoke any of those methods. For example, in the previous code we pass the message variable, which is of type Unit, to println(), and that internally calls the toString() method of Unit. Let's take a look at the output:

```
Well, hello
The result of sayHello is kotlin.Unit
```

The toString() method of Unit merely returns a String with value kotlin.Unit, the full name of the class.

Since all functions return something useful, or a Unit at the very least, they all serve as expressions and the result may be assigned to a variable or used for further processing.

The functions we've used so far in this chapter didn't take any parameters, but in reality functions typically accept parameters. Let's now focus on defining parameters and passing arguments to functions.

Defining Parameters

Some languages like Haskell and F# can dive into functions and infer the types of the parameters. Personally, I'm not a fan of that; changing the implementation of a function may result in change to the types of the parameters. That's unsettling for me. Kotlin insists on specifying the types for parameters to functions and methods. Provide the type of the parameter right after the parameter's name, separated by :.

Let's change the greet() function to take a parameter of String type.

```
functions/passingarguments.kts
fun greet(name: String): String = "Hello $name"

println(greet("Eve")) //Hello Eve
```

The type specification in Kotlin has the consistent form candidate : Type, where the candidate can be one of the following: variable declaration using val or var, function declaration to specify the return type, function parameters, and an argument passed to the catch block.

While the type of the parameter name is required, we may omit the return type if we want Kotlin to infer the return type. If you have more than one parameter, list them comma separated within the parenthesis.

You saw in Prefer val over var, on page 26, that we should prefer immutability over mutability and that Kotlin forces you to choose between val and var when defining local variables. But when defining the greet() function, we didn't specify val or var for the parameter. That has a good reason.

Effective Java, Third Edition [Blo18] advises programmers to use final and prefer immutability as much as possible. Kotlin doesn't want us to make a choice here for function and method parameters; it decided that modifying parameters passed to functions is a bad idea. You can't say val or var for parameters—they're implicitly val, and any effort to change the parameters' values within functions or methods will result in compilation errors.

We've seen really short functions so far. Let's look at writing more complex functions.

Functions with Block Body

When a function is small, a single expression, we can separate the body of the function from the declaration using the = operator. If the function is more complex than that, then place the body in a block {} and don't use =. You have to specify the return type for any function with a block body; otherwise, the return type is inferred as Unit.

Let's write a function that returns the maximum among numbers in a given array.

functions/multilinefunction.kts
```kotlin
fun max(numbers: IntArray): Int {
  var large = Int.MIN_VALUE

  for (number in numbers) {
    large = if (number > large) number else large
  }

  return large
}

println(max(intArrayOf(1, 5, 2, 12, 7, 3))) //12
```

The max() function takes an array as a parameter, specifies Int as the return type, and has a body wrapped in a block {}. In this case the return type isn't optional—you must specify it since the body of the function is a block. Also, the return keyword is required.

A word of caution—don't use = followed by a block {} body. If you explicitly specify the return type, and follow it with the =, and then a block body, the compiler will raise an error.

What if we omit the return type, but used = and then a block body instead of a single expression? For example, what if we write something like the following?

```kotlin
fun notReally() = { 2 }
```

Kotlin won't infer the return type by stepping into the code block. But, it will assume the entire block to be a lambda expression or an anonymous function—a topic we'll cover later in the book. Kotlin thinks that notReally() is a function that returns a lambda expression—oops.

For the sake of fun, admittedly a skewed definition of fun, let's explore the effect of using = with a block, but without a return type.

functions/caveat.kts
```kotlin
fun f1() = 2
fun f2() = { 2 }
fun f3(factor: Int) = { n: Int -> n * factor }
```

```
println(f1()) //2
println(f2()) //() -> kotlin.Int
println(f2()()) //2
println(f3(2)) //(kotlin.Int) -> kotlin.Int
println(f3(2)(3)) //6
```

The function f1() is inferred to return an Int. But Kotlin inferred that the function f2() is returning a lambda expression that takes no parameters and returns an Int. Likewise, it inferred that the function f3() is returning a lambda that takes Int and returns Int.

It's highly unlikely that someone who writes such code will have many friends—no point writing code like that and spending the rest of your life alone. If you want to create functions that return lambdas, we'll see better ways to do that later. In short, don't mix = with block body.

You know how to create functions; let's next see how we can evolve existing functions easily in Kotlin.

Default and Named Arguments

Overloading of functions is common in Java and is the way to create functions that can take different number and type of arguments. That's an option in Kotlin as well, but the feature of default arguments is a simpler and better way to evolve functions, though it requires recompilation as it breaks binary compatibility. Also, named arguments is a great way to create readable code. We'll focus on those two features now.

Evolving Functions with Default Arguments

Quickly glance at the greet() function we wrote earlier, repeated here for convenience.

```
fun greet(name: String): String = "Hello $name"
```

```
println(greet("Eve")) //Hello Eve
```

The greet() function has a hardcoded string "Hello", but what if we want to provide the flexibility to the caller of the function to provide a pleasantry of its choice?

If we add a new parameter to the function, then any existing code that calls the function will break because those will be shy of the much needed, albeit new, parameter. In languages like Java we use overloading for this purpose, but that may lead to code duplication. Kotlin makes this task easy with default arguments.

A default argument is a parameter that takes a default value right after the declaration. If the caller doesn't pass a value for that parameter, then the default value is used. Specify the name of the parameter, colon, type, followed by the assignment to the default value, using =. Let's change the greet method to take on an additional parameter, but with a default value.

```
functions/defaultarguments.kts
fun greet(name: String, msg: String = "Hello"): String = "$msg $name"

println(greet("Eve")) //Hello Eve
println(greet("Eve", "Howdy")) //Howdy Eve
```

The existing code that calls greet() with only one argument for name continues to work. Any new call to greet() may pass either one argument, for name, or two arguments, for name and msg. In the first call, since msg isn't provided a value, the default argument Hello is used. In the second call the given argument Howdy is used and the default argument is ignored.

In greet(), the parameter with default argument is placed after the regular parameter—that is, the one with no default argument. You may wonder if it makes sense to swap their order of appearance. Yes, but with consequences:

- Since a value will be required for the regular parameter, the caller will be forced to provide a value for the parameter with default argument as well—that defeats the purpose of having the default argument.

- The caller may skip the default parameter if they use named arguments—we'll see this in Improve Readability with Named Arguments, on page 45.

- A parameter with default argument may precede a last parameter that stands for a lambda expression—we'll see the benefit of this in Use Lambda as the Last Parameter, on page 182.

In short, to make default arguments effective, use them on trailing parameters and follow them, optionally, only with parameters for lambda expressions.

The default argument doesn't have to be a literal; it may be an expression. Also, you may compute the default arguments for a parameter using the parameters to its left.

The default argument used in the greet() function has a hardcoded value. Let's change that to use the parameter to its left:

```
functions/defaultcompute.kts
fun greet(name: String, msg: String = "Hi ${name.length}") = "$msg $name"

println(greet("Scott", "Howdy")) //Howdy Scott
println(greet("Scott")) //Hi 5 Scott
```

Once again, when two arguments are passed to greet(), the default argument is ignored; it's not computed. On the other hand, when only the value for the name parameter is passed, then the value for the msg parameter is computed from the default argument expression. In the second call to greet(), we pass only the name and the result; msg is computed based on the value of the name parameter—a geeky high five to good friend Scott.

In this example, swapping the position of name and msg will result in a compilation error that name is uninitialized in the default argument expression—another reason for placing parameters with default arguments in the trailing positions.

Improve Readability with Named Arguments

Code is written once but read and updated many times. Anything we can do to reduce the burden on the readers is a welcome step. In a call like greet("Scott", "Howdy") it's not hard to surmise what the arguments stand for. But you might come across a call like this:

functions/namedarguments.kts
```
createPerson("Jake", 12, 152, 43)
```

You may wonder what those numbers mean, and that's certainly no fun when dealing with impending deadlines. You'll have to switch context and look at the documentation for the function or its declaration to find the meaning of these magic numbers.

functions/namedarguments.kts
```
fun createPerson(name: String, age: Int = 1, height: Int, weight: Int) {
  println("$name $age $height $weight")
}
```

Poorly written code can turn the politest human into a terrible cusser—readability matters. Kotlin is a language of fluency, and that principle shines in method calls as well.

Without changing anything in how a function is defined, you can make calls to methods more readable, with little effort. This is where named arguments come in.

Let's make the call to createPerson() readable:

functions/namedarguments.kts
```
createPerson(name = "Jake", age = 12, weight = 43, height = 152)
```

That's a lot better—no guessing and no fussing over what those parameters mean. You can assign a value to a parameter's name right there in the function call. Even though the function takes weight as the last parameter, it isn't required to be the last in the call; named arguments may be placed in any order.

The confusion in this code is among the different integer values; the value for name in createPerson is intuitive. We can place named arguments after positional arguments, as shown in the following two examples:

functions/namedarguments.kts
```
createPerson("Jake", age = 12, weight = 43, height = 152)
```

functions/namedarguments.kts
```
createPerson("Jake", 12, weight = 43, height = 152)
```

While the last one is valid Kotlin syntax, from the readability point of view it may be better to use named argument for age as well.

Since age has a default argument, we may leave it out if we used either named values for all other parameters, or positional arguments for all parameters to its left and named arguments for all other parameters.

For example, the following two calls that leave out the argument for age are valid:

functions/namedarguments.kts
```
createPerson(weight = 43, height = 152, name = "Jake")

createPerson("Jake", weight = 43, height = 152)
```

Named arguments make method calls readable and also eliminate potential errors when adding new parameters to existing functions. Use them when the parameters passed in aren't obvious. Let's now turn our attention to two other features of Kotlin that can reduce the noise in method calls.

vararg and Spread

Functions like println() take a variable number of arguments. The vararg feature of Kotlin provides a type-safe way to create functions that can receive a variable number of arguments. The spread operator is useful to explode or spread values in a collection as discrete arguments. We'll look at vararg first and spread next.

Variable Number of Arguments

In Functions with Block Body, on page 42, we wrote a max() function that took an array of numbers. In the call to the function, as expected, we passed an array of values. If we already have an array of values, then it's not a big deal;

but if we have a discrete set of values, then to call the function we'll have to create a temporary array of those values and then pass that array. Tedious.

In Kotlin, functions may take a variable number of arguments. Let's convert the max() function to be more flexible for the caller.

functions/vararg.kts
```
fun max(vararg numbers: Int): Int {
  var large = Int.MIN_VALUE

  for (number in numbers) {
    large = if (number > large) number else large
  }

  return large
}
```

Compared to the max() function we wrote previously, this version has two changes, both in the parameter list. First, the parameter numbers is prefixed with the keyword vararg. Second, the type of the parameter is specified as Int instead of IntArray. The real type of the parameter numbers is an array; the vararg annotates the parameter to be an array of the specified type.

Let's make a couple of calls to the function, passing a few discrete values.

functions/vararg.kts
```
println(max(1, 5, 2)) //5
println(max(1, 5, 2, 12, 7, 3)) //12
```

That worked nicely—we can pass any number of arguments and Kotlin's type checking will ensure that the different arguments are of the right type.

The max() function took only one parameter, but you can use vararg when a function takes more than one parameter as well. But only one parameter may be annotated as vararg.

Here's a function that takes two parameters, but only the trailing one is marked as vararg.

functions/mixvararg.kts
```
fun greetMany(msg: String, vararg names: String) {
  println("$msg ${names.joinToString(", ")}")
}

greetMany("Hello", "Tom", "Jerry", "Spike") //Hello Tom, Jerry, Spike
```

In the call, the first argument binds to the first parameter, and the remaining arguments are passed to the vararg parameter.

The type of the vararg parameter may be independent of the type of any of the other parameters the function takes.

The vararg parameter isn't required to be the trailing parameter, but I highly recommend that it is. Consider the following version of the greetMany() function:

```
fun greetMany(vararg names: String, msg: String) {
  println("$msg ${names.joinToString(", ")}")
}
```

When calling the function, if you pass any number of unnamed String arguments the compiler will assume all of them are for the vararg parameter. For it to know that a value is for the msg parameter, you'll have to use a named argument, like so:

```
greetMany("Tom", "Jerry", "Spike", msg = "Hello") //Hello Tom, Jerry, Spike
```

If you annotate a non-trailing parameter with vararg, then the caller is forced to use named arguments.

Here are some recommendations on where to place the vararg parameter:

- Place it in trailing position so callers aren't forced to use named arguments.
- Place it before the last parameter if the last argument is expected to be a lambda expression—we'll explore this further later in the book.

We saw how Kotlin makes it easy to pass a variable number of arguments, but what if we have an array with values already? The spread operator comes to the rescue in that case.

Spread Operator

Take another look at the max() function with vararg in the previous example—it made it easier to pass different numbers of arguments. Sometimes, though, we may want to pass values that are in an array or list to a function with vararg. Even though the function may take a variable number of arguments, we can't directly send an array or a list. This is where the spread operator comes in. To look at an example of using this operator, let's start with the following instance:

```
functions/vararg.kts
val values = intArrayOf(1, 21, 3)
```

The vararg implies that we may pass any number of arguments to this single parameter. But if we pass an array as argument, we'll get an error:

```
println(max(values)) //ERROR
//type mismatch: inferred type is IntArray but Int was expected
```

Even though internally the type of vararg parameter is an array, Kotlin doesn't want us to pass an array argument. It'll only accept multiple arguments of the specified vararg type.

To use the data in the array, we may try the following:

functions/vararg.kts
```
println(max(values[0], values[1], values[2])) //SMELLY, don't
```

But that's verbose, and you'll never be able to proudly show that code to anyone, not even to mom.

Where the parameter is annotated as vararg, you may pass an array—of right type, of course—by prefixing it with the spread operator *. Let's pass the array values as an argument to the numbers parameter of max():

functions/vararg.kts
```
println(max(*values)) //21
```

That's much better. By placing a * in front of the argument, you're asking Kotlin to spread the values in that array as discrete values for the vararg parameter. No need to write verbose code; the combination of vararg and spread restores harmony.

If we have an array, we can use spread, but often we work with lists instead of arrays. If we want to pass a list of values, then we can't use the spread operator on the list directly. Instead, we have to convert the list to an array, of the desired type, and then use spread. Here's an example of how that would look:

functions/vararg.kts
```
println(max(*listOf(1, 4, 18, 12).toIntArray()))
```

If the elements in the list and the type of vararg are of a different type than Int, then use the appropriate to…Array() method of List<T> to convert to an array of the desired type.

Destructuring

Structuring, or construction, is creating an object from values in different variables. Destructuring is the opposite—to extract values into variables from within an existing object. This facility is useful to remove noisy, repetitive code. Kotlin has the destructuring capability much like in languages such as JavaScript. But unlike JavaScript, the destructuring in Kotlin is based on the position of properties instead of the names of the properties.

Let's start with a piece of code that is verbose and then refactor that code, using destructuring, to make it concise. Triple is a class in the Kotlin standard library that represents a tuple. We'll look at it further in Using Pair and Triple, on page 66. For now, we'll use Triple to return a group of three values:

functions/destructuring.kts
```
fun getFullName() = Triple("John", "Quincy", "Adams")
```

Here's a traditional, boring, call to the above function, to receive the result and assign to three different variables.

functions/destructuring.kts
```
val result = getFullName()
val first = result.first
val middle = result.second
val last = result.third

println("$first $middle $last") //John Quincy Adams
```

That took multiple lines of code and a few dot operations. But when the return type of a function is a Pair, Triple, or any data class, we can use destructuring to extract the values into variables, elegantly and concisely. Let's rewrite the code, this time to use destructuring.

functions/destructuring.kts
```
val (first, middle, last) = getFullName()

println("$first $middle $last")   //John Quincy Adams
```

Four lines reduced to a concise single line of code. It appears like the getFull-Name() function suddenly returned multiple values—a nice illusion. The three immutable variables first, middle, and last are defined in that line and are immediately assigned the three properties of the result Triple, in the order first, second, and third, respectively. In reality, this works because the Triple class has specialized methods to assist with destructuring; you'll learn about this later in the book. The order in which the properties are destructured is the same as the order in which the properties are initialized in the source object's constructor.

Suppose we don't care about one of the properties of the object being returned. For example, if we don't want the middle name, we can use an underscore (_) to skip it.

functions/destructuring.kts
```
val (first, _, last) = getFullName()

println("$first $last")   //John Adams
```

Similarly, you may skip more than one property by using multiple _s, like so:

functions/destructuring.kts
```
val (_, _, last) = getFullName()

println(last)   //Adams
```

You may place _ at any position that you want to ignore. If you want to stop at a particular position and ignore the rest, you don't need to fill all remaining spaces with _s. For example, to get only the middle name we can write:

functions/destructuring.kts
```
val (_, middle) = getFullName()

println(middle)   //Quincy
```

In addition to using destructuring when the return type is a data class, you can also use destructuring to extract key and value from Map entries—see Using Map, on page 73.

If you're curious how destructuring works under the hood and what those special methods that I alluded to are, stay tuned; we'll revisit destructing and explore further in Data Classes, on page 129.

Wrapping Up

Kotlin doesn't force you to create methods; you can create top-level functions as well. This opens a few more design choices in Kotlin than Java has—applications aren't required to comprise of objects only, they can be composed of functions too. This allows you to create procedural, object-oriented, or functional-style code, whichever is a better choice in a given context. The compiler can infer return types for single-expression, non-block functions. The types of parameters are always required, and that's good.

Default arguments make it a lot easier to extend functions in Kotlin and reduce the need to overload functions. vararg parameters offer the flexibility to pass a discrete number of arguments with type safety, and the spread operator gives you a nice way to explode an array argument into a vararg parameter. Using named arguments is a great way to make code readable; it's a way to write self-documenting code. Finally, destructuring is a capability that can reduce noise in code and make the code highly concise.

In the next chapter, we'll learn about iterating over a range of values and processing data using the argument-matching facility of Kotlin.

CHAPTER 4

External Iteration and Argument Matching

Count the number of times you've used for loops in your code. Shocking. Something that's so widely used and fundamental as iterating should be fluent, concise, easy to write, and effortless to understand. Yet, in C-like languages, for loops have rather been primitive and verbose. Not so in Kotlin.

Kotlin provides both external iterators, used in the imperative style of programming, and internal iterators, used in the functional style. With external iteration, you, as the programmer, control the sequence of iteration explicitly, for example, with i++, i--, and so on. Internal iteration takes charge of the sequencing and lets programmers focus on the actions or computations for each iteration, resulting in less code and fewer errors. We'll explore the benefits of internal iteration in Chapter 10, Functional Programming with Lambdas, on page 175, but in this chapter we'll focus on the fluency Kotlin provides for working with the common external iteration.

In this chapter, you'll learn the features in Kotlin to concisely and elegantly iterate over ranges of values and through objects in collections. You'll see that code you write to sift through data and make decisions doesn't have to be a series of repeated if-else blocks. Kotlin's elegant argument-matching capabilities will remove so much cruft and make the decision logic highly transparent to the reader.

Once you pick up the facilities provided in Kotlin, you'll never want to go back to the old ways of iterating. Concise, pleasant, and expressive syntax will keep you moving, motivated, and focused on the problem at hand. As a result, you'll write less code to implement your business rules.

Since we often work with ranges of values, you can readily use the classes and functions in the kotlin.ranges package to nicely iterate, turning the task of writing that code into a pleasant experience. The enhanced for loop is not only for a range of values; you may use it to iterate over values in a collection as well.

We'll also look at the elegant argument-matching syntax and the powerful when expression, which will save you from drowning in deeply nested code. This will become your go-to syntax for taking different actions on different pieces of data.

1, 2, 3… let's start the iteration.

Range and Iteration

Imagine telling someone to count from one to five by uttering "set i equal to 1 but while keeping i less than 6, increment i and report the value." If we had to communicate with a fellow human that way, it would have ended civilization a long time ago. Yet that's how programmers have been writing code in many C-like languages. But we don't have to, at least not in Kotlin.

Range Classes

Kotlin raises the level of abstraction to iterate over a range of values with specialized classes. For instance, here's a way to create a range of numbers from 1 to 5.

iteration/ranges.kts
```
val oneToFive: IntRange = 1..5
```

The type IntRange, which is part of the kotlin.ranges package, is provided for clarity, but you may leave it out and let type inference figure out the variable's type.

If you want a range of letters in the English alphabet, the process is the same:

iteration/ranges.kts
```
val aToE: CharRange = 'a'..'e'
```

You're not limited to primitives like int, long, and char. Here's a range of strings:

iteration/ranges.kts
```
val seekHelp: ClosedRange<String> = "hell".."help"
```

That's nifty. Take the initial value, place the .. operator, followed by the last value in the range. The range includes both the values before and after the .. operator. Let's quickly check if a couple of values exist in that range.

iteration/ranges.kts
```
println(seekHelp.contains("helm")) //true
println(seekHelp.contains("helq")) //false
```

The first call verifies that the range includes the value "helm", which is in the lexical order of words between the values "hell" and "help". The second call confirms that the value "helq" is not in the range.

Forward Iteration

Once we create a range, we can iterate over it using the for (x in ..) syntax. Let's iterate over a range of values 1 to 5.

iteration/ranges.kts
```
for (i in 1..5) { print("$i, ") } //1, 2, 3, 4, 5,
```

Not only is the syntax elegant, it's safe as well. As you may have guessed—even though we didn't explicitly say it—the variable i is a val and not a var; that is, we can't mutate the variable i within the loop. And, of course, the variable i's scope is limited; it's not visible outside of the loop.

Likewise we can iterate over the range of characters:

iteration/ranges.kts
```
for (ch in 'a'..'e') { print(ch) } //abcde
```

All that went well, but the iteration from "hell" to "help", like the following, will run into issues:

```
for (word in "hell".."help") { print("$word, ") } //ERROR
//for-loop range must have an 'iterator()' method
```

The reason for the failure is whereas classes like IntRange and CharRange have an iterator() function/operator, their base class ClosedRange<T> doesn't. But brave-at-heart programmers won't sulk and take *no* for an answer. Stay tuned—we'll create an extension function to iterate over elements of Close-dRange<String> in Injecting into Third-Party Classes, on page 228.

Reverse Iteration

The previous examples showed iterating forward, but we should be able to iterate over the range in reverse just as easily. Creating a range of values 5..1 won't cut it, though. This is where downTo comes in.

Let's iterate from 5 *down to* 1:

iteration/reverse.kts
```
for (i in 5.downTo(1)) { print("$i, ") } //5, 4, 3, 2, 1,
```

The call to the downTo() method creates an instance of IntProgression, which is also part of the kotlin.ranges package. That works, but it's a bit noisy. We can remove the dot and parenthesis near downTo with the *infix* notation to make the code easier to read—we'll see in Function Fluency with infix, on page 235, how to make dot and parenthesis optional for our own code. Let's rewrite the iteration with less noise:

iteration/reverse.kts
```
for (i in 5 downTo 1) { print("$i, ") } //5, 4, 3, 2, 1,
```

Both .. and downTo() produced a range of every single value from the start to the end value. It's not uncommon to skip some values in the range, and there are other methods to achieve that.

Skipping Values in Range

When iterating over a range of numbers, you can skip the ending value in the range by using until(). Unlike .., the until() method will stop one value shy of the end value. Just like the downTo() method, we can drop the dot and parenthesis when using the until() method. Let's give that a try:

iteration/skipvalues.kts
```
for (i in 1 until 5) { print("$i, ") } //1, 2, 3, 4,
```

This iteration created using until() didn't include the ending value 5, whereas the range we created previously using .. did.

In the traditional for-loop in C-like languages we can skip some values by using, for example, i = i + 3, but that's mutating i and we know that's a no-no in Kotlin. To skip some values during iteration, Kotlin provides a step() method—that's definitely a step in the right direction for fluency and fewer errors. Let's use the step() method, again with the infix notation for fluency:

iteration/skipvalues.kts
```
for (i in 1 until 10 step 3) { print("$i, ") } //1, 4, 7,
```

The step() method transforms an IntRange or IntProgression created using .., until, downTo, etc. into an IntProgression that skips some values. Let's use step() to iterate in reverse order while skipping some values:

iteration/skipvalues.kts
```
for (i in 10 downTo 0 step 3) { print("$i, ") } //10, 7, 4, 1,
```

That was an easy way to methodically skip some values, but there are other methods to skip values that don't fall into a rhythm. For example, if you want to iterate over all values divisible by 3 and 5, use the filter() method:

iteration/skipvalues.kts
```
for (i in (1..9).filter { it % 3 == 0 || it % 5 == 0 }) {
  print("$i, ") //3, 5, 6, 9,
}
```

The filter() method takes a predicate—a lambda expression—as argument. We'll discuss lambdas and functional style later.

So far you've seen rudimentary iteration over a range of values. Next, let's take a look at iterating over a collection of values.

Iterating over Arrays and Lists

You can seamlessly use any of the JDK collection classes and interfaces in Kotlin. Thus, you can use Java's array and java.util.List in Kotlin as well. Creating instances of these in Kotlin is simpler than in Java, and you can iterate over the values in these collections with greater ease in Kotlin.

Let's first create an array of numbers and examine its type:

iteration/iterate.kts
```
val array = arrayOf(1, 2, 3)

println(array.javaClass) //class [Ljava.lang.Integer;
```

To create an array of values, use the arrayOf() function that belongs to the kotlin package. The functions that belong to the kotlin package may be called without the kotlin prefix—kotlin.arrayOf(), for example—or without any explicit imports.

Since all the values given are of type Int, the array created in this example is an array of Integer values. To create a primitive int array, instead of an array of Integer objects, use the intArrayOf() function. Irrespective of which function we pick, we can iterate over the array of values using the for(x in ...) syntax like before.

iteration/iterate.kts
```
for (e in array) { print("$e, ") } //1, 2, 3,
```

Likewise, you can create an instance of List<T> using the listOf() function and then iterate over its values using for:

iteration/iterate.kts
```
val list = listOf(1, 2, 3)

println(list.javaClass) //class java.util.Arrays$ArrayList

for (e in list) { print("$e, ") } //1, 2, 3,
```

Just like in the iterations we saw earlier, the variable e—for element of the collection—is immutable, leading to safe iteration.

The preceding iteration using for provided the values in the collection. But sometimes we need the index in addition to the value. The traditional for loop in C-like languages gives us the index, but not the value so easily. In this iteration we got the values easily, but getting the index, well, that shouldn't be hard either. The indices property provides a range of index values. Let's use that to iterate over a list of String values.

iteration/index.kts
```
val names = listOf("Tom", "Jerry", "Spike")

for (index in names.indices) {
  println("Position of ${names.get(index)} is $index")
}
```

Once we get the index value from the indices property we can obtain the value from the list at that position.

```
Position of Tom is 0
Position of Jerry is 1
Position of Spike is 2
```

Alternatively, we can get both the index and the position in one shot, using the withIndex() function along with an application of destructuring, which we saw in Destructuring, on page 49, like so:

iteration/withIndex.kts
```
for ((index, name) in names.withIndex()) {
  println("Position of $name is $index")
}
```

You've seen how you can use the Java collections in Kotlin and also iterate over the values with greater ease. Later in the book we'll see how to achieve greater fluency using internal iterators, when we discuss the functional style of programming.

When iterating over a collection of values, we often want to process the values, sometimes differently, depending on the value or its type. The handy argument-matching syntax will remove so much boilerplate code, as we'll see next.

When It's Time to Use when

Kotlin doesn't have switch; instead it has when, and that comes in different flavors: as expression and as statement.

When as an Expression

Here's an implementation of the function to determine if a cell will be alive in the next generation in Conway's Game of Life.[1]

---

1. https://en.wikipedia.org/wiki/Conway%27s_Game_of_Life

iteration/boring.kts
```kotlin
fun isAlive(alive: Boolean, numberOfLiveNeighbors: Int): Boolean {
  if (numberOfLiveNeighbors < 2) { return false }
  if (numberOfLiveNeighbors > 3) { return false }
  if (numberOfLiveNeighbors == 3) { return true }
  return alive && numberOfLiveNeighbors == 2
}
```

This code tells if a cell will live in the next generation, but any programmer reading such code may quickly lose motivation to live; the code is too noisy, verbose, repetitive, and error prone.

In the simplest form, when can replace a series of if-else statements or expressions. Now is a great time to refactor that code to use Kotlin's when.

iteration/when.kts
```kotlin
fun isAlive(alive: Boolean, numberOfLiveNeighbors: Int) = when {
    numberOfLiveNeighbors < 2 -> false
    numberOfLiveNeighbors > 3 -> false
    numberOfLiveNeighbors == 3 -> true
    else -> alive && numberOfLiveNeighbors == 2
  }
```

The previous version of the function specified the return type and used the block structure for the method body. In this version, the refactored code uses type inference and the single-expression function syntax. Here, when is used as an expression. The value returned by the function is the value returned by one of the branches in when.

The two versions of the isAlive() function produce the same results for the same inputs, but the one using when is less noisy in comparison. when is succinct when compared to if in general, but as an observant reader you may further refactor the above code to replace the entire when expression with a simple alive && numberOfLiveNeighbors == 2 || numberOfLiveNeighbors == 3 after the = separator.

In the case where when is used as an expression, the Kotlin compiler will verify that either the else part exists or that the expression will result in a value for all possible input values. This compile-time check has a direct impact on the accuracy of code and reduces errors that often arise from conditions that were accidentally overlooked.

In the previous example, the when expression isn't taking any arguments, but we may pass a value or an expression to it. Let's look at an example of that by using it in a function that takes a parameter of Any type—see more about this in Any, the Base Class, on page 78.

We'll use Any in the next example to illustrate the versatility of when. Occasionally, you may find it useful to receive Any—for example, in an application tier where a message broker may receive messages of different types. Consider those cases to be an exception rather than a norm, and, in general, avoid defining methods that take Any as a parameter. With those words of caution, let's take a look at the code.

```
iteration/activity.kts
fun whatToDo(dayOfWeek: Any) = when (dayOfWeek) {
  "Saturday", "Sunday" -> "Relax"
  in listOf("Monday", "Tuesday", "Wednesday", "Thursday") -> "Work hard"
  in 2..4 -> "Work hard"
  "Friday" -> "Party"
  is String -> "What?"
  else -> "No clue"
}

println(whatToDo("Sunday")) //Relax
println(whatToDo("Wednesday")) //Work hard
println(whatToDo(3)) //Work hard
println(whatToDo("Friday")) //Party
println(whatToDo("Munday")) //What?
println(whatToDo(8)) //No clue
```

In this example, we passed to when the variable dayOfWeek. Unlike the previous example, where each of the conditions within when were Boolean expressions, in this example we have a mixture of conditions.

The first line within when checks if the given value is one of the comma separated values—you're not restricted to two values. In the next two lines we check if the given parameter is a member of the list or the range, respectively. In the line with "Friday" we look for an exact match. In addition to matching if the given value is in a list or range, you may also perform type checking—that's what we're doing in the line starting with is String. That branch is taken if the given input doesn't match with any of the previous conditions and is of type String. Finally, the line with else takes care of the default situation. Once again, the compiler will insist on having the else part in this case.

A word of caution. The Kotlin compiler won't permit the else part to appear anywhere but as the last option within when. But it doesn't complain if a more general condition, for example, if is String is placed before a more specific condition, like "Friday". The order in which the conditions are placed matters—the execution will follow the path corresponding to the first satisfying condition.

In the examples we've seen so far, the code that follows the -> was a short single expression. Kotlin permits that part to be a block as well. The last expression within the block becomes the result of the execution of that path.

Even though Kotlin allows blocks after ->, from the readability point of view, avoid that. If more complex logic than a single expression or statement is needed, refactor that into a separate function or method and call it from within the path after ->. Friends don't let friends write large, ugly when expressions.

when as a Statement

If you want to perform different actions based on the value of one or more variables, you can use when as a statement instead of as an expression. Let's convert the previous code to print the activities instead of returning a String response and, along the way, give a new name to the function.

```kotlin
iteration/printActivity.kts
fun printWhatToDo(dayOfWeek: Any) {
  when (dayOfWeek) {
    "Saturday", "Sunday" -> println("Relax")
    in listOf("Monday", "Tuesday", "Wednesday", "Thursday") ->
      println("Work hard")
    in 2..4 -> println("Work hard")
    "Friday" -> println("Party")
    is String -> println("What?")
  }
}

printWhatToDo("Sunday") //Relax
printWhatToDo("Wednesday") //Work hard
printWhatToDo(3) //Work hard
printWhatToDo("Friday") //Party
printWhatToDo("Munday") //What?
printWhatToDo(8) //
```

The return type of the function printWhatToDo() is Unit—it returns nothing. Within when each of the conditions is taking an action, printing something to the standard out. Kotlin doesn't care if you don't provide the else condition in the case where when is used as a statement. No action is taken when no condition matches, like when 8 is passed.

when and variable Scope

In the previous examples the variables used for matching came from outside the when expression or statement. But that's not a requirement; the variables used for matching may be limited to the scope of when. Designing code with such a restriction, where possible, is a good thing, as it will prevent variable scope bleeding and make the code easier to maintain.

Let's look at limiting a variable's scope with an example. Here's a function that uses when to examine the number of cores on a system.

iteration/cores.kts
```
fun systemInfo(): String {
  val numberOfCores = Runtime.getRuntime().availableProcessors()

  return when (numberOfCores) {
    1 -> "1 core, packing this one to the museum"
    in 2..16 -> "You have $numberOfCores cores"
    else -> "$numberOfCores cores!, I want your machine"
  }
}
```

The systemInfo() function returns a response based on the number of cores, but the code is a tad noisy. The function had to first invoke the availableProcessors() method of Runtime to determine the number of cores. Then that variable was passed to when for its evaluation. We can reduce the noise and limit the scope of the variable numberOfCores to the when block by rewriting the code as follows:

```
fun systemInfo(): String =
  when (val numberOfCores = Runtime.getRuntime().availableProcessors()) {
    1 -> "1 core, packing this one to the museum"
    in 2..16 -> "You have $numberOfCores cores"
    else -> "$numberOfCores cores!, I want your machine"
  }
```

Placing the val in the argument to when gives us some benefits. First, we can directly return the result of when and remove the outer block {} and return; that's less noise and fewer lines of code too. Second, in cases where we want to take the result of when and do further processing, the variable numberOfCores won't be available beyond the point it's needed. Limiting scope for variables is good design.

Wrapping Up

Using the imperative style to iterate is a lot more fluent in Kotlin than in many mainstream languages. With a higher level of abstraction, through specialized classes for range of values, Kotlin makes it easier to do forward iteration, reverse iteration, skip values in the range, and so on. The same approach may be used for iterating over a collection of values as well. And, to process different values, of different types, the argument-matching syntax—the when construct—removes a lot of noisy conditional code.

We've covered a lot of ground so far in this part about fundamental everyday programming tasks. Next we'll take a look at the collections that are available when programming with Kotlin.

CHAPTER 5

Using Collections

We use collections of objects in every single application, whether it's business, scientific, or game development. You can pretty much use any collection available in Java directly from within Kotlin. But, Kotlin also offers a few view interfaces over Java collections, which provide a pleasant and a safer coding experience.

For example, Kotlin provides Pair and Triple for a collection of two or three values, respectively. For larger fixed-size collections we can use an array, but for more flexibility we may use lists. We also often use sets and associative maps. Kotlin offers all of them.

Kotlin provides both a mutable and an immutable flavor for collection interfaces that serve as views to Java collections. If the application is simple and single threaded you may use mutable interfaces to access the underlying collections. For more complex behaviors, functional and asynchronous programming, the immutable interfaces are safer to use.

In this chapter, you'll learn about the different flavors of collections in Kotlin to gain a high-level understanding of what's there. Then we'll dive into using Pair, arrays, lists, sets, and maps, both the mutable and immutable versions. We'll use the facilities for external iteration that we looked at in the previous chapter, and here we'll see how to use them with collections. With the knowledge you gain from this chapter, you'll be ready to reach for the right collection for your projects.

Flavors of Collections

In Java, we're used to different types of collections: List, Set, Map, and so on. We can use them in Kotlin as well. The mutable collection interfaces of Java are split into two interfaces in Kotlin: an immutable read-only interface and a mutable read-write interface. Kotlin also provides a number of convenience methods on collections in addition to those from the JDK.

When you're ready to iterate over the elements in any of these collections, Kotlin makes that task easier and much more fluent than in Java. At a high level, you may use the following collections in Kotlin:

- Pair—a tuple of two values.
- Triple—a tuple of three values.
- Array—indexed fixed-sized collection of objects and primitives.
- List—ordered collection of objects.
- Set—unordered collection of objects.
- Map—associative dictionary or map of keys and values.

Since Java already offers a wide range of collections in the JDK, you may wonder what role Kotlin plays when working with collections. The improvement comes in two forms: through extension functions and views. Let's discuss each of these separately.

Convenience Methods Added by Kotlin

Through the kotlin.collections[1] package, of the standard library, Kotlin adds many useful convenience functions to various Java collections. You can use the Java collections from within Kotlin, in ways you're familiar with. For the same collections, when coding in Kotlin, you can also use the methods that Kotlin has added.

For example, in Java, we may iterate over the elements of a List of String stored in a reference names using the traditional for-loop like so:

```
//Java code
for(int i = 0; i < names.size(); i++) {
  System.out.println(names.get(i));
}
```

Alternatively, for greater fluency, we may use the for-each iterator:

```
//Java code
for(String name : names) {
  System.out.println(name);
}
```

The latter is less noisy than the former, but we get only the elements and not the index in this case. This is also true if you use the functional style forEach in Java instead of the imperative style for-each iterator. Kotlin makes

---

1.   https://kotlinlang.org/api/latest/jvm/stdlib/kotlin.collections/index.html

it convenient to get both the index and then value, by adding a withIndex() method. Here's an example of using it:

```
collections/extension.kts
val names = listOf("Tom", "Jerry")

println(names.javaClass)

for ((index, value) in names.withIndex()) {
  println("$index $value")
}
```

In this example, we call the withIndex() method on an instance of ArrayList obtained from the JDK, using Kotlin's listOf() method. This method returns a special iterator over an IndexedValue, which is a data class. As we saw in Destructuring, on page 49, Kotlin makes it easy to extract values from data classes using destructuring. Using that facility, we obtained both the index and the value in the code. Here's the output:

```
class java.util.Arrays$ArrayList
0 Tom
1 Jerry
```

The output shows that the instance at hand is the JDK ArrayList class, but we're able to iterate more conveniently in Kotlin than in Java. The withIndex() is but one example of the vast number of convenience methods that Kotlin has added to the JDK classes. Take some time to familiarize yourself with the methods in the kotlin.collections package.

Views

Immutable collections are much safer to use when programming in the functional style, using concurrency, or programming asynchronous applications. Most collections in Java are mutable, but in recent years Java has introduced immutable versions. One downside, though, is that both mutable and immutable versions of the collections in Java implement the same interfaces. So any attempt to modify an immutable collection, like using the add() method on a List, for example, will result in an UnsupportedOperationException at runtime. Kotlin doesn't want you to wait that long to know that the operation is invalid. This is where the views come in.

Kotlin provides two different views for lists, sets, and maps: the read-only or immutable view, and the read-write or mutable view. Both views simply map to the same underlying collection in Java. There's no runtime overhead, and there are no conversions at compile time or runtime when you use these views instead of the original collection. The read-only view permits only read operations; any attempt to write using a read-only reference will fail at compile time.

For example, both List and MutableList are Kotlin views around ArrayList, but operations to add an element or set a value at an index using a List reference will fail at compile time.

A word of caution—don't assume that the use of read-only views provides thread safety. The read-only reference is to a mutable collection and, even though you can't change the collection, it's not guaranteed that the referenced collection isn't changed in another thread. Likewise, if you use multiple views on a same instance, where some views are read-only and the others are read-write, you have to be extra careful to verify that no two threads use the read-write interface to modify the collection at the same time.

We'll first look at Pair and Triple, and then we'll move on to other, more complex and powerful, collections.

Using Pair and Triple

Tuples are sequences of objects of small, finite size. Unlike some languages that provide a way to create tuples of different sizes, Kotlin provides two specific types: Pair for a tuple of size two and Triple for a size of three. Use these two when you want to quickly create two or three objects as a collection.

Here's an example of creating a Pair of Strings:

```
println(Pair("Tom", "Jerry")) //(Tom, Jerry)
println(mapOf("Tom" to "Cat", "Jerry" to "Mouse")) //{Tom=Cat, Jerry=Mouse}
```

First we create an instance of Pair using the constructor. Then we use the to() extension function, that's available on any object in Kotlin, to create pairs of entries for a Map. The to() method creates an instance of Pair, with the target value as the first value in the Pair and the argument provided as the second value in the Pair.

The ability to create a pair of objects with such concise syntax is useful. The need to work with a pair of objects is common in programming. For example, if you have a list of airport codes and want to get the temperature at each of these airports, then representing the airport code and temperature as a pair of values is natural. In Java, if you hold the values in an array, it'll get cumbersome to work with. Besides, we'll lose type safety since airport code is a String and temperature is a double, and the array will end up being of type Object—smelly. In Java we normally create a specialized class to hold the two values. This approach will provide type safety and remove some noise in code, but it increases the burden on us to create a separate class just for this purpose. Java provides no pleasant way to deal with this. Kotlin Pair solves the issue elegantly.

To see the benefit of Pair, let's create an example to collect the temperature values for different airport codes.

collections/airporttemperatures.kts
```
val airportCodes = listOf("LAX", "SFO", "PDX", "SEA")

val temperatures =
  airportCodes.map { code -> code to getTemperatureAtAirport(code) }

for (temp in temperatures) {
  println("Airport: ${temp.first}: Temperature: ${temp.second}")
}
```

We iterate over the collection airportCodes using the functional-style map() iterator (which you'll learn about in Chapter 11, Internal Iteration and Lazy Evaluation, on page 203) to transform each airport code in the list to the pair of (code, temperature). The result is a list of Pair<String, String>. Finally, we loop through the values in the list of Pairs to print the details of each airport code and temperature at that location. For each Pair, we obtain the two contained values using the first and second property, respectively.

If you're curious about the getTemperatureAtAirport() function used in this code, we'll implement a working code to talk to a web service later in the book. For now, let's implement a fake function to keep the focus on the benefits of Pair.

collections/airporttemperatures.kts
```
fun getTemperatureAtAirport(code: String): String =
  "${Math.round(Math.random() * 30) + code.count()} C"
```

Run the code and watch the program output the fake temperatures for the given airports. Here's a sample of what I got on a run:

```
Airport: LAX: Temperature: 25 C
Airport: SFO: Temperature: 21 C
Airport: PDX: Temperature: 30 C
Airport: SEA: Temperature: 27 C
```

This example shows the use of Pair in a practical setting. Use it anywhere you'll need a pair of objects or tuple. You not only get concise code, it's type safe at compile time as well.

Pair is useful when working with two values. While it looks special, it's just another class written in the Kotlin standard library. You may create your own classes like that where you need.

If you have a need for three objects, then instead of Pair use Triple. For example, if you need to represent the position of a circle, you don't have to rush to create a Circle class. Instead, you may create an instance of Triple<Int, Int, Double> where its first value represents the center X, the second value the center Y, and finally the third value, of type Double, holds the radius. That's less code while getting type safety.

Both Pair and Triple are immutable and are useful to create a grouping of two and three values, respectively. If you need to group more than three immutable values, then consider creating a *data class* (see Data Classes, on page 129).

The Kotlin standard library takes care of your needs to keep two or three immutable values. But if you need a mutable collection of values, Array may be a good choice, as we'll see next.

Arrays of Objects and Primitives

The Array<T> class represents an array of values in Kotlin. Use arrays only when low-level optimization is desired; otherwise, use other data structures like List, which we'll see later in this chapter.

The easiest way to create an array is using the arrayOf() top-level function. Once you create an array, you may access the elements using the index [] operator.

To create an array of Strings, for example, pass the desired values to the arrayOf() function:

collections/arrays.kts
```
val friends = arrayOf("Tintin", "Snowy", "Haddock", "Calculus")

println(friends::class) //class kotlin.Array
println(friends.javaClass) //class [Ljava.lang.String;
println("${friends[0]} and ${friends[1]}") //Tintin and Snowy
```

The friends variable holds a reference to the newly created array instance. The type of the object is Kotlin.Array, that is Array<T>, but the underlying real type, when run on the JVM, is a Java array of Strings. To get the values of the elements, the index operator [] is used and that, in turn, will invoke the get() method of Array<T>. When used on the left-hand side, the index operator [] will invoke the set() method of Array<T>.

The previous code created an array of Strings; to create an array of integers we may be tempted to use the same method, as in this example:

collections/arrays.kts
```
val numbers = arrayOf(1, 2, 3)
println(numbers::class) //class kotlin.Array
println(numbers.javaClass) //class [Ljava.lang.Integer;
```

That works, but it may not be a smart way. When numbers were passed to arrayOf(), the instance created was Array<T>, as expected, but internally it is an array of boxed Integer types. That overhead is unnecessary when working with primitive types.

The specialized functions like intArrayOf() are better alternatives to create specialized arrays that don't have the boxing overhead. To create an array of ints instead of an array of Integers, change the previous code to the following:

collections/arrays.kts
```
val numbers = intArrayOf(1, 2, 3)
println(numbers::class) //class kotlin.IntArray
println(numbers.javaClass) //class [I
```

The same operations that are available on Array<T> are available on the specialized classes like IntArray as well. So even though they are different types, you may use them as if they were the same type.

In addition to using the index operator [] to get and set values, you may determine the size of the array using the size property. Also, you may use one of many functions on Array[2] to conveniently work with arrays. Let's exercise the size property and one useful method—average—on the array we just created:

collections/arrays.kts
```
println(numbers.size) //3
println(numbers.average()) //2.0
```

Explore the Kotlin.Array<T> class to learn about the different methods you may use on an array of objects and primitives.

Instead of hard-coding the values when creating an array, you may also compute the values if you like. For example, in the code that follows we're computing the square of values from 1 to 5 into an array and then totaling the values in the array:

collections/arrays.kts
```
println(Array(5) { i -> (i + 1) * (i + 1) }.sum()) //55
```

The Array constructor takes two parameters, the size of the array and a function that takes the index, starting with 0, and returns the value to be placed at that index. The syntax for this function in the example uses a lambda expression, which we'll explore further in Chapter 10, Functional Programming with Lambdas, on page 175.

If you want an ordered collection of elements with flexible size, then you may want to consider a list instead of an array. Also, unlike an array, which is mutable, list comes in both mutable and immutable flavors.

---

2.   https://kotlinlang.org/api/latest/jvm/stdlib/kotlin/-array/index.html

Using List

As a first step in creating a list, Kotlin wants you to declare your intent—immutable or mutable. To create an immutable list, use listOf()—immutability is implied, which should also be our preference when there's a choice. But if you really need to create a mutable list, then use mutableListOf().

The function listOf() returns a reference to an interface kotlin.collections.List<T>. In the following code the reference fruits is of this interface type, specialized to String for the parametric type:

```
collections/lists.kts
val fruits: List<String> = listOf("Apple", "Banana", "Grape")
println(fruits) //[Apple, Banana, Grape]
```

To access an element in the list you may use the traditional get() method, but the index operator [], which routes to the same method, may be used as well.

```
collections/lists.kts
println("first's ${fruits[0]}, that's ${fruits.get(0)}")
  //first's Apple, that's Apple
```

The index operator [] is less noisy than get() and is more convenient—use it freely instead of get(). You may check if a value exists in the collection using the contains() method or using the in operator—we'll dig into operator overloading in Overloading Operators, on page 222.

```
collections/lists.kts
println(fruits.contains("Apple")) //true
println("Apple" in fruits) //true
```

In the previous code we asked if the list contains a value and if that value is *in* the list—the latter is more fluent and is preferred in Kotlin.

Using the reference returned by listOf(), we can't modify the list. If you're the good type that won't take *no* for an answer, go ahead and verify that with the following code:

```
collections/lists.kts
fruits.add("Orange") //ERROR: unresolved reference: add
```

The interface kotlin.collections.List<T> acts as a compile-time view around the widely used object in the JDK that you'd create using Arrays.asList() in Java, but the interface doesn't have the methods that permit mutation or change to the list. That's the reason the call to the add() method failed at compile time. By providing such views, Kotlin is able to make the code safer from the immutability point of view, but without introducing any runtime overhead or conversions.

That protection is nice, but that shouldn't stop us from having another fruit. This is where the + operator comes in handy.

```
collections/lists.kts
val fruits2 = fruits + "Orange"
println(fruits) //[Apple, Banana, Grape]
println(fruits2) //[Apple, Banana, Grape, Orange]
```

The operation didn't mutate the list fruits; instead, it created a new list with all the values from the original copied over, plus the new element.

If there's a plus, then it's only logical to expect a minus. The - operator is useful to create a new list without the first occurrence of the specified element, like this:

```
collections/lists.kts
val noBanana = fruits - "Banana"
println(noBanana) //[Apple, Grape]
```

If the specified element isn't present in the list, then the result is a list with the original elements, nothing removed.

The List<T>[3] interface shines nicely in the previous examples, and Kotlin provides a long list of methods. The fruits interface is of type List<T>, but what's the real class under the hood? you may wonder. Let's answer that question with the next piece of code:

```
collections/lists.kts
println(fruits::class) //class java.util.Arrays$ArrayList
println(fruits.javaClass) //class java.util.Arrays$ArrayList
```

The output shows that the instance is of the type provided in the JDK, even though we accessed it using a view interface in Kotlin.

The listOf() method returns a read-only reference, but if you feel the urge to create a mutable list, call a helpline so they can convince you not to. But, after enough thought and discussions, if you decide that's the right choice, you can create one using the mutableListOf() function. All the operations you were able to perform on List<T> are readily available on the instance of MutableList<T> as well. The instance created using this method, though, is an instance of java.util.ArrayList instead of java.util.Arrays$ArrayList.

---

3. https://kotlinlang.org/api/latest/jvm/stdlib/kotlin.collections/-list/index.html

In the next piece of code, we get access to the read-write interface instead of the read-only interface:

```
val fruits: MutableList<String> = mutableListOf("Apple", "Banana", "Grape")
println(fruits::class) //class java.util.ArrayList
```

Using this interface we may alter the list. For example, we can add an element to it:

```
fruits.add("Orange")
```

Instead of interacting with the ArrayList<T> through the MutableList<T> interface, obtained using the mutableListOf() function, you may directly obtain a reference of type ArrayList<T> using the arrayListOf() function.

Where possible, use listOf() instead of mutableListOf() and arrayListOf()—only reluctantly bring in mutability.

Once you create a list, you may iterate over it using the imperative style like we saw in Iterating over Arrays and Lists, on page 57, or using the functional style like we'll see in Chapter 11, Internal Iteration and Lazy Evaluation, on page 203.

If you don't care about ordering of the elements, you may want to use a set instead of a list, and Kotlin has top-level functions for that.

Using Set

Sets are unordered collections of elements. Like the methods for creating List<T>, which has both immutable/read-only and mutable/read-write versions, you may create instances of Set<T> using setOf() or instances of MutableSet<T> using mutableSetOf(). You may also use hashSetOf() to get a reference of type java.util.HashSet<T>: linkedSetOf() for LinkedHashSet, and sortedSetOf() for TreeSet<T>.

Here's a set of fruits, with a duplicate element:

```
collections/sets.kts
val fruits: Set<String> = setOf("Apple", "Banana", "Apple")
```

Since sets guarantee uniqueness of elements, the duplicate is discarded in the set created:

```
collections/sets.kts
println(fruits) //[Apple, Banana]
```

The instance created by setOf() is of the type Set<T> interface, but the underlying implementation, the class, is from the JDK:

collections/sets.kts
```
println(fruits::class) //class java.util.LinkedHashSet
println(fruits.javaClass) //class java.util.LinkedHashSet
```

Just like on List<T>, there are plenty of functions on Set<T> and MutableSet<T>: operations like +, -, contains or in, and so on. The chances are the library already contains a method to accomplish the operation you'd like to carry out on a set. Take time to familiarize with the methods of Set<T>[4] and its mutable counterpart.

Instead of keeping a collection of values or objects, often we want a collection of key-value pairs, and kotlin.collections.Map<K, V> is exactly for that.

Using Map

A map keeps a collection of key-value pairs. Much like the way Kotlin provides a read-only immutable interface and a read-write mutable interface for the JDK List, the language also provides two interfaces for the JDK Map. All methods of the JDK Map interface are available through the mutable interface, and the read-only methods are available through the immutable interface.

You may use mapOf() to create a map and get a reference to the read-only interface Map<K, V>. Alternatively, use mutableMapOf() to get access to MutableMap<K, V>. Also, you may obtain a reference to the JDK HashMap using hashMapOf(), LinkedHashMap using linkedMapOf(), and SortedMap using sortedMapOf().

Let's create an example using the immutable/read-only interface Map<K, V> and look at ways to access the elements. Here's a piece of code to create a map of site names and their corresponding URLs, where both keys and values are Strings:

collections/usingmap.kts
```
val sites = mapOf("pragprog" to "https://www.pragprog.com",
  "agiledeveloper" to "https://agiledeveloper.com")

println(sites.size) //2
```

The key-value pairs are created using the to() extension function, available on any object in Kotlin, and mapOf(), which takes a vararg of Pair<K, V>. The size property will tell you the number of entries in the map.

You may iterate over all the keys in the map using the keys property or all the values using the values property. You may also check if a particular key or value exists using the containsKey() and containsValue() methods, respectively.

---

4. https://kotlinlang.org/api/latest/jvm/stdlib/kotlin.collections/-set/index.html

Alternatively, you may use the contains() method or the in operator to check for a key's presence:

```
collections/usingmap.kts
println(sites.containsKey("agiledeveloper")) //true
println(sites.containsValue("http://www.example.com")) //false
println(sites.contains("agiledeveloper")) //true
println("agiledeveloper" in sites) //true
```

To access the value for a key you may use the get() method, but there's a catch. The following won't work:

```
collections/usingmap.kts
val pragProgSite: String = sites.get("pragprog") //ERROR
```

It's not guaranteed that a key exists in the map, so there may not be a value for it. The get() method returns a nullable type—see Nullable References, on page 80. Kotlin protects us at compile time and wants us to use a nullable reference type:

```
collections/usingmap.kts
val pragProgSite: String? = sites.get("pragprog")
```

The get() method is also used for the index operator [], so instead of using get() we may use that operator:

```
collections/usingmap.kts
val pragProgSite2: String? = sites["pragprog"]
```

That's convenient, but we can avoid the nullable reference type by providing an alternative, default, value if the key doesn't exist:

```
collections/usingmap.kts
val agiledeveloper =
  sites.getOrDefault("agiledeveloper", "http://www.example.com")
```

If the key "agiledeveloper" doesn't exist in the map, then the value provided as the second argument will be returned. Otherwise, the actual value will be returned.

The mapOf() function provides a read-only reference, so we can't mutate the map. But we may create a new map with additional key-value pairs, like so:

```
collections/usingmap.kts
val sitesWithExample = sites + ("example" to "http://www.example.com")
```

Similarly, we can use the - operator to create a new map without a particular key that may be present in the original map, like this:

```
collections/usingmap.kts
val withoutAgileDeveloper = sites - "agiledeveloper"
```

To iterate over the entries in the map, you may use the for loop we saw in Chapter 4, External Iteration and Argument Matching, on page 53. Let's use the for loop here:

collections/usingmap.kts
```
for (entry in sites) {
  println("${entry.key} --- ${entry.value}")
}
```

The variable entry refers to a Map entry, and we can get the key and value from that object. But instead of that extra step, we may use the destructuring feature we saw in Destructuring, on page 49, to extract the key and value, like so:

collections/usingmap.kts
```
for ((key, value) in sites) {
  println("$key --- $value")
}
```

As the iteration progresses, Kotlin automatically extracts the key and the value from each entry into the immutable variables named key and value, thanks to the feature of destructuring.

We used the imperative style to loop here. Later in the book, when we explore internal iterators, we'll revisit this to see how to iterate over the values using the functional style—in Chapter 10, Functional Programming with Lambdas, on page 175.

The Map interface also has two special methods, getValue() and setValue(), which enable us to use maps as delegates—a powerful concept we'll dive into in Chapter 9, Extension Through Delegation, on page 149.

Wrapping Up

Kotlin extends Java collections and at the same time brings along improved compile-time safety via read-only views. Use the read-only views when working with functional style, writing concurrent code, or when programming asynchronously.

Kotlin's Pair and Triple are useful to create finite small-sized collections. For a larger fixed-sized collection, reach for the Array class. However, for flexibility to grow the collection, choose between List or Set. When working with collections, you have to choose methods, like listOf() to get a read-only view of the JDK collection, or methods like mutableListOf(), to get a read-write view. To work with associative maps, use the Kotlin view interfaces to interact with Java's Map implementations.

We've been exploring the imperative way to use iterators in this chapter. A functional style, using internal iterators, is a very powerful way to iterate, but there are performance consequences to it. We'll explore that later in the book, along with when to use iterators vs. sequences for lazy evaluation.

Next, you'll learn how Kotlin takes compile-time type safety to a whole new level.

CHAPTER 6

Type Safety to Save the Day

The more statically typed a language is, the more readily it should ensure type safety, but without the need to excessively specify types. Kotlin works hard to make your code more type safe and less error prone with enhanced null checks, smart type casting, and fluent type checking. In this chapter, you'll learn about a few basic types in Kotlin and the effective type checking capabilities built in to the compiler. We'll also look at how Kotlin fails fast at compile time to prevent many errors from sneaking into runtimes—this will make your programming efforts more productive.

Can you imagine turning on the television and getting a NullPointerException? That happened to my friend Brian Sletten[1] after he turned on his TV to watch his favorite show, and saw that error instead—with programs like that who needs horror movies? Kotlin will help you prevent NullPointerExceptions *at compile time*.

With Kotlin's design-by-contract approach, you clearly express if and when a function or a method may receive or return a null reference. If a reference may possibly be null, then you're forced to perform a null check before you can access any useful methods or properties of the object that's referenced. With this facility, Kotlin makes the code safe, which can save the day from debugging and embarrassing blowups in production. Also, Kotlin provides a number of operators to work with null types, which reduces the noise in code when dealing with references that may be null. What's even more exciting about this capability is that these checks are purely at compile time and don't add anything to the bytecode.

Much like Java's Object, all classes in Kotlin inherit from the Any class. This class brings under one fold a few common methods that are useful on

---

1. https://twitter.com/bsletten/status/587441266863943680

instances of just about any class in Kotlin. When working with multiple types, if a need to cast between types arises, the smart cast feature of Kotlin will take care of automatically casting so you don't have to write mundane code that's obvious to both you and the compiler. This not only saves keystrokes but also greatly reduces the verbosity in code, leading to code that is easier to maintain. And, in case you need to perform an explicit type cast, Kotlin has elegant syntax for that too, as you'll soon see.

One of the more advanced concepts in Kotlin is the nice support for working with covariance and contravariance of generics parametric types. That sounds complicated—and it is—but this chapter will demystify those concepts so you can use generics more effectively in Kotlin than in Java. We'll also explore reified type parameters that reduce clutter and error when creating and calling generic functions that require type information at runtime.

In this chapter you'll learn about the Any and Nothing classes, about the nullable references and related operators, and the benefits of smart casts. You'll also learn how to safely perform type casts and how to create extensible generic functions that are type safe. This will help you to design code that is less error prone and easier to maintain.

Any and Nothing Classes

Some methods like equals() and toString() are pervasive. In Java you'd expect to find them in the Object base class. In Kotlin, these methods are included in the Any class, along with a number of other methods that are useful on instances of any class. Any is Kotlin's counterpart of Java's Object class, except Any has a lot of special methods that come in through extension functions. Kotlin also has a class named Nothing that serves to stand in as type when a function literally is expected to return *nothing*—this is useful for type-checking methods when one or more branches is expected to return nothing. Nothing in Java is equivalent to Kotlin's Nothing. In this section you'll learn about the facilities offered by the ubiquitous Any and the purpose of Nothing.

Any, the Base Class

All classes in Kotlin inherit from Any, which maps to Object in Java. If a function will take objects of different types as a parameter, then you can specify its type as Any. Likewise, if you can't put your finger on a specific type to return, you may return Any. The Any class gives you the maximum—often too much—flexibility from the type point of view, so use it sparingly.

The purpose of Any isn't to let us define variables, parameters, or return types as Any, though occasionally we may want to, but to provide some common methods that are available on all Kotlin types. For example, methods like equals(), hashCode(), and toString() may be called on any type in Kotlin because those methods are implemented in Any.

Even though Any maps to Object in Java in the bytecode, they're not identical. Also, Any offers some special methods through extension functions. For example, the to() extension function that we saw in Using Pair and Triple, on page 66, is an excellent example. Since creating a Pair of different objects is such a common operation and Pair is used widely with helper functions to create maps, Kotlin decided to make the to() method, which creates a Pair of objects of any type, universally available on objects of every single type.

Likewise, executing a block of code in the context of an object can remove a lot of verbose and repetitive code. To facilitate this, Any has extension functions like let(), run(), apply(), and also()—we'll explore these in Fluency with Any Object, on page 236. By using these methods you can remove a lot of clutter. These are also useful for creating highly fluent internal DSLs in Kotlin, as you'll see in Chapter 13, Creating Internal DSLs, on page 249.

Nothing Is Deeper Than void

In languages like Java we use void to indicate that a method returns nothing. In Kotlin we use Unit, instead, to tell us when functions, which are expressions, return nothing useful. But there are situations where a function truly returns nothing...nada; that's where the Nothing class comes in. The class Nothing has no instances and it represents a value or result that will never exist. When used as a return type of a method it means that the function never returns—the function call will only result in an exception.

One unique capability of Nothing is that it can stand in for anything—that is, Nothing is substitutable for any class, including Int, Double, String, and so on. For example, take a look at the following code:

```
fun computeSqrt(n: Double): Double {
  if(n >= 0) {
    return Math.sqrt(n)
  } else {
    throw RuntimeException("No negative please")
  }
}
```

The if part returns a Double, while the else part throws an exception. The exception part is represented by the type Nothing. Cumulatively, the compiler can determine the return type of the if expression, in this case, to be a Double type. Thus the sole purpose of Nothing is to be able to help the compiler verify that the integrity of types in a program is sound.

Nullable References

null is a smell in Java that we can't avoid all the time. If a function that returns an object doesn't have anything to return at times, then the solution in Java is to return null. This unfortunately leads to an accidental NullPointerException if the caller of the function doesn't—that is, forgets to—perform an explicit null check. In more recent versions of Java, Optional is used as a solution to this issue, but this approach has three disadvantages. First, the programmer has to use Optional and the compiler won't force that. Second, Optional involves a small overhead to wrap the object's reference, or an empty null reference, when there's no object. Third, a programmer may still return null instead of an instance of Optional and the Java compiler won't complain. Kotlin avoids these issues and at the same time offers great compile-time support to ensure that necessary null check is done by the programmer.

We'll first discuss why null references are generally not pleasant to use. Then we'll see how the Kotlin compiler doesn't permit assigning null to any arbitrary reference and requires the references that can accept null to be a special nullable type. Then we'll look at nice operators that Kotlin provides to safely and conveniently dereference nullable references, with full compile-time verification that necessary null checks are done. Finally, we'll look at how the when expression interplays with null checks.

null Is a Smell

Effective Java, Third Edition [Blo18], suggests that if a function is returning a collection but at runtime there's nothing to return, then we should return an empty collection instead of null. That's because the receiver of the result will otherwise fail and will have to perform an explicit null check to avoid the issues. Good advice.

What if the result of a function is an object and not a collection? The traditional solution in Java was to return null if there's nothing to return as reference, and a more recent recommendation is to return Optional<T>. These solutions present a few issues though.

It's not possible, in Java, to prevent a programmer from returning null from a method that expects a reference to be returned. Programmers have to opt in to use Optional<T>, and it's confusing when and where to use it. In addition, with Optional<T> there's extra overhead just for the sake of avoiding null.

Kotlin handles this situation safely, elegantly, and gracefully. To begin with, assigning null to a non-nullable reference or returning null where the reference type is non-nullable will result in a compilation error.

Here's a piece of code that will make the Kotlin compiler complain:

```
types/nonull.kts
fun nickName(name: String): String {
  if (name == "William") {
    return "Bill"
  }

  return null //ERROR
}

println("Nickname for William is ${nickName("William")}")
println("Nickname for Venkat is ${nickName("Venkat")}")
println("Nickname for null is ${nickName(null)}") //ERROR
```

In the current form, the nickName() function wants to return the nickname for only the popular name "William" and null for everything else. Not so fast, Kotlin says.

Similar code in Java would have compiled and then failed at runtime, but Kotlin doesn't want us to write code that will crash and burn, at least not so easily. Kotlin doesn't permit returning null from within the method since the return type is String, which is not nullable. Likewise, it doesn't allow us to pass null as argument since the function parameter type is also String, non-nullable. Here are the murmurs from the compiler:

```
nonull.kts:6:10: error: null can not be a value of a non-null type String
  return null //ERROR
         ^
nonull.kts:11:42: error: null can not be a value of a non-null type String
println("Nickname for null is ${nickName(null)}") //ERROR
                                         ^
```

In general, unless you're interoperating with code written in Java, avoid null and nullable types. But if you have to receive and/or return null, then you have to make your intention abundantly clear so Kotlin can enforce a few checks at compile time to prevent accidental NullPointerException at runtime. Let's focus on getting that compile-time safety for null references next.

Using Nullable Types

Non-nullable types have a nullable counterpart. Where the type is a non-nullable reference, you can pass only a valid reference that is non-null. However, you may pass either a valid reference or a null to a nullable reference type. On the receiving side, you can't use the object held by a nullable reference without first performing a null check.

The nullable types have a ? suffix—that is, the counterpart for non-nullable String is String?. Likewise, Int vs. Int?, List<String> vs. List<String>?, and YourOwnClass vs. YourOwnClass?.

Mapping of Nullable Types to Bytecode

You may wonder how nullable types are mapped to Java bytecode, since they don't have a direct representation on the JVM. A nullable type is erased to its non-nullable counterpart; for example, String? becomes String, along with extra meta-instructions in the bytecode. The Kotlin compiler uses these meta-instructions to perform compile-time null checks with no runtime performance overhead.

Let's fix the issues in the previous code, one at a time, starting with the effort to safely return null. To convey that we may return a reference or null from within the nickName() function, we have to change the return type of the function from String to its nullable counterpart String?. That's the only change to fix that compilation error:

```
types/returnnull.kts
fun nickName(name: String): String? {
  if (name == "William") {
    return "Bill"
  }

  return null
}

println("Nickname for William is ${nickName("William")}")
println("Nickname for Venkat is ${nickName("Venkat")}")
//println("Nickname for null is ${nickName(null)}")
```

Since the last line, where we pass null, is commented out, the code will have no issues to run and produce the following output:

```
Nickname for William is Bill
Nickname for Venkat is null
```

It's almost good; for the sake of record, trust me, null is not a nickname for Venkat. If instead of merely printing out the response, we had done some processing with it, then Kotlin would have required a null check on the response. Instead of trying to do more work on the response, let's modify the code to permit null as argument to the parameter. That will help you to learn how to process a nullable reference, while keeping the example short.

Let's enhance the nickName() function. In its new form the function will return the correct nickname for "William", the reversed name for any other non-null name, and null for null argument. For this we have to change the parameter type from String to String?, to allow a null argument.

types/receivenullerror.kts
```
fun nickName(name: String?): String? {
  if (name == "William") {
    return "Bill"
  }

  return name.reversed() //ERROR
}
println("Nickname for William is ${nickName("William")}")
println("Nickname for Venkat is ${nickName("Venkat")}")
println("Nickname for null is ${nickName(null)}")
```

Passing null in the last line of code presents no problem. But within the function, the line where we call reversed() on name fails compilation. Kotlin requires method calls on nullable references to be prefixed with either the safe-call operator or the non-null assertion operator—we'll see these operators soon. The compiler insists on this because, in this example, name may be null and calling a method on a null reference will… you know. The compiler is readily protecting us from the otherwise runtime impending doom. Thank you, Kotlin.

Before we can access the object held by the nullable reference, we have to perform a null check, like so:

```
if (name != null) {
  return name.reversed()
}

return null
```

Kotlin nudges us down the path of safety and defensive programming. With a nullable type, we can't forget to perform a null check. It's almost safe—we'll see the caveats soon. Let's run the code with the null check change and take a look at the output:

```
Nickname for William is Bill
Nickname for Venkat is takneV
Nickname for null is null
```

That worked, but the code with null check is noisy. Next we'll see how to retain the safety but remove the clutter.

Safe-Call Operator

We can merge the null check and the call to a method or property into one step using ?.—the *safe-call* operator. If the reference is null, the safe-call operator will result in null. Otherwise, the result will be the property or the result of the method call. In any case, the type will be the nullable counterpart of the method's return type or property's type.

Out with the clutter, in with the concise safe-call operator. Let's replace the following code:

```
if (name != null) {
  return name.reversed()
}
return null
```

This single line is beautiful:

```
return name?.reversed()
```

Suppose we want to convert the reversed name to uppercase. We can combine multiple calls to the safe-call operator, like so:

```
return name?.reversed()?.toUpperCase()
```

That's pretty awesome, right? Yes, but not as awesome as Elvis.

Elvis Operator

The safe-call operator returns null if the target is null. But, what if we want to return something else, a non-null? Let's further enhance the nickName() function to return "Joker" if the caller passes in null. For this, we can change the return type to a more restrictive String instead of String?. Here's the change, but it's going to get a bit smelly, again, before we refactor to restore elegance.

```
fun nickName(name: String?): String {
  if (name == "William") {
    return "Bill"
  }

  val result = name?.reversed()?.toUpperCase()

  return if (result == null) "Joker" else result
}

println("Nickname for William is ${nickName("William")}")
println("Nickname for Venkat is ${nickName("Venkat")}")
println("Nickname for null is ${nickName(null)}")
```

Let's quickly look at the output of the code:

```
Nickname for William is Bill
Nickname for Venkat is TAKNEV
Nickname for null is Joker
```

The function now takes String? to allow null arguments, but the return type is String. If the name is not "William", we reverse the value in the given parameter using reversed() and convert to uppercase, just like before. But, in this version, we store the result of the two consecutive uses of safe-call to a temporary variable named result. Then we perform a null check and return "Joker" if result is null and the value otherwise. These null checks are like a nasty villain in a terrible movie series—they keep coming back.

We have good news and bad news. To return the value after null check there's no ceremony. We're able to return result as is in the end, after the else, even though result is of type String? and the return type of the function is String. In general, we can't return an instance of String? where String is expected. But Kotlin knows we've paid our dues with a null check and so doesn't mess with us anymore here. For the bad news: we wrote two lines of code and created a temporary variable. It'd be great to reduce that noise; Elvis operator—?:—to the rescue.

The Elvis operator will return the result of the expression to the left if it's not null, otherwise it will evaluate and return the result of the expression on the right. The Elvis operator short circuits evaluation—that is, it doesn't evaluate what's on the right if that won't be used.

In the previous code, let's replace the verbose part:

```
val result = name?.reversed()?.toUpperCase()

return if (result == null) "Joker" else result
```

It becomes elegant, like so:

```
return name?.reversed()?.toUpperCase() ?: "Joker"
```

The Elvis operator is pretty cool, like its namesake singer Mr. Presley. In a skewed imagination, you can see his hairstyle ? above his eyes : in the emoticon ?:, hence this operator's name.

The safe-call operator and the Elvis operator are your friends, but sometimes you'll have the urge to leave them behind for a greater conciseness with the operator !!, but that may not be a good idea, as you'll see next.

Don't Use the Unsafe Assertion Operator !!

Here is one more operator, the not-null assertion operator !!, which I'd like to officially name *the Joker operator* because it's an epitome of badness, like the super-villain in *Batman*. At first it may appear cool, until you realize its true nefarious nature.

We saw that given a nullable type, we can't call the methods of the non-nullable counterpart on it without null check. For example, given a reference of type String?, we can't call the reversed() method on it without performing a null check. But what if you know for sure that the reference isn't null? Then you can tell Kotlin to stand down from its rigorous check and let you call the methods and properties of String on the nullable counterpart.

If we know that name, which is of type String?, isn't null, then we can replace the code with ?., and ?: with this:

```
return name!!.reversed().toUpperCase() //BAD CODE
```

That's concise—what could possibly go wrong?

That operator has two ! for a reason. Here, we've put all our bets on name not being null. But what if that reference turns out to be null? Oops. At runtime we'll end up with a NullPointerException—yep, the very exception we tried to avoid in the first place with the nullable type. Don't use !!, forget it even exists, pretend I never mentioned it.

As you've seen, the safe-call and Elvis operators are powerful ways to process nullable types. However, we can make the code more intuitive using the when argument-matching operator.

Using when

Every effort that can reduce clutter and make the logic in code easier to follow is well worth it. When working with a nullable reference, if you want to perform different computations or take different actions based on the value in the reference, including null, then consider using when instead of ?. or ?: (see When It's Time to Use when, on page 58). In other words, use the safe-call or Elvis operator to extract values, and use when to make decisions on nullable references.

Since the nickName() function decides what to return based on the values in the nullable reference, and doesn't merely extract the values, we can change this function:

```
fun nickName(name: String?): String {
  if (name == "William") {
    return "Bill"
  }

    return name?.reversed()?.toUpperCase() ?: "Joker"
}
```

Instead of the previous code, the following works nicely:

```
fun nickName(name: String?) = when (name) {
  "William" -> "Bill"
  null -> "Joker"
  else -> name.reversed().toUpperCase()
}
```

In this code, when is used as an expression, and the value it produces is returned as the result of the function. The else clause is required in this case and should be the last. The path with null may appear anywhere above else.

Since we have a check for null, all other paths within when will be executed only if the reference isn't null. You know this and the compiler knows too. So within any of the non-null paths you don't have to perform a null check, nor do you have to use a safe-call operator or the Elvis operator. That's sweet—less work, less noise.

Kotlin not only provides safety when dealing with null, it also reduces clutter in code with elegant operators. You'll also find that same elegance in the features that perform type checks and explicit type casting.

Type Checking and Casting

Sometimes you may wonder if the object at hand is of a particular type you expect. And, once you verify, you often cast the reference to that type so you can invoke the methods you desire—well, at least, that's the case in Java. Here we'll see how Kotlin supports these two operations of type checking and type casting. Along the way you'll see how to benefit from Kotlin's type safety, and at the same time see how the language removes your need to write mundane code.

Type Checking

"Is it a feature or a flaw?" is an unsettled debate about runtime type checking. It's necessary to check an object's type occasionally, but from the extensibility point of view, we should use it sparingly. Checking for arbitrary types can make the code brittle when new types are added and lead to failure of the Open-Closed Principle—see *Agile Software Development, Principles, Patterns, and Practices [Mar02]*. Think many times before writing code to check for runtime types.

Having said that, checking for runtime type is useful and unavoidable in two situations. One is in the implementation of the equals() method—we need to know if the instance at hand is of the current class. The other is within when, if the path to take depends on the type of an instance.

Let's first look at how to check for the runtime type, and then at a nice little feature that removes the burden of casting once the type is confirmed.

Using is

The equals() method of Object performs reference-based comparison, but classes may override that method to determine equality. Continuing that tradition, all Kotlin classes, which extend from the Any class (discussed in Any, the Base Class, on page 78), may override the equals() method. We also saw in Improved Equality Check, on page 28, that Kotlin maps the == operator to the equals() method. Even though we've not looked at classes in Kotlin yet, let's move forward to implement the equals() method in a class for the sake of exploring type checking.

In the code below, an Animal class overrides the equals() method with an implementation that wants to treat all Animal instances as being equal. But if the parameter given—which has to be of type Any? due to the signature of the method being overridden from Any—is not an instance of Animal, it wants to return false.

```
types/equals.kts
class Animal {
  override operator fun equals(other: Any?) = other is Animal
}
```

The is operator is used to check if the object pointed to by a reference, other in this example, is of a particular type, Animal in this case. If the instance is of the expected type, then the result of that expression is true; otherwise it's false.

Let's use that equals() method in an example:

```
types/equals.kts
val greet: Any = "hello"
val odie: Any = Animal()
val toto: Any = Animal()

println(odie == greet) //false
println(odie == toto) //true
```

In Improved Equality Check, on page 28, we saw the difference between ==
and ===. In this example we access the equals() method using the == operator.
Comparing an instance of Animal with a String returns false, but comparing two
instances of Animal results in true. All the references in this example are of
type Any. If the reference types were of the specific class types—for example,
if the greet reference were defined as type String and the odie reference as type
Animal—then the Kotlin compiler would barf at the equality check due to a
type mismatch that can be detected from the source code. We kept the references types as Any to get around that check, to illustrate type checking.

The is operator can be used on any type of reference. If the reference is null,
then the result of using the is operator is false. But if the instance is either of
the type specified after is or one of its derived types, then the result is true.

You may use the is operator with negation as well. For example, you can use
other !is Animal to check if the given reference isn't pointing to an instance of
Animal.

Kotlin comes with a buy-one, get-one-free offer—if you buy the use of is or !is,
you get casting for free. Let's see how.

Smart Casts

Suppose the Animal class has an age property and we need to use that property
when comparing objects. In the equals() method, the reference type of the
parameter is Any, so we can't directly get the age value from that reference. If
we were programming in Java, the equals() method for the Animal class would
look like this:

```
//Java code
@Override public boolean equals(Object other) {
  if(other instanceof Animal) {
    return age == ((Animal) other).age;
  }

  return false;
}
```

It's not enough that we used instanceof to ask Java if the type of the reference
other was Animal. In addition, to access age, we had to write ((Animal)(other)).age.
What's that feature of Java in that code snippet called?

Punishment, but some call it casting.

Kotlin can perform automatic or smart casts once the type of a reference is confirmed. Let's change the Animal class we wrote earlier to include age and then modify the equals() method:

types/smartcast.kts
```
class Animal(val age: Int) {
  override operator fun equals(other: Any?):Boolean {
    return if (other is Animal) age == other.age else false
  }
}
```

Within the equals() method, we're able to use other.age directly without any casts. That's because within the if expression's condition, Kotlin confirmed that other is an instance of Animal. If you try to access other.age before the if, you'll get a compilation error. But once you've paid for the is check, so to speak, you get the casting for free.

Let's use this modified version of the Animal class in an example before refactoring further to reduce some noise.

types/smartcast.kts
```
val odie = Animal(2)
val toto = Animal(2)
val butch = Animal(3)

println(odie == toto) //true
println(odie == butch) //false
```

The example confirms the behavior of the type checking with smart casts. Smart casts work as soon as Kotlin determines the type. It may also be used after the || and && operators, for example, not just with an if expression.

Let's refactor the equals() method we wrote to make use of this capability:

```
override operator fun equals(other: Any?) =
  other is Animal && age == other.age
```

Kotlin will apply smart casts automatically where possible. If it can determine with confidence that the type of a reference is of a particular type, then it'll let you avoid casts. Likewise, once Kotlin determines that an object reference isn't null, it can apply smart casts to automatically cast a nullable type to a non-nullable type, again saving you an explicit cast.

Using Type Checking and Smart Cast with when

We can use is and !is and the smart casts within a when expression or statement.

We saw the following whatToDo() function in When It's Time to Use when, on page 58:

```
fun whatToDo(dayOfWeek: Any) = when (dayOfWeek) {
  "Saturday", "Sunday" -> "Relax"
  in listOf("Monday", "Tuesday", "Wednesday", "Thursday") -> "Work hard"
  in 2..4 -> "Work hard"
  "Friday" -> "Party"
  is String -> "What?"
  else -> "No clue"
}
```

One of the paths in when is performing type check, using the is operator, to verify if the given parameter is of type String at runtime. We can go further and use the properties and methods of String within that path without any explicit casts. For example, we can change that path for String type to:

```
is String -> "What, you provided a string of length ${dayOfWeek.length}"
```

Even though dayOfWeek is of type Any in the parameter list for the function, within this path—and only in this path—we're able to use that reference as type String. That's Kotlin's smart casts capability in action again. Smart cast is our ally; rely on it as much as possible.

Occasionally you'll want to do explicit casts, and Kotlin offers a few options for that.

Explicit Type Casting

Use explicit casts only in situations where smart casts aren't possible—that is, when the compiler can't determine the type with confidence. For example, if a var variable were to change between the check and its use, then Kotlin can't guarantee the type. In such cases it won't apply smart casts, and we have to take the responsibility for casts.

Kotlin provides two operators to perform explicit cast: as and as?. Let's create an example that illustrates how to use both of them.

Suppose we have a function that returns a message of different types, like this one:

```
types/unsafecast.kts
fun fetchMessage(id: Int): Any =
  if (id == 1) "Record found" else StringBuilder("data not found")
```

Now suppose that we want to receive the message by calling the above function, and print some details about it, but only if the result is a String type. One approach to writing such code would be to store the result of the call to fetchMessage() in a temporary variable. Then we can use is to check the type, and if it is of String type, then we can use smart casts to get the details we need from that temporary variable.

That will work. It's defensive coding, and so it's a prudent solution. But at times, we all are tempted to reduce the number of lines of code to an unhealthy extent and in the process may introduce unintended behavior in code. If we give in to that urge here, we could be tempted to use as to write code like this:

types/unsafecast.kts
```
for (id in 1..2) {
  println("Message length: ${(fetchMessage(id) as String).length}")
}
```

Casting using as is like putting all your money into a lottery—the outcome won't be pleasant. If the type of the object is different from what's expected, the result is a runtime exception. No fun.

```
Message length: 12
java.lang.ClassCastException: java.base/java.lang.StringBuilder cannot be cast
        to java.base/java.lang.String
```

To avoid this possibility we may fall back and use the is operator, but the safe alternative as? works in this particular example.

The as operator results in a reference of the same type as the one specified to the right of the operator, as in this example:

```
val message: String = fetchMessage(1) as String
```

On the other hand, as? results in a nullable reference type, like in this one:

```
val message: String? = fetchMessage(1) as? String
```

Whereas the as operator blows up if the casting fails, the safe cast operator as? will assign null to the reference upon failure.

Instead of using the as operator, let's switch over to using the safe alternative as?. Here's the one line of code that has changed from the previous example:

```
println("Message length: ${(fetchMessage(id) as? String)?.length ?: "---"}")
```

Since the safe cast operator assigns the reference to null if the cast fails, we use the Elvis operator to provide an alternative to length when necessary.

This is the output after the change:

```
Message length: 12
Message length: ---
```

The safe cast operator as? is better than the unsafe as. Here are some recommendations to take to the office:

- Use smart casts as much as possible.
- Use safe cast only when smart cast isn't an option.
- Use unsafe cast if you want to see the application crash and burn.

Kotlin's support for making your code type safe doesn't end with simple types. The language walks a few extra miles to make code that uses generics type safe as well. We often use generic types in code, and learning about the flexibility that Kotlin offers with generics' parametric types will help us not only create better code but also, more importantly, understand code that uses these features.

Dealing with generics in general isn't easy, and when we mix in terms like covariance and contravariance, it can get frustrating. The following are some advanced capabilities of the language that are worth the effort to learn, but take it slow for the concepts to sink in. Take a short walk first, refill your caffeinated beverage, and when you come back, get ready to practice the code as you read along—that will help you absorb this advanced topic more easily.

Generics: Variance and Constraints of Parametric Types

The desire to reuse code shouldn't come at a cost of compromising type safety. Generics bring a nice balance to this issue. With generics you can create code that can be reused for different types. At the same time, the compiler will verify that a generic class or a function isn't used with unintended types. We've enjoyed a fairly good amount of type safety with generics in Java. So, you may wonder, what could Kotlin possibly provide to improve? It turns out, quite a bit.

By default, in Java, generics impose type invariance—that is, if a generic function expects a parametric type T, you're not allowed to substitute a base type of T or a derived type of T; the type has to be exactly the expected type. That's a good thing, as we'll discuss further in this section. But what good are rules if there are no exceptions?—and it's in the area of exceptions that Kotlin comes out ahead.

We'll first look at type invariance and how Kotlin, just like Java, nicely supports that. Then we'll dig into ways to change the default behavior.

Sometimes you want the compiler to permit covariance—that is, tell the compiler to permit the use of a derived class of a parametric type T—in addition to allowing the type T. In Java you use the syntax <? extends T> to convey covariance, but there's a catch. You can use that syntax when you use a generic class, which is called *use-site variance*, but not when you define a class, which is called declaration-site variance. In Kotlin you can do both, as we'll see soon.

Other times you want to tell the compiler to allow contravariance—that is, permit a super class of a parametric type T where type T is expected. Once again, Java permits contravariance, with the syntax <? super T> but only at use-site and not declaration-site. Kotlin permits contravariance both at declaration-site and use-site.

In this section we'll first review type variance, which is available in Java. Going over it here will help set the context for the much deeper discussions to follow. Then, you'll learn the syntax for covariance both for declaration-site and use-site. After that, we'll dive into contravariance and, finally, wrap up with how to mix multiple constraints for variance.

Type Invariance

When a method receives an object of a class T, you may pass an object of any derived class of T. For example, if you may pass an instance of Animal, then you may also pass an instance of Dog, which is a subclass of Animal. However, if a method receives a generic object of type T, for example, List<T>, then you may not pass an object of a generic object of derived type of T. For example, if you may pass List<Animal>, you can't pass List<Dog> where Dog extends Animal. That's type invariance—you can't vary on the type.

Let's use an example to illustrate type invariance first, and then we'll build on that example to learn about type variance. Suppose we have a Fruit class and two classes that inherit from it:

types/typeinvariance.kts
```
open class Fruit
class Banana : Fruit()
class Orange: Fruit()
```

Now suppose a basket of Fruits is represented by Array<Fruit> and we have a method that receives and works with it.

types/typeinvariance.kts
```
fun receiveFruits(fruits: Array<Fruit>) {
  println("Number of fruits: ${fruits.size}")
}
```

Right now, the receiveFruits() method is merely printing the size of the array given to it. But, in the future, it may change to get or set an object from or into the Array<Fruit>. Now if we have a basket of Bananas, that is Array<Banana>, then Kotlin, like Java, won't permit us to pass it to the receiveFruits() method:

types/typeinvariance.kts
```
val bananas: Array<Banana> = arrayOf()
receiveFruits(bananas) //ERROR: type mismatch
```

This restriction is due to Kotlin's type invariance with generic types—a basket of Bananas doesn't inherit from a basket of Fruits. There's a really good reason for this. Inheritance means substitutability—that is, an instance of derived may be passed to any method that expects an instance of base. If an instance of Array<Banana> were allowed to be passed as argument where an instance of Array<Fruit> was expected, we may be in trouble if the receiveFruits() method were to add an Orange to the Array<Fruit>. In this case, when processing Array<Banana>, we'll run into a casting exception later when we try to treat that instance of Orange as Banana—no orange ever likes that kind of treatment. Alternatively, we may attempt to implement the receiveFruits() method so that it adds an Orange only if the given parameter isn't an Array<Banana>, but such a type check will result in the violation of the Liskov Substitution Principle—see *Agile Software Development, Principles, Patterns, and Practices [Mar02]*.

Even though Banana inherits from Fruit, by disallowing the Array<Banana> to be passed in where Array<Fruit> is expected, Kotlin makes the use of generics type safe.

Before we move forward, let's make a slight change to the code to understand what at first appears like a quirk but is actually the sign of a sound type system.

```
fun receiveFruits(fruits: List<Fruit>) {
  println("Number of fruits: ${fruits.size}")
}
```

We changed the parameter type from Array<Fruit> to List<Fruit>. Now, let's pass an instance of List<Banana> to this function:

```
val bananas: List<Banana> = listOf()
receiveFruits(bananas) //OK
```

After this change, the Kotlin compiler doesn't complain. That seems unfair—the language seems to restrict Arrays but not List. But the reason for this difference in behavior is a good one. Array<T> is mutable, but List<T> is immutable. You may add an Orange to Array<Fruit>, but you can't add anything to List<Fruit>. That makes sense, but you may be curious how Kotlin knows how to tell the difference. The answer to that lies in how the two types are defined: class Array<T> vs. interface List<out E>. That out is the secret sauce. Let's dig into that next.

Using Covariance

Kotlin protects us from passing an Array<Banana> where Array<Fruit> is expected and thus prevents us from inadvertently adding some arbitrary fruit into an array of Banana. That's great, but sometimes we want to tell Kotlin to relax the rules a bit, but without compromising type safety, of course. In other words, we want the Kotlin compiler to allow covariance—accept a generic of derived type where a generic of base type is expected. This is where type-projections come in.

Let's create an example where Kotlin will block our approach and then find ways to make progress, but without lowering type safety.

As you code along the examples in the rest of this chapter, anywhere the classes Fruit, Banana, and Orange are needed, bring them along from the examples we created in the previous section. Here's a copyFromTo() function that uses two arrays of Fruit:

```
types/copy.kts
fun copyFromTo(from: Array<Fruit>, to: Array<Fruit>) {
  for (i in 0 until from.size) {
    to[i] = from[i]
  }
}
```

The copyFromTo() function iterates over the objects in the from parameter and copies them into the to array. It assumes that the size of the two arrays are equal, since that detail isn't relevant to what we're interested in here. Now, let's create two arrays of Fruits and copy the contents of one into the other:

```
types/copy.kts
val fruitsBasket1 = Array<Fruit>(3) { _ -> Fruit() }
val fruitsBasket2 = Array<Fruit>(3) { _ -> Fruit() }

copyFromTo(fruitsBasket1, fruitsBasket2)
```

The copyFromTo() method expects two Array<Fruit>, and we're passing exactly those types. No complaints.

Now, let's change the parameter that we pass to the copyFromTo() function:

```
types/copyerr.kts
val fruitsBasket = Array<Fruit>(3) { _ -> Fruit() }
val bananaBasket = Array<Banana>(3) { _ -> Banana() }

copyFromTo(bananaBasket, fruitsBasket) //ERROR: type mismatch
```

Kotlin blocks us from passing an Array<Banana> where Array<Fruit> is expected since it's worried that the method copyFromTo() may potentially add a Fruit that's not a Banana to the Array<Banana>, which should be a no-no; as we discussed earlier, Array<T> is type invariant.

We can tell Kotlin that we intend to only read *out* of the Array passed to the from parameter; there's no risk of passing any Array<T> where T is either of type Fruit or a derived class of Fruit. This intent is called covariance on the parametric type—to accept a type itself or any of its derived types in its place.

The syntax from: Array<out Fruit> is used to convey covariance on the Fruit parametric type. Kotlin will assert that no method call is made on the from reference that would allow data to be passed *in*. Kotlin will determine this by examining the signature of the methods being called.

Let's fix the code by using a covariant parametric type:

types/copyout.kts
```
fun copyFromTo(from: Array<out Fruit>, to: Array<Fruit>) {
  for (i in 0 until from.size) {
    to[i] = from[i]
  }
}
```

Kotlin will now verify that within the copyFromTo() function, no call to send in an argument of the parametric type Fruit is made on the parameter with covariance. In other words, the following two calls, if present within the loop in copyFromTo(), will fail compilation:

```
from[i] = Fruit()   //ERROR
from.set(i, to[i])  //ERROR
```

With only code to read from the from parameter and code to set into the to parameter, we'll have no trouble passing Array<Banana>, Array<Orange> or Array<Fruit> where Array<Fruit> is expected for the from parameter:

types/copyout.kts
```
copyFromTo(bananaBasket, fruitsBasket) //OK
```

The Array<T> class has methods to both read *out* and set *in* an object of type T. Any function that uses Array<T> may call either of those two types of methods. But using covariance, we're promising to the Kotlin compiler that we'll not call any method that sends in any value with the given parametric type on Array<T>. This act of using covariance at the point of using a generic class is called *use-site variance* or *type projection*.

Use-site variance is useful for the user of a generic class to convey the intent of covariance. But, on a broader level, the author of a generic class can make the intent of covariance—for all users of that class—that any user can only read out and not write into the generic class. Specifying covariance in the declaration of a generic type, rather than at the time of its use, is called *declaration-site variance*. A good example of declaration-site variance can be found in the declaration of the List interface—which is declared as List<out T>. That use of declared-site variance is what permitted passing List<Banana> to receiveFruits(), whereas passing Array<Banana> was disallowed.

In other words, List<out T> by definition guarantees to Kotlin that receiveFruits(), or any method for that matter, won't write into the parameter of type List<T>. On the other hand, Array<out T> guarantees to Kotlin that the receiver of that covariant parameter won't write into that parameter. Declaration-site variance achieves universally what use-site variance achieves tactically for just the parameter it's applied to.

Using covariance, you tell the compiler to accept a derived parametric type in place of a parametric type. You can ask the compiler to take base types as well. That's contravariance, which we'll explore next.

Using Contravariance

Looking at the copyFromTo() method, it makes sense to copy objects from any Array<T> where T is of type Fruit or one of Fruit's derived classes. Covariance helped to convince Kotlin that it's safe to be flexible with the from parameter. Now let's turn our attention to the to parameter. The type of the parameter is the invariant Array<Fruit>.

No issue arises if we pass an Array<Fruit> to the to parameter. But what if we want to pass a Fruit or one of the derived classes of Fruit into a collection of Fruit or any class that is collection of a base of Fruit. If we desire that kind of flexibility, we can't simply pass an instance of Array<Any> as an argument to the to parameter. We have to explicitly ask the compiler to permit contravariance—that is, to accept a parametric type of base where an instance of a parametric type is expected.

Without using contravariance, let's first try passing an instance of Array<Any> to the parameter to and see what Kotlin says:

```
types/copyinerr.kts
val things = Array<Any>(3) { _ -> Fruit() }
val bananaBasket = Array<Banana>(3) { _ -> Banana() }

copyFromTo(bananaBasket, things) //ERROR: type mismatch
```

That's a no go, again due to the default type invariant behavior of Kotlin to protect us. We can once again ask Kotlin to relax, but this time to permit the parametric type to be a type or a base type—*contravariant*—of the parametric type.

types/copyin.kts

```
fun copyFromTo(from: Array<out Fruit>, to: Array<in Fruit>) {
  for (i in 0 until from.size) {
    to[i] = from[i]
  }
}
```

The only change was to the second parameter, what was to: Array<Fruit> is now to: Array<in Fruit>. The in specification tells Kotlin to permit method calls that set *in* values on that parameter and not permit methods that read *out*.

Now, let's retry the call we tried before:

types/copyin.kts

```
copyFromTo(bananaBasket, things) //OK
```

That's no problem. This again is a use-site variance, but this time for contravariance (in) instead of covariance (out). Just like declaration-site variance for covariance, classes may be defined with parametric type <in T> to universally specify contravariance—that is, that type can only receive parametric types and can't return or pass out parametric types.

Designing generic functions and classes isn't an easy task; we have to take the time to think about types, variances, and consequences. One more thing we have to consider when working with parametric types is to constrain the type that can be passed. We'll see that next.

Parametric Type Constraints Using where

Generics offer the flexibility to use different types in place of parametric types, but sometimes that much flexibility isn't the right option. We may want to use different types but within some constraint.

For instance, in the following code the type T is expected to support a close() method:

types/closeerr.kts

```
fun <T> useAndClose(input: T) {
  input.close() //ERROR: unresolved reference: close
}
```

But arbitrary types don't have a close() method and so the compiler fails on the call to close(). We can, however, tell Kotlin to constraint the parametric type to only types that have that method, via an interface with a close()

method—for example, the AutoCloseable interface. Let's rework the function declaration to use a constraint:

types/closeable.kts
```
fun <T: AutoCloseable> useAndClose(input: T) {
  input.close() //OK
}
```

The function useAndClose() expects a parameteric type T as parameter, but only one that conforms to being AutoCloseable. Now we can pass any object that can satisfy the AutoCloseable constraint, as here for example:

types/closeable.kts
```
val writer = java.io.StringWriter()
writer.append("hello ")
useAndClose(writer)
println(writer) // hello
```

To place a single constraint, modify the parametric type specification to place the constraint after colon. But if there are multiple constraints, that technique won't work. We need to use where in that case.

In addition to saying that the parametric type should conform to AutoCloseable, let's also ask it to conform to Appendable, so we can call the append() method:

types/where.kts
```
fun <T> useAndClose(input: T)
  where T: AutoCloseable,
        T: Appendable {
  input.append("there")
  input.close()
}
```

At the end of the method declaration, place a where clause and list all the constraints, comma separated. Now, we can use both the close() and the append() method on the parameter. Let's exercise this modified version of useAndClose() function:

types/where.kts
```
val writer = java.io.StringWriter()
writer.append("hello ")
useAndClose(writer)
println(writer) //hello there
```

We passed an instance of StringWriter which implements both AutoCloseable and Appendable, but we may pass any instance as long as it conforms to both of those constraints.

Star Projection

Kotlin's declaration-site variance isn't the only difference from Java's support for generics. In Java you may create raw types, like ArrayList, but that's generally not type safe and should be avoided. Also, in Java we may use the ? to specify that a function may receive a generic object of any type, but with a read-only constraint. Star projection, which is defining the parametric type with <*>, is the Kotlin equivalent of both specifying generic read-only type and raw type.

Use star projection when you want to convey that you simply don't know enough about the type but nevertheless want type safety. The star projection will permit only read-out and not write-in. Here's a piece of code to use star projection:

```
types/star.kts
fun printValues(values: Array<*>) {
  for (value in values) {
    println(value)
  }

  //values[0] = values[1] //ERROR
}

printValues(arrayOf(1, 2)) //1\n2
```

The function printValues() takes an Array<*> as its parameter, and any change to the array isn't permitted within the function. Had we written the parameter as Array<T>, then the commented out line, marked as ERROR, would have compiled if uncommented. That would result in potentially modifying the collection, when the intent is to iterate over it. The star projection protects us from such inadvertent errors. The star projection here, <*>, is equivalent to out T but is more concise to write. If star projection is used for a contravariant parameter, which is defined as <in T> in the declaration-site variance, then it's equivalent to in Nothing, to emphasize that writing anything will result in a compilation error. Thus, star projection prevents any writes and provides safety.

Reified Type Parameters

When using generics in Java we sometimes get into smelly situations where we have to pass Class<T> parameters to functions. This becomes necessary when the specific parametric type is needed in a generic function but the type details are lost due to Java's type erasure. Kotlin removes this smell with reified type parameters.

To get a clear understanding of reification, we'll first explore some verbose and unpleasant code where we pass the class details as a parameter to a function, and then we'll refactor the code to use type reification.

Suppose we have a base class Book and a couple of derived classes, like so:

```
types/reifiedtype.kts
abstract class Book(val name: String)
class Fiction(name: String) : Book(name)
class NonFiction(name: String) : Book(name)
```

Here's a list that includes different kinds of books:

```
types/reifiedtype.kts
val books: List<Book> = listOf(
  Fiction("Moby Dick"), NonFiction("Learn to Code"), Fiction("LOTR"))
```

The list contains a mixture of Fiction and NonFiction instances in the List<Book>. Now, suppose we want to find the first instance of a particular type, either a Fiction or a NonFiction from the list. We may write a function like this in Kotlin, much like how we'd write it in Java:

```
fun <T> findFirst(books: List<Book>, ofClass: Class<T>): T {
  val selected = books.filter { book -> ofClass.isInstance(book) }

  if(selected.size == 0) {
    throw RuntimeException("Not found")
  }

  return ofClass.cast(selected[0])
}
```

Since the parameteric type T will be erased when the code is compiled to bytecode, we can't use T within the function to perform operations like book is T or selected[0] as T. As a work-around, both in Java and Kotlin, we pass the type of the object we desire as a parameter, like ofClass: Class<T> in this example. Then within the code, we use the ofClass to perform type checking and type cast, which makes the code verbose and messy. This approach also burdens the user of the function, like so:

```
println(findFirst(books, NonFiction::class.java).name) //Learn to Code
```

Each time the function is called, programmers have to pass the runtime type information as an additional argument. That's smelly both on the caller side and the callee side. And such effort makes the code error prone.

Thankfully, we have a much better alternatively in Kotlin—reified type parameters.

Kotlin still has to work with the limitations of type erasure—at runtime the parametric type isn't available. However, Kotlin permits us to use the parametric type within the function when the parametric type is marked as reified and the function itself is marked as inline. We'll discuss the benefits of inline in Inlining Functions with Lambdas, on page 194, but for now, let's simply say that inlined functions are expanded at compile time, thus removing a function call overhead.

Let's refactor the findFirst() function to use reified.

types/reifiedtype.kts
```
inline fun <reified T> findFirst(books: List<Book>): T {
  val selected = books.filter { book -> book is T }

  if(selected.size == 0) {
    throw RuntimeException("Not found")
  }

  return selected[0] as T
}
```

We marked the parametric type T as reified and removed the Class<T> parameter. Within the function we use T to perform type checking and for casting. Since the function is marked as inline—we can use reified only for inline functions—the body of the function will be expanded at the site of a function call. Thus, the type T will be replaced in the expanded code with the actual type that is known at compile time.

In addition to removing the noise in the function, this feature also benefits the callers of the functions that use reified type parameters. Let's rewrite the call to the findFirst() function, like so:

types/reifiedtype.kts
```
println(findFirst<NonFiction>(books).name) //Learn to Code
```

Reified type parameters are useful to reduce clutter and also to alleviate potential errors in code. Reified type parameters eliminate the need to pass extra class information to functions, help to write code with safe casts, and customize the return type of functions with compile-time safety.

Keep your eyes open for functions that use reified type parameters as you work along with Kotlin code—for example, functions like listOf<T>() and mutableListOf<T>() of the Kotlin standard library you saw in Chapter 5, Using Collections, on page 63, and parse<T> of the Klaxon library, as you'll see in Chapter 16, Asynchronous Programming, on page 309.

Wrapping Up

Kotlin doesn't want to be an average statically typed language, and it takes type safety to a whole new level. By setting nullable reference types apart from non-nullable types, the compiler introduces greater type safety but without introducing memory overhead. Kotlin also provides a number of operators to fetch objects from nullable references with great ease and fluency. The smart casts feature removes unnecessary casting wherever possible, which reduces noise in code. When working with generic functions and classes, you can enjoy type safety, along with greater flexibility, by tailoring the parametric type variance to meet your needs. Additionally, the reified type parameters reduce clutter and error in code by enhancing compile-time type safety when working with parametric types.

In the next part, we will dig into Kotlin's support for object-oriented programming.

Part II

Object-Oriented Kotlin

Kotlin supports the object-oriented paradigm, but with a few twists. The compiler does a healthy dose of code generation to remove boilerplate code and also provides a few special types of classes not available in Java. In this part, you'll learn the benefits of data classes, sealed classes, companion objects, singletons, and more. From the design point of view, you'll learn when to use inheritance vs. delegation, both of which are directly supported by Kotlin. It's time for your OO code to enjoy a serious makeover.

CHAPTER 7

Objects and Classes

Kotlin is determined to make your code fluent, concise, and expressive, whether you're writing procedural, functional, or object-oriented code. Kotlin doesn't require classes, and you can work with top-level functions when they suffice. When object-oriented programming is the right design choice for your applications, Kotlin will get you moving fast in that direction without insisting on verbose boilerplate code to create classes. You can write classes with less effort, fewer lines of code, and with greater speed and ease.

Kotlin's facility to create and work with classes and objects is more akin to the features in Scala than in Java. But Kotlin takes the low-ceremony approach further than Scala in a few ways. You invoke class constructors like functions—there's no new keyword in Kotlin. You don't waste your time and effort to define fields—that's an implementation detail that Kotlin takes care of. Instead, you define properties, and Kotlin proceeds to generate the backing fields where necessary. If your focus is on representing data rather than behavior, you can achieve that using data classes, for which Kotlin generates a few conventional methods.

In this chapter you'll learn to create classes with constructors, properties, methods, companion objects, and data classes. You'll see how to define instance methods, and how defining static methods in Kotlin is different than in Java. You'll also learn how to create generic classes with constraints of parameterized types. But first we'll start with absolutely zero ceremony—working just with objects.

Objects and Singletons

The Singleton Design Pattern, discussed in *Design Patterns: Elements of Reusable Object-Oriented Software [GHJV95]*, is one of the easiest to understand and yet one of the most difficult to implement. It turns out that controlling the number of instances of a class isn't a trivial task—you need to prevent reflective access to constructors, ensure thread safety, and, at the same time, not introduce any overhead to check if an instance exists. By providing support for singletons directly, Kotlin removes the burden of implementing the pattern and the risks of getting it wrong. When you need, you can directly create an object without being forced to first define a class. For simple situations you can use objects, and for more complex cases, where you want to define an abstraction, you may create classes. In this section we'll focus on objects, how to create them, and how to make use of singletons.

Anonymous Objects with Object Expressions

If you want an object, then you should have an object—no fluff, no ceremony, no tax. Kotlin object expressions are like JavaScript objects and Anonymous Types in C#, although they're also useful to create instances of anonymous classes, like in Java.

In its most basic form, an object expression is the keyword object followed by a block {}. Such a trivial object expression is limited in use but not entirely purposeless. Suppose we want to represent a few pieces of data related to a circle. One option would be to create a Circle class, but that may be overkill. Another option is to keep around multiple local variables, but that doesn't give us a sense these are closely related values. Object expression can help here, as in this example:

```
oop/object.kts
fun drawCircle() {
  val circle = object { //an expression
    val x = 10
    val y = 20
    val radius = 30
  }

  //Pass circle.x, circle.y, circle.radius to a draw function here

  println("Circle x: ${circle.x} y: ${circle.y} radius: ${circle.radius}")
  //Circle x: 10 y: 20 radius: 30
}

drawCircle()
```

The circle object simply provides a grouping of the three values: x, y, and radius—it's just that, a grouping of a few local variables. Likewise, you may create an alien object, in a game, with different properties that belong to a dreadful creature that doesn't deserve the status of a full-blown class.

Instead of defining the properties as val, you may make them mutable with var. You may add methods to the object as well. But if you're going that far, you might as well create a class instead of defining an anonymous object. That's because classes don't have the limitations that anonymous objects have—and there are a few:

- The internal type of anonymous objects can't stand as return types to functions or methods.

- The internal type of anonymous objects can't be used as types of parameters to functions or methods.

- If they're stored as properties in classes, they'll be considered Any type and none of their properties or methods will then be available for direct access.

In short, the most rudimentary object expression is useful only to group a few local variables together.

With a slight change, anonymous objects can be useful as implementors of interfaces—that is, as anonymous inner classes like in Java. An anonymous inner class typically implements an interface on the fly. Between the object keyword and the block {}, mention the names of the interfaces you'd like to implement, comma separated. Oh, and follow the keyword with a : in this case. Let's implement the popular Runnable interface from the JDK, here using Kotlin's object expression.

oop/anonymous.kts
```
fun createRunnable(): Runnable {
  val runnable = object: Runnable {
    override fun run() { println("You called...") }
  }

  return runnable
}

val aRunnable = createRunnable()
aRunnable.run() //You called...
```

The variable runnable holds a reference to an instance of the anonymous inner class. The type of this variable is Runnable. You may return this instance from the function in which it's created, and the return type will take the type of the interface the anonymous inner class implements. If the instance is created by extending an existing class instead of an interface, then that class will serve as the type.

If the interface implemented by the anonymous inner class is a single abstract method interface (what Java 8 calls a functional interface), then we can directly provide the implementation without the need to specify the method name, like so:

```
fun createRunnable(): Runnable = Runnable { println("You called...") }
```

In addition to using the single abstract method implementation syntax, in the above example, we turned the createRunnable() function into a concise single-expression function by removing the block body and the return keyword.

If the anonymous inner class implements more than one interface, you have to specify the type the instance should represent upon return. Let's take a look at how to do that by changing the previous example to implement both Runnable and AutoCloseable interface, even though the method still chooses Runnable as the return type.

```
fun createRunnable(): Runnable = object: Runnable, AutoCloseable {
    override fun run() { println("You called...") }

    override fun close() { println("closing...") }
}
```

Outside of the function, we're able to access the instance of the anonymous inner class through an interface it implements—Runnable in this case.

In Kotlin, use object expressions anywhere you'd use anonymous inner classes in Java.

Singleton with Object Declaration

If you place a name between the object keyword and the block {}, then Kotlin considers the definition a statement or declaration instead of an expression. Use an object expression to create an instance of an anonymous inner class and an object declaration to create a singleton—a class with a single instance. Unit is an example of a singleton in Kotlin, but you can create your own singletons using the object keyword.

Let's create a singleton utility object to get some details about the system on which the code is run:

```
oop/util.kts
object Util {
    fun numberOfProcessors() = Runtime.getRuntime().availableProcessors()
}
```

The Util object we created using the object declaration is a singleton. We can't create objects of Util—it's not considered to be a class by the Kotlin compiler; it's already an object. Think of it like a Java class with a private constructor and only static methods. Internally, however, Kotlin represents the singleton object as a static instance of a Util class. The method itself isn't static in the bytecode unless the @JvmStatic annotation is used (which we'll see soon in Creating static Methods, on page 339. You can call the methods of a singleton like you'd call static methods on classes in Java.

Let's call the numberOfProcessors() method of the singleton:

oop/util.kts
```
println(Util.numberOfProcessors()) //8
```

The call to Util.numberOfProcessors() reports 8 on my machine. What does it say on yours? More? Showoff :).

Singletons aren't limited to having methods. They may have properties as well, both val and var. Object declarations may implement interfaces or may extend from existing classes, like object expressions do. If a singleton has a base class or interface, then that single instance may be assigned to a reference or passed to a parameter of the base type. Let's explore these with an example:

oop/singleton.kts
```
object Sun : Runnable {
  val radiusInKM = 696000
  var coreTemperatureInC = 15000000

  override fun run() { println("spin...") }
}

fun moveIt(runnable: Runnable) {
  runnable.run()
}

println(Sun.radiusInKM) //696000

moveIt(Sun)   //spin...
```

We can pass the singleton Sun to functions like moveIt(), since it's expecting an instance of Runnable. We can also access properties of the singleton, like radiusInKM, much like the way we'd access properties on instance of classes. A word of caution: even though this example illustrates the capability of the language, placing mutable state in a singleton isn't a good idea, especially in a multithreaded application.

Kotlin is highly flexible and unopinionated, in a good way, and lets us choose between top-level functions and singletons. Before we get deeper into the object-oriented concepts, let's discuss when to choose singletons instead of top-level functions.

Top-Level Functions vs. Singletons

Modularization is key to maintain sanity in any nontrivial application. But we don't want to also take things to the extreme of death-by-modularity. You can maintain a sensible balance with Kotlin based on the needs of your applications.

Should we choose top-level functions—that is, functions placed directly within a package—or singletons? Before we discuss which is better, let's take a look at an example of a package with both top-level functions and singletons.

oop/com/agiledeveloper/util/Util.kt

```
package com.agiledeveloper.util

fun unitsSupported() = listOf("Metric", "Imperial")

fun precision(): Int = throw RuntimeException("Not implemented yet")

object Temperature {
  fun c2f(c: Double) = c * 9.0/5 + 32
  fun f2c(f: Double) = (f - 32) * 5.0/ 9
}

object Distance {
  fun milesToKm(miles: Double) = miles * 1.609344
  fun kmToMiles(km: Double) = km / 1.609344
}
```

In the file Util.kt, we've defined a package with the package keyword—the syntax for this in Kotlin is just like in Java, minus the semicolon, which is optional. Next we have a few top-level functions placed directly in the file, within the package. Then we have a few singletons, each of which groups methods that closely belong together.

To use a top-level function, like unitsSupported(), we may refer to its fully qualified name, like com.agiledeveloper.util.unitsSupported(), or just the name unitsSupported(), after importing either com.agiledeveloper.util.unitsSupported or com.agiledeveloper.util.*. To access the methods within a singleton we can use similar techniques.

If there's a conflict in the names imported, we can either use the fully qualified name or define an alias, like import somepackage.SingletonName as ALocalName and then use ALocalName to refer to somepackage.SingletonName.

Let's use some of the methods from the com.agiledeveloper.util package.

oop/com/agiledeveloper/use/UseUtil.kt

```
package com.agiledeveloper.use

import com.agiledeveloper.util.*
import com.agiledeveloper.util.Temperature.c2f
```

```
fun main() {
  println(unitsSupported())
  println(Temperature.f2c(75.253))
  println(c2f(24.305))
}
```

The code to use the functions in com.agiledeveloper.util is placed in a new package, com.agiledeveloper.use in this example. It imports all members of the package com.agiledeveloper.util and the c2f method of the Temperature singleton. Within the main() method, we're calling the top-level function unitsSupported() and the c2f() method of the Temperature singleton without any qualifiers since they're visible from the imports. But to call the method f2c() of Temperature, we're qualifying it with the name of the singleton Temperature, which has been imported using the broader import com.agiledeveloper.util.*.

To compile the above two files and execute the code in UseUtil.Kt, use the following commands (use backslash instead of forward slash on Windows):

```
$ kotlinc-jvm ./com/agiledeveloper/util/Util.kt \
  ./com/agiledeveloper/use/UseUtil.kt \
  -d Util.jar
```

```
$ kotlin -classpath Util.jar com.agiledeveloper.use.UseUtilKt
```

In addition to showing how to use packages, functions, and singletons, this example shows why we may choose a top-level function or a singleton. If a group of functions are high level, general, and widely useful, then place them directly within a package. If on the other hand, a few functions are more closely related to each other than the other functions, like f2c() and c2f() are more closely related to each other than to milesToKm(), then place them within a singleton. Also, if a group of functions needs to rely on state, you can place that state along with those related functions in a singleton, although a class may be a better option for this purpose. Use caution: placing mutable state in a singleton may cause issues in multithreaded applications. In short, place functions at the top-level and use singletons to group and modularize functions further, based on application needs.

Functions and singletons make good sense when we're focused on behaviors, computations, and actions. But if we want to deal with state, then classes are a better choice, and Kotlin offers great support for creating those as well.

Creating Classes

Kotlin differs quite a bit from Java in how classes are defined. Writing classes in Java involves so much boilerplate code. To alleviate the pain of typing all that, programmers rely a lot on IDEs to generate code. Good news, you don't need to type as much. Bad news, you'll have to wade through all that code each day. Kotlin moves the code generation from the IDE to the compiler—kudos for that, especially for a language created by the company that makes the best IDEs in the world.

The syntax for creating a class in Kotlin is closer to the facilities in Scala than in Java. The number of options and flexibilities seem almost endless; let's start small and grow the code for creating a class incrementally.

Smallest Class

Here's the minimum syntax for a class—the class keyword followed by the name of the class:

oop/empty.kts
```
class Car
```

We didn't provide any properties, state, or behavior for this class, so it's only fair that it does nothing useful.

Read-Only Properties

Let's define a property in the class:

oop/property.kts
```
class Car(val yearOfMake: Int)
```

We made a few design decisions right there in that highly concise syntax. We wrote a constructor to take an integer parameter and initialize a read-only property named yearOfMake of type Int—yep, all that in one line. The Kotlin compiler wrote a constructor, defined a field, and added a getter to retrieve the value of that field.

Let's take a closer look at the class definition. That line is a shortcut for this:

```
public class Car public constructor(public val yearOfMake: Int)
```

By default, the access to the class and its members is public and the constructor is public as well. In Kotlin, the line that defines the class is actually defining the primary constructor. The keyword constructor isn't needed unless we want to change the access modifier or place an annotation for the primary constructor.

Creating Instances

Let's use the class to create an instance. New in Kotlin, related to creating objects, is there's no new keyword. To create an object use the class name like it's a function:

oop/property.kts
```
val car = Car(2019)
println(car.yearOfMake) //2019
```

The immutable variable car holds a reference to a Car instance created by calling the constructor with the value 2019. The property yearOfMake is accessible directly on the instance car. Efforts to modify it will run into issues, like so:

```
car.yearOfMake = 2019 //ERROR: val cannot be reassigned
```

Much like val local variables, val properties are immutable too.

Read-Write Properties

You can design a property to be mutable if you like:

oop/readwrite.kts
```
class Car(val yearOfMake: Int, var color: String)

val car = Car(2019, "Red")
car.color = "Green"
println(car.color) //GREEN
```

The newly added property color of type String is initialized with the constructor. But, unlike yearOfMake, we may change the value of color anytime on an instance of Car.

Use val to define read-only properties and var for properties that may change.

A Peek Under the Hood—Fields and Properties

In the previous example, yearOfMake and color seem like fields rather than properties to my Java eyes. However, those are properties and not fields. Kotlin doesn't expose fields of classes.

When you call car.yearOfMake, you're actually calling car.getYearOfMake()—the good old JavaBean convention is honored by the compiler. To prove this, let's examine the bytecode generated by the Kotlin compiler.

First, write the class Car in a separate file named Car.kt:

oop/Car.kt
```
class Car(val yearOfMake: Int, var color: String)
```

Next, compile the code and take a look at the bytecode using the javap tool, by running these commands:

```
$ kotlinc-jvm Car.kt
$ javap -p Car.class
```

Here the excerpt of the bytecode generated by the Kotlin Compiler for the Car class is:

```
Compiled from "Car.kt"
public final class Car {
  private final int yearOfMake;
  private java.lang.String color;
  public final int getYearOfMake();
  public final java.lang.String getColor();
  public final void setColor(java.lang.String);
  public Car(int, java.lang.String);
}
```

That concise one line of Kotlin code for the Car class resulted in the creation of two fields—the backing fields for properties, a constructor, two getters, and a setter. Nice.

Let's confirm that when using the object we're not directly accessing the fields. For this, create a file UseCar.kt with the following code:

oop/UseCar.kt
```
fun useCarObject(): Pair<Int, String> {
  val car = Car(2019, "Red")

  val year = car.yearOfMake

  car.color = "Green"

  val color = car.color

  return year to color
}
```

Let's compile using the following commands and take a look at the bytecode generated:

```
$ kotlinc-jvm Car.kt UseCar.kt
$ javap -c UseCarKt.class
```

The formatted excerpt from the output that follows shows that we're not accessing the fields directly; the code follows the JavaBean convention and doesn't breach encapsulation.

```
//...
      7: ldc             #11                 // String Red
      9: invokespecial #15
                                  // Method Car."<init>":(ILjava/lang/String;)V
     12: astore_0
     13: aload_0
     14: invokevirtual #19                 // Method Car.getYearOfMake:()I
     17: istore_1
     18: aload_0
     19: ldc             #21                 // String Green
```

```
21: invokevirtual #25
                              // Method Car.setColor:(Ljava/lang/String;)V
24: aload_0
25: invokevirtual #29
                              // Method Car.getColor:()Ljava/lang/String;
//...
```

In Kotlin you access properties by providing the name of the property instead of the getter or setter.

Controlling Change to Properties

In our Car class, yearOfMake is immutable but color is mutable. Immutability is safe, but uncontrolled change to a mutable property is unsettling. Kotlin will prevent someone changing or setting color to null since it's a String and not String? type—that is, it's not a nullable reference type. But what if someone sets it to an empty string? Let's fix the class to prevent that. Along the way we'll add another property to the class, but this one won't be given a value through the constructor.

oop/setter.kts
```
class Car(val yearOfMake: Int, theColor: String) {
  var fuelLevel = 100

  var color = theColor
    set(value) {
      if (value.isBlank()) {
        throw RuntimeException("no empty, please")
      }

      field = value
    }
}
```

To reiterate, in Kotlin you never define fields—backing fields are synthesized automatically, but only when necessary. If you define a field with both a custom getter and custom setter and don't use the backing field using the field keyword, then no backing field is created. If you write only a getter or a setter for a property, then a backing field is synthesized.

In our constructor we defined one property, yearOfMake, and one parameter, not field, named theColor—we didn't place val or var for this parameter. If you really wanted to call this color, you could have done that as well.

Within the class, we created a property named fuelLevel and initialized it to a value of 100. Its type is inferred to be Int by the compiler. This property isn't being set using any parameter of the constructor.

Then we created a property named color and assigned it to the value in the constructor parameter theColor. If we had called the constructor parameter color instead of theColor, then this line would have read like this:

```
var color = color
```

But named thecolor, it reads as follows:

```
var color = theColor
```

Using the same name for a property and a parameter is like the practice in Java where the this.color = color syntax is used for assignment, but if it's confusing, use different names for properties and parameters.

Kotlin will synthesize a getter and a setter for the fuelLevel property. For the color property it will only synthesize a getter, but use the setter provided in code. The setter throws an exception if the value given for the property is empty. You may call the parameter something other than value if you like. Also, you may specify the type for the parameter of set if you desire, but in this case the compiler knows the type, based on the type of the property initialization. If the given value is acceptable, then assign it to the field which is referenced by a special keyword field. Since Kotlin synthesizes fields internally, it doesn't give access to that name in code. You may refer to it using the keyword field only within getters and setters for that field.

Let's use the modified class to access the fields.

oop/setter.kts
```
val car = Car(2019, "Red")
car.color = "Green"
car.fuelLevel--

println(car.fuelLevel) //99

try {
  car.color = ""
} catch(ex: Exception) {
  println(ex.message) //no empty, please
}

println(car.color) //Green
```

No issue arose to change fuelLevel or to set color to "Green". But the attempt to change color to an empty string failed with a runtime exception. Following Kotlin convention, we got the details of the exception from the message property instead of using the getMessage() method of the Exception class. In the last line we verify that the color property is the same as what was set before the try expression.

Access Modifiers

The properties and methods of a class are public by default in Kotlin. The possible access modifiers are: public, private, protected, and internal. The first two have the same meaning as in Java. The protected modifier gives permission to the methods of the derived class to access that property. The internal modifier gives permission for any code in the same module to access the property or method, where a module is defined as all source code files that are compiled together. The internal modifier doesn't have a direct bytecode representation. It's handled by the Kotlin compiler using some naming conventions without posing any runtime overhead.

The access permission for the getter is the same as that for the property. You may provide a different access permission for the setter if you like. Let's change the access modifier for fuelLevel so that it can be accessed from only within the class.

oop/privatesetter.kts
```
var fuelLevel = 100
  private set
```

To make the setter private, simply place the keyword private before the keyword set. If you don't have an implementation to provide for the setter, then leave out the parameter value and the body. If you don't write a setter, or if you don't specify the access modifier for the setter, then its permission is the same as that of the property.

Initialization Code

The primary constructor declaration is part of the first line. Parameters and properties are defined in the parameter list for the constructor. Properties not passed through the constructor parameters may also be defined within the class. If the code to initialize the object is more complex than merely setting values, then we may need to write the body for the constructor. Kotlin provides a special space for that.

A class may have zero or more init blocks. These blocks are executed as part of the primary constructor execution. The order of execution of the init blocks is top-down. Within an init block you may access only properties that are already defined above the block. Since the properties and parameters declared in the primary constructor are visible throughout the class, any init block within the class can use them. But to use a property defined within the class, you'll have to write the init block after the said property's definition.

Just because we can define multiple init blocks doesn't mean we should. Within your class, first declare your properties at the top, then write one init block, but only if needed, and then implement the secondary constructors (again only if needed), and finally create any methods you may need.

If you're curious to see an init block, here's one to set the value of the fuelLevel based on the yearOfMake property.

```
oop/initialization.kts
class Car(val yearOfMake: Int, theColor: String) {
  var fuelLevel = 100
    private set

  var color = theColor
    set(value) {
      if (value.isBlank()) {
        throw RuntimeException("no empty, please")
      }

      field = value
    }
  init {
    if (yearOfMake < 2020) { fuelLevel = 90 }
  }
}
```

Within the init block we change the value of fuelLevel based on the value of yearOfMake. Since this requires access to fuelLevel, it can't be earlier than the declaration of fuelLevel.

You may wonder if, instead of the init block, could we have accomplished the task at the location of fuelLevel definition? Sure thing—you may remove the above init block entirely and write the following:

```
var fuelLevel = if (yearOfMake < 2020) 90 else 100
  private set
```

Don't write more than one init block, and avoid it if you can. The less work we do in constructors, the better from the program safety and also performance point of view.

Secondary Constructors

If you don't write a primary constructor, then Kotlin creates a no-argument default constructor. If your primary constructor has default arguments for all parameters, then Kotlin creates a no-argument constructor in addition to the primary constructor. In any case, you may create more constructors, called secondary constructors.

Your secondary constructors are required to either call the primary constructor or call one of the other secondary constructors. Also, secondary constructors' parameters can't be decorated with val or var; they don't define any properties. Only the primary constructor and declarations within the class may define properties.

Let's define a few constructors for a Person class.

```
oop/secondary.kts
class Person(val first: String, val last: String) {
  var fulltime = true
  var location: String = "-"

  constructor(first: String, last: String, fte: Boolean): this(first, last) {
    fulltime = fte
  }

  constructor(
    first: String, last: String, loc: String): this(first, last, false) {
    location = loc
  }

  override fun toString() = "$first $last $fulltime $location"
}
```

The primary constructor for Person defines two properties, first and last, through the two parameters annotated as val. The keyword constructor is optional here. The two secondary constructors are declared using the keyword constructor. The first secondary constructor calls the primary constructor, referring to it using this. Within the body, this secondary constructor initializes one of the fields. The second secondary constructor calls the first secondary constructor. It could have instead called the primary constructor.

Any secondary constructor may call either the primary constructor or any of the other secondary constructors, as long as the call doesn't fall into a cyclic chain that leads up to the constructor being defined.

Let's verify this class works by creating a few instances to use the different constructors:

```
oop/secondary.kts
println(Person("Jane", "Doe"))          //Jane Doe true -
println(Person("John", "Doe", false))  //John Doe false -
println(Person("Baby", "Doe", "home")) //Baby Doe false home
```

From the caller point of view, whether they're using the primary constructor or one of the secondary constructors makes no difference—they keep their focus on creating an object with the desired parameters.

Defining Instance Methods

Define methods in classes using the fun keyword. By default methods are public, but you may mark them as private, protected, or internal before the fun keyword if you want to change the access permission.

Here's a fullName() method, marked internal, and a private method yearsOfService() in the Person class:

```
oop/methods.kts
class Person(val first: String, val last: String) {
  //...

  internal fun fullName() = "$last, $first"

  private fun yearsOfService(): Int =
    throw RuntimeException("Not implemented yet")
}
```

The methods within a class are defined much like top-level functions, except they appear within the class body {}. The methods have access to the properties and other methods of the class, just like in Java. You may also use this to refer to the instance or the receiver on which the instance method is being executed.

Any effort to access a method that's not accessible—private for example—will result in an error. For instance, in the previous code, the yearsOfService() method isn't visible outside the class, and any effort to access it will result in a compilation error:

```
oop/methods.kts
val jane = Person("Jane", "Doe")
println(jane.fullName()) //Doe, Jane
//jane.yearsOfService() //ERROR: cannot access...private in 'Person'
```

Kotlin classes have the same semantics as classes written in Java, but the language has a special feature to erase classes at compile time—let's explore that next.

Inline Classes

Classes represent abstractions, and so do primitive types. During design, sometimes we debate between using a class or using a primitive type. For example, should Social Security Number, or any other form of government issued identification, be represented using an SSN class or merely a String. Creating a class gives the distinctive advantage of clarity. We wouldn't be able to accidentally pass an arbitrary string, like "John Doe", where SSN is expected. But if all that it represents is a String in reality, that overhead of wrapping a string inside of an object of SSN may be overkill and may result in poor performance—more overhead of object creating and memory usage. inline classes, which are experimental in Kotlin at the time of this writing, strike a great balance. You get the benefit of classes at compile time but you get the benefits of using a primitive at runtime—the class is transformed into a primitive in the bytecode.

Calls to inline functions—which we discuss in Inlining Functions with Lambdas, on page 194—are replaced with their body, and thus they don't incur the overhead of a function call. Likewise, inline classes are expanded or replaced by their underlying member where they are used.

For example, in the following code we mark the class SSN as inline:

```
oop/ssn.kt
inline class SSN(val id: String)

fun receiveSSN(ssn: SSN) {
  println("Received $ssn")
}
```

If the code is compiled with the -XXLanguage:+InlineClasses command-line option, to indicate that we're using an experimental feature, then the function receiveSSN() will be compiled to receive a String instead of an instance of SSN. When invoking, however, the Kotlin compiler will verify that the receiveSSN() function is invoked with an instance of SSN and not a raw string, like so:

```
receiveSSN(SSN("111-11-1111"))
```

Once the compiler verifies that an instance of SSN is passed to receiveSSN(), it will unwrap the embedded instance of String and pass that directly to receiveSSN(), thus removing the wrapper and any potential overhead both in terms of memory and object creation.

inline classes may have properties and methods and may implement interfaces as well. Under the hood, methods will be rewritten as static methods that receive the primitive types that are being wrapped by the inline class. inline classes are required to be final and aren't allowed to extend from other classes.

Creating classes with properties and instance methods is straightforward. In Java we're used to static methods too, but you can't simply place the static keyword before the keyword fun in Kotlin. Kotlin provides companion objects for creating class members.

Companion Objects and Class Members

The classes we created so far had properties and instance methods. If a property or a method is needed at the class level and not on a specific instance of the class, we can't drop them into the class. Instead, place them in a companion object. In Singleton with Object Declaration, on page 110, we created singletons. Companion objects are singletons defined within a class—they're singleton companions of classes. In addition, companion objects may implement interfaces and may extend from base classes, and thus are useful with code reuse as well.

Class-Level Members

In the next example, a MachineOperator class needs a property and a method at the class level; we achieve that using a companion object:

```
oop/companion.kts
class MachineOperator(val name: String) {
  fun checkin() = checkedIn++
  fun checkout() = checkedIn--

  companion object {
    var checkedIn = 0

    fun minimumBreak() = "15 minutes every 2 hours"
  }
}
```

Within the class, the companion object, literally defined using those keywords, is nested. The property checkedIn within the companion object becomes the class-level property of MachineOperator. Likewise, the method minimumBreak doesn't belong to any instance; it's part of the class.

The members of the companion object of a class can be accessed using the class name as reference, like so:

```
oop/companion.kts
MachineOperator("Mater").checkin()

println(MachineOperator.minimumBreak()) //15 minutes every 2 hours

println(MachineOperator.checkedIn) //1
```

Use caution: placing mutable properties within companion objects may lead to thread-safety issues in multithreaded scenarios.

Instance methods like checkin() need an instance as a target, but methods like minimumBreak(), which are part of the companion object, can't be accessed using an instance. They can only be accessed using the class name as a reference.

That's true for properties, like checkedIn, that are defined within the companion objects as well.

Accessing the Companion

Sometimes we need a reference to the companion object instead of one of its members. This is especially true when the companion object implements an interface, for example, and we want to pass that singleton instance to a function or method that expects an implementor of the interface. You may access the companion of a class using .Companion on the class—that's an uppercase C. For example, here's the way to get the companion of the Machine-Operator class:

oop/companion.kts
```
val ref = MachineOperator.Companion
```

If you don't expect the users of your class to directly need a reference to the companion too often, then the above is fine. But for frequent use, you may want to give a nicer name than Companion. The name Companion is used only if the companion object doesn't have an explicit name. Here's a way to give an explicit name for the companion object of MachineOperator:

```
//companion object {
companion object MachineOperatorFactory {
  var checkedIn = 0
  //...
```

The name Companion is no longer available on MachineOperator. To refer to the companion use the explicit name:

```
val ref = MachineOperator.MachineOperatorFactory
```

The explicit name for the companion object may be any legal name in Kotlin, but the Factory suffix alludes to an intent of the companion object to serve as a factory, as we'll explore next.

Companion as Factory

Whether you give an explicit name or not, the companion object can serve as a factory to create instances of the class they are part of.

The constructors initialize an object to a valid state, but there are times when we may have to perform some extra steps before an object becomes available for use. For example, we may want to register an object as an event handler or register with a timer to execute a method. Registering within the constructor isn't a good idea; you don't want a reference to the object to become available anywhere before the construction is completed. Providing a method to be called after construction isn't good either: the user of the class may forget to register or may invoke other methods before registering. The companion object for the class, acting as a factory, can help with this design concern.

To use a companion as a factory, provide a private constructor for the class. Then, provide one or more methods in the companion object that creates the instance and carries out the desired steps on the object before returning to the caller.

Revisiting the previous example, we can change the MachineOperator class to use a factory.

```kotlin
class MachineOperator private constructor(val name: String) {
  //...
  companion object {
    //...

    fun create(name: String): MachineOperator {
      val instance = MachineOperator(name)
      instance.checkin()
      return instance
    }
  }
}
```

The constructor of the MachineOperator class is marked as private. Outside the class, we can't directly create any instances. Within the companion object, we have a new create() method that takes name as a parameter, creates an instance of the MachineOperator, invokes the checkin() method on it, and returns the instance to the caller. The create() method is the only way to create an instance of the class, thus the companion object acts as a factory for the class.

To create an instance, we have to use the create() method:

```kotlin
val operator = MachineOperator.create("Mater")
```

```kotlin
println(MachineOperator.checkedIn) //1
```

The create() method is invoked directly on the MachineOperator class and it is routed to the companion object. We may have more than one method in a companion object, taking different parameters to create instances of a class.

Not Quite Static

Looking at how we access the members of the companion objects, through a reference to the class name, we may get the impression that members of companion objects turn into static members, but that's not true. Don't assume that the methods in a companion are static methods of a class.

When you reference a member of a companion object, the Kotlin compiler takes care of routing the call to the appropriate singleton instance. But this will pose a problem from the Java interoperability point of view, especially if a programmer is looking for static methods. The @JvmStatic annotation is useful to resolve this issue. You'll learn about this facility, its purpose, and the benefits it offers soon in Creating static Methods, on page 339.

The classes we created so far have properties of specific types, but their types may be parameterized as well. We'll see how to create generic classes next.

Creating Generics Classes

Often the classes we create deal with specific types; for example, a Book may have title of type String and a list of Authors, a Publisher, and so on. Sometimes though, especially when working with collections, we may not want to tie the members of a class to specific types. For example, a list of Books vs. a list of Authors are both lists. The list should be general enough to support members of either of those types, or other types, but specific enough to disallow, for example, adding an Author to a list of Books. Generics classes are used to create such generalized lists with type safety. Kotlin support for generics is much like the support in Java in many ways, but variance and constraints are declared differently; we discussed these in the context of generic functions in Generics: Variance and Constraints of Parametric Types, on page 93.

We frequently use generic classes, but, as application programmers, we tend not to create these types of classes as often as we create nongeneric classes. Still, it's useful to learn how to create a generic class. We'll achieve that goal with an example.

Kotlin has a class named Pair that holds two objects of two different types. We'll create here a PriorityPair that will hold a pair of objects of the same type, but based on ordering, with the larger object first and the smaller one second. We'll use a compareTo() method, of the Comparable<T> interface, to determine the objects' ordering.

Before we jump into code, let's think through the features of the class we're about to create. Once we create an instance, there's no need to modify the members that are part of the PriorityPair, thus there's no need for any mutable operations. Since the objects will be ordered, the parametric class needs to be constrained to implement the Comparable<T> interface. The class permits only read and not write, so we may be tempted to mark the parametric type with the out annotation, like the way class Pair<out A, out B> is defined in Kotlin. But since the properties of our class will be passed to the compareTo() method of Comparable<T>, we can't annotate with the out keyword. That's enough thinking—let's jump into the code now.

Here's the PriorityPair class with parametrized type T constrained to implement Comparable<T>:

oop/prioritypair.kts
```
class PriorityPair<T: Comparable<T>>(member1: T, member2: T) {
  val first: T
  val second: T

  init {
    if (member1 >= member2) {
      first = member1
      second = member2
    } else {
      first = member2
      second = member1
    }
  }

  override fun toString() = "${first}, ${second}"
}
```

Following the class name, the parametric type and the constraint are specified within the angle brackets <>. Since there's only one constraint, we didn't need the where clause and instead used the concise colon : syntax we saw in Generics: Variance and Constraints of Parametric Types, on page 93. The class receives two primary constructor parameters, member1 and member2, of the parametric type T. Two properties—first and second—are defined as val, that is immutable, but their initialization is postponed to determine the ordering of the members.

Within the init block we initialize first and second based on the order of priority of the two members passed to the constructor, where the ordering is done using the compareTo() method of the Comparable interface. Instead of using the compareTo() method directly, we're using the >= operator—see Overloading Operators, on page 222. Finally, the toString() method returns a String with the properties first and second.

Let's use this generic class to create two instances:

oop/prioritypair.kts
```
println(PriorityPair(2, 1))     //2, 1
println(PriorityPair("A", "B")) //B, A
```

An instance of PriorityPair<T> may be created using any type that implements the Comparable<T> interface to specialize the parametric type. A generic class builds on the syntax of a regular class with the added complexity of constraints and variance specifications. When designing a generic class, we have to do a lot more testing to ensure that the generics work properly for the specialized types.

Looking at the PriorityPair class, we haven't implemented the equals() and hashCode() methods. We could implement those methods in minutes if needed, but you don't have to write all the code manually all the time. Even though Kotlin makes it easier to define properties and create methods in classes, it can generate some common things, as we'll see next.

Data Classes

Much like the case classes of Scala, the *data classes* of Kotlin are specialized classes that are intended to carry mostly data rather than behavior. The primary constructor is required to define at least one property, using val or var. Non-val or var parameters aren't allowed here. You may add other properties or methods to the class, within the body {}, if you desire.

For each data class Kotlin will automatically create the equals(), hashCode(), and toString() methods. In addition, it provides a copy() method to make a copy of an instance while providing updated values for select properties. It also creates special methods that start with the word component—component1(), component2(), and so on—to access each property defined through the primary constructor. We'll refer to these methods as componentN() methods for convenience.

Here's an example data class that represents a task or a to-do item, annotated with the data keyword to convey the intent:

```
oop/taskdataclass.kts
data class Task(val id: Int, val name: String,
  val completed: Boolean, val assigned: Boolean)
```

Any property defined within the class body {}, if present, will not be used in the generated equals(), hashCode(), and toString() methods. Also, no componentN() method will be generated for those.

Continuing with the same example, let's create an object of the data class and exercise one of the generated methods, toString().

```
oop/taskdataclass.kts
val task1 = Task(1, "Create Project", false, true)
println(task1)
  //Task(id=1, name=Create Project, completed=false, assigned=true)
println("Name: ${task1.name}") //Name: Create Project
```

The String returned by toString() has properties and their values listed in the same order in which they appeared in the primary constructor's parameter list. You may access any of the properties by their name, like the name property is accessed in our example.

For data classes, Kotlin generates a copy() method that creates a new object with all the properties of the receiver object copied into the result object. Unlike the equals(), hashCode(), and the toString() methods, the copy() method includes any property defined within the class, not just those presented in the primary constructor. Each parameter to the method receives a default argument, and we may pass an alternative value to any property using named arguments. Let's use this technique to copy task1 but provide a different value for a couple of properties:

oop/taskdataclass.kts
```
val task1Completed = task1.copy(completed = true, assigned = false)
println(task1Completed)
  //Task(id=1, name=Create Project, completed=true, assigned=false)
```

The newly created instance has copies of all properties from the original, but it has new values assigned to the completed and assigned properties. The copy() function only performs a shallow copy of primitives and references. The objects referenced internally are not deep copied by the method. This isn't an issue if the entire hierarchy of nested objects is immutable.

The main purpose of the componentN() methods is for destructuring—see Destructuring, on page 49. Any class, including Java classes, that has componentN() methods can participate in destructuring.

Here's an example to extract the id and assigned properties from an instance of Task:

```
val id = task1.id
val isAssigned = task1.assigned
println("Id: $id Assigned: $isAssigned") //Id: 1 Assigned: true
```

But that's boring and takes as many lines as the number of properties we want to extract. Instead, we can use the destructuring capability of data classes.

To destructure, we have to extract the properties in the same order as they appear in the primary constructor. However, we're not required to extract each and every property. If you don't want a property, simply leave it out from the request. If you need the value of a property that comes after a property you want to ignore, then use underscore—which is the international symbol for "I don't care." An example will help clarify this:

oop/taskdataclass.kts
```
val (id, _, _, isAssigned) = task1
println("Id: $id Assigned: $isAssigned") //Id: 1 Assigned: true
```

The local variables into which the properties should be extracted may be defined as val, as in the code we just used, or var. The id local variable is assigned the value of the id property from task1—for this Kotlin invokes the component1() method. We ignore the name and completed properties. Then we assign the assigned property's value to the local variable named isAssigned—here again, Kotlin uses the component4() method. If there were any more properties—which there aren't in this example—they'd be ignored and _ wouldn't be required in the trailing positions.

The destructuring of data classes in Kotlin comes with a significant limitation. In JavaScript, object destructuring is based on property names, but, sadly, Kotlin relies on the order of properties passed to the primary constructor. If a developer inserts a new parameter in between current parameters, then the result may be catastrophic.

For example, suppose we add a new parameter in between the name and the completed parameter of Task's primary constructor. Any use of the constructor will now have to be modified and recompiled. But, the effect on destructuring is severe. For example, the previous destructuring code won't cause any compilation error, but the isAssigned variable will now be assigned the value of the completed property instead of the assigned property, due to the change in the ordering of the parameters.

Instead of using type inference, if we specify the type during destructuring, we might get some relief in some situations, but specifying types won't entirely solve the issue in all cases. Whereas we can agree that changing the order of parameters is a poor programming practice, this issue reinforces the need to perform good automated testing, even for statically typed languages like Kotlin.

With the choices offered by Kotlin we have to decide when to use a data class vs. a regular class. Use a data class in these situations:

• You're modeling data more than behavior.

• You want equals(), hashCode(), toString(), and/or copy() to be generated, knowing that you may override any of these methods if you like.

• It makes sense for the primary constructor to take at least one property—no-argument constructors are not allowed for data classes.

• It makes sense for the primary constructor to take only properties.

• You want to easily extract data from the object using the destructuring facility (be aware that the extraction is based on the order of properties and not their names).

Wrapping Up

Kotlin's support for object-oriented programming goes beyond what we're used to in Java. Kotlin generates fields and synthesizes getters and setters so you don't have to spend the time writing boilerplate code. Instance members go into classes and class members go into companion objects. Singleton is a first-class citizen in the language. Data classes are useful to represent data more than behavior, and you can enjoy the destructuring capability to extract properties fluently from data classes. The support for generic classes is almost the same as in Java, except for improved type safety that comes from better support for variance and constraints.

We've seen how to create classes in this chapter, but classes rarely live alone. In the next chapter, we'll work with multiple classes to create class hierarchies using inner classes and inheritance.

CHAPTER 8

Class Hierarchies and Inheritance

Classes are more like social creatures than hermits. Classes relate to and build on top of the abstractions defined in other classes. To build complex applications, it should be easy to create hierarchies of abstractions. Kotlin does that well—you can create interfaces, define nested and inner classes, and also use inheritance.

Being a statically typed language, Kotlin promotes design by contract, where interfaces serve as specifications and classes as implementors of those contracts. You can also reuse implementations, in addition to specifications, by creating abstract classes.

From the safety point of view, classes are final by default and you have to explicitly annotate them as open to serve as a base class. Further, Kotlin doesn't work in a binary state of inheritable vs. non-inheritable. You can define classes as sealed and thus state which specific classes may extend from those. This gives you the capability to model closed sets of classes, to create what are called algebraic data types in type theory—a powerful idea and something that's not currently possible in Java.

We'll start this chapter with creating interfaces and abstract classes. Then we'll look at creating nested and inner classes—good design options when two classes are closely related to each other. We'll then follow that with how to use inheritance if we want to substitute the objects of one class where instances of another are expected. Then you'll learn how to restrict subclasses using sealed classes. Finally, we'll look at enums, which are a way to create classes that work together to represent multiple values of a single abstraction.

Creating Interfaces and Abstract Classes

Object-oriented programming is programming with hierarchies of abstractions—complex applications typically have multiple interfaces, abstract classes, and implementation classes. We heavily rely on interfaces to specify behavior of abstractions and use abstract classes to reuse implementations. So learning about interfaces and abstract classes is a good starting point for learning about building object-oriented hierarchies.

In recent years interfaces have dramatically evolved in Java. In the past, interfaces were permitted to carry only method declarations and no implementation: they could tell a lot about what's possible, but never did anything—kinda like my boss. In recent versions of Java, interfaces can have default methods, static methods, and even private methods. With such improvements in Java, it's fair to ask how interfaces in Kotlin measure up to interfaces in modern Java. We'll start with that question and explore how Kotlin interfaces fare in comparison. Then we'll explore how abstract classes differ in Kotlin when compared to Java.

Creating Interfaces

Semantically, Kotlin interfaces are a lot like Java interfaces, but they differ widely in syntax. You can honor the original design-by-contract intent of interfaces by writing abstract methods in them. In addition, you may also implement methods within interfaces, but without the default keyword that Java requires. Much like the way static methods in Kotlin classes are placed in companion objects, interfaces can also have static methods, but only via companion objects written within the interfaces.

To get a good feel for interfaces in Kotlin, we'll create an interface with a few abstract methods and a method with implementation. Then we'll inherit from that interface to see how the implementation gets carried over to the derived class. Finally, we'll look at the Kotlin way to define static methods for interfaces.

Let's start with a Remote interface that represents a remote control device.

```
inheritance/remote.kts
interface Remote {
  fun up()
  fun down()

  fun doubleUp() {
    up()
    up()
  }
}
```

Abstract methods, like up(), are merely declared within the interface. Implementing a method, like doubleUp(), in an interface is much like implementing a method in a class—no extra syntax or ceremony. Any class implementing the interface will have to override the abstract methods. However, they get the implementation in the doubleUp() method for free and may optionally override the implementation as well.

The methods implemented within interfaces—that is, Kotlin-type default methods—work even in Java 1.6, even though default methods were introduced only in Java 8. To make the Kotlin default methods visible as default methods in the bytecode, you can use the @JvmDefault annotation, which we'll cover in More Annotations, on page 345.

To see how the interface interplays with an implementor, let's implement the Remote interface in a TVRemote class that may be used to control the volume of a TV:

```
inheritance/remote.kts
class TV {
  var volume = 0
}

class TVRemote(val tv: TV) : Remote {
  override fun up() { tv.volume++ }
  override fun down() { tv.volume-- }
}
```

To convey that the class TVRemote is implementing the Remote interface, we place Remote following the colon : after the primary constructor's parameter list. Kotlin follows the Ruby and C# style for inheritance syntax. The TVRemote is required to implement the abstract methods of Remote, and the override keyword is required for any method that is overriding a method of a base class or an interface. The TVRemote class isn't overriding the implementation of doubleUp() in Remote.

To see how these classes and the interface work together, let's exercise the methods of Remote through an instance of TVRemote.

```
inheritance/remote.kts
val tv = TV()
val remote: Remote = TVRemote(tv)

println("Volume: ${tv.volume}") //Volume: 0
remote.up()
println("After increasing: ${tv.volume}") //After increasing: 1
remote.doubleUp()
println("After doubleUp: ${tv.volume}") //After doubleUp: 3
```

The reference remote is of type Remote but refers to an instance of TVRemote at runtime. The call to up() was handled by the TVRemote instance, but the call to doubleUp() landed in the implementation within Remote.

In Java, interfaces may have static methods too, but in Kotlin we can't place static methods directly in interfaces, just like we can't place them directly in classes. Use companion objects to create static methods in interfaces. For example, let's create a combine() method that will bind two remotes so that the operations are performed on both remotes, one after the other:

inheritance/remote.kts
```
companion object {
  fun combine(first: Remote, second: Remote): Remote = object: Remote {
    override fun up() {
      first.up()
      second.up()
    }

    override fun down() {
      first.down()
      second.down()
    }
  }
}
```

This companion object goes directly into the Remote interface. To access the method in the companion object, use the Remote interface, like so:

inheritance/remote.kts
```
val anotherTV = TV()

val combinedRemote = Remote.combine(remote, TVRemote(anotherTV))

combinedRemote.up()
println(tv.volume) //4
println(anotherTV.volume) //1
```

When implementing an interface, you must implement all the abstract methods. When implementing multiple interfaces, any methods that collide—that is, have the same name and signature—must be implemented in the class as well.

Creating Abstract Classes

Kotlin also supports abstract classes. The classes have to be marked abstract to be considered abstract, and abstract methods have to be marked abstract in abstract classes.

Here's an example of an abstract base class and a class that extends from it.

inheritance/abc.kts
```
abstract class Musician(val name: String, val activeFrom: Int) {
  abstract fun instrumentType(): String
}

class Cellist(name: String, activeFrom: Int) : Musician(name, activeFrom) {
  override fun instrumentType() = "String"
}

val ma = Cellist("Yo-Yo Ma", 1961)
```

Since the instrumentType() method isn't implemented in the base class, it has to be marked as abstract. When overriding it in the derived class, the override keyword is required. The derived class Cellist's primary constructor receives the two parameters and passes them to the base class. It may receive additional parameters not needed by the base, and those additional parameters may be declared using val or var to become properties in the derived class.

The main differences between an abstract class and an interface are these:

- The properties defined within interfaces don't have backing fields; they have to rely on abstract methods to get properties from implementing classes. On the other hand, properties within abstract classes can use backing fields.

- You may implement multiple interfaces but can extend from at most one class, abstract or not.

Interface or Abstract Class?

Should you create an interface or an abstract class instead? Interfaces can't contain fields, but a class may implement multiple interfaces. On the other hand, abstract base classes can have fields, but a class may only extend from at most one abstract class. So each has pros and cons. Let's discuss how to choose between them.

If you want to reuse state between multiple classes, then an abstract class is a good choice. You can implement the common state in the abstract class and have implementing classes override the methods, while reusing the state provided by the abstract class.

If you want multiple classes to abide by one or more contracts or specifications, but you want those classes to choose their own implementations, then interfaces are the better choice. If you choose this route, you may also move some common methods into the interfaces, while still letting the implementing classes choose how they implement the state.

In both modern Java and Kotlin, interfaces have a slight advantage over abstract classes. Interfaces have the ability to carry method implementations, but without state. A class may implement multiple interfaces. Where possible, prefer interfaces over abstract or base classes, as this offers more flexibility.

In the example for interfaces, the TVRemote relied on a public property volume of TV to implement the methods of the Remote interface. Next we'll explore an alternative to this approach.

Nested and Inner Classes

In the previous example, you may wonder why TV didn't directly implement the Remote interface instead of having a separate class TVRemote that implements the interface. Having a separate class like TVRemote instead of directly implementing the interface has a few pros and cons. Let's discuss the pros first, then the cons, and arrive at a solution to give us the best of both options.

The first benefit of having a TVRemote is that we may have multiple instances of TVRemote for a single instance of TV, much like how cars and garage doors have multiple remotes. This design capability can save relationships where each person can amiably control a TV instance without bothering someone else near a single remote to do it. Second, the instances of TVRemote may carry their internal state separate from any state contained in a TV instance. For example, a TVRemote instance used by one person may have a dim light on the remote turned on to help operate in the dark.

Implementing an interface in a separate class has drawbacks—the methods of TVRemote that implement the Remote interface have to use the public methods of the TV. If the TV implements the interface, then we don't have to rely on any public methods, and also the implementation can efficiently use internals visible only within the class. And, instead of passing an instance of TV to the constructor of TVRemote, if we implement the interface directly in TV, we don't need the extra references kept within instances of TVRemote.

An alternative design option can help us keep the pros and at the same time avoid the cons. Using inner classes we can get the benefits offered by having the separate class, but without compromising efficiency. While the solution that follows may appear esoteric at first sight, this technique is used extensively in C#, Java, and Kotlin to implement iterators on collections.

In Kotlin a class may be nested—placed inside—another class. Unlike in Java, Kotlin nested classes can't access the private members of the nesting outer class. But if you mark the nested class with the inner keyword, then they turn into inner classes and the restriction goes away.

Let's move the TVRemote class from the previous example to be an inner class of TV:

inheritance/nestedremote.kts
```
class TV {
  private var volume = 0

  val remote: Remote
    get() = TVRemote()

  override fun toString(): String = "Volume: ${volume}"

  inner class TVRemote : Remote {
    override fun up() { volume++ }
    override fun down() { volume-- }

    override fun toString() = "Remote: ${this@TV.toString()}"
  }
}
```

Unlike the TV class in the previous version, in this example the volume property of TV is private and can't be directly accessed from outside the instance of TV. TVRemote, though, is defined as an inner class, and its methods up() and down() access volume as if it were a property of TVRemote. The inner class has direct access to the members of the outer class, including private members. The TV class now provides a public property remote that returns an instance of TVRemote.

Let's use the modified version of TVRemote:

inheritance/nestedremote.kts
```
val tv = TV()
val remote = tv.remote

println("$tv") //Volume: 0
remote.up()
println("After increasing: $tv") //After increasing: Volume: 1
remote.doubleUp()
println("After doubleUp: $tv") //After doubleUp: Volume: 3
```

A user of a TV instance can obtain a reference to a Remote for the TV instance using the remote property. The getter of this property has been designed so that each call to remote will result in a different instance, much like each call to the iterate() method on a collection will return a new iterator instance.

If a property or method in the inner class shadows a corresponding member in the outer class, you can access the member of the outer class from within a method of the inner using a special this expression. You can see this in the toString() method of TVRemote, shown here again for convenience:

```
override fun toString() = "Remote: ${this@TV.toString()}"
```

Read the syntax this@TV within the string template as "this of TV"—that is, this will refer to the TVRemote instance but this@TV refers to the instance of the outer class TV. Let's verify that the access to the outer instance from the inner instance worked:

inheritance/nestedremote.kts
```
println(remote) //Remote: Volume: 3
```

What if you want to access the toString() of Any—that is, the base class of TV from a method of TVRemote? Instead of asking for this of TV ask for super of TV—the base class of the outer class:

```
override fun toString() = "Remote: ${super@TV.toString()}"
```

Use super@Outer syntax sparingly; it's a design smell to bypass a class to get to its base class, defeating the intent of polymorphism and method overriding.

If we need a special state within the nested or inner classes, we may place properties in them much like how we keep state in outer classes. Also, instead of creating an inner class within a class, we may create an anonymous inner class within a method as well. Let's turn the inner class from the previous example to an anonymous inner class within the remote property's getter:

```
class TV {
  private var volume = 0

  val remote: Remote get() = object: Remote {
      override fun up() { volume++ }
      override fun down() { volume-- }

      override fun toString() = "Remote: ${this@TV.toString()}"
    }

  override fun toString(): String = "Volume: ${volume}"
}
```

The inner keyword isn't used for anonymous inner classes. The anonymous instance implements the Remote interface and, of course, has no name. Other than those differences, the class isn't any different from the TVRemote inner class it replaced.

We've looked at ways to implement interfaces and to create nested and inner classes. Next, let's look at extending classes.

Inheritance

When you use inheritance, you'll feel the extra layer of safety and protection that Kotlin provides. Since inheritance is one of the misused concepts in OO programming, Kotlin helps you make sure that your intentions are laid out very explicitly to the users of your classes.

Kotlin doesn't want classes to accidentally serve as a base class. As an author of a class, you have to provide explicit permission for your class to be used as a base class. Likewise, when writing a method, you have to tell Kotlin that it's OK for a derived class to override that method. Let's take a look at how Kotlin provides this safety net.

Unlike interfaces, classes in Kotlin are final by default—that is, you can't inherit from them. Only classes marked open may be inherited from. Only open methods of an open class may be overridden in a derived class and have to be marked with override in the derived. A method that isn't marked open or override can't be overridden. An overriding method may be marked final override to prevent a subclass from further overriding that method.

You may override a property, either defined within a class or within the parameter list of a constructor. A val property in the base may be overridden with a val or var in the derived. But a var property in the base may be overridden only using var in the derived. The reason for this restriction is that val only has a getter and you may add a setter in the derived by overriding with var. But you shouldn't attempt to withdraw the setter that's for a base's var by overriding with a val in the derived.

All these concepts will take shape in the next example. The Vehicle class that follows is marked as open and so can serve as a base class.

```
inheritance/inheritance.kts
open class Vehicle(val year: Int, open var color: String) {
  open val km = 0

  final override fun toString() = "year: $year, Color: $color, KM: $km"

  fun repaint(newColor: String) {
    color = newColor
  }
}
```

The class takes two parameters in the constructor: the first defines a property that can't be overridden in any derived class of Vehicle, and the second is a property that may be overridden since it's marked as open. The property km defined within the class may also be overridden in a derived class. This class overrides the toString() method of its own base class Any, but prohibits any inheriting class from overriding that method. The method repaint() is final since it's not marked as open.

Next we'll create a derived class of Vehicle:

inheritance/inheritance.kts
```
open class Car(year: Int, color: String) : Vehicle(year, color) {
  override var km: Int = 0
    set(value) {
      if (value < 1) {
        throw RuntimeException("can't set negative value")
      }

      field = value
    }

  fun drive(distance: Int) {
    km += distance
  }
}
```

The class Car derives from Vehicle and at the same time can serve as a base class for any class that likes to extend it. The parameters of the constructor of Car are passed as arguments to the constructor of Vehicle. The colon notation is used to express inheritance of a class from another class, much like how inheritance from an interface was specified. Unlike Java, Kotlin doesn't distinguish between implements and extends—it's just inheritance.

The class overrides the km property, provides a setter that checks the value to be greater than zero, and sets the acceptable value into the backing field for this property. There's no explicit getter, and the value in the backing field will be returned automatically when requested. The drive() method modifies the km property stored in Car and is final since it isn't marked open.

Let's create an instance of the Car class to study its behavior.

inheritance/inheritance.kts
```
val car = Car(2019, "Orange")
println(car.year)  // 2019
println(car.color) // Orange

car.drive(10)
println(car) // year: 2019, Color: Orange, KM: 10

try {
  car.drive(-30)
} catch(ex: RuntimeException) {
  println(ex.message) // can't set negative value
}
```

The instance of Car takes values for year and color properties. Both these properties are passed on to the base and stored there. When drive() is called the first time, the km property stored in Car, and not the one in Vehicle, is modified. This value is displayed in the implicit call to toString() within println(car).

Even though the toString() method is implemented in Vehicle and not in Car, when the km property is accessed within the toString() method, the overridden implementation in Car is used due to polymorphism. The second call to drive() fails since the value set into the km property can't be less than 1.

We may derive further from Car if we like. The FamilyCar class that follows extends Car:

inheritance/inheritance.kts
```
class FamilyCar(year: Int, color: String) : Car(year, color) {
  override var color: String
    get() = super.color
    set(value) {
      if (value.isEmpty()) {
        throw RuntimeException("Color required")
      }

      super.color = value
    }
}
```

Unlike the km property in Car, which kept its value locally in its backing field, the FamilyCar doesn't store the value of color locally. Instead, by overriding both getter and setter, it fetches and forwards the value in these methods, respectively, from the base class. Since Car doesn't override color, the FamilyCar uses the color from Vehicle. But if the value set is empty, the change won't be accepted due to the overridden setter.

The constructor of FamilyCar passes the values to the base, but due to polymorphism the getter and setter in the derived will be used appropriately.

Let's use an instance of FamilyCar to see its behavior.

inheritance/inheritance.kts
```
val familyCar = FamilyCar(2019, "Green")

println(familyCar.color) //Green

try {
  familyCar.repaint("")
} catch(ex: RuntimeException) {
  println(ex.message) // Color required
}
```

Even though color is stored within the Vehicle, the instance of FamilyCar takes over the validation of the property's value and doesn't permit a blank color.

In addition to the reasonable restrictions Kotlin places, it also ensures that when overriding, you may be more generous with the access restriction, but not stricter. For example, you may make a private or protected member public in the derived, but you can't make a public member of base protected in the derived.

We've seen Kotlin's support for inheritance—any class that's open may be used as a base class. Sometimes, though, we may want to restrict the derived classes to some select classes. Kotlin provides sealed classes for that purpose.

Sealed Classes

In Kotlin, on one extreme we have final classes—that is, classes not marked as open—which can't have any derived classes. On the other extreme we have open and abstract classes, and there's no telling which class may inherit from them. It'll be nice to have a middle ground for a class to serve as a base to only a few classes, which the author of the class specifies.

Kotlin's sealed classes are open for extension by other classes defined in the same file but closed—that is, final or not open—for any other classes.

Here's a sealed class Card, along with a few classes that inherit from it, all within the same file Card.kt.

```
inheritance/Card.kt
sealed class Card(val suit: String)

class Ace(suit: String) : Card(suit)

class King(suit: String) : Card(suit) {
  override fun toString() = "King of $suit"
}

class Queen(suit: String) : Card(suit) {
  override fun toString() = "Queen of $suit"
}

class Jack(suit: String) : Card(suit) {
  override fun toString() = "Jack of $suit"
}

class Pip(suit: String, val number: Int) : Card(suit) {
  init {
    if (number < 2 || number > 10) {
      throw RuntimeException("Pip has to be between 2 and 10")
    }
  }
}
```

The constructors of sealed classes aren't marked private, but they're considered private. The derived classes of a sealed class, like Ace, for example, may have any number of instances and may have state—that is, their own properties—and methods. In addition to deriving classes, you may also derive singleton objects from sealed classes. In this example, there can be only five derived classes of Card. Any attempt to inherit from Card by any classes written in any other files will fail compilation.

Since the constructors of sealed classes are considered to be private, we can't instantiate an object of these classes. However, we can create objects of classes that inherit from sealed classes, assuming their constructors aren't marked private explicitly. Let's create instances of the derived classes of Card:

inheritance/UseCard.kt
```
fun process(card: Card) = when (card) {
  is Ace -> "${card.javaClass.name} of ${card.suit}"
  is King, is Queen, is Jack -> "$card"
  is Pip -> "${card.number} of ${card.suit}"
}

fun main() {
  println(process(Ace("Diamond")))     // Ace of Diamond
  println(process(Queen("Clubs")))     // Queen of Clubs
  println(process(Pip("Spades", 2)))   // 2 of Spades
  println(process(Pip("Hearts", 6)))   // 6 of Hearts
}
```

Creating instances of the derived classes of a sealed class is straightforward. However, when used within a when expression, you should not write the else path. If there's a path for all the derived types of a sealed class in when, then placing an else will result in a warning for the path that will never be taken. If there's no path for any of the derived class, the compiler will insist that you add a path for the missing cases or that you add an else path. Even if the compiler suggests adding an else path, do not add it, and don't ignore any warnings the compiler may generate. If you were to add it, and later on a new sealed class is added, then instead of getting a compilation error to alert that the new case isn't handled properly, the program may execute an unintended piece of code in the else path.

The derived classes of a sealed class may have any number of instances. A special case of this is enum, which restricts the number of instances to one for each subclass.

Creating and Using Enums

In the previous example we used String to represent a suit, but that's smelly. We don't need arbitrary values for suit. We may create a sealed class Suit and derived classes for each of the four permissible types. In fact, there can be only four values for suit. In short, we don't need classes, we simply need four instances. The enum class solves that problem elegantly.

Here's an excerpt of code where the suits properties are converted to use an enum class Suit instead of being a String:

```
inheritance/CardWithEnum.kt
enum class Suit { CLUBS, DIAMONDS, HEARTS, SPADES }

sealed class Card(val suit: Suit)

class Ace(suit: Suit) : Card(suit)

class King(suit: Suit) : Card(suit) {
  override fun toString() = "King of $suit"
}
//...
```

Likewise, instead of passing a String to the constructor, we can now pass an instance of the enum class Suit:

```
inheritance/UseCardWithEnum.kt
println(process(Ace(Suit.DIAMONDS)))    // Ace of DIAMONDS
println(process(Queen(Suit.CLUBS)))     // Queen of CLUBS
println(process(Pip(Suit.SPADES, 2)))   // 2 of SPADES
println(process(Pip(Suit.HEARTS, 6)))   // 6 of HEARTS
```

The reference Suit.DIAMONDS represents an instance of class Suit and is a static property in the enum class.

Not only are enum classes suitable for creating a bunch of enumerated values, we may customize them and iterate over them easily as well.

Given a String we can obtain the corresponding enum instance using the valueOf() method:

```
inheritance/iteratesuit.kts
val diamonds = Suit.valueOf("DIAMONDS")
```

If the String argument provided to valueOf() doesn't match for any of the values defined for the target enum class, then a runtime exception will be thrown.

We can also iterate over all the values for a enum class:

```
inheritance/iteratesuit.kts
for (suit in Suit.values()) {
  println("${suit.name} -- ${suit.ordinal}") //CLUBS -- 0, etc.
}
```

The values() method provides an array of all the instances of the enum class. The name and ordinal properties of an enum instance will return the name and an index of the instance in the definition.

We may also hold state and provide methods in enum classes, but a semicolon has to separate the list of values from the methods. Let's add a symbol property for each value of the Suit enum and provide a method to return the name and symbol.

inheritance/initlizeenum.kts
```kotlin
enum class Suit(val symbol: Char) {
  CLUBS('\u2663'),
  DIAMONDS('\u2666'),
  HEARTS('\u2665') {
    override fun display() = "${super.display()} $symbol"
  },
  SPADES('\u2660');

  open fun display() = "$symbol $name"
}
```

The enum class Suit now takes a parameter for the symbol property of type Char. It also has a method display() to return the name and symbol for a suit. Had we defined it as abstract, then each of the suit values would be required to implement that method. Had we defined it without open, then none of the suit values could override it. We took the middle ground here—those suits that want to override that method may do so and the other suits will use the implementation provided.

Each of the values CLUBS, DIAMONDS, and so on, pass the appropriate Unicode value to the constructor as argument. The HEARTS is special, as you'd suspect. Instead, being an instance of Suit, it's an anonymous inner class which overrides its own display() method. After the last enum value, SPADES, a semicolon indicates the end of values and the beginning of properties and methods of the enum class.

To see the above changes in action, let's iterate over the values of Suit and call the display() method for each value:

inheritance/initlizeenum.kts
```kotlin
for (suit in Suit.values()) {
  println(suit.display())
}
```

The output below shows that the specialized display() method is called where available:

```
♣ CLUBS
♦ DIAMONDS
♥ HEARTS ♥
♠ SPADES
```

If you query for the javaClass on an instance of Suit with the call suit.javaClass, you'll see that CLUBS, DIAMONDS, and SPADES are instances of Suit but HEARTS is an instance of an anonymous inner class of Suit.

The Kotlin compiler takes care of minimally creating instances of the enum class where possible and specializes with anonymous inner classes when needed. Without regard to that, we can use enums in a type-safe manner, to create expressive code that's easier to maintain.

Wrapping Up

Kotlin's support to build a hierarchy of classes goes beyond the support provided in Java. Interfaces are almost the same in both languages, except in the way they are defined—Kotlin has no default keyword, and static methods go into companion objects even for interfaces. Kotlin's nested and inner classes also differ from the same concepts in Java—unlike Java, Kotlin makes a clear distinction between nested and inner classes, to make the intent clear. Classes are final by default, but not all open classes are widely inheritable—you can control inheritance using sealed classes if you like. Kotlin places restrictions around inheritance so classes don't accidentally serve as a base class. This forces you to make the intent explicit and makes code safer to use. Finally, the instances of enum classes are created as static members, and where specialization is needed, they turn into anonymous inner classes.

Good design guidelines often suggest preferring delegation over inheritance, but many OO languages offer little direct support for delegation. Kotlin is keen on helping you make the right design choices. In the next chapter, we'll learn how to use the delegation feature of Kotlin.

CHAPTER 9

Extension Through Delegation

Both inheritance and delegation, which are distinctive design tools in OO programming, promote reuse by way of extending one class from another. We have to wisely choose between them. Languages' capabilities often limit our choices, and this is where Kotlin's ability to support both comes into play.

While powerful and often used, inheritance—where a class derives properties, methods, and implementation from another class—leads to tight coupling and is inflexible. Most languages that provide inheritance don't permit a class to choose between different base classes. Whatever a class inherits from, you're stuck with it, like biological parents—whether you like them or not, you don't have a choice.

Delegation is more flexible than inheritance. An object may delegate or pass some of its responsibilities to an instance of another class. Different instances of a class may delegate to instances of different classes. It's like the way siblings, with the same parents, can and do choose different friends.

Design books like *Design Patterns: Elements of Reusable Object-Oriented Software [GHJV95]* advise us to prefer delegation over inheritance where possible. *Effective Java, Third Edition [Blo18]* makes that a strong recommendation for Java programs as well. Yet we see reuse via inheritance more often than delegation in Java, because the language provides good support for inheritance and little for delegation. Kotlin takes the design recommendations of those books to heart and provides facilities for delegation.

In this chapter, you'll learn when to use delegation instead of inheritance, and how to use it. We'll also look at a few built-in delegates in Kotlin. Since we don't delegate fun things like learning to someone else, let's get moving.

When to Choose Delegation over Inheritance?

Both delegation and inheritance are useful, but you have to decide when one is a better choice than the other. Inheritance is common, highly used, and is a first-class feature in OO languages. Though delegation is more flexible, there's no special support for it in many OO languages. We often shy away from delegation since it takes more effort to implement than inheritance. Kotlin supports both inheritance and delegation, so we can freely choose between them based on the problem at hand. The following rules will serve you well in deciding which one to choose:

- Use inheritance if you want an object of a class *to be used in place of* an object of another class.

- Use delegation if you want an object of a class *to simply make use of* an object of another class.

You can see the two design choices in the following figure—a Candidate class using inheritance on the left and delegation on the right.

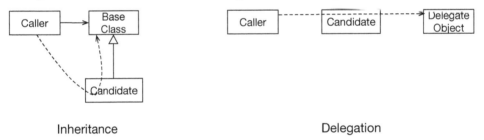

Inheritance   Delegation

When a Candidate class inherits from the BaseClass—like in the design on the left in the figure—an instance of the Candidate class carries an instance of the BaseClass within. Not only is that base instance (BaseClass) inseparable from the derived instance (Candidate) but its class is set in stone. The Caller, which references an instance of the base class at compile time, may actually be using an instance of derived at runtime without knowing. We celebrate this as the charm of polymorphism that's enabled through inheritance in statically typed OO languages. But achieving this behavior to freely interchange instances of derived—where an instance of base is expected—can be a slippery slope, as cautioned by Liskov's Substitution Principle (LSP)—see *Agile Software Development, Principles, Patterns, and Practices [Mar02]*. The issue is that the creator of the derived class must make sure that the implementation that overrides the base methods maintains the external observable behavior of the base class. In short, using inheritance greatly limits the degree of freedom for the designer of the derived class.

When a Candidate class delegates to a DelegateObject—like in the design on the right in the figure—an instance of the Candidate class holds a reference to a delegate. The actual class of the delegate may vary, within reason. In some languages that support delegation, like Groovy, Ruby, and JavaScript, you may even change the delegated object on a Candidate instance at runtime. Unlike in inheritance, the instances aren't inseparable, and that offers greater flexibility. The Caller sends its call to the Candidate, which then forwards the call, as appropriate, to the delegate.

With these two distinctive design choices being available, programmers have to choose wisely between the two. Use inheritance to specialize the implementation of a class and to substitute an instance of one class in place of another—that is, to design the *kind-of* relationship, like in Dog is a *kind of* Animal. To merely reuse an object in the implementation of another, use delegation, like a Manager *has an* Assistant, to do part of the work.

If delegation is the right choice for your design, you'll have to write a lot of duplicated code in languages like Java. That leads to bloated code that can be hard to maintain. Kotlin uses a better, declarative approach to delegation—you concisely convey your intent, and the compiler runs off to generate the necessary code.

Designing with Delegates

In the previous chapter, you saw that Kotlin offers a different and safer way to use inheritance than Java. Likewise, Kotlin has much better support than Java for delegation. Before we dive into the syntax for delegation, we'll take a small problem and design it using inheritance, to better understand the reasons to use delegation over inheritance. Soon we'll run into issues where inheritance begins to become a hindrance, and you'll see how delegation may be a better choice for the problem. We'll then look at how Kotlin is able to readily support our new design using delegation, without flinching.

A Design Problem

Imagine an application that simulates the execution of software projects by corporate teams (don't worry, we'll limit the scope so our program, unlike some enterprise projects, actually completes). We need workers to get real stuff done—let's start with a Worker interface:

delegation/version1/project.kts
```
interface Worker {
  fun work()
  fun takeVacation()
}
```

A worker may perform two tasks: does work and occasionally takes vacation. Let's implement two classes, JavaProgrammer and CSharpProgrammer, that specialize in two different languages—the idea of being polyglot has not caught this company's attention yet.

delegation/version1/project.kts
```
class JavaProgrammer : Worker {
  override fun work() = println("...write Java...")
  override fun takeVacation() = println("...code at the beach...")
}
class CSharpProgrammer : Worker {
  override fun work() = println("...write C#...")
  override fun takeVacation() = println("...branch at the ranch...")
}
```

The programmers perform their work() based on their language specialty and enjoy their vacations according to the established industry standards.

The company wants to have a software development manager for their teams—let's write that class:

delegation/version1/project.kts
```
class Manager
```

The Manager class is very small, agile, and highly efficient, and as you'd expect, does nothing. A call to work() on an instance of this manager won't lead anywhere. We need to design some logic into the Manager, but that's not easy.

The Inheritance Misroute

Now that we have the interface Worker and the two implementations, JavaProgrammer and CSharpProgrammer, let's focus on using them with the Manager class. The company will want to rely on the Manager to execute and deliver the project. The Manager, in turn, will need a programmer to get the actual work done. In the most simple form, a call to work() on the Manager will have to be executed on an implementation of Worker. One way to achieve this is to use inheritance, which is a common approach we use in Java. By inheriting Manager from JavaProgrammer, we won't have to write the work() method in the Manager class, and that often serves as a temptation to use inheritance. Let's take this approach and see where it leads.

As a first step, we have to annotate the JavaProgrammer class as open:

delegation/version2/project.kts
```
open class JavaProgrammer : Worker {
```

Then, we can enhance the Manager class to inherit from the JavaProgrammer class:

delegation/version2/project.kts
```
class Manager : JavaProgrammer()
```

Now we can call work() on an instance of Manager:

delegation/version2/project.kts
```
val doe = Manager()
doe.work() //...write Java...
```

That worked, but this design has a drawback. This Manager class is stuck to the JavaProgrammer class and can't use what's offered by a CSharpProgrammer class (or any other classes that implement Worker in the future). That's not fair, but that's the consequence of inheritance. And let's examine another unintended consequence—substitutability.

We didn't mean Manager is a JavaProgrammer or a *kind-of* JavaProgrammer, but sadly that was implied from inheritance. As a result, the following code will compile:

delegation/version2/project.kts
```
val coder: JavaProgrammer = doe
```

Even though this wasn't intended by the design, we can't stop it. Our real intention here is that Manager should rely upon or use a JavaProgrammer or any worker that can get the tasks done. But that's delegation, not inheritance. We want to be able to delegate work from a Manager instance to the instance of any Worker. Let's move toward that design and see how it solves the problem at hand, but without bringing along the aforementioned unintended behaviors.

Delegation, the Hard Way

Although in languages like Java we have a syntax for inheritance, there's nothing to specify delegation. You may use a reference to refer to another object, but the language leaves you with the full burden to implement the design.

Let's look at an example of delegation. Even though the code here is in Kotlin, for a few minutes we'll use only facilities that are available in Java. Here's Kotlin code with the Java approach to delegate Manager to a Worker.

delegation/version3/project.kts
```
class Manager(val worker: Worker) {
 fun work() = worker.work()

 fun takeVacation() = worker.work() //yeah, right, like that's gonna happen
}
```

Before we discuss the quality of this design, let's use the modified Manager class:

```
delegation/version3/project.kts
val doe = Manager(JavaProgrammer())
doe.work() //...write Java...
```

We created an instance of Manager and passed an instance of JavaProgrammer as an argument to the constructor. The benefit this design has over inheritance is that the Manager isn't tightly coupled to the JavaProgrammer class. Thus, we may instead pass to the constructor an instance of CSharpProgrammer class, or just about any class that implements the Worker interface. In other words, an instance of Manager may delegate to an instance of any class that implements Worker—JavaProgrammer, CSharpProgrammer, and so on.

An additional benefit in this solution is that the JavaProgrammer class no longer has to be marked as open since we're not inheriting from it.

But an undesirable aspect to this design is that the code is verbose and violates a few fundamental software design principles. Let's discuss the issues one at a time.

Within the Manager class, we implement the work() method that merely routes the call to the instance of Worker that's referenced by the Manager instance. Likewise, in the takeVacation() method, we're merely routing the call to the worker reference. Imagine having more methods in Worker—that's even more routing code in Manager. All the routing code looks the same, except for the method routed to. That's a violation of the Don't Repeat Yourself or DRY principle presented in *The Pragmatic Programmer: From Journeyman to Master [HT00]*.

Besides not being DRY, the code also fails the Open-Closed Principle (OCP) coined by Bertrand Meyer and discussed in *Agile Software Development, Principles, Patterns, and Practices [Mar02]*. The principle says that a software module—classes, functions, and so on—should be open for extension but closed from modification. In other words, to extend a class we shouldn't have to change it. Sadly, though, in the current implementation of the design, suppose we add a method deploy() to Worker, and the Manager wants to delegate calls to that method, then we'll have to change the Manager class to add the routing method—OCP violation.

These issues give us a sense of why Java programs use inheritance more than delegation—delegation has issues due to lack of language support, and inheritance is so easy to reach for. But Manager isn't a JavaProgrammer, and modeling it using inheritance will lead to violation of LSP. The programmers are left with a "doomed if you do, doomed if you don't" kind of solution.

Kotlin solves this problem by supporting delegation at the language level.

Delegation Using Kotlin's by

In the previous example we implemented delegation by hand, routing method calls from Manager to the Worker delegate. The body of the Manager is smelly with all these duplicated method calls and the DRY and OCP violations. That's the only option if we were programming in Java. But in Kotlin, instead, we can ask the compiler to generate the crufty routing code for us, and then the Manager can route like a boss without any fuss.

Let's take a small step to explore the simplest use of delegation in Kotlin for this problem at hand.

delegation/version4/project.kts
```
class Manager() : Worker by JavaProgrammer()
```

This version of Manager doesn't have any methods of its own, at least not at code-writing time. It implements the Worker interface *by way of* or via the JavaProgrammer. Upon seeing the by keyword, the Kotlin compiler will implement, at the bytecode level, the methods in the Manager class that belong to Worker, and route the call to the JavaProgrammer instance supplied after the by keyword. In other words, the by keyword in this example does at compile time what we painstakingly did manually in the previous example where we implemented delegation by hand.

Kotlin requires the left side of the by to be an interface. The right side is an implementor of that interface.

Let's exercise this version of the Manager class by creating an instance:

delegation/version4/project.kts
```
val doe = Manager()
doe.work() //...write Java...
```

It was easy to create an instance of Manager and call the work() method on it.

At first sight, this solution almost looks like the inheritance solution, but there are some key differences. First, the class Manager isn't inheriting from JavaProgrammer. Recall that with the inheriting solution we were able to assign an instance of Manager to a reference of type JavaProgrammer. Thankfully, that's no longer possible, and the following will result in an error:

delegation/version4/projecterror.kts
```
val coder: JavaProgrammer = doe //ERROR: type mismatch
```

Second, in the inheritance solution, calls to methods like work() weren't implemented in Manager; instead they were sent to the base class. In the case of Kotlin delegation, the compiler internally creates methods within the Manager class and does the routing. In effect, when we call doe.work() we are calling the invisible method work() within the Manager class. This method, synthesized by the Kotlin compiler, routes the call to the delegate, the instance of JavaProgrammer given in the class declaration.

The above solution is the simplest form of delegation but has some limitations. We'll identify those and resolve them next.

Delegating to a Parameter

In the previous example we wrote Worker by JavaProgrammer(), which says that the Manager instance is delegating to an implicitly created instance of the JavaProgrammer, but that poses two issues. First, the instances of Manager class can only route to instances of JavaProgrammer, not to instances of any other Worker implementors. Second, an instance of Manager doesn't have access to the delegate; that is, if we were to write a method in the Manager class, we can't access the delegate from that method. It's easy to fix those limitations by tying the delegate to the parameter passed to the constructor instead of to an implicitly created instance.

```
delegation/version5/project.kts
class Manager(val staff: Worker) : Worker by staff {
  fun meeting() =
    println("organizing meeting with ${staff.javaClass.simpleName}")
}
```

The constructor of the Manager class receives a parameter named staff which also serves as a property, due to val in the declaration. If the val is removed, staff will still be a parameter, but not a property of the class. Irrespective of whether or not val is used, the class can delegate to the parameter staff.

In the meeting() method of the Manager class, we're able to access staff since it's a property of the object. Calls to methods like work() will go to staff due to delegation. Let's confirm this behavior by creating a couple of instances of this version of Manager.

```
delegation/version5/project.kts
val doe = Manager(CSharpProgrammer())
val roe = Manager(JavaProgrammer())

doe.work() //...write C#...
doe.meeting()//organizing meeting with CSharpProgrammer

roe.work() //...write Java...
roe.meeting()//organizing meeting with JavaProgrammer
```

The first instance of Manager receives an instance of CSharpProgrammer, and the second instance receives an instance of JavaProgrammer. That shows that the delegation is flexible; it's not tied to one class, JavaProgrammer, and may use different implementations of Worker. When work() is called on the two instances of Manager, Kotlin routes the calls automatically to the respective delegates. Also, when meeting() is called on the Manager instances, those calls send an invitation to the respective staff properties that are part of the Manager instances.

Dealing with Method Collisions

The Kotlin compiler creates a wrapper in the delegating class for each method that's in the delegate. What if there's a method in the delegating class with the same name and signature as in the delegate? Kotlin resolves this conflict in favor of the delegating class. As a consequence, you can be selective and don't have to delegate every single method of the delegate class—let's explore this further.

In the previous example, the Worker has a takeVacation() method and the Manager is delegating calls to that method to the Worker delegate. Although that's the default behavior for delegation in Kotlin, it's unlikely that any Manager would settle for that; while it makes perfect sense for a Manager to delegate work(), one would expect the takeVacation() to be executed on the instance of Manager and not be delegated.

Kotlin requires the delegating class to implement a delegate interface, but without actually implementing each of the methods of the interface. We saw this in the Manager—it implements Worker, but didn't provide any implementations for the work() or takeVacation() methods. For every method of the delegate interface, the Kotlin compiler creates a wrapper. But that's true only if the delegating class doesn't already have an implementation of a method. If the delegating class has an implementation for a method that's in the interface, then it must be marked as override, that implementation takes precedence, and a wrapper method isn't created.

To illustrate this behavior, let's implement the takeVacation() method in the Manager:

```
delegation/version6/project.kts
class Manager(val staff: Worker) : Worker by staff {
  override fun takeVacation() = println("of course")
}
```

With the override keyword, you're making it very clear to the reader of the code that you're implementing a method from the interface, not some arbitrary function that happens to accidentally have the same name as a method in the delegate. Seeing this, the Kotlin compiler won't generate a wrapper for takeVacation(), but it will generate a wrapper for the work() method.

Let's invoke the methods of the interface on an instance of this version of the Manager class.

delegation/version6/project.kts
```
val doe = Manager(CSharpProgrammer())
doe.work()            //...write C#...
doe.takeVacation() //of course
```

The call to the work() method on the instance of Manager is routed to the delegate, but the call to the takeVacation() method is handled by the Manager—no delegation there. Kotlin nicely takes care of resolving method collisions and also makes it easy to override select methods of the delegate interface in the delegating class.

In the examples so far, we've looked at delegating the methods of a single interface to an implementing class. A class may delegate to multiple interface implementors as well. If there are any method collisions between the interfaces, then the candidate class should override the conflicting methods. The next example will illustrate this behavior.

Let's modify the Worker interface to add a new method:

delegation/version7/project.kts
```
interface Worker {
  fun work()
  fun takeVacation()
  fun fileTimeSheet() = println("Why? Really?")
}
```

The new method fileTimesheet() is implemented within the interface. The classes that implement the Worker interface can readily reuse it but may override that method if they dare.

Let's now look at a new interface, Assistant, with a few methods:

delegation/version7/project.kts
```
interface Assistant {
  fun doChores()
  fun fileTimeSheet() = println("No escape from that")
}
```

This interface has two methods, one of which is implemented in it. Here's a class that implements the Assistant interface:

delegation/version7/project.kts
```
class DepartmentAssistant : Assistant {
  override fun doChores() = println("routine stuff")
}
```

Let's see the effect of delegating to both interfaces.

delegation/version7/project.kts
```
class Manager(val staff: Worker, val assistant: Assistant) :
  Worker by staff, Assistant by assistant {

  override fun takeVacation() = println("of course")

  override fun fileTimeSheet() {
    print("manually forwarding this...")
    assistant.fileTimeSheet()
  }
}
```

The Manager class now has two properties defined as the primary constructor parameters. It also delegates to both of those objects, the first for the Worker interface and the second for the Assistant interface. If we don't implement the fileTimeSheet() method in the Manager class, we'll get a compilation error due to the collision of the fileTimeSheet() methods in the two interfaces. To resolve this conflict, we have implemented that method in the Manager class.

Let's use the latest version of the Manager class to see the delegation to two objects in action:

delegation/version7/project.kts
```
val doe = Manager(CSharpProgrammer(), DepartmentAssistant())
doe.work()           //...write C#...
doe.takeVacation()   //of course
doe.doChores()       //routine stuff
doe.fileTimeSheet() //manually forwarding this...No escape from that
```

The call to the work() method was delegated to the implementation of the Worker interface. The call to takeVacation() wasn't delegated; it was executed on the Manager instance. The call to doChores() method was delegated to the implementation of the Assistant interface. Finally, the call to fileTimeSheet() method was executed on the Manager instance. Thus, the Manager instance has intercepted the call to fileTimeSheet(), avoiding any conflict or ambiguity to a call on Worker or on an Assistant. The Manager instance can decide to manually route the call to either the Worker implementation, or the Assistant implementation, or to both. In this example, the Manager intercepted the call to fileTimeSheet() and then delegated manually to the implementor of the Assistant interface via the assistant property.

Kotlin's facility for delegation is a breath of fresh air when you consider what's lacking in Java. But we have to be careful about a few things when using delegation. Let's go over those to avoid any surprises later.

Caveats of Kotlin Delegation

In the example we've created so far, the Manager may delegate calls to an instance of a JavaProgrammer, but a reference to a Manager may not be assigned to a reference of a JavaProgrammer—that is, a Manager may use a JavaProgrammer, but a Manager may not be used as a JavaProgrammer. In other words, a Manager *has a* JavaProgrammer but is not a *kind of* JavaProgrammer. Thus, delegation offers reuse without accidentally leading to substitutability as inheritance does.

However, there's one small consequence of how Kotlin implements delegation. The delegating class implements the delegating interface, so a reference to the delegating class may be assigned to a reference of the delegating interface. Likewise, a reference to a delegating class may be passed to methods that expect a delegate interface. In other words, for example, the following isn't valid:

```
val coder: JavaProgrammer = doe //ERROR: type mismatch
```

But the following is possible in Kotlin:

```
val employee: Worker = doe
```

This means a Manager is a, or kind of a, Worker. The true intention of delegation is for a Manager to use a Worker, but Kotlin's delegate implementation introduces a side effect that a Manager may be treated as a Worker.

Also, use caution when delegating to a property. We passed a parameter of type Worker to the constructor of Manager, using val. In Prefer val over var, on page 26, we discussed why we should prefer val over var. That recommendation is useful here too. If we decide to change the property that's used as a delegate from val to var, a few consequences arise. Let's see what those are with an example.

Here's the full listing we'll use for this example:

```
delegation/version8/project.kts
interface Worker {
  fun work()
  fun takeVacation()
  fun fileTimeSheet() = println("Why? Really?")
}

class JavaProgrammer : Worker {
  override fun work() = println("...write Java...")
  override fun takeVacation() = println("...code at the beach...")
}

class CSharpProgrammer : Worker {
  override fun work() = println("...write C#...")
  override fun takeVacation() = println("...branch at the ranch...")
}
```

```
class Manager(var staff: Worker) : Worker by staff

val doe = Manager(JavaProgrammer())

println("Staff is ${doe.staff.javaClass.simpleName}")
doe.work()

println("changing staff")
doe.staff = CSharpProgrammer()
println("Staff is ${doe.staff.javaClass.simpleName}")
doe.work()
```

The Manager's primary constructor defines a mutable property named staff and delegates to that same object. We created the instance doe by passing an instance of JavaProgrammer. Then we get the property staff from the instance doe and ask for the type. When we call work() on doe we expect the work method of the JavaProgrammer attached to the staff property to be called.

Then we change the staff property to an instance of the CSharpProgrammer class and check the type of the object referenced by the staff property, to confirm it is CSharpProgrammer now and not JavaProgrammer. Finally, we invoke the work() method. Which work method does this call land in, CSharpProgrammer or JavaProgrammer?

Let's look carefully at the declaration once again:

```
class Manager(var staff: Worker) : Worker by staff
```

It's easy to mistake what the delegate is. The delegate at the far right is the parameter and not the property. The declaration is really taking a parameter named staff and assigning it to a member named staff, like so: this.staff = staff. So there are two references to the given object: one held inside the class as a backing field and one held for the purpose of delegation. When we change the property to an instance of CSharpProgrammer, though, we only modified the field and not the reference to the delegate. Hence the following output:

```
Staff is JavaProgrammer
...write Java...
changing staff
Staff is CSharpProgrammer
...write Java...
```

Kotlin doesn't delegate to a property of an object but to the parameter passed to the primary constructor—this behavior may change in the future.

Another problem arises with the code we just used. When we replace staff with an instance of CSharpProgrammer, the originally attached instance of JavaProgrammer is no longer attached to the object as its property. But it can't get garbage collected since the delegate holds on to it. Thus, the lifetime of the delegate is the same as the object's lifetime, though the properties may come and go along the way.

Knowing these caveats will help you safely benefit from the delegates feature. But there's more to delegates than applying on an entire class. Let's dig in further.

Delegating Variables and Properties

In the examples so far, we focused on delegation at the class level. You may delegate get and set access to properties of objects and local variables too.

When you read a property or a local variable, internally Kotlin calls a getValue() function. Likewise, when you update a property or a variable, it calls a setValue() function. By providing as delegate an object with these two methods, you may intercept calls to read and write local variables and objects' properties.

Delegating Variables

You can intercept access, both read and write, to local variables and alter what is returned and where and how the data is stored. To illustrate this facility, let's create a custom delegate to intercept access of String variables.

Suppose we're creating an application that takes users' comments. The text they enter may be displayed to other users, and we definitely want to be polite. So let's write a delegate that filters out an offensive word, like "stupid".

Let's look at a small script with no filtering:

```
var comment: String = "Some nice message"
println(comment)

comment = "This is stupid"
println(comment)

println("comment is of length: ${comment.length}")
```

Running this will produce the rude output, no surprise:

```
Some nice message
This is stupid
comment is of length: 14
```

Our objective is to replace the word "stupid" so when the string is printed it's not as rude. For that, let's create a class named PoliteString that has getValue() and setValue() methods with special signatures:

delegation/com/agiledeveloper/delegates/PoliteString.kt
```
package com.agiledeveloper.delegates

import kotlin.reflect.KProperty

class PoliteString(var content: String) {
  operator fun getValue(thisRef: Any?, property: KProperty<*>) =
    content.replace("stupid", "s*****")

  operator fun setValue(thisRef: Any, property: KProperty<*>, value: String) {
    content = value
  }
}
```

The class PoliteString is all set to act as a delegate. Kotlin doesn't require any interface to be implemented, no ceremony—all it wants is the get method. If the delegate will target a mutable property or variable, then it demands the set method also. It's that simple. If you're unsure of the signature of these methods, refer to the interfaces kotlin.properties.ReadOnlyProperty and kotlin.properties.ReadWriteProperty. Though you don't have to implement these interfaces, the getValue() and setValue() methods are the same as the ones in these symbolic interfaces.

The PoliteString class receives a mutable property named content. From the getValue() function we return the value in the contents string after cleansing any offending words in it. In the setValue() function we merely store the given value into the content property. The methods are marked with the annotation operator since they stand for the assignment operator = used for get and set.

We'll have to compile this code into a jar file since it's in a separate package. We'll see the command for that soon. Let's make use of this delegate with the code that contains the impolite comment.

delegation/politecomment.kts
```
import com.agiledeveloper.delegates.PoliteString

var comment: String by PoliteString("Some nice message")
println(comment)

comment = "This is stupid"
println(comment)

println("comment is of length: ${comment.length}")
```

We imported PoliteString and changed the comment variable to use the PoliteString in the declaration. It's a String that will delegate access to PoliteString.

Here are the steps to compile and execute this example:

```
$ kotlinc-jvm com/agiledeveloper/delegates/PoliteString.kt -d polite.jar
$ kotlinc-jvm -classpath polite.jar -script politecomment.kts
```

The output from the code shows the offending word replaced:

```
Some nice message
This is s*****
comment is of length: 14
```

In the example, we're passing an instance of PoliteString as delegate. That's fine, but if you'd rather use a function that returns a delegate instance, instead of calling the constructor of a class after by, you may do so easily. Let's introduce a top-level function in the file PoliteString.kt within the package com.agiledeveloper.delegates:

delegation/com/agiledeveloper/delegates/PoliteString.kt
```
//This function goes at the end of class PoliteString
fun beingpolite(content: String) = PoliteString(content)
```

We can now use this function instead of the PoliteString class:

```
import com.agiledeveloper.delegates.beingpolite
```

```
var comment: String by beingpolite("Some nice message")
```

We can improve on the PoliteString delegate to filter out many rude words. Then anywhere we want to keep things polite, we can pass the variable to the delegate to achieve that goal.

Delegating Properties

Using the previous approach, we can not only delegate access to local variables but also to properties of objects. When defining a property, instead of assigning a value, specify by and follow it with a delegate. Again here, delegate may be any object that implements getValue() for a val or read-only property, and both getValue() and setValue() for a read-write property.

In the next example, we'll use a variation of PoliteString delegate that we created earlier. Instead of storing the comment within the instance of PoliteString, we'll store it in a data source.

By design, the Kotlin standard libraries, Map and MutableMap (that we discussed in Using Map, on page 73), can serve as delegates—the first for val properties and the second for var properties. That's because, in addition to providing the get() method, Map also has getValue(). Likewise, in addition to set, MutableMap also has the setValue() method. In the example, we'll use these as delegates to handle property access.

We'll first create the variation of PoliteString to store the comment value in a MutableMap that will serve as a data source:

delegation/postcomment.kts

```kotlin
import kotlin.reflect.KProperty
import kotlin.collections.MutableMap

class PoliteString(val dataSource: MutableMap<String, Any>) {
  operator fun getValue(thisRef: Any?, property: KProperty<*>) =
    (dataSource[property.name] as? String)?.replace("stupid", "s*****") ?: ""

  operator fun setValue(thisRef: Any, property: KProperty<*>, value: String) {
    dataSource[property.name] = value
  }
}
```

Instead of receiving a String parameter, here we receive a reference to a Muta-bleMap<String, Any> that will hold the comment value. In the getValue() method, we return the value from the map for the property's name as key. If the value exists, we safely cast to String and cleanse it; otherwise, return an empty string. In the setValue() we merely save the given value into the map.

Next, we'll create a PostComment class that represents a blog post comment. Instead of storing the fields locally, its properties will delegate the get/set operations to a map. Let's take a look at the code, and then we'll discuss it further.

delegation/postcomment.kts

```kotlin
class PostComment(dataSource: MutableMap<String, Any>) {
  val title: String by dataSource
  var likes: Int by dataSource
  val comment: String by PoliteString(dataSource)

  override fun toString() = "Title: $title Likes: $likes Comment: $comment"
}
```

The primary constructor receives a parameter dataSource of type MutableMap<String, Any>, which will serve as a delegate to the properties of this class. The title is a read-only property of type String and is delegated to dataSource. Likewise, likes, which is of type Int but is a read-write property, is delegated to the same object, dataSource. The comment property, however, is delegated to PoliteString, which in turn will store and retrieve data from the same dataSource.

When the title property of an instance of PostComment is read, Kotlin will invoke the getValue() method of the delegate dataSource by passing the property name title to it. Thus, the map will return the value for the key title, if present.

The behavior for reading the likes property is similar to that of reading the title property. Unlike title, likes is mutable. When the likes property is written or set, Kotlin will invoke the setValue() method of the delegate passing the property name likes and the value. This will result in the value being stored for the key likes within the dataSource that is the MutableMap<String, Any>.

Read and write of the comment property will result in calls to getValue() and set-Value(), respectively, on the PoliteString delegate. Via this delegate, the comment value will be fetched from or stored into the dataSource.

Let's create some sample data for a couple of blog post comments. We'll store them in a list of MutableMap instances.

```
delegation/postcomment.kts
val data = listOf(
    mutableMapOf(
      "title" to "Using Delegation",
      "likes" to 2,
      "comment" to "Keep it simple, stupid"),
    mutableMapOf(
      "title" to "Using Inheritance",
      "likes" to 1,
      "comment" to "Prefer Delegation where possible"))
```

Now we can create an instance of PostComment using the data in the list.

```
delegation/postcomment.kts
val forPost1 = PostComment(data[0])
val forPost2 = PostComment(data[1])

forPost1.likes++

println(forPost1)
println(forPost2)
```

The instances of PostComment act as a façade around the MutableMaps—they delegate any access to their properties to their dataSource. Here's the output from the above code:

```
Title: Using Delegation Likes: 3 Comment: Keep it simple, s*****
Title: Using Inheritance Likes: 1 Comment: Prefer Delegation where possible
```

An object doesn't have to delegate all its properties. As we saw here, it may delegate properties to different delegates and may also internally store a few in its own fields.

We've seen how to create our own delegates. Next, we'll see some delegates that are built in to the Kotlin standard library.

Built-in Standard Delegates

Kotlin provides a few built-in delegates that we can readily benefit from. The Lazy delegate is useful to defer creating objects or executing computations until the time the result is truly needed. The observable delegate is useful to observe or monitor changes to the value of a property. The vetoable delegate can be used to reject changes to properties based on some rules or business logic. We'll explore these features in this section.

It's OK to Get a Little Lazy

Decades ago John McCarthy introduced *short-circuit evaluation* to eliminate redundant computations in Boolean logic—the execution of an expression is skipped if the evaluation of an expression ahead of it is enough to yield the result. Most programming languages support this feature, and programmers quickly learn about the efficiency of this approach. The Lazy delegate pushes the boundaries of this approach—let's see how.

Suppose we have a function that gets the current temperature for a city (the following implementation merely returns a fake response):

delegation/shortcircuit.kts
```
fun getTemperature(city: String): Double {
  println("fetch from webservice for $city")
  return 30.0
}
```

Calling this hypothetical function getTemperature() is going to consume some time due to the remote access it requires to a web service. Also, there may be cost associated with the service usage. It's better to avoid calls where possible. The short-circuit evaluation naturally does that, like in this example:

delegation/shortcircuit.kts
```
val showTemperature = false
val city = "Boulder"

if (showTemperature && getTemperature(city) > 20) //(nothing here)
  println("Warm")
else
  println("Nothing to report") //Nothing to report
```

Since the value of showTemperature variable is false, due to short-circuit evaluation the execution of getTemperature() method will be skipped. That's efficient—if the result of a task isn't used, we don't bother doing that work.

However, a slight refactoring of this code will result in loss of that efficiency.

delegation/eagerevaluation.kts
```
val temperature = getTemperature(city) //fetch from webservice

if (showTemperature && temperature > 20)
  println("Warm")
else
  println("Nothing to report") //Nothing to report
```

We stored the result of getTemperature() into a local temporary variable and then used that within the Boolean expression of the if expression. But we incur the execution overhead with this change, even though we're not using the value of the temperature variable, again due to short-circuit evaluation. How sad.

Why can't Kotlin be smart to avoid this call? you may wonder. Because a function or method call may have side effects, its execution isn't skipped, in general. In the context of short-circuit, though, the execution may be skipped. The reason, simply put, is a well-known behavior of programs—programmers are familiar with short-circuit evaluation in Boolean expressions, and language specifications convey that expressions within Boolean expressions are not guaranteed to execute.

But, you protest, there must be a way to skip execution of expressions outside the context of Boolean expressions. Kotlin heard you—you can tell the compiler to be lazy about executing an expression until the point where its result is truly needed; otherwise, skip the execution entirely.

Let's modify the previous code to use the Lazy delegate, but instead of directly using the lazy delegate class, we'll use the lazy convenience wrapper function.

```
delegation/lazyevaluation.kts
val temperature by lazy { getTemperature(city) }

if (showTemperature && temperature > 20) //(nothing here)
  println("Warm")
else
  println("Nothing to report") //Nothing to report
```

We turned the simple variable temperature into a delegate property using the by keyword. The lazy function takes as argument a lambda expression that will perform the computation, but only on demand and not eagerly or immediately. The computation within the lambda expression will be evaluated if and when the value of the variable is requested. It's deferred until that time and, potentially, the execution may never happen, as in this example.

If we change the value of showTemperature to true, then the execution of getTemperature() will take place—not where temperature is defined, but where the comparison to > 20 happens, which is after the evaluation of the expression showTemperature in the Boolean condition.

Once the expression within the lambda is evaluated, the delegate will memoize the result and future requests for the value will receive the saved value. The lambda expression is not reevaluated.

The lazy function by default synchronizes the execution of the lambda expression so that at most one thread will execute it. If it's safe to execute the code concurrently from multiple threads or if you know the code will be executed only on a single thread, like in the case of Android UI application code, then you may provide an argument of the enum type LazyThreadSafetyMode to the lazy function to specify different synchronization options.

It's OK to get a little lazy where that can lead to more efficiency. Next, we'll see how to observe change to variables' values.

The Observable Delegate

The singleton object kotlin.properties.Delegates has an observable() convenience function to create a ReadWriteProperty delegate that will intercept any change to the variable or property it's associated with. When a change occurs, the delegate will call an event handler you register with the observable() function.

The event handler receives three parameters of type KProperty which hold the metadata about the property, the old value, and the new value. It doesn't return anything—that is, it's a Unit or void function. Let's create a variable with the observable delegate.

delegation/observe.kts
```
import kotlin.properties.Delegates.observable

var count by observable(0) { property, oldValue, newValue ->
  println("Property: $property old: $oldValue: new: $newValue")
}

println("The value of count is: $count")

count++

println("The value of count is: $count")

count--

println("The value of count is: $count")
```

The variable count is initialized with the value 0 that is provided as the first argument to the observable() function. The second argument to observable() is a lambda expression, the event handler. It merely prints the details of the property: the value of the variable before the change and the new value given for the variable. The increment operation on count will result in a call to that event handler. Here's the output of the code:

```
The value of count is: 0
Property: var Observe.count: kotlin.Int old: 0: new: 1
The value of count is: 1
Property: var Observe.count: kotlin.Int old: 1: new: 0
The value of count is: 0
```

Use the observable delegate to keep an eye on changes to local variables or properties within objects. It can be useful for monitoring and debugging purposes. Instead of merely observing, if you want to partake in deciding if a change should be accepted or rejected, then use the vetoable delegate.

Exercise Your Vetoable Rights

Unlike the handler registered with observable, whose return type is Unit, the handler we register with vetoable returns a Boolean result. A return value of true means a favorable nod to accept the change; false means reject. The change is discarded if we reject.

Let's modify the previous code to use vetoable() instead of observable().

delegation/veto.kts
```
import kotlin.properties.Delegates.vetoable

var count by vetoable(0) { _, oldValue, newValue -> newValue > oldValue }

println("The value of count is: $count")

count++

println("The value of count is: $count")

count--

println("The value of count is: $count")
```

In this version of code we're not using the property parameter—to avoid Kotlin compiler's warning for unused variables we use _ in that position. The lambda expression returns true if the new value for the variable is more than the previous value; otherwise it returns false. In other words, only increasing changes to the value of count are accepted. Let's take a look at the output of the code:

```
The value of count is: 0
The value of count is: 1
The value of count is: 1
```

Use the vetoable delegate anywhere you like to keep an eye on a local variable or property and want to reject certain changes based on some business logic.

Wrapping Up

Good design guidelines often recommend that we should prefer delegation over inheritance. Yet that was a hard sell in many OO languages, due to lack of direct support for delegation. Kotlin fixes that by providing facilities to delegate calls on objects, and access to both local variables and properties. Using the by keyword, you may delegate reads to any object that implements a getValue() method and writes to any object with setValue() method. Using these low-ceremony facilities, you may create your own custom delegates easily. You can also benefit from a few built-in standard delegates in the Kotlin standard library, like the Lazy delegate for example.

Being a multiparadigm language, Kotlin not only offers extensive OO programming features, as we've seen, it also provides phenomenal support for functional programming, as we'll see next. In the next chapter, we'll explore functional style and lambda expressions.

Part III

Functional Kotlin

The functional style is less complex compared to the imperative style of programming. Code reads like a problem statement in the functional style and so is easier to understand. With the ability to pass functions to functions, we can use functional decomposition in addition to object decomposition in Kotlin.

In this part, we'll focus on the functional programming capabilities of Kotlin. You'll learn how to create lambda expressions, why and where to use them, and how to ensure we don't compromise performance to gain fluency. You'll also learn to use internal iterators, sequences, and design patterns that can benefit from using lambda expressions.

Functional Programming with Lambdas

Functional-style code is declarative—you focus on what to do and assign the details of how to do it to underlying libraries of functions. In contrast, in the imperative style of programming you have to deal with both the whats and hows. As applications become complicated, having to deal with the hows makes the code highly complex. The functional style is inherently less complex—you can get more accomplished with not only fewer lines of code but also code that is expressive, easier to understand, and a breeze to maintain.

The imperative style of programming has been the mainstream for a few decades now. Languages like Java have offered a combination of imperative style and object-oriented programming. Object-oriented programming is helpful to abstract and encapsulate concepts. The goal of functional programming is not to replace OO, which greatly reduces complexity; the real concern is the imperative style. That's one of the reasons why Java has moved forward to accommodate the functional style of programming in recent years. Now we can do both imperative and functional styles of programming along with object-oriented programming in Java. While Java has evolved, Kotlin was born that way, as a mixed paradigm language that supports the imperative, functional, and object-oriented paradigms.

In this chapter you'll learn the benefits of the functional style, how to create and use lambda expressions, or lambdas for short, and the dos and don'ts with lambdas. You'll also learn about lexical scoping, passing methods where lambdas are expected, and when to create anonymous functions instead of lambdas.

Sometimes appearances can be deceiving, and the functional style may result in poor performance if we're not careful. We'll also see how to keep the fluency in code without compromising performance.

The Functional Style

The functional style of programming has been around for a very long time, although it hasn't been the mainstream. In recent years, it's been gaining in popularity. Let's first look at what it is, and then why that's significant.

What's the Functional Style?

"Computers are stupid; you have to tell them every detail," were the words of my teenager learning to program. Sadly, feeling that pain every single day is the job of most professional programmers. Anything that can alleviate those troubles is a step in the right direction. Functional programming is one such solution.

In the imperative style of programming, we have to key in every step. Create a variable named i, set the initial value to 0, check if the value is less than k—wait, is it less than or less than or equal to? Hmm.

The declarative style is where you say what you want and let the functions you call figure out how to do it. For example, to find if our friend Nemo exists in a list of names, the imperative style will demand iterating over each element to compare the values at each position in the collection. In the declarative style, we'll call a contains() method and be done quickly.

"How does that method work?" is a reasonable question. The short answer is "We don't care," but that sounds rather rude—let's rephrase: "It's encapsulated," meaning we shouldn't care. But as programmers, we know that such details are important.

The difference is that in the imperative style, the details are in your face all the time, whether you need them or not. In the declarative style, they are encapsulated in a layer below. You can seek the details, at your will, anytime you deem it important and not be bothered at other times.

Functional style builds on declarative style. It mixes the expressive nature of the declarative style with higher-order functions. We're used to passing objects to functions and returning objects from functions. Higher-order functions may receive functions as parameters and/or may return functions as a result. We can nicely compose a chain of function calls—known as functional composition—to accomplish tasks, and that leads to fluent and easier-to-understand code.

The imperative style is familiar to most programmers, but it can get complex and hard to read. Part of the reason is that it contains too many moving parts. The following small example illustrates that point.

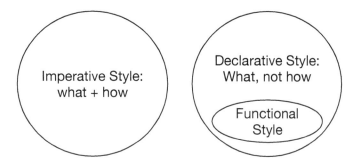

Functional Style: Declarative style + higher-order functions

lambdas/doubleofeven.kts
```
var doubleOfEven = mutableListOf<Int>()

for (i in 1..10) {
  if (i % 2 == 0) {
    doubleOfEven.add(i * 2)
  }
}

println(doubleOfEven) //[4, 8, 12, 16, 20]
```

To compute the double of all even numbers in the range 1 to 10, we first created an empty mutable list. Then we picked each value in the collection, checked if the value is even, and if so, added the double of the value to the list.

The functional style is less familiar to a lot of programmers, but it's simple. We can use higher-order functions, filter() and map(), on the IntRange class to achieve the same thing in the functional style. We can pass lambdas to these functions, as you can see in this next example. Ignore the syntax for now and focus on the concept; we'll explore the syntax shortly.

lambdas/doubleofeven.kts
```
val doubleOfEven = (1..10)
  .filter { e -> e % 2 == 0}
  .map { e -> e * 2 }

println(doubleOfEven) //[4, 8, 12, 16, 20]
```

Instead of creating a mutable list and repeatedly adding values to it, we have a better flow of logic in this code. Given a range of values from 1 to 10, we filter (or pick) only even values, and then map (or transform) the ones picked to double their values. The result is an immutable list of values. And during the execution of code, we didn't use any explicit mutable variables—that's fewer moving parts.

Before getting deep into the functional style, let's discuss the reasons, why and when, this is a better approach when compared to the imperative style.

Why and When to Use Functional Style

Declarative style is taking root beyond programming; the world is embracing this style.

For example, look at cars—when rental car agencies ask me what kind I'd like to rent, I say, "Give me one with four wheels, please." Driving a stick-shift car is the equivalent of the imperative style of programming—though you'll see me use imperative style from time to time, you'll never catch me driving a stick-shift. Auto-transmission is like adding fluency to imperative style. I'm more of an Uber or Lyft kind of person—code away in the back seat while the driver takes care of getting me to the destination. As a bonus, the streets are safer with me not behind the wheel.

As the world is heading toward autonomous vehicles so we can focus on where to go, not how to get there, the programming world is likewise heading in the direction of being more declarative. We see this with frameworks and libraries that remove the drudgery of programming using low-level APIs.

As you ease into the functional style, which is declarative in nature, you may realize:

- Imperative style is familiar, but complex; it's easier to write, due to our familiarity, but is hard to read.

- Functional style is less familiar, but simpler; it's harder to write, due to our unfamiliarity, but is easier to read.

Once you get comfortable with the functional style, you'll see that it has less complexity baked in compared to imperative-style code. And it's much easier to make functional code concurrent than to make imperative code concurrent. It's less complex, easier to change, and safer to run concurrently.

The functional style is less complex, but that doesn't make it better than imperative style all the time. Use the functional style when the code is mostly focused on computations—you can avoid mutability and side effects—and for the problems that can be expressed in terms of series of transformations. But if the problem at hand involves a lot of IO, has unavoidable state mutation or side effects, or if code will have to deal with many levels of exceptions, then imperative style may be a better option. We'll see this aspect further in Chapter 16, Asynchronous Programming, on page 309.

Let's next look at lambdas, their structure, and how to create and use them.

Lambda Expressions

A few years ago a conference organizer asked if I'd like to talk about Lambada expressions. Dancing is a form of expression, but I'm far from being qualified to talk about it—I chose lambda expressions instead. Lambdas are also a form of expression—they're concise, expressive, and elegant.

Lambdas are short functions that are used as arguments to higher-order functions. Rather than passing data to functions, we can use lambdas to pass a piece of executable code to functions. Instead of using data to make decisions or perform calculations, the higher-order functions can rely on the lambdas to make decisions or perform calculations. In essence, it's like instead of giving someone a fish, you're giving them a fishing lesson. Let's dive into lambdas.

Structure of Lambdas

A lambda expression is a function with no name whose return type is inferred. Generally a function has four parts: name, return type, parameters list, and body. Lambdas carry over only the most essential parts of a function—the parameters list and body. Here's the syntax of lambdas in Kotlin:

```
{ parameter list -> body }
```

A lambda is wrapped within {}. The body is separated from the parameter list using a hyphenated arrow (->), and the body is generally a single statement or expression, but it may also be multiline.

When passing a lambda to a function as argument, avoid the urge to create multiline lambdas unless it's the last argument. Having multiple lines of code in the middle of the argument list makes the code very hard to read, defeating the benefits of fluency we aim to get from lambdas. In such cases, instead of multiline lambdas, use function references, which we'll see in Using Function References, on page 183.

Passing Lambdas

Thinking functionally and using lambdas takes some effort and time to get comfortable with. Given a problem, we have to think in terms of transformational steps and look for functions that can help us with intermediate steps.

For example, let's implement a function, in the functional style, to tell if a given number is a prime number or not. Let's first formulate the problem in words and then translate that into code. Think of the simplest way to find if a number is a prime number—no fancy optimization for efficiency needed here. A number is a prime number if it is greater than 1 and is not divisible by any number in the range between 2 and the number. Let's reword that: a number is a prime number if greater than one and *none* (nothing) in the range 2 until n divides the number. The functional-style code becomes visible with one more coat of polish over those words:

```
fun isPrime(n: Int) = n > 1 && (2 until n).none({ i: Int -> n % i == 0 })
```

Let's discuss how the lambda is passed as a parameter in this code and how, in this example, the functional style is as efficient as an imperative implementation would be. The code snippet 2 until n returns an instance of the IntRange class. This class has two overloaded versions of none(), where one of them is a higher-order function that takes a lambda as a parameter. If the lambda returns true for any of the values in the range, then none() returns false; otherwise, it returns true. The none() function will short-circuit the evaluation—that is, anytime a call to the lambda returns true, no further elements will be evaluated, and none() will immediately return false. In short, none() will break out of the iteration upon finding a divisor. This behavior shows that none(), which is functional-style code, is as efficient as the equivalent imperative-style code for this problem.

The parameter list of the lambda passed to none() specifies the type of the parameter, i: Int. You know that Kotlin requires the type for each parameter of a function since there's no type inference for parameters. However, Kotlin doesn't insist on types for lambdas' parameters. It can infer the type for these based on the parameter of the function to which the lambdas are passed. For example, the signature none(predicate: (Int) -> Boolean): Boolean of the none() method says that the lambda passed should have one parameter of type Int when none() is called on IntRange—the actual method uses parametric type T which is specialized to Int in this context. Thus, we can drop the type from the lambda's parameter list:

```
fun isPrime(n: Int) = n > 1 && (2 until n).none({ i -> n % i == 0 })
```

That reduced the noise a tad, but we can take this one step further. Since the version of none() we're using takes only one parameter, we can drop the parenthesis () in the call—we'll discuss this further in Use Lambda as the Last Parameter, on page 182. Let's get rid of the () around the argument passed to none():

```
fun isPrime(n: Int) = n > 1 && (2 until n).none { i -> n % i == 0 }
```

Feel free to leave out the type and also () where possible. It's less work for your fingers and less parsing for the eyes of everyone who reads the code.

Using the Implicit Parameter

If the lambdas passed to a function take only one parameter, like i in the previous example, then we can omit the parameter declaration and use a special implicit name it instead. Let's change the lambda passed to none() to use it:

```
fun isPrime(n: Int) = n > 1 && (2 until n).none { n % it == 0 }
```

For short lambdas with only a single parameter, feel free to leave out the parameter declaration and the arrow, ->, and use it for the variable name. The only downside is you can't quickly tell if a lambda is a no-parameter lambda or if it takes one parameter that's referenced using it. Again, if the lambda is extremely short, this isn't a real concern. But what about long lambdas? Lambdas that have many lines are hard to maintain and should be avoided.

Receiving Lambdas

We saw how to pass a lambda to a higher-order function. Let's now look at creating a function that receives a lambda. Here's a function that takes an Int and a lambda as parameters. It iterates over values from 1 to the given number and calls the given lambda expression with each value in the range. Let's take a look at the code and then discuss the syntax.

lambdas/iterate.kts
```
fun walk1To(action: (Int) -> Unit, n: Int) =
  (1..n).forEach { action(it) }
```

In Kotlin we specify the variable name and then the type, like n: Int for parameters. That format is used for lambda parameters as well. In this example, the name of the first parameter is action. Instead of the type being something simple like Int, it defines a function. The function that walk1To() wants to take should take an Int and return nothing—that is, return Unit. This is specified using the transformational syntax (types list) -> output type—in this example, (Int) -> Unit. The syntax signifies that the function takes some inputs of the type specified to the left of -> and returns a result of the type specified on the right of ->.

Let's call this function passing two arguments: a lambda expression and an Int:

lambdas/iterate.kts
```
walk1To({ i -> print(i) }, 5) //12345
```

The first argument is a lambda, and the type of the parameter i of the lambda is inferred as Int. The second argument is 5, which conforms to the required type Int.

That code works, but it's a bit noisy. We can improve the signal-to-noise ratio a bit by rearranging the parameters.

Use Lambda as the Last Parameter

In the previous example the lambda was the first argument. It's not uncommon for a function to take more than one lambda parameter. In the call we separated the first argument, which is of type lambda, from the second argument with a comma. Both the arguments live within the (). With the {}, comma, and (), that call is a bit noisy. And if the lambda passed as the first argument is going to be more than a single line, the code will be hard to read, with }, 5) hanging on a separate line at the end. At the very least, such code is far from being pleasant to read.

Kotlin makes a concession: it bends the rules for a lambda in the trailing position, like how parents are more lenient toward their last child—I know this well because I wasn't that privileged one. But this feature of Kotlin is a good one; it makes the code less noisy. For this reason, when designing functions with at least one lambda parameter, use the trailing position for a lambda parameter.

Let's rearrange the parameter positions in the previous example:

```
fun walk1To(n: Int, action: (Int) -> Unit) = (1..n).forEach { action(it) }
```

After this change, we may still place the lambda within the parenthesis, but as second argument, like so:

```
walk1To(5, { i -> print(i) })
```

However, we can reduce some noise, get rid of the comma, and place the lambda outside the parenthesis:

```
walk1To(5) { i -> print(i) }
```

This is just a bit less noisy than the previous call. But the difference is significant if we plan to write multiline lambdas. For example, let's split the short lambda into multiple lines to get a feel:

```
walk1To(5) {i ->
  print(i)
}
```

We could go a step further if we choose and use implicit it instead of i here to reduce the noise even further:

```
walk1To(5) { print(it) }
```

In this example we placed the first argument 5 within the (). If the function takes only one parameter of a lambda type, then we don't have to use an empty (). We can follow the method's name with the lambda. You saw this in the call to the none() method earlier.

Using Function References

We've seen how Kotlin bends the rules a bit to reduce noise. But we can take this noise reduction further if the lambdas are pass-through functions.

Glance at the lambdas passed to the filter(), map(), and none() in the earlier examples. Each of them used the parameter received for some comparison or computation, like e * 2, for example. But, the lambdas passed to forEach() and to walk1To() didn't really do anything with their parameters except to pass them through to some other function. In the case of forEach(), the lambda passed the parameter i to the lambda action. Likewise, within the lambda passed to walk1To(), the parameter was passed to print(). We can replace pass-through lambdas with references to the functions the parameter is passed through.

For example, look at the following code:

```
({x -> someMethod(x) })
```

We can replace it with this:

```
(::someMethod)
```

If the pass-through is to another lambda, then we don't need the ::. Let's modify the previous example to use these Kotlin niceties. While at it, we'll expand the example a little to see a few other variations of function references as well.

First, let's modify the walk1To() function. We can replace the lambda that's passed to the forEach() method with action—that is, we might have the following code:

```
fun walk1To(n: Int, action: (Int) -> Unit) = (1..n).forEach { action(it) }
```

But we can change it to read like this:

```
fun walk1To(n: Int, action: (Int) -> Unit) = (1..n).forEach(action)
```

We got rid of the middle agent that was merely taking the parameter and sending to action. No need for a lambda that doesn't add any value—overall less noise, work, and overhead.

Now, in the call to walk1To() we can also get rid of the lambda. But, unlike action, the function print() isn't a lambda. So we can't replace the lambda with print like we replaced the previous lambda with action. If a function is qualified to stand in for a lambda, then it should be prefixed with ::. Let's take a look at the call to walk1To() with the lambda and with the function reference to get a clear view of the change:

```
walk1To(5) { i -> print(i) }
walk1To(5, ::print)
```

Now, suppose we're passing the parameter to System.out.println(). We can replace the lambda with a function reference, but, in this case, we can replace the dot with ::. Let's take a look at an example of this. You might have the following code:

```
walk1To(5) { i -> System.out.println(i) }
```

We change it to this:

```
walk1To(5, System.out::println)
```

In the previous example, println() was called on the instance System.out, but the reference may be an implicit receiver this. In that case, replace the lambda with a function reference on this, like in this example where send() is called on the implicit receiver this:

```
fun send(n: Int) = println(n)

walk1To(5) { i -> send(i) }
walk1To(5, this::send)
```

The same structure is used if the function call is on a singleton, like so:

```
object Terminal {
  fun write(value: Int) = println(value)
}

walk1To(5) { i -> Terminal.write(i) }
walk1To(5, Terminal::write)
```

If a lambda is a pass-through lambda, then replace it with either a reference to another lambda or a function reference, as appropriate.

Function Returning Functions

Functions may return functions—that's intriguing. We ran into this accidentally in Functions with Block Body, on page 42, when type inference was used with = in a block-bodied function. We do encounter legitimate situations where we'd want to return functions.

Suppose we have a collection of names and we want to find the first occurrence of a name of length 5 and also of length 4. We may write something like this:

lambdas/returnlambda.kts
```
val names = listOf("Pam", "Pat", "Paul", "Paula")

println(names.find {name -> name.length == 5 }) //Paula

println(names.find { name -> name.length == 4 }) //Paul
```

Both the lambdas in this example do the same thing, except for two different lengths. That may not be a big deal, but duplicating code is often a bad taste, and if the code within the lambda has any complexity, we definitely don't want to write that logic twice, or many times, and fall into the Write Every Time (WET) anti-pattern. We can refactor the code to create a function that will take the length as a parameter and return a lambda, a predicate, as the result. Then we can reuse calls to that function, like so:

lambdas/returnlambda.kts
```
fun predicateOfLength(length: Int): (String) -> Boolean {
  return { input: String -> input.length == length }
}

println(names.find(predicateOfLength(5))) //Paula

println(names.find(predicateOfLength(4))) //Paul
```

The parameter passed to predicateOfLength() is of type Int, but the return type isn't that simple. The return type is the signature of a function that takes String as parameter and returns Boolean as output. Within the function we return a lambda that takes a String parameter input, and compares its length with the value in the length parameter passed to predicateOfLength().

In the function, we specified the return type of predicateOfLength(). We may also ask Kotlin to infer the type. That's only possible if the function is short, with a non-block body. In this case, it can be, so let's remove the return type details:

lambdas/returnlambda.kts
```
fun predicateOfLength(length: Int) =
  { input: String -> input.length == length }

println(names.find(predicateOfLength(5))) //Paula

println(names.find(predicateOfLength(4))) //Paul
```

Always specify return type for block-body functions, and use type inference only for functions with a non-block body. That's true for functions that return objects and for those that return functions as well.

We've looked at various options Kotlin provides for working with lambdas. Next we'll look at saving lambdas into variables for reuse.

Lambdas and Anonymous Functions

Lambdas are often passed as arguments to functions, but if the same lambda is needed on multiple calls, that may lead to code duplication. We can avoid that in a couple of ways. One is to store a lambda into a variable for reuse. Or we may create anonymous functions instead of lambdas—but consequences follow that design decision. Let's explore these two options and discuss when to use each.

In the previous example, we wrote a function to generate the lambdas. If the same lambda is used multiple times, we may save it into a variable and reuse it. There's one catch, though. When a lambda is passed as argument to a function, Kotlin can infer the type of the parameters. But if we define a variable to store a lambda, Kotlin doesn't have any context about the types. So, in this case, we need to provide sufficient type information.

Let's create a variable to store one of the lambdas we passed earlier to the find() method:

lambdas/savelambdas.kts
```
val checkLength5 = { name: String -> name.length == 5 }
println(names.find(checkLength5)) //Paula
```

The variable checkLength5 refers to a lambda that takes a String parameter. The return type of this lambda is inferred by Kotlin because there are enough details to deduce the type information. We then pass the variable as an argument to the function where a lambda, of the appropriate type, is expected. We may reuse that variable any number of times in other suitable calls.

In this example, we specified the type of the lambda's parameter, and Kotlin inferred the type of the variable to be (String) -> Boolean. Alternatively, we may ask Kotlin to infer in the opposite direction; we can specify the type of the variable and ask it to infer the type of the lambda's parameter. Let's give that a try:

lambdas/savelambdas.kts
```
val checkLength5: (String) -> Boolean = { name -> name.length == 5 }
```

In this case, if the lambda doesn't return the expected type that's specified in the variable declaration, then the compiler will complain.

Another undesirable alternative is that one may be tempted to specify both the type of the variable and of the lambda parameters, as here for example:

```
lambdas/savelambdas.kts
val checkLength5: (String) -> Boolean = { name: String -> name.length == 5 }
//Not Preferred
```

This feature is used only by programmers at the Department of Redundancy—the rest of us should avoid it.

Specify the type of the variable if you'd like to convey and enforce the return type of the lambda. If you want the return type to be inferred, then specify the type of the lambda parameters.

If you define the type of the variable to which a lambda is assigned, you should specify the return type. If you only specify the lambda parameter's type, then the return type is inferred. Another option to specify the return type while inferring the variable's type is *anonymous functions*.

An anonymous function is written like a regular function, so the rules of specifying the return type—no type inference for block-body, return required for block-body, and so on—apply, with one difference: the function doesn't have a name. Let's convert the assignment to the variable in the previous example to use an anonymous function instead of a lambda.

```
lambdas/savelambdas.kts
val checkLength5 = fun(name: String): Boolean { return name.length == 5 }
```

Instead of storing an anonymous function in a variable, you may use it directly as an argument in a function call, in place of a lambda. For instance, here's an example to pass an anonymous function to the find() method:

```
lambdas/savelambdas.kts
names.find(fun(name: String): Boolean { return name.length == 5 })
```

That's a lot more verbose than passing a lambda, so there's no good reason to do this except in some rare situations.

Some restrictions apply when an anonymous function is used instead of a lambda. The return keyword is required for block-body anonymous functions that return a value. The return will always return from the anonymous function, and not from the encompassing function—we'll discuss return and lambdas in Non-Local and Labeled return, on page 190. Also, if the lambda parameter is in the trailing position, then you may pass the lambda outside of the ()—we discussed this in Use Lambda as the Last Parameter, on page 182. However, anonymous functions are required to be within the (). In short, the following isn't allowed:

```
names.find { fun(name: String): Boolean { return name.length == 5 } } //ERROR
```

Prefer lambdas over anonymous functions where possible, and use anonymous functions selectively only in those rare occasions when they are suitable instead of lambdas—one such situation we'll see in Chapter 16, Asynchronous Programming, on page 309.

Closures and Lexical Scoping

Functional programmers talk about lambdas and closures. Many programmers use those two terms interchangeably, which is acceptable, as long as we know the difference and can discern which one we're using based on the context. Let's take a closer look at how lambdas bind to variables and how that relates to the concept of closures.

A lambda is stateless; the output depends on the values of the input parameters. For example, the output of the following lambda is twice the value of the given parameter:

lambdas/closures.kts
```
val doubleIt = { e: Int -> e * 2 }
```

Sometimes we want to depend on external state. Such a lambda is called a *closure*—that's because it closes over the defining scope to bind to the properties and methods that aren't local. Let's turn the previous lambda into a closure.

lambdas/closures.kts
```
val factor = 2

val doubleIt = { e: Int -> e * factor }
```

In this version, e is still the parameter. But within the body, the variable or property factor isn't local. The compiler has to look in the defining scope of the closure—that is, where the body of the closure is defined—for that variable. If it doesn't find it there, the compiler will have to continue the search in the defining scope of the defining scope, and so on. This is called *lexical scoping*.

In our example, the compiler binds the variable factor within the body of the closure to the variable right above the closure—that is, val factor = 2.

We used lexical scoping earlier in Function Returning Functions, on page 184, and it felt so natural that it may have gone unnoticed. Here's the relevant code from that section, repeated for your convenience:

```
fun predicateOfLength(length: Int): (String) -> Boolean {
  return { input: String -> input.length == length }
}
```

The lambda being returned has a parameter named input. Within the body of the lambda we compare the value of the length property of this input parameter with the value in the length variable. But, the variable length isn't part of the lambda—it's from the closure's lexical scope, which happens to be the parameter passed to the predicateOfLength() function.

Mutability is taboo in functional programming. However, Kotlin doesn't complain if from within a closure we read or modify a mutable local variable. In the earlier example, the variable factor is immutable since it's defined as a val. If we change it to a var—that is, turn it into a mutable variable—then potentially we may modify factor from within the closure. The Kotlin compiler won't warn in this case, but the result may surprise or, at the very least, confuse the reader.

In the following code we transform values in two collections, one created using listOf() and the other created using sequenceOf(). After that, we modify the value in the variable factor and, finally, print the values of the transformed collections. Without running the code, try guessing the output of the code.

```
lambdas/mutable.kts
var factor = 2

val doubled = listOf(1, 2).map { it * factor }
val doubledAlso = sequenceOf(1, 2).map { it * factor }

factor = 0

doubled.forEach { println(it) }
doubledAlso.forEach { println(it) }
```

Is it 2, 4, 2, 4 on separate lines, 0, 0, 0, 0, or 2, 4, 0, 0?

It's certainly not worth the trouble thinking through the different behaviors of list vs. sequence (which we'll cover in Chapter 11, Internal Iteration and Lazy Evaluation, on page 203), even though the structure of the code to transform the two collections are so similar. Using mutable variables from within a closure is often a source of error and should be avoided. Keep closure as pure functions to avoid confusion and to minimize errors—see Prefer val over var, on page 26.

Non-Local and Labeled return

By default lambdas aren't allowed to have the return keyword, even if they return a value. This is a significant difference between lambdas and anonymous functions—the latter is required to have return if returning values and it signifies only a return from the immediate lambda and not the outer calling function. In this section, we'll look at why return is not allowed by default, how to use labeled return, and when non-local return is permitted.

return Not Allowed by Default

return is not valid in lambdas by default, but you can use it under some special situations. This can be quite confusing if you don't take the time to fully understand the context and the consequences. Take this topic a bit slow for the details to sink in.

We'll use a function to illustrate the concepts in this section. This function takes two parameters, an Int and a lambda, and returns Unit.

lambdas/noreturn.kts
```
fun invokeWith(n: Int, action: (Int) -> Unit) {
  println("enter invokeWith $n")
  action(n)
  println("exit invokeWith $n")
}
```

Within the invokeWith() function, we pass the given Int parameter to the given lambda referenced using action(). Quite simple, nothing exciting yet.

Let's call invokeWith() from within a caller() function and then call the caller() function.

lambdas/noreturn.kts
```
Line 1  fun caller() {
          (1..3).forEach { i ->
            invokeWith(i) {
              println("enter for $it")
     5
              if (it == 2) { return } //ERROR, return is not allowed here

              println("exit for $it")
            }
          }
    10  }

        println("end of caller")
      }

    15  caller()
      println("after return from caller")
```

The caller() function iterates over values 1 to 3 and calls the invokeWith() function for each value. The lambda attached to the invokeWith() function prints a message when we enter it and then again when we exit it. If the value of the lambda's parameter, referenced using the implicit reference it, is equal to 2 we request an immediate return using the return keyword.

The line with return will fail compilation. The reason for this becomes clear if we look at that line in the overall context of the entire code. When we call return on line 6, Kotlin doesn't know if we mean (1) to exit the immediate lambda and continue executing code within invokeWith() right after the call to action(n), or (2) we mean to exit the for loop we entered on line 2, or (3) exit the function caller() we entered on line 1. To avoid this confusion, Kotlin doesn't permit return by default. However, Kotlin makes two exceptions to this rule—labeled return and non-local return. We'll see these next, one at a time.

Labeled return

If you want to exit the current lambda immediately, then you may use a labeled return, that is return@label where label is some label you can create using the syntax label@. Let's use a labeled return in a modified version of the caller().

```
lambdas/labeledreturn.kts
Line 1  fun caller() {
          (1..3).forEach { i ->
            invokeWith(i) here@ {
              println("enter for $it")

  5
              if (it == 2) {
                return@here
              }

              println("exit for $it")
 10
            }
          }

          println("end of caller")
 15  }

     caller()
     println("after return from caller")
```

We replaced the return with return@here on line 7 and, in addition, added a label here@ on line 3. The compiler won't complain at this use of return.

The labeled return causes the control flow to jump to the end of the labeled block—that is, exit the lambda expression. The behavior here is equivalent to the continue statements used in imperative-style loops where the control skips to the end of the loop. In this case, it skips to the end of the lambda expression. We can observe this behavior from the output of the previous code, shown here:

```
enter invokeWith 1
enter for 1
exit for 1
exit invokeWith 1
enter invokeWith 2
enter for 2
exit invokeWith 2
enter invokeWith 3
enter for 3
exit for 3
exit invokeWith 3
end of caller
after return from caller
```

Instead of using an explicit label, like @here, we can use an implicit label that is the name of the function to which the lambda is passed. We can thus replace return@here with return@invokeWith and remove the label here@, like so:

```kotlin
fun caller() {
  (1..3).forEach { i ->
    invokeWith(i) {
      println("enter for $it")

      if (it == 2) {
        return@invokeWith
      }

      println("exit for $it")
    }
  }
  println("end of caller")
}
```

Even though Kotlin permits the use of method names as labels, prefer explicit labels instead. That makes the intention clearer and the code easier to understand.

The compiler won't permit labeled return to arbitrary outer scope—you can only return out of the current encompassing lambda. If you want to exit out of the current function being defined, then you can't do that by default, but you can if the function to which the lambda is passed is inlined. We looked at the default behavior in the previous subsection. Let's explore the inlining option next.

Non-Local return

The return keyword is not allowed by default in lambdas. You may use a labeled return and that restricts the control flow to only return out of the current lambda. Non-local return is useful to break out of the current function that's being implemented, right from within a lambda. Let's modify the caller() function once again to see this feature.

```
Line 1  fun caller() {
          (1..3).forEach { i ->

            println("in forEach for $i")
        5   if (i == 2) { return }

            invokeWith(i) {
              println("enter for $it")

       10     if (it == 2) { return@invokeWith }

              println("exit for $it")
            }
          }
       15   println("end of caller")
        }

        caller()
        println("after return from caller")
```

In the caller() function, within the lambda passed to forEach() we return if i == 2 on line 5. We know that on line 10, Kotlin doesn't permit return but only a labeled return. But, in line 5 it doesn't have any qualms about it. Curious—before we discuss the why, let's address the what; that is, let's understand the behavior of this return. Unlike the labeled return which exits the encompassing lambda, this return on line 5 will exit the encompassing function being defined—caller() in this example. Thus, it's called the non-local return.

Let's verify this behavior by executing the caller() function:

```
in forEach for 1
enter invokeWith 1
enter for 1
exit for 1
exit invokeWith 1
in forEach for 2
after return from caller
```

When the execution hits the return statement, it bails all the way out of the caller(), and the code following the call to caller() is executed after return.

Now to the question: Why did Kotlin disallow return, without label, of course, within the lambda we passed to invokeWith(), but didn't flinch at the return within the lambda passed to forEach()? The answer is hidden in the definition of the two functions.

We defined invokeWith() as the following:

```
fun invokeWith(n: Int, action: (Int) -> Unit) {
```

On the other hand, forEach() is defined, in the Kotlin standard library, like this:

```
inline fun <T> Iterable<T>.forEach(action: (T) -> Unit): Unit {
```

The answer lies in the keyword inline. We'll focus on this keyword in the next section—let's recap the behavior of return before we move forward:

- return is not allowed by default within lambdas.
- You may use a labeled return to step out of the encompassing lambda.
- Use of non-local return to exit from the encompassing function being defined is possible only if the function to which the lambda is passed is defined with inline.

Here are some ways to deal with the complexity associated with the behavior of return:

- You can use labeled return anytime to return out of the lambda.

- If you're able to use return, remember that it will exit out of the encompassing function that's being defined and not merely from within the encompassing lambda or from within the caller of the lambda.

- If you're not allowed to use return, don't worry; Kotlin will let you know in no uncertain terms.

Inlining Functions with Lambdas

Lambdas are elegant, and it's convenient to pass functions to functions, but there's a catch—performance. Kotlin provides the inline keyword to eliminate the call overhead in order to improve performance, to provide non-local control flow such as a return from within forEach(), and to pass reified type parameters as we saw in Reified Type Parameters, on page 101.

Before we delve into ways to improve performance of functions that use lambdas, let's set some context. Every higher-order function we write doesn't need the solutions we'll see in this section. A good amount of code we write will enjoy a reasonable performance and need nothing special. But in some situations—such as when a higher-order function contains a loop and excessively calls a lambda expression from within the loop, for example—the overhead of calling the higher-order function and the lambdas within it may be measurable. In that case, and only in that case, measure the performance first, and then consider these added complexities to improve the performance where necessary.

No inline Optimization by Default

To learn about inline, let's create an invokeTwo() function that takes an Int and two lambdas. It also returns a lambda. We'll modify this function a few times in this section, but the following is a good starting point without any inline:

lambdas/noinline.kts
```
fun invokeTwo(
  n: Int,
  action1: (Int) -> Unit,
  action2: (Int) -> Unit
): (Int) -> Unit {

  println("enter invokeTwo $n")

  action1(n)
  action2(n)

  println("exit invokeTwo $n")
  return { _: Int -> println("lambda returned from invokeTwo") }
}
```

The short function invokes the two lambdas given and returns a lambda created within the function. The lambda that's returned ignores the input parameter and merely prints a message. Let's call this function from within another function named callInvokeTwo(). And, right after defining that function, let's call callInvokeTwo().

lambdas/noinline.kts
```
fun callInvokeTwo() {
  invokeTwo(1, { i -> report(i) }, { i -> report(i) })
}

callInvokeTwo()
```

Within the callInvokeTwo() function we pass the value 1 as the first argument to invokeTwo(). For the second and third arguments we pass two identical lambdas that call a function named report. That function doesn't exist yet, but we'll write it now to print the parameter it receives along with the depth of the call stack.

lambdas/noinline.kts
```kotlin
fun report(n: Int) {
  println("")
  print("called with $n, ")

  val stackTrace = RuntimeException().getStackTrace()

  println("Stack depth: ${stackTrace.size}")
  println("Partial listing of the stack:")
  stackTrace.take(3).forEach(::println)
}
```

The function reports the number of levels of call stack below the current execution of report(). Let's run the code to take a look at the calls and the number of levels in the call stack:

```
enter invokeTwo 1

called with 1, Stack depth: 31
Partial listing of the stack:
Noinline.report(noinline.kts:31)
Noinline$callInvokeTwo$1.invoke(noinline.kts:20)
Noinline$callInvokeTwo$1.invoke(noinline.kts:1)

called with 1, Stack depth: 31
Partial listing of the stack:
Noinline.report(noinline.kts:31)
Noinline$callInvokeTwo$2.invoke(noinline.kts:20)
Noinline$callInvokeTwo$2.invoke(noinline.kts:1)
exit invokeTwo 1
```

The call to callInvokeTwo() results in a call to invokeTwo(). That function call in turn results in a call to action1(), the first lambda passed as parameter. The lambda calls report(). Likewise, when invokeTwo() calls the second lambda, action2(), it calls report(). Between the place of call to invokeTwo() and within each call to report(), we have three levels of stack. That's the top three out of the depth of 31.

Inline Optimization

You may improve performance of functions that receive lambdas using the inline keyword. If a function is marked as inline, then instead of making a call to the function, the bytecode for that function will be placed inline at the call location. This will eliminate the function call overhead, but the bytecode will be larger since the inlining will happen at every location where the function is called. It's usually a bad idea to inline long functions.

Though you may annotate any non-recursive function with inline, Kotlin will give you a warning if it sees no benefit to inlining, for example, if the function isn't receiving any lambda parameters.

Let's optimize the invokeTwo() function using inline:

```
inline fun invokeTwo(
  n: Int,
  action1: (Int) -> Unit,
  action2: (Int) -> Unit
): (Int) -> Unit {
```

The function's body has no change; the inline annotation prefixes the function declaration—that's enough to tell the compiler to optimize the call.

Let's run the code after this change and take a look at the depth of the call stack.

```
enter invokeTwo 1

called with 1, Stack depth: 28
Partial listing of the stack:
Inlineoptimization.report(inlineoptimization.kts:31)
Inlineoptimization.callInvokeTwo(inlineoptimization.kts:20)
Inlineoptimization.<init>(inlineoptimization.kts:23)

called with 1, Stack depth: 28
Partial listing of the stack:
Inlineoptimization.report(inlineoptimization.kts:31)
Inlineoptimization.callInvokeTwo(inlineoptimization.kts:20)
Inlineoptimization.<init>(inlineoptimization.kts:23)
exit invokeTwo 1
```

The three top levels of call stack we discussed earlier, before adding the inline annotation, are gone. Within the callInvokeTwo() function the compiler expands the bytecode for the invokeTwo() function. And within the invokeTwo() functions body, the compiler inlines or expands the bytecode for the two lambdas, instead of making the calls. That optimization continues to eliminate the call overhead to report() as well.

By using the inline annotation you can eliminate the call overhead. But if the function being inlined is very large and if it's called from a lot of different places, the bytecode generated may be much larger than when inline isn't used. Measure and optimize—don't optimize blindly.

Selective noinline of Parameter

If for some reason we don't want to optimize the call to a lambda, we can ask that optimization to be eliminated by marking the lambda parameter as noinline. We can use that keyword only on parameters when the function itself is marked as inline.

Let's ask the compiler to inline the invokeTwo() function, and as a result inline the call to action1(), as well, but specifically exclude the optimization for action2() call, using noinline on that parameter:

```
inline fun invokeTwo(
  n: Int,
  action1: (Int) -> Unit,
  noinline action2: (Int) -> Unit
  ): (Int) -> Unit {
```

Kotlin won't allow us to hold a reference to action1 since it's inlined, but we may create a reference to action2 within the invokeTwo() function, if we like, since action2 is defined as noinline.

Also, since the action2 parameter is marked with noinline, there'll be no optimization to its call. Thus, the second call to report(), from within the lambda passed to action2 will be deeper than the call to report() from within the lambda passed to action1. We can see this in the output of the code we used:

```
enter invokeTwo 1

called with 1, Stack depth: 28
Partial listing of the stack:
Noinlineoptimization.report(noinlineoptimization.kts:31)
Noinlineoptimization.callInvokeTwo(noinlineoptimization.kts:20)
Noinlineoptimization.<init>(noinlineoptimization.kts:23)

called with 1, Stack depth: 30
Partial listing of the stack:
Noinlineoptimization.report(noinlineoptimization.kts:31)
Noinlineoptimization$callInvokeTwo$2.invoke(noinlineoptimization.kts:20)
Noinlineoptimization$callInvokeTwo$2.invoke(noinlineoptimization.kts:1)
exit invokeTwo 1
```

In addition to inlining the code, the inline keyword also makes it possible for lambdas called from inlined functions to have non-local return. We saw this in the context of forEach() earlier. Let's revisit that for our invokeTwo() function.

Non-Local return Permitted in Inlined Lambdas

In the previous example, the invokeTwo() function has the inline annotation and, as a result, the first lambda action1() will also be inlined. However, the second lambda action2() is marked as noinline. Thus, Kotlin will permit non-local return and labeled return from within the lambda passed as an argument for the action1 parameter. But, from within the lambda passed as the argument for the action2 parameter, only labeled return is permitted. This is because, whereas an inlined lambda expands within a function, the non-inlined lambda will be a separate function call. While the return from the former will exit the function, the return from the latter won't do the same since it's in a more nested level of stack.

Let's see this behavior in action.

```
Line 1  fun callInvokeTwo() {
          invokeTwo(1, { i ->
            if (i == 1) { return }

     5      report(i)
          }, { i ->
            //if (i == 2) { return }| //ERROR, return not allowed here
            report(i)
          })
    10  }

        callInvokeTwo()
```

Within the first lambda passed to invokeTwo(), we call return if the value of the parameter i == 1. This is a non-local return and will result in the exit from the function being defined—that is, callInvokeTwo(). We can verify this in the output that follows. On the other hand, within the second lambda passed to invokeTwo(), the Kotlin compiler won't permit using non-local return. Any attempt to uncomment line 7 will result in compilation failure.

```
enter invokeTwo 1
```

In addition to annotating functions with inline, you may also mark methods and properties of classes with inline if you choose. When using inline you can not only eliminate the function call overhead, but also gain the ability to place a non-local return from within the inlined lambdas. Any lambda that is not inlined can't have a non-local return. That's good, but what if a lambda that's intended to be inlined can't really be inlined? Let's discuss next how this may happen and how Kotlin lets us know about this situation.

crossinline Parameters

If a function is marked inline, then the lambda parameters not marked with noinline are automatically considered to be inlined. At the location where a lambda is invoked within the function, the body of the lambda will be inlined. But there's one catch. What if instead of calling the given lambda, the function passes on the lambda to yet another function, or back to the caller? Tricky, you can't inline what is not being called.

In the case where the lambda is passed on instead of being called, not placing any annotation on the lambda parameter makes no sense. One solution is to mark it as noinline. But what if you want the lambda to be inlined wherever it may be called. You can ask the function to pass on your request for inlining *across* to the caller; that's what crossinline is for.

Let's understand this scenario and how crossinline helps with an example. Let's make two changes to the invokeTwo() function. First, let's remove the noinline annotation of the action2 parameter. Second, let's modify the lambda returned in the end of invokeTwo() to call action2—that is, invokeTwo() passes on action2 so that it may be called eventually by the caller of invokeTwo().

```
inline fun invokeTwo(
  n: Int,
  action1: (Int) -> Unit,
  action2: (Int) -> Unit //ERROR
): (Int) -> Unit {

  println("enter invokeTwo $n")

  action1(n)

  println("exit invokeTwo $n")
  return { input: Int -> action2(input) }
}
```

When invokeTwo() is inlined, the internal call action1(n) can be inlined. But since invokeTwo() isn't directly calling action2, the action2(input) call embedded within the lambda on the last line can't be inlined. Since there is no noinline annotation on the second parameter to invokeTwo(), we're in a conflict situation and the compiler will give us an error.

Besides the error, we need to document for the programmers using invokeTwo() that they can't use a non-local return from the second lambda passed to invokeTwo(). We can achieve this goal and resolve the compilation error in one of two ways:

- Mark the second parameter as noinline. In this case, the call to action2 won't be inlined, period. There'll be no performance benefit and a non-local return won't be permitted within the lambda passed for action2.

- Mark the second parameter as crossinline. In this case, the call to action2 will be inlined, not within the invokeTwo() function but wherever it is called.

You're not allowed to place a non-local return within a lambda passed to the parameter marked with crossinline. The reason is that by the time the lambda is executed, you would have exited from the function to which it is passed as a parameter; no point trying to return from a function that has already completed.

Let's modify the above code so it will pass compilation, by using crossinline:

```kotlin
inline fun invokeTwo(
  n: Int,
  action1: (Int) -> Unit,
  crossinline action2: (Int) -> Unit
  ): (Int) -> Unit {
```

Now that we marked action2 as crossinline, the compiler is happy that we understood the consequences.

In summary,

- inline performs inline optimization, to remove function call overhead.

- crossinline also performs inline optimization, not within the function to which the lambda is passed, but wherever it is eventually called.

- Only lambdas passed for parameters not marked noinline or crossinline can have non-local return.

Good Practices for inline and returns

The concepts related to inline, return from lambda, and non-local returns is not trivial and can get overwhelming. Take some time to review, practice the examples, and try out your own code examples to get a better grip of the concepts.

Here's a summary and some good practices related to returns and inline:

- Unlabeled return is always a return from a function and not from a lambda.

- Unlabeled returns are not permitted in non-inlined lambdas.

- Function names are the default labels, but don't rely on them, always provide custom names if you choose to use labeled returns.

- Measure performance before deciding to optimize code; this is true in general, and in particular for code that uses lambdas.

- Use inline only when you see measurable performance improvements.

Wrapping Up

The functional style of programming is less complex when compared to the imperative style of programming. Using higher-order functions and functional composition, we can write fluent code that is easier to understand and to maintain. Lambdas are functions with no name and may be easily passed around as arguments to functions. Kotlin provides a variety of options to write lambdas. Where a lambda is expected, you may also pass function references to reuse functions or methods. Whereas lambdas are stateless, closures carry state. However, avoid messing with mutable state as that may lead to potential errors and confusing behavior in code. Kotlin has strict rules about using return from within lambdas; it permits the use of labeled returns, and non-local returns under special situations. In addition, Kotlin provides a facility to eliminate function and lambda call overhead with the help of the inline keyword.

You've learned how to create lambdas in this chapter. In the next, we'll use lambdas for internal iteration and working with sequences.

CHAPTER 11

Internal Iteration and Lazy Evaluation

Unlike the imperative style where external iterators are prominent (see Chapter 4, External Iteration and Argument Matching, on page 53), in functional programming we use internal iterators. Internal iterators put iterations on autopilot; instead of focusing on iteration, you can keep your eyes on what to do for each element in a collection or a range. As well, internal iterators avoid explicit mutability and thus the iteration can be easily parallelized without the risk of race conditions.

Internal iterators are higher-order functions; that is, we pass lambdas to functions that perform various tasks related to iteration, like selecting particular values, transforming data, and so on. The higher-order functions provide common code for the iteration, and the lambdas tailor them for the problem at hand. For example, the filter() higher-order function will iterate over the elements in a collection and return selected values. The lambda passed to filter() decides the actual elements that get selected. For instance, given a list of languages, the filter() function can be used to return a sublist of only statically typed languages from among the original list. To accomplish this, the lambda that's passed to filter() can take a language as argument and return true if the language is statically typed and false otherwise.

Internal iterators in Kotlin are concise, expressive, and have reduced complexity compared to external iterators. But performance may occasionally be a drawback when using them. In some situations, as we'll explore later, internal iterators may end up performing some extra computations when compared to the corresponding external iterators. This may not have much impact when a collection is relatively small, such as a few hundred elements. On the other hand, if we're dealing with a very large collection of data, like thousands of elements, then the overhead will become an issue. This is where Kotlin sequences come in. Sequences are internal iterators and look almost the same as other internal iterators to the human eyes. Internally, though, they're implemented differently; they defer execution—hence they are lazy—and evaluate parts of the iteration only if necessary.

In this chapter, we'll first discuss the key differences between external and internal iterators, then explore different internal iterators built into the Kotlin standard library, and, finally, look at the benefits of lazy evaluations with sequences.

External vs. Internal Iterators

Programmers with experience in Java and other C-like languages are used to external iterators. They are common but complex; we're very familiar with them, but they involve many moving parts. Internal iterators are less familiar to a lot of programmers, but they are less complex than external iterators.

External iterators in Kotlin are already an improvement when compared to external iterators in Java, but even then, the internal iterators have much less ceremony, are more concise, and are expressive when compared to Kotlin's external iterators. Let's compare Kotlin's external iterators with internal iterators using some examples.

Here's a list of numbers stored in a numbers variable:

internal/iterate.kts
```
val numbers = listOf(10, 12, 15, 17, 18, 19)
```

To print only the even numbers in this list we can use the for...in loop of Kotlin, like so:

internal/iterate.kts
```
for (i in numbers) {
  if (i % 2 == 0) {
    print("$i, ") //10, 12, 18,
  }
}
```

As the iteration progresses, the variable i holds different values from the collection, one per iteration. The if expression, used as a statement here, checks if the value currently held in i is even, and if it is, we print the value. That's external iteration. We may easily add break and continue if we choose to further alter the flow of iteration.

Let's rewrite the iteration using internal iterators.

internal/iterate.kts
```
numbers.filter { e -> e % 2 == 0 }
  .forEach { e -> print("$e, ") } //10, 12, 18,
```

Kotlin standard library has added a number of extension functions to collections. In this example we use two of them, the filter() and the forEach() functions. Both are higher-order functions and so we pass lambdas to them.

The lambda that is given to the filter() function returns true if the value passed as a parameter to the lambda is even and returns false otherwise. Thus, the filter() function will return a list of only the even values from the given collection numbers. The forEach() function works on that resulting collection of even numbers and passes the values, one at a time, to the given lambda. The lambda attached to forEach() prints the given value.

Even though the for loop of the external iterator isn't verbose in Kotlin, the internal iterator to achieve the same result is a tad more concise. The code naturally reads like the problem statements: given the numbers, filter only even numbers and print each. The difference between these two styles will widen as the complexity of the tasks performed is increased. Let's dig in further to see this.

Suppose instead of printing the even numbers, we want to collect the doubles of the even numbers into another result collection. Here's the code using an external iterator to perform that task:

internal/iterate.kts
```kotlin
val doubled = mutableListOf<Int>()

for (i in numbers) {
  if (i % 2 == 0) {
    doubled.add(i * 2)
  }
}

println(doubled) //[20, 24, 36]
```

The first smell in this code is the definition of an empty mutable list. Then, within the loop we add the double of each even number to that list. If you hear a programmer say "That's not bad," it's just a sign of the Stockholm syndrome—it's not their fault. The code has a few moving parts and is more complex than the corresponding internal iterator code, but many programmers are familiar with external iterators and often feel comfortable with that style.

Let's take a look at the internal iterator version for the same task:

internal/iterate.kts
```kotlin
val doubledEven = numbers.filter { e -> e % 2 == 0 }
  .map { e -> e * 2 }

println(doubledEven) //[20, 24, 36]
```

Instead of using the forEach() function, we used the map() function here. The map() function transforms the given collection into a result collection by applying the lambda to each element. The internal iterators form a *functional pipeline*—that is, a collection of functions that will be applied on objects or values that flow through the pipeline. The result of this functional pipeline is a read-only list containing the doubles of the even numbers from the original collection.

External iterators in Kotlin are good, but internal iterators are better. You can use whichever you're comfortable with, and you also can refactor your code at any time to the style you feel is the best fit for the problem at hand. Let's dive into see some internal iterators built into the Kotlin standard library.

Internal Iterators

We mostly use for to program external iterators. But internal iteration involves many specialized tools like filter(), map(), flatMap(), reduce(), and so on. Much like the way a professional mechanic uses different specialized tools to fix a car, and doesn't settle for just a hammer, in functional programming we use a combination of the right tools for different tasks. The Kotlin standard library provides plenty of higher-order functions for internal iteration. We'll visit some of the most commonly used functions.

filter, map, and reduce

filter(), map(), and reduce() are the three amigos of functional programming; they are fundamental functions used as internal iterators. The filter() function picks certain values from a given collection while dropping the others. The map() function transforms the values in a collection using a given function or lambda. Finally, the reduce() function performs a cumulative operation on the elements, often to arrive at a single value. All these functions perform their operations without mutating or changing the given collection—they return a copy with the appropriate values.

The size of the collection returned by filter() may vary from 0 to n where n is the number of elements in the original collection. The result is a sub-collection; that is, the values in the output collection are values present in the original collection. The lambda passed to filter() is applied on each element in the original collection. If and only if the lambda returns true, when evaluated for an element, the element from the original collection is included in the output collection.

The size of the collection returned by map() is the same as the original collection. The lambda passed to map() is applied on each element in the original collection, and the result is a collection of these transformed values.

A lambda passed to both filter() and map() takes only one parameter, but a lambda passed to reduce() takes two parameters. The first is an accumulated value and the second is an element from the original collection. The result of the lambda is the new accumulated value. The result of reduce() is the result of the last invocation of the lambda.

An example will help to illustrate the behavior and purpose of these three functions. For that, let's start with a Person class and a people collection with some sample values.

internal/iterators.kts
```
data class Person(val firstName: String, val age: Int)

val people = listOf(
  Person("Sara", 12),
  Person("Jill", 51),
  Person("Paula", 23),
  Person("Paul", 25),
  Person("Mani", 12),
  Person("Jack", 70),
  Person("Sue", 10))
```

Let's use internal iterators to create the names, in uppercase and comma separated, of everyone who is older than 20.

internal/iterators.kts
```
val result = people.filter { person -> person.age > 20 }
  .map { person -> person.firstName }
  .map { name -> name.toUpperCase() }
  .reduce { names, name -> "$names, $name" }

println(result) //JILL, PAULA, PAUL, JACK
```

The filter() function extracts from the given collection only Persons who are older than 20. That list is then passed on to map(), which then transforms the list of Persons who are older than 20 to a list of names. The second map() then transforms the names list into a list of names in uppercase. Even though we could have combined the two map() calls into one, keeping them separate makes the code more cohesive, where each line focuses on one operation. Finally, we combine the uppercase names into one string, comma separated, using the reduce() function. The figure on page 208 illustrates the operations in the example.

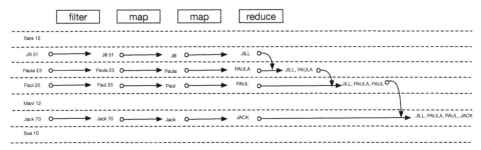

The filter() and map() functions operate within their swim lanes, where their lambdas return a value based only on the respective elements in the collection, whereas the lambda passed to reduce() operates by cutting across the swim lanes. The lambda combines the result of computation for previous elements in the collection with the operation on the subsequent element.

Kotlin provides a number of specialized reduce functions for different operations like sum, max, and even to join strings. We can replace the previous reduce() call with the following, to make the code more concise:

internal/iterators.kts
```
.joinToString(", ")
```

If we want to total the age of every Person in the list instead, we can use map() and reduce(), like so:

internal/iterators.kts
```
val totalAge = people.map { person -> person.age }
  .reduce { total, age -> total + age }

println(totalAge) //203
```

Again, instead of reduce(), we may use the specialized reduce operation sum(), like so:

internal/iterators.kts
```
val totalAge2 = people.map { person -> person.age }
  .sum()
```

Whereas reduce() is a more general cumulative operation on the values in a collection, specialized functions are available for some operations like join and sum. Use the specialized functions where they're available as that makes the code more expressive, less error prone, and easier to maintain as well.

Getting the First and the Last

Much like the specialized reduce operation sum() Kotlin also has a function first() to return the first element from a given collection. When used with filter()

and map(), we can perform filtering and transformation before extracting the first element from the resulting collection.

For example, using the first() function, let's get the name of the first adult, where adulthood is defined based on the age being greater than 17 rather than the maturity of a person:

internal/iterators.kts
```
val nameOfFirstAdult = people.filter { person -> person.age > 17 }
  .map { person -> person.firstName }
  .first()

println(nameOfFirstAdult) //Jill
```

The filter() function returns a collection of everyone who is older than 17, and the map() function returns the names of those adults. Finally, the first() function returns the first element from that list of the names of the adults.

If instead of the first adult's name you want to get the last adult's name, replace the call to first() with last(). This will result in "Jack" in the above example.

flatten and flatMap

Suppose we have a nested list, such as List<List<Person>>, where the top-level list contains families and the members of the families are in sublists of Persons. What if we want to convert it to one flat list of Persons? Kotlin, like languages such as Ruby, has a flatten() function for that.

Given an Iterable<Iterable<T>> the flatten() function will return a Iterable<T> where all the elements in the nested iterables are combined into the top level, thus flattening the hierarchy.

Let's use flatten() in a short example.

internal/iterators.kts
```
val families = listOf(
    listOf(Person("Jack", 40), Person("Jill", 40)),
    listOf(Person("Eve", 18), Person("Adam", 18)))

println(families.size) //2
println(families.flatten().size) //4
```

The variable families refers to a nested list of Person objects. A call to size property on families tells us there are 2 lists contained inside of the outer list. A call to flatten() returns a new list which has at the top level the four elements in the nested list.

In the previous example we intentionally created nested lists within a list. Sometimes such nesting may be the result of a map() operation on another collection. Let's explore one such scenario and see how flatten() plays a role in that context.

Let's revisit the people collection and get in lowercase the first name and the reverse of the first name for each person. From the people collection, we can get the list of first names using a call to the map() function. From that, we can get the first names in lowercase again using another call to map(). Finally, we can use map() a third time to get the name in lowercase and its reverse. Let's start with these steps and observe the result.

internal/iterators.kts
```
val namesAndReversed = people.map { person -> person.firstName }
  .map(String::toLowerCase)
  .map { name -> listOf(name, name.reversed())}

println(namesAndReversed.size) //7
```

In the last step we returned a list of two strings for each Person in the original list. The type of namesAndReversed is List<List<String>> and the size of the result is 7, which is the number of elements in the original list. But instead of List<List<String>>, we really want List<String>. That can be achieved readily with a call to flatten(). Let's verify that works.

internal/iterators.kts
```
val namesAndReversed2 = people.map { person -> person.firstName }
  .map(String::toLowerCase)
  .map { name -> listOf(name, name.reversed())}
  .flatten()

println(namesAndReversed2.size) //14
```

The type of namesAndReversed2 is List<String> and the number of elements in it is 14, as expected. Although that worked, it will be nice if we can combine the map operation with the flatten operation because our intention is to create one flat list and not a nested list. Thus, it would be great if there were a map-flatten function.

Before we explore this idea further let's work together on a small verbal exercise. Say this aloud three or four times: *map-flatten*.

That resulted in a rather awkward movement of the jaw and a noticeable discomfort. Now imagine there was a function called map-flatten and a generation of programmers grew up saying that name. This may have resulted in the evolution of a species with a weird-shaped jaw to accommodate the odd vocal movement. The designers of functional programming saved the human race by naming it flatMap(), even though the actual operation is map followed by a flattening operation.

Let's combine the last two steps in the previous code into one call to flatMap():

internal/iterators.kts
```
val namesAndReversed3 = people.map { person -> person.firstName }
  .map(String::toLowerCase)
  .flatMap { name -> listOf(name, name.reversed())}

println(namesAndReversed3.size) //14
```

The type of namesAndReversed3 is also List<String> and there are 14 values in it, just like in namesAndReversed2.

If you're trying to decide if you should use map() or flatMap(), here are some tips that will help:

- If the lambda is a one-to-one function—that is, it takes an object or value and returns an object or value—then use map() to transform the original collection.

- If the lambda is a one-to-many function—that is, it takes an object or value and returns a collection—then use map() to transform the original collection into a collection of collections.

- If the lambda is a one-to-many function, but you want to transform the original collection into a transformed collection of objects or values, then use flatMap().

Sorting

In addition to iterating over the values in a collection, you can also sort anywhere in the middle of the iteration. You can use as criteria for sorting any details available in that stage of the functional pipeline.

For example, let's get the names of adults from the people collection in the sorted order of age, with the youngest Person's name first.

internal/iterators.kts
```
val namesSortedByAge = people.filter { person -> person.age > 17 }
  .sortedBy { person -> person.age }
  .map { person -> person.firstName }

println(namesSortedByAge) //[[Paula, Paul, Jill, Jack]
```

We first filtered the Persons who are older than 17 and then used the sortedBy() function to sort the Person objects based on their age property. The collection returned by sortedBy() is a new collection, where the elements are in the sorted order of age. In the final step of the functional pipeline we used map() to extract only the firstName properties from the sorted collection. The result is the first names in the order of age from the youngest adult to the eldest adult in the original list.

If we want to sort in the descending order of the age properties, or any other property, we can use the sortedByDescending() function. Let's replace the sortedBy() call in the above example with sortedByDescending() to see this in action:

internal/iterators.kts
```
.sortedByDescending { person -> person.age }
  //[Jack, Jill, Paul, Paula]
```

The output of the first names will be in the reverse order, with the eldest Person's first name coming first.

Grouping Objects

The idea of transforming data through the functional pipeline goes far beyond the basics of filter, map, and reduce. You can group or place into buckets objects based on different criteria or properties.

For example, let's group the Persons in the people collection based on the first letter of their first name, using the groupBy() function.

internal/iterators.kts
```
val groupBy1stLetter = people.groupBy { person -> person.firstName.first() }

println(groupBy1stLetter)
//{S=[Person(firstName=Sara, age=12), Person(firstName=Sue, age=10)], J=[...
```

The groupBy() function invokes the given lambda for each element in the collection. Based on what the lambda returns it places the element in an appropriate bucket. In this example, Persons whose first names start with the same letter are placed in the same bucket or group. The result of the operation is a Map<L, List<T>>, where the lambda determines the type of the key of the resulting Map. The type of the value is a List<T> where groupBy() is called on a Iterable<T>. In the previous example, the result is of type Map<String, List<Person>>.

Instead of grouping the Person, if we want to group only their names, we can do that using an overloaded version of groupBy() that takes two arguments. The first parameter is a lambda that maps the element in the original collection to the key. The second lambda maps the element to the value that should be placed into the list. Instead of List<Person> for the values, let's create List<String> where String represents the first names.

internal/iterators.kts

```
val namesBy1stLetter =
  people.groupBy({ person -> person.firstName.first() }) {
    person -> person.firstName
  }

println(namesBy1stLetter)
//{S=[Sara, Sue], J=[Jill, Jack], P=[Paula, Paul], M=[Mani]}
```

Since groupBy() is taking two lambdas as parameters, the first is placed inside the parenthesis () and the second floats freely outside the parenthesis—see Use Lambda as the Last Parameter, on page 182.

If instead of grouping the first names, you want to group the age values, replace the second lambda's body with person.age instead of person.firstName.

With such a variety of powerful tools available combined with elegant and expressive code for internal iterators, you may wonder, Why not use them all the time instead of external iterators or any other alternatives? Appearances can be deceiving and we need to be cognizant of the performance implications of this style. We'll look at that next and discuss some alternatives to improve performance.

Sequences for Lazy Evaluation

Simply put, collections are eager and sequences are lazy. Sequences are optimized wrappers around collections intended to improve performance. In this section, we'll look at what that means and how to decide when to use collections and when to use sequences.

Unlike Java, the methods like filter(), map(), and so on are available in Kotlin directly on collections like List<T>, instead of only on a Stream<T>. The designers of Java made a decision against offering these methods on collections for performance reasons. The designers of Kotlin, on the other hand, decided to lean toward convenience, and they expect us to choose wisely.

Use the internal iterators on collections directly in Kotlin when the collection size is small. For larger collections, use the internal iterators through a sequence. The reason for this is that unlike operations on collections that are evaluated eagerly, the function calls on sequences are evaluated lazily. Laziness defers execution of code to the point where they may be eliminated if unnecessary. That optimization can save time and resources that may otherwise be spent on computations whose results may never be used. And laziness also makes it possible to create infinite sequences that are evaluated on demand. We'll explore these ideas and discuss their benefits here.

Improve Performance with Sequences

Let's revisit the example from the previous section where we obtained the first adult in a given list. We'll use the same Person class and the people list we created earlier. Using the internal iterators filter(), map(), and first(), we get the name of the first adult in the group. Instead of passing lambdas to filter() and map(), we'll pass function references. The filter() method takes a reference to an isAdult() function, and the map() method takes a reference to the fetchFirstName() function.

```kotlin
fun isAdult(person: Person): Boolean {
  println("isAdult called for ${person.firstName}")
  return person.age > 17
}

fun fetchFirstName(person: Person): String {
  println("fetchFirstName called for ${person.firstName}")
  return person.firstName
}

val nameOfFirstAdult = people
  .filter(::isAdult)
  .map(::fetchFirstName)
  .first()

println(nameOfFirstAdult)
```

As you would expect, the value stored in nameOfFirstAdult is Jill, no surprises there. But the effort to get that result is significant. The filter() method executes eagerly to call the isAdult() function and creates a list of adults. Then the map() method also executes eagerly to call the fetchFirstName() function and creates yet another list of names of adults. Finally, the two intermediate temporary lists are discarded when first() gets just the first element from the list returned by map(). Although only one value is expected as the final result, the execution ends up performing a lot of work, as we can see from the output:

```
isAdult called for Sara
isAdult called for Jill
isAdult called for Paula
isAdult called for Paul
isAdult called for Mani
isAdult called for Jack
isAdult called for Sue
fetchFirstName called for Jill
fetchFirstName called for Paula
fetchFirstName called for Paul
fetchFirstName called for Jack
Jill
```

This was a small collection, but what if we had hundreds of thousands of elements in the collection. That would result in a lot of computations whose results aren't used in the end—what a waste.

This is where the lazy evaluation capabilities of *sequences* come in. We can wrap a collection into a sequence using the asSequence() method and then apply the same internal iterator methods that we used on the collection, but this time on the sequence. Let's change the previous code to do that.

```
val nameOfFirstAdult = people.asSequence()
  .filter(::isAdult)
  .map(::fetchFirstName)
  .first()

println(nameOfFirstAdult)
```

The only difference between the previous code and this one is the call to asSequence() before the filter() call. A small change but a huge gain in performance, as we see from the output:

```
isAdult called for Sara
isAdult called for Jill
fetchFirstName called for Jill
Jill
```

Instead of eagerly creating a list of adults, the filter() method, when called on a sequence, returns another sequence. Likewise, the call to map() on a sequence returns yet another sequence. But the lambdas passed to filter() or map() haven't been called yet. When the first() method is called, the actual evaluation that was deferred so long is triggered. Unlike the other methods on sequence that return a sequence, the terminal methods like first() return a result of executing the pipeline of operations. By nature, sequences defer evaluation until a terminal method is called and then minimally perform operations to get the desired result.

Both the direct use of internal iterators on collections and their use via sequences lead to elegant functional-style code. Whereas the computations are performed eagerly when internal iterators are run on collections, the same operations execute lazily when run on sequences.

Since sequences do less work, should we use them all the time instead of calling the internal iterators on collections directly? The short answer is no. If the collection is very small, the difference in performance will be rather negligible. Eager evaluation, which is easier to debug and easier to reason, may be better in that case. However, if the collection size is large, in the hundreds of thousands of elements, then using sequence will remove the significant overhead of creating intermediate collections and eliminated computations.

Infinite Sequences

Performance isn't the only benefit of laziness. Laziness can also help perform on-demand computation and that, in turn, can help to create infinite or unbounded sequences of elements. An infinite sequence starts with a value and is followed by a sequence of numbers that follow a particular pattern of occurrence. For example, the Fibonacci sequence 1, 1, 2, 3, 5, 8,... follows the pattern that the value at a position is equal to the sum of values at the previous two positions. The numbers 2, 4, 6, 8, 10,... form an infinite sequence of even numbers that start with 2.

Kotlin provides a few different ways to create an infinite sequence. The generateSequence() function is one way. Let's use that function to create an infinite sequence of prime numbers as a way to illustrate the power of sequences to create unbounded sequences of values. We'll start with some convenience functions to lead up to the use of generateSequence().

Given a number n, the isPrime() function returns true if the number is prime and false otherwise:

internal/primes.kts
```
fun isPrime(n: Long) = n > 1 && (2 until n).none { i -> n % i == 0L }
```

The nextPrime() function takes a number n and returns the prime number after that value. For example, if we provide 5 or 6 as input, it will return the next prime number 7. The method is marked as tailrec to prevent the possibility of StackOverflowError—see Chapter 14, Programming Recursion and Memoization, on page 269, for a discussion of tail call optimization.

internal/primes.kts
```
tailrec fun nextPrime(n: Long): Long =
  if (isPrime(n + 1)) n + 1 else nextPrime(n + 1)
```

Given the above two functions, we can create an infinite sequence of prime numbers starting with any prime number, using the generateSequence() function, like so:

internal/primes.kts
```
val primes = generateSequence(5, ::nextPrime)
```

One overloaded version of the generateSequence() function takes a seed value as the first parameter and a function, a lambda expression, as the second parameter. The lambda takes in a value and returns a result value. In this example, we use a function reference to the nextPrime() function which, given a number, returns the next prime number. Thus, primes holds an infinite sequence of prime numbers starting with 5.

In the call to generateSequence(), if the second argument, which is a call to the nextPrime(), were executed immediately and repeatedly, then we'd end up with an infinite collection of values. Such execution doesn't make sense both from the time and space points of view. The trick here is that generateSequence() is lazy and it doesn't execute the nextPrime() function until we ask for the values. We can ask for any number of values using the take() method. This method gives us a view into the regions of the infinite sequence that we're interested in viewing or using. Let's use the take() method to get 6 values from the primes infinite series of prime numbers.

internal/primes.kts
```
System.out.println(primes.take(6).toList()) //[5, 7, 11, 13, 17, 19]
```

The call to toList() triggers the evaluation of the elements in the sequence, but take() produces only the given number of values.

With the ability to create infinite sequences, we can model problems with lazy evaluation to create sequence of values whose bounds aren't known ahead of time.

Instead of writing the nextPrime() recursive function and then using the generate-Sequence() function, we can also use the sequence() function. This function takes a lambda that runs as a continuation, which is an advanced and relatively new topic in Kotlin. We'll dive extensively into continuations and coroutines later in this book. For now, when you see the yield() call, read it as "return a value to the caller and then continue executing the next line of code." In other words, continuations give an illusion of writing a function with multiple return points.

Let's replace the nextPrime() function and the call to generateSequence() in the previous example with the following:

```
val primes = sequence {
  var i: Long = 0

  while (true) {
    i++

    if (isPrime(i)) {
      yield(i)
    }
  }
}
```

The result of the call to sequence() is an instance that implements the Sequence interface. Within the lambda provided to the sequence() function, we have an infinite loop that yields prime numbers. The code within the lambda is executed on demand, only when a value is requested or taken from the sequence. The iteration starts with the value i being 0 and the first prime number yielded by the code is 2. We can take as many values as we like from this infinite sequence, but we can also skip or drop some values. Since the sequence of primes starts with 2, let's use drop() to throw away a couple of initial values and then take six values after that:

```
println(primes.drop(2).take(6).toList()) //[5, 7, 11, 13, 17, 19]
```

If you have a separate function, like nextPrime(), that can produce the next value in a sequence, then use that function with generateSequence() to generate an infinite sequence. On the other hand, if you want to combine the code to generate the next value in a sequence with the code to create the infinite sequence, then use the sequence() function.

Wrapping Up

External iterators are common in imperative-style programming, whereas internal iterators are the way of life in functional programming. Internal iterators are less complex, more fluent, expressive, and concise when compared to external iterators. Kotlin provides internal iterators directly on collections. However, the execution of these methods on collections is eager. This isn't an issue for small collections, but for larger collections it may result in poor performance due to evaluations that may not be necessary. For such situations, Kotlin provides sequences as wrappers that will postpone evaluations. By lazily evaluating operations, you may eliminate computations that are otherwise not needed, resulting in better performance while retaining all the other benefits of internal iterators.

Internal iterators are concise, expressive, and elegant, but Kotlin takes the characteristics to a whole new level with its capabilities to create fluent code. That's the topic we'll explore in the next part.

Part IV

Elegant and Efficient Kotlin

Programmers often say that Kotlin code is beautiful, and there are good reasons for that. Kotlin code is concise, has less ceremony, and the language provides hygienic syntax to extend the capabilities of existing classes to add domain-specific methods and properties. You'll see the fluency of Kotlin shine in this part, and you'll learn to apply the capabilities of the language to implement your own fluent APIs and internal domain-specific languages. You'll also learn about the optimization Kotlin provides for recursion so you can make use of this intriguing programming construct for large input parameters.

CHAPTER 12

Fluency in Kotlin

The famous words of Blaise Pascal, "If I had more time I would have written a shorter letter," apply as much to programming as writing. In this chapter I urge you to take the time to learn some useful ways to write shorter yet readable code.

Code is written just once, but is read, refactored, enhanced, and maintained continuously through the lifetime of the application. Verbose, poor-quality, hard-to-understand code can turn even the politest person on the planet into a cusser. By increasing quality you can lower the cost of maintaining code.

Fluent code is concise, easy to read and understand, and is a gift we give to ourselves and to the rest of the team. It's pleasing to read, makes us productive, and can serve as a great motivator to develop better-quality software.

Fluent code has a direct economic impact on developing software. Most teams are in a perpetual state of urgency and rarely have the luxury to fix bugs when they have plenty of time and are relaxed. Cluttered code that is verbose and hard to read greatly increases the stress level, which in turn makes it harder to see through and resolve issues. It takes less effort and time to parse through code that is fluent than code that is long, noisy, and verbose. While some programmers may be able to write more fluent code in any language, a language that offers greater fluency lets all of us create more fluent code with less effort. When fluency becomes a natural part of coding, everyone benefits—the developers and the business.

In this chapter, we'll focus on how to make Kotlin code fluent, expressive, and concise. We'll start with the controversial operator overloading capability, then we'll cover how to inject methods and properties into existing third-party classes, to extend functions, to make function calls fluent, and to reduce code when using any object. We'll wrap up the chapter by looking at an advanced feature that allows attaching a receiver to lambda expressions. The techniques you learn here will be a nice segue into creating DSLs in the next chapter.

Overloading Operators

Traditionally we use operators on numeric types to create expressions, for example, 2 + 3 or 4.2 * 7.1. Operator overloading is a feature where the language extends the capability to use operators on user-defined data types.

Compare the two lines in the following code snippet:

```
bigInteger1.multiply(bigInteger2)
bigInteger1 * bigInteger2
```

The first line uses the multiply method from the JDK. The second line uses the * operator on the instances of BigInteger; that operator comes from the Kotlin standard library. The second line takes less effort—both to write and to read—than the first line, even though they both accomplish the same thing. The operator * makes the code look more natural, fluent, less code-like than the use of the multiply() method. Java doesn't permit us to overload operators on user-defined datatypes, but Kotlin does. That leads to greater fluency, less clutter, and makes it a joy to program in Kotlin.

In addition to using operators like +, -, and * on numeric types, languages that support operator overloading also permit using such operators on objects. For instance, given a reference today of a Date class, today + 2 may mean that's two days from now.

Don't Overuse Operator Overloading

Programmers have a love-hate relationship with operator overloading because it's a feature that can be abused easily. For example, does today + 2 mean two days or two months from now? It's not clear, and that's frustrating to the person reading the code. Don't use operator overloading unless it'll be obvious to the reader.

When used correctly, the benefits of operator overloading are amazing. For example, wishList + appleWatch is fairly intuitive; we're appending an item to a List. When overloading an operator on a user-defined class, we have to be careful to honor the intended behavior of the operator. For example, we know that + is a pure function; it doesn't modify either of the operands. The writer of + on the class List shouldn't modify either of the operands provided to the + operator. That's part of the "used correctly" effort. The names used for the variables also contribute to the readability of code with operators, so pick names judiciously. For example, wishList + appleWatch, rather than w + x, is better to convey that we're using overloaded operator + on an instance of List.

Since the JVM doesn't support operator overloading (and Kotlin compiles down to Java bytecode), Kotlin makes operator overloading possible by mapping operators to specially named methods. For example, + will result in a call to a plus() method. By writing these specialized methods, you may overload operators on your own classes, although the precedence of operators is fixed and you can't change the precedence. Also, using the extension functions that we'll see soon, you may overload operators on third-party classes.

To overload an operator, define a function and mark it with the operator keyword. Here's an example of overloading + on a Pair<Int, Int> to add a pair of numbers:

fluency/pairplus.kts
```
operator fun Pair<Int, Int>.plus(other: Pair<Int, Int>) =
  Pair(first + other.first, second + other.second)
```

The function is named plus() which is the specialized method name for +. It operates on an implicit object, the left operand, referenced using this and on the right operand other. Instead of writing this.first + other.first, we used a short form first + other.first to compute the sum of the first values in the two pairs. The plus() extension function returns a new Pair<Int, Int>, where the first value is sum of the first values in each of the given pairs and second is the sum of the second values in each of the given pairs.

To overload operators for your own classes, write the appropriate specialized methods as member functions within your classes. For example, here's how you'd overload *, on a class that represent a complex number, to multiply two complex numbers:

fluency/complex.kts
```
import kotlin.math.abs

data class Complex(val real: Int, val imaginary: Int) {
  operator fun times(other: Complex) =
    Complex(real * other.real - imaginary * other.imaginary,
        real * other.imaginary + imaginary * other.real)

  private fun sign() = if (imaginary < 0) "-" else "+"

  override fun toString() = "$real ${sign()} ${abs(imaginary)}i"
}
println(Complex(4, 2) * Complex(-3, 4)) //-20 + 10i
println(Complex(1, 2) * Complex(-3, 4)) //-11 - 2i
```

How could one not love a language where fun times is a valid syntax—the times()
method marked as operator stands in for the * operator. If you don't mark it
as operator, but try to use *, then you'll get an error. Also, if you mark a method
with a non-specialized name with operator, you'll get an error.

The mapping from operator to the corresponding special name for methods,
shown in the following table, is fairly easy to remember and it's often intuitive.
All operations are pure—they don't mutate or cause side effects, unless otherwise noted.

Operator	Corresponds To	Observations
+x	x.unaryPlus()	
-x	x.unaryMinus()	
!x	x.not()	
x + y	x.plus(y)	
x - y	x.minus(y)	
x * y	x.times(y)	
x / y	x.div(y)	
x % y	x.rem(y)	
++x	x.inc()	x must be assignable
x++	x.inc()	x must be assignable
--x	x.dec()	x must be assignable
x--	x.dec()	x must be assignable
x == y	x.equals(y)	
x != y	!(x.equals(y))	
x < y	x.compareTo(y)	Also used for <=, >, >=
x[i]	x.get(i)	
x[i] = y	x.set(i, y)	
y in x	x.contains(y)	Also used for !in
x..y	x.rangeTo(y)	
x()	x.invoke()	
x(y)	x.invoke(y)	

The functions for the composite operators +=, -=, *=, /=, and %= take on the
word *Assign* after the special name for the first operator, for example, plusAssign()
for +=. You shouldn't implement both plus() and plusAssign() for the same class.
Likewise, for other composite operators. If you implement plus(), for example,
then += will use that method appropriately. If not, to resolve +=, the compiler
will look for plusAssign(). If neither plus() nor plusAssign() are found, then the

compilation of += for instances of your class will fail. While plus() is a pure function and returns a new instance, plusAssign() will change the state of the instance on which it operates and thus expects the object to be mutable.

You have to abide by some rules when overloading operators. Honor the conventional wisdom of the behavior associated with an operator. For instance, don't mutate an object in the + or - operator-overloaded functions. This rule extends even to operators that are normally perceived as mutating. For example, let's overload the increment and decrement operators. The function inc() is used both for pre-increment ++x and post-increment x++. Likewise, dec() is used for both pre-decrement and post-decrement.

fluency/counter.kts
```
class Counter(val value: Int) {
  operator fun inc() = Counter(value + 1)

  operator fun dec() = Counter(value - 1)

  override fun toString() = "$value"
}

var counter = Counter(2)
println(counter)     //2
println(++counter)   //3
println(counter)     //3
println(counter++)   //3
println(counter)     //4
```

Within the inc() method we're not mutating anything. Instead, we return a new object with new state. When used as pre-increment, Kotlin will save the returned value into the variable on which the operator is applied. That's the reason why we see 3 as a result of ++counter. On the other hand, when used as a post-increment operator, Kotlin will save the result into the said variable but return the previous value as a result of the expression. That explains why the result of counter++ is 3 instead of the more recent value 4, which is the value held in the object that counter now refers to.

Operator overloading is a powerful feature, but follow a few recommendations when using it:

- Use sparingly.
- Overload only when the use will be obvious to the readers.
- Abide by the commonly understood behavior of the operators.
- Use meaningful names for variables so it's easier to follow the context of overloading.

Operators reduce noise and, when used correctly, can make the code intuitive and readable. Next, we'll see how we can take readability further, beyond operators.

Injecting Using Extension Functions and Properties

From the readability and ease points of view, having application-specific convenience methods on third-party classes will make the lives of your fellow programmers better. And, that's possible because Kotlin permits you to inject methods and properties into any class, including classes written in other JVM languages. Unlike other languages that offer metaprogramming, Kotlin performs injection without patching the runtime or class loading. In Kotlin, classes are open for extension, even though they may not be available for inheritance. Extension functions and extension properties are techniques to add methods and properties, but without altering the bytecode of the targeted classes. When you create an extension function for a class, it gives an illusion that you've implemented an instance method for that class. Don't create an extension function for a method if that method already exists in the class. Members of a class always win over extension functions if there's a conflict. When the Kotlin compiler sees a method call, it checks to see if an instance method is available and uses it if found. If an instance method isn't found, Kotlin looks for an extension function for the targeted class.

You can inject methods and properties into existing classes, including final classes, and even those classes that you didn't write—that's the spirit of a free society.

Let's explore injecting methods into existing classes first, then look into injecting an operator, followed by injecting a property.

Injecting Methods Using Extension Functions

Suppose our large enterprise application has two classes Point and Circle, defined like so:

fluency/circle.kts
```
data class Point(val x: Int, val y: Int)
data class Circle(val cx: Int, val cy: Int, val radius: Int)
```

These classes don't have any methods at this time, and the two classes are independent of each other.

Suppose we want to find if a point is located within a circle. It would be nice to have a convenience method in either of the classes for that. But we don't have to bribe the creator of the Circle class or the Point class to introduce that method. We can add methods, right from outside, to any of these classes. Let's inject an extension function named contains() into the Circle class, like so:

fluency/circle.kts
```
fun Circle.contains(point: Point) =
  (point.x - cx) * (point.x - cx) + (point.y - cy) * (point.y - cy) <
    radius * radius
```

This code sits outside any of the classes, at the top level of a package—a default package in this example. Within the contains() extension function, we access the member of the implicit Circle instance exactly like we'd access it if this extension function were written as an instance method within the class. If we'd written this method within the Circle class, the only difference is that we would have written fun contains(point: Point) instead of fun Circle.contains(point: Point).

As long as this method is visible—that is, it's either in the same file or we've imported it from the package where it resides—we can use it, like so:

fluency/circle.kts
```
val circle = Circle(100, 100, 25)
val point1 = Point(110, 110)
val point2 = Point(10, 100)

println(circle.contains(point1)) //true
println(circle.contains(point2)) //false
```

Even though the class Circle doesn't have the contains() method, we're able to call it on an instance of that class. When Kotlin sees the extension function, it creates a static method in the package where the extension function exists and passes the context object—Circle in the example—as the first argument to the function, and the actual parameters as the remaining parameters. When the compiler sees the call to a method, it figures we're calling the extension function and routes the context object circle as the first argument to the method. In short, what appears to be a method call is really a call to a static method when extension functions are involved.

Extension functions have a few limitations. When there's a conflict between an extension function and an instance method of the same name, the instance method always wins. And unlike instance methods, which can reach into the encapsulation boundaries of an instance, extension functions can access only the parts of an object visible from within the package they are defined in.

Injecting Operators Using Extension Functions

The extension function may be an operator as well. In the list of operators mentioned in Overloading Operators, on page 222, we saw that in is an operator and it maps to the contains() method. A circle contains a point, possibly, but we'd ask if a point is in a circle. It turns out the in operator when called like aPoint in aCircle will compile down to aCircle.contains(aPoint). But for that to work, we have to annotate the contains() method in Circle with operator. Let's do that:

```
operator fun Circle.contains(point: Point) =
  (point.x - cx) * (point.x - cx) + (point.y - cy) * (point.y - cy) <
    radius * radius
```

We simply added the keyword operator to the front of the extension function—that's it.

Now, we may use the contains() method like before or use the in operator, like this:

```
println(circle.contains(point1)) //true
println(point1 in circle) //true
println(point2 in circle) //false
```

Injecting Properties Using Extension Properties

Taking a quick detour from extension functions, we may add extension properties as well. Since these are also not part of the internals of the class, extension properties can't use backing fields—that is, they can't access field like actual properties can. They may use other properties or methods on the class to get their work done. Let's add a area property to the Circle class.

```
val Circle.area: Double
  get() = kotlin.math.PI * radius * radius
```

From the object user's perspective, we can use extension properties much like we use real properties:

```
val circle = Circle(100, 100, 25)
println("Area is ${circle.area}") //1963.49...
```

Where it makes sense, we may also write setters for var extension properties. The setter will have to rely upon other methods of the class to accomplish its goals; just like the getters for extension properties, the setters for extension properties can't use backing fields.

Injecting into Third-Party Classes

You may add extension functions to third-party classes and also route the extension functions to existing methods. Here's an extension function for the good old java.lang.String class:

```
fluency/stringext.kts
fun String.isPalindrome(): Boolean {
  return reversed() == this
}
```

The isPalindrome() method uses the Kotlin extension function reversed() to determine if a given string is a palindrome. Instead of defining a code block, we may route the call to an existing method, using a single line expression, like so:

fluency/stringext.kts
```
fun String.shout() = toUpperCase()
```

Here's an example to use these two methods:

fluency/stringext.kts
```
val str = "dad"
println(str.isPalindrome()) //true
println(str.shout()) //DAD
```

The first line shows that the extension function isPalindrome() works for String. The second line shows that shout() is merely using the toUpperCase() method to evoke a response I normally hear from my children after I tell a joke.

Don't Change Behavior of Existing Methods

Once, in a Kotlin class I was teaching, a developer with unsurmountable enthusiasm toward extension functions asked if we could replace an existing method with an extension function. In the spirit of live coding, I cranked up the following in class:

fluency/shadow.kts
```
fun String.toLowerCase() = toUpperCase() //BAD CODE
```

Not only did I replace the implementation of an existing method, but I gave it exactly the opposite behavior than what the name indicates. We can see the effect of this by calling the method—the result of calling the toLowerCase() is the string in all uppercase:

fluency/shadow.kts
```
val str = "Please Don't"
println(str.toLowerCase()) //PLEASE DON'T
```

What bothered me most is not that Kotlin permits this, but how pleased the developer was upon seeing the ridiculous result.

While instance methods always win, it's possible to replace an extension function from another package, like toLowerCase(), which is defined in the Kotlin standard library, with an extension function in your own package. As the message says, please don't. File that under "Just because we can doesn't mean we should." Changing behavior of well-known methods will cause hard-to-maintain code, loss of hair for your friends, and loss of their friendship when they find out who caused it.

Before we leave the topic of extension functions, we have to complete a long-pending task. Back in Forward Iteration, on page 55, we tried to iterate over a range of Strings from "hell" to "help", which failed. Here's the code we tried:

```
for (word in "hell".."help") { print("$word, ") } //ERROR
//for-loop range must have an 'iterator()' method
```

Now we're ready to fix that error, with an extension function.

The error says that the compiler didn't find the iterator() method on the ClosedRange<String> class. Let's review a few things that can help us to inject that method into the class:

- We can create an iterator as an anonymous object, as you learned in Anonymous Objects with Object Expressions, on page 108.

- We can access the first element of the range using the start property and the last element using endInclusive of the ClosedRange<T> class.

- Kotlin will invoke the compareTo() method when the >= operator is used, as we discussed in Overloading Operators, on page 222.

- We can use the StringBuilder class from the JDK to hold a mutable String.

- The + operator of kotlin.Char can be used to get the next character, and we can use that to increment the last character in the StringBuilder.

Let's apply these ideas to create the extension function for the iterator():

```
fluency/forstringrange.kts
operator fun ClosedRange<String>.iterator() =
  object: Iterator<String> {
    private val next = StringBuilder(start)
    private val last = endInclusive

    override fun hasNext() =
      last >= next.toString() && last.length >= next.length

    override fun next(): String {
      val result = next.toString()

      val lastCharacter = next.last()

      if (lastCharacter < Char.MAX_VALUE) {
        next.setCharAt(next.length - 1, lastCharacter + 1)
      } else {
        next.append(Char.MIN_VALUE)
      }

      return result
    }
  }
```

Kotlin expects the iterator() method to be annotated as operator. In the extension function, we create an implementation of Iterator<String>. In that, we store the start value of the range into the next property and the endInclusive value into the last property. The hasNext() method returns true if we've not gone past the last element in the iteration and if the length of the last element isn't less than the string generated in the iteration. Finally, the next() method returns the current String value in next and increments the last character in that variable. If the last character reaches the Char.MAX_VALUE, then a new character is appended to the generated string. This implementation of next() was inspired by a similar implementation in the Groovy library.

Let's call the loop again and see the effect of this injected method:

```
fluency/forstringrange.kts
for (word in "hell".."help") { print("$word, ") }
```

No error this time, and here's the output:

```
hell, helm, heln, helo, help,
```

We can simplify the implementation of the iterator further using yield from Kotlin coroutines—we'll see this in Interleaving Calls with Suspension Points, on page 291.

Injecting Static Methods

You can inject static methods into classes by extending their companion object—that is, injecting method into the companion instead of the class. As a result, you may inject static methods only if the class has a companion object.

For example, Kotlin has extended and added a companion to String, so you can add a static method to String, like so:

```
fun String.Companion.toURL(link: String) = java.net.URL(link)
```

Once you add that extension function, you may call the toURL() on the String class, to take a String and return an instance of URL, like in this example:

```
val url: java.net.URL = String.toURL("https://pragprog.com")
```

Adding a static or class-level method to String took little effort. However, you can't add a static method to all third-party classes from Kotlin. For example, you can't add a class-level method to the java.net.URL class of the JDK since Kotlin hasn't added a companion class to this class.

Injecting from within a Class

All the extension functions we injected so far were at the top level—that is, we added them from outside of any class. Those extension functions are visible from any code that imports the package in which they're located at the top level. Extension functions may also be injected from within classes.

As a designer of a class, you may occasionally come to realize that having some convenience methods on third-party classes may ease the implementation of your own class. For instance, when implementing an InsurancePolicy class you may find it useful to have methods on Date that tell you the number of days until the policy expires, if a policy is valid on a given date, and so on. Thus, you may want to create extension functions on third-party classes right within your classes.

If you create an extension function within a class, then that extension function is visible only within the class and its inner classes. Also, within the extension function there are two receivers; that is, in a sense there are two this context objects. Let's create an example to grasp these concepts.

Earlier we created a Point data class that had two properties, x and y. Let's create a variation of that class here, but this time we'll store the values in a Pair instead of keeping them directly within the Point. That will give us an excuse to create a convenience method on Pair to be used within our new Point class.

The Point class's primary constructor will take two parameters x and y. We create them as parameters instead of as properties and then store those two parameters in a Pair<Int, Int>. We'll create two private properties within Point, to return the sign of the x and y values, now stored within the Pair. We'll call these firstsign and secondsign. Then, we'll override the toString() method and in the implementation we'll call the method on Pair<Int, Int> that we'll extend from within the Point class. As the last step in the example, we'll implement the extension function point2String(), which is called from within the toString() method. Let's take a look at the code for the Point class before discussing further about the extension function.

fluency/innerextension.kts
```kotlin
class Point(x: Int, y: Int) {
  private val pair = Pair(x, y)

  private val firstsign = if (pair.first < 0) "" else "+"
  private val secondsign = if (pair.second < 0) "" else "+"

  override fun toString() = pair.point2String()
```

```
  fun Pair<Int, Int>.point2String() =
    "(${firstsign}${first}, ${this@Point.secondsign}${this.second})"
}

println(Point(1, -3)) //(+1, -3)
println(Point(-3, 4)) //(-3, +4)
```

The extension function is injected into the Pair<Int, Int> from within the Point class. So any effort to use that extension function on an instance of Pair<Int, Int> from outside the class will result in compilation error. Let's take a closer look at the extension function alone.

```
fun Pair<Int, Int>.point2String() =
  "(${firstsign}${first}, ${this@Point.secondsign}${this.second})"
```

Since the extension function is created within a class, it has two receivers: this and this@Point. These two receivers have distinct names in Kotlin, *extension receiver* and *dispatch receiver*, respectively. An extension receiver is the object that the extension function is executing on—that is, the object that received the extension function. A dispatch receiver is the instance of the class from within which we added the extension function—that is, the class from within which we did the injection of the method.

The following figure shows a clear view of the two receivers in the extension function.

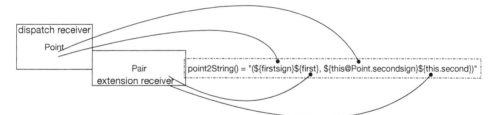

A property or method mentioned within the extension function refers to the extension receiver if it exists on that instance. Otherwise, it binds to the corresponding property or method, if present, on the dispatch receiver. The extension receiver takes precedence for binding to properties and methods.

Within the method, first binds to the property of Pair<Int, Int> the extension receiver. Likewise, this.second binds to the second property on the same instance. Since the extension receiver, Pair<Int, Int>, doesn't have a property named firstsign but the dispatch receiver, Point, does, the reference to firstsign binds to the dispatch receiver. If there's a conflict, and we want to bypass the extension receiver and reference the dispatch receiver, we can use the this@Outer syntax for that—we saw this in Nested and Inner Classes, on page 138. That's the same syntax used to refer to the outer class from within the inner class. The reference this@Point.secondsign illustrates this explicit access to a property on dispatch receiver.

Extension functions defined within a class, and even a method of a class, are useful to narrow the scope of the extension functions for use within the particular class or particular method.

So far, we've seen adding methods to classes. Next, we'll see how to add a method to a function—that'll make the interesting feature of extension functions even more intriguing.

Extending Functions

Functions are objects in Kotlin, and you can inject methods into functions, like you can inject methods into classes. In Java 8, the functional interface Function<T, R> has an andThen() method to combine two functions, and we can use this to compose operations—see *Functional Programming in Java [Sub14]*. Kotlin's Function doesn't have that method, but we can inject an andThen() method into Kotlin functions like this, for example:

fluency/extendfunctions.kts
```
fun <T, R, U> ((T) -> R).andThen(next: (R) -> U): (T) -> U =
  { input: T -> next(this(input)) }
```

The extension function signature says that andThen() is added to a function that takes a parametrized type T and returns a result of type R. The parameter passed to andThen() has to be a function that takes as a parameter a variable of type R—the return type of the function on which andThen() is called—and it returns a result of parameterized type U. The resulting composed function created by andThen() takes a parameter of type T and returns a result of type U. In the body of andThen() we return a lambda expression. This lambda passes its parameter to the function on which andThen() is called and passes the result to the next function—that is, the parameter to andThen(). Thus, andThen() passes the result of one function as input to the next.

Let's write two standalone functions that we'll use to exercise the above function:

fluency/extendfunctions.kts
```
fun increment(number: Int): Double = number + 1.toDouble()
fun double(number: Double) = number * 2
```

Now we can use andThen() to combine the result of increment() with a call to the double() function, like this:

fluency/extendfunctions.kts
```
val incrementAndDouble = ::increment.andThen(::double)
```

```
println(incrementAndDouble(5)) //12.0
```

On a reference to the increment() function, obtained using the :: construct, we call the andThen() method and pass a reference to the double() method. The result is a function that will combine calls to these two functions, increment() and then double().

We'll apply this technique in Memoization, the Groovy Way in Kotlin, on page 275, to inject a memoize() method into functions.

Function Fluency with infix

Dots and parenthesis are common in code we write, but on many occasions leaving those out can make the code less noisy and easier to follow. For example, the following is familiar code in Java:

```
//Java
if(obj instanceof String) {
```

Imagine Java had insisted that we write if(obj.instanceOf(String)) {—what a clutter that would have been. Instead, we used a nice syntax if(obj instanceof String) {—that's much easier to read, and it uses what is called the infix notation, where an operator is infixed or implanted in the middle of its operands. That syntax is nice, but in Java such fluency is limited to predefined operators. In Kotlin you can use the infix notation—that is, leave out dots and parenthesis—for your own code and thus make the code expressive, less noisy, and easier to read.

In the earlier example with Circle and Point, we saw this:

```
println(circle.contains(point1)) //true
println(point1 in circle) //true
```

We used the dot and parenthesis to invoke contains() but didn't use those with in. The reason is obvious: contains() is a method, but in is an operator, like +. Operators always enjoy infix notation automatically in Kotlin, but methods don't by default. That's a good reason for the difference, but we don't have to accept that and settle quietly. If we want to use contains much like the way we used in, we can do that in Kotlin, but after a change.

If we mark a method with infix annotation, then Kotlin will allow us to drop the dot and parenthesis. infix may be combined with operator, but operator isn't required for infix—they are orthogonal to each other.

To see infix notation in action, we'll start with this:

```
operator fun Circle.contains(point: Point) =
  (point.x - cx) * (point.x - cx) + (point.y - cy) * (point.y - cy) <
    radius * radius
```

Let's change it to the following:

```
operator infix fun Circle.contains(point: Point) =
  (point.x - cx) * (point.x - cx) + (point.y - cy) * (point.y - cy) <
    radius * radius
```

Now, we can write:

```
println(circle.contains(point1)) //true
```

And we can also write:

```
println(circle contains point1) //true
```

What's the big deal in not having dot and parenthesis? you may ask. It leads to more fluent code and less noise—characteristics that are helpful for creating DSLs—we'll see this in Chapter 13, Creating Internal DSLs, on page 249.

Kotlin offers some flexibility for infix functions but also comes with some limitations: infix methods are required to take exactly one parameter—no vararg and no default parameters.

Fluency with Any Object

infix reduces some noise, but when working with just about any object, Kotlin makes code less verbose and more expressive. The language does this by adding a few convenience functions. Learning those methods can make your everyday coding a pleasant experience and make your code more fluent.

Coding in Kotlin involves invoking functions, methods, and passing lambda expressions, among other things. The language offers some support for minimizing noise with these day-to-day operations.

Specifically, Kotlin has four significant methods that can make code fluent: also(), apply(), let(), and run(). Each of these methods takes a lambda expression as a parameter and returns something back after invoking the given lambda. The format of a call to one of these methods, on a context object, looks like this:

```
result = context.oneOfTheseFourMethods { optionalParameter ->
        ...body...
        ...what's this (receiver) here?...
        optionalResult
}
```

Depending on the method you call, the optionalParameter and this, the receiver of the call, will be assigned differently. The optionalResult received from the call will differ as well. Once we learn a bit more about these functions, we'll see how we can benefit from these functions to create concise and expressive code. Stay tuned.

Behavior of the Four Methods

Let's exercise these four methods and report back on the arguments received by the lambdas passed, the this receiver within each lambda expression, the result returned by them, and the result received on the calling side of these four methods.

fluency/anymethods.kts
```
val format = "%-10s%-10s%-10s%-10s"
val str = "context"
val result = "RESULT"

fun toString() = "lexical"

println(String.format("%-10s%-10s%-10s%-10s%-10s",
  "Method", "Argument", "Receiver", "Return", "Result"))
println("==============================================")

val result1 = str.let { arg ->
  print(String.format(format, "let", arg, this, result))
  result
}
println(String.format("%-10s", result1))

val result2 = str.also { arg ->
  print(String.format(format, "also", arg, this, result))
  result
}
println(String.format("%-10s", result2))

val result3 = str.run {
  print(String.format(format, "run", "N/A", this, result))
  result
}
println(String.format("%-10s", result3))

val result4 = str.apply {
  print(String.format(format, "apply", "N/A", this, result))
  result
}
println(String.format("%-10s", result4))
```

Each of the lambdas ends with an expression result, but some of them may get ignored, as we'll see. The first two lambdas receive a parameter arg and the last two don't. Study the output to learn about the behavior of the methods:

```
Method    Argument  Receiver  Return   Result
=================================================
let       context   lexical   RESULT   RESULT
also      context   lexical   RESULT   context
run       N/A       context   RESULT   RESULT
apply     N/A       context   RESULT   context
```

The let() method passes the context object, the object on which it's called, as an argument to the lambda. The lambda's this, or receiver, is lexically scoped and bound to the this in the defining scope of the lambda—we discussed lexical scoping in Closures and Lexical Scoping, on page 188. The result of the lambda is passed as the result of the call to let().

The also() method also passes the context object as the argument to its lambda, and the receiver is tied to this in lexical scoping. However, unlike let(), the also() method ignores the result of its lambda and returns the context object as the result. The return types of the lambda that also() receives is Unit, thus the result returned is ignored.

The run() method doesn't pass any argument to its lambda but binds the context object to the this, or receiver, of the lambda. The result of the lambda is returned as the result of run().

The apply() method also doesn't pass any argument to its lambda and binds the context object to the this, or receiver, of the lambda. But unlike the run() method, the apply() method ignores the result of the lambda—Unit type used for return—and returns the context object to the caller.

Let's summarize these four methods' behaviors:

- All four methods execute the lambdas given to them.

- let() and run() execute the lambda and return the result of lambda to the caller.

- also() and apply() ignore the result of the lambda and, instead, return the context object to their callers.

- run() and apply() run the lambda in the execution context—this—of the context object on which they are called.

Let that sink in. Don't try to memorize these, it will fall in place with practice. The key is to understand that there are differences in the receiver and what is returned from these methods.

From a Verbose and Noisy Code

We'll now use these four methods to make a piece of code fluent. For this purpose, we start by defining a Mailer class:

```
class Mailer {
  val details = StringBuilder()
  fun from(addr: String) = details.append("from $addr...\n")
  fun to(addr: String) = details.append("to $addr...\n")
  fun subject(line: String) = details.append("subject $line...\n")
  fun body(message: String) = details.append("body $message...\n")
  fun send() = "...sending...\n$details"
}
```

The fluency of code to interact with the methods of the class is the focus here, thus the class doesn't do anything useful other than registering the calls into a StringBuilder.

Here's a rather verbose example of using this Mailer class.

```
val mailer = Mailer()
mailer.from("builder@agiledeveloper.com")
mailer.to("venkats@agiledeveloper.com")
mailer.subject("Your code sucks")
mailer.body("...details...")
val result = mailer.send()
println(result)
```

Before we discuss the quality of the code, let's make sure it works:

```
...sending...
from builder@agiledeveloper.com...
to venkats@agiledeveloper.com...
subject Your code sucks...
body ...details......
```

The code worked, but the calls to the methods on Mailer were noisy, repetitive, and not very pleasant. This is where the four convenience methods we discussed come into play.

Removing Repetitive References with apply

Refer back to the output table from the example in Behavior of the Four Methods, on page 237; the apply() method executes the lambda in the context of the object on which it's called and returns the context object back to the caller. The apply() method can form a chain of method calls, like so: obj.apply{...}.apply{...}...

Let's rewrite the previous code that uses Mailer to use apply():

```
val mailer =
  Mailer()
    .apply { from("builder@agiledeveloper.com") }
    .apply { to("venkats@agiledeveloper.com") }
    .apply { subject("Your code sucks") }
    .apply { body("details") }

val result = mailer.send()

println(result)
```

None of the methods of Mailer return back the Mailer instance on which they were called. That means we can't combine multiple calls to Mailer methods. The apply() solves that issue nicely. With each call to apply(), we start with a Mailer and end with the same instance. This allows us to chain—that is, continue making multiple calls on a Mailer instance—without repeating the reference name. The good news is less repetition of the reference, but the code is now noisy with all these apply {... calls.

The apply() method executes the lambda in the context of its target object. As a result we may place multiple calls to Mailer within the lambda, like so:

```
val mailer = Mailer().apply {
    from("builder@agiledeveloper.com")
    to("venkats@agiledeveloper.com")
    subject("Your code sucks")
    body("details")
}
val result = mailer.send()

println(result)
```

Without changing the Mailer class, the user of the Mailer is able to make multiple calls on an instance without repeatedly using the reference dot notation. That reduces the noise significantly in code. Also, a builder-pattern like expressions can be used for any class, even those that were not designed for chaining of calls to setters.

Getting Results Using run

In the previous example, we made multiple calls to methods of Mailer, but eventually we wanted to get the result of the send() method call. apply() is a great choice if we want to keep the Mailer reference at the end of the calls and do more work with the instance. But if we're after the result of a sequence of calls on an object and don't care for the instance, we may use run(). The run()

method returns the result of the lambda, unlike apply(); but just like apply(), it runs the lambda in the context of the target object.

Let's modify the code to use run() instead of apply():

```
val result = Mailer().run {
    from("builder@agiledeveloper.com")
    to("venkats@agiledeveloper.com")
    subject("Your code sucks")
    body("details")
    send()
}

println(result)
```

Each of the method calls within the lambda executed on the Mailer instance that was used as a target to run(). The result of the send() method, the String, is returned by the run() method to the caller. The Mailer instance on which run() was called isn't available anymore.

To keep the target object at the end of a sequence of calls, use apply(); to keep the result of the last expression within the lambda instead, use run(). In either case, use these methods only if you want to run the lambda in the context of the target.

Passing an Object as Argument Using let

Suppose you receive an instance from a function but want to pass that instance to another method as argument. That sequence of operation will break the flow of code, the fluency in general. The let() method will help restore the fluency in that case.

Let's look at an example to illustrate this point. Here are two functions—one that returns a Mailer object and one that takes that in as a parameter:

```
fun createMailer() = Mailer()

fun prepareAndSend(mailer: Mailer) = mailer.run {
    from("builder@agiledeveloper.com")
    to("venkats@agiledeveloper.com")
    subject("Your code suks")
    body("details")
    send()
  }
```

The internals of the createMailer() and prepareAndSend() aren't important for this discussion. Let's focus on the code that uses these two functions:

```
val mailer = createMailer()
val result = prepareAndSend(mailer)
println(result)
```

We first stored the result of createMailer() into a variable, then passed it to pre-pareAndSend() and stored that result into a variable named result for final printing. That's boring. Where's the flow? you protest.

Ignoring the println(), we could change the calls to the two functions like this:

```
val result = prepareAndSend(createMailer())
```

That'll work, but fluency is definitely missing there; it feels heavy with multiple parenthesis, like the regular code we write. We want to be able to take the result of one operation and perform the next step on it, to nicely compose one call to the next. Let the let() method lead us there.

```
val result = createMailer().let { mailer ->
  prepareAndSend(mailer)
}
```

On the output from createMailer() we call let() and pass a lambda expression to it. Within the lambda, the Mailer instance—that is, the target of let(), the result of createMailer()—is available as a parameter. We are then passing it to the pre-pareAndSend() function. Hmm, really, this is an improvement? That's a reasonable question, but this code is like a delicious meal being prepared—it's not fully baked yet.

We can make one teeny-tiny change, to get rid of that parameter name:

```
val result = createMailer().let {
  prepareAndSend(it)
}
```

A notch better, but... The lambda isn't doing much; it's taking a parameter and passing it to the prepareAndSend() method. Instead of using a lambda here, we may use a method reference—we saw this in Using Function References, on page 183.

```
val result = createMailer().let(::prepareAndSend)
```

Now that's a lot better. The result of createMailer() is passed to let(), which then passes that to the prepareAndSend() method, and whatever that function returns, let() hands it back to us.

If you want to use the result of the lambda we passed to let() as argument, then the method let() is a good choice. But to continue doing some work with the target on which let() was called, also() is the method you're looking for.

Chaining void Functions Using also

The also() method is useful to chain a series of void functions that otherwise don't fall into a call chain.

Suppose we have a bunch of void functions—returning Unit in Kotlin—like these:

```kotlin
fun prepareMailer(mailer: Mailer):Unit {
  mailer.run {
    from("builder@agiledeveloper.com")
    to("venkats@agiledeveloper.com")
    subject("Your code suks")
    body("details")
  }
}

fun sendMail(mailer: Mailer): Unit {
  mailer.send()
  println("Mail sent")
}
```

Using the createMailer() function we saw earlier, we can create a Mailer instance and then pass it to a series of functions that don't return anything. But that won't have a good flow:

```kotlin
val mailer = createMailer()
prepareMailer(mailer)
sendMail(mailer)
```

We can restore the chain of function calls using also() since also() passes the target to the lambda as a parameter, ignores the return from the lambda, and returns back the target of the call. Here's the fluent code to use these void functions:

```kotlin
createMailer()
  .also(::prepareMailer)
  .also(::sendMail)
```

By using these four functions, we can make the code we write each day a tad more fluent, not just pleasing to our eyes, but reducing the stress of reading the code as well.

Getting used to writing such fluent code takes some effort and practice.

Implicit Receivers

Unlike the let() and also() methods, the run() and apply() methods executed their lambdas in the context of their own target. What's cool about Kotlin is that the language and library implementors didn't keep that as a privileged execution for themselves. Instead, they made it accessible very elegantly to every one using the language. If you're eager to learn and execute such methods for your own code, the wait is over. And this technique is one of the most essential to create fluent syntax for DSLs, so it's all the more exciting.

Passing a Receiver

In JavaScript, functions may take zero or more parameters, but you may also pass a context object—a receiver—using either the call() method or apply() function. Kotlin's ability to tie a receiver to a lambda expression is heavily influenced by that JavaScript capability.

Before we dive into dealing with receivers, let's look at a regular lambda expression for a moment.

fluency/lambda.kts
```
var length = 100

val printIt: (Int) -> Unit = { n: Int ->
  println("n is $n, length is $length")
}

printIt(6)
```

In this code, printIt refers to a lambda, which receives an Int as its parameter and returns nothing. Within the lambda we print a property named length and the value of the parameter n. It's clear what n is, but where does length come from? The variable length isn't in the internal scope of the lambda. Thus, the compiler binds length to the variable in the lexical scope—that is, from above the lambda expression. Let's confirm that from the output:

```
n is 6, length is 100
```

Kotlin gives us a nice way to set a receiver for lambdas. To do this we have to change the signature of the lambda a little. Let's do that in the next example:

fluency/lambdareceiver.kts
```
var length = 100

val printIt: String.(Int) -> Unit = { n: Int ->
  println("n is $n, length is $length")
}
```

We still have the length property in the scope of the script. The only change in the definition of the lambda is in the parameter signature: String.(Int) -> Unit instead of (Int) -> Unit. The syntax String.(Int) says that the lambda will execute in the context of an instance of String. If you have more than one parameter for the lambda, for example, (Int, Double), then to say that the lambda will get a receiver during a call, write it as Type.(Int, Double), where Type is the type of the receiver. When resolving the scope of variables, the compiler will first look for the variable in the scope of the receiver, if present. If the receiver isn't present or if the variable isn't in the receiver, then the compiler looks for the variable in the lexical scope.

When calling a lambda that expects a receiver, we need to pass an additional argument—that is, the context or the receiver that will be bound to this inside the lambda. Here's one way, though not the most elegant way, to achieve that goal:

fluency/lambdareceiver.kts
```
printIt("Hello", 6)
```

The receiver is passed in as the first argument, and the actual parameters of the lambda follow that. That'll work, but it's not the preferred syntax in Kotlin. That's like, in JavaScript, doing func.call(context, value) instead of context.func(value). You can invoke the lambda like it's a member function, a method, of the receiver, like so:

```
"Hello".printIt(6)
```

That's wicked cool.

The lambda acts like it's an extension function for the receiver. In fact, that's exactly what Kotlin did. It treated the lambda as an extension function of the receiver.

Whether we pass the receiver as a parameter (and risk being chided as boring) or use it as a target of the call, the this within the lambda now refers to the receiver passed instead of the lexical this. As a result, the access to property length will be the length of the target receiver "Hello" and not the length property defined above the lambda. Let's verify this by running the modified version of the lambda with the receiver.

```
n is 6, length is 5
```

The output shows the length of the receiver String and not the value from the lexical scope. The receiver may be an object of any type, not only a String. We'll exploit this feature when building DSLs in the next chapter.

Multiple Scopes with Receivers

Lambda expressions may be nested within other lambda expressions. In this case, the inner lambda expression may appear to have multiple receivers: its direct receiver and the receiver of its parent. If the parent itself were nested into another lambda expression, then the innermost lambda expression may appear to have three or more receivers. In reality, a lambda has only one receiver but may have multiple scopes for binding to variables, depending on the levels of nesting. This concept of perceived multiple receivers for lambdas is much like the use of receivers we saw for extension functions defined within classes in Injecting from within a Class, on page 232, and the receivers of an inner class that we looked at in Nested and Inner Classes, on page 138. In both of those cases, we were able to refer to the outer receiver using the syntax this@OuterClassName. In the case of lambda expressions, though, the outer is a function instead of a class. Thus, we can use the syntax this@Outer-FunctionName to refer to the outer scope. Let's examine this with an example.

We'll define two functions, top() and nested(), that will receive a parameter that's a lambda expression with a receiver. Each of the functions will invoke the lambda expressions provided to them, in the context of a target or receiver object. We'll then examine the receivers by nesting the calls.

```kotlin
fluency/multiplereceivers.kts
fun top(func: String.() -> Unit) = "hello".func()

fun nested(func: Int.() -> Unit) = (-2).func()

top {
  println("In outer lambda $this and $length")

  nested {
    println("in inner lambda $this and ${toDouble()}")
    println("from inner through receiver of outer: ${length}")
    println("from inner to outer receiver ${this@top}")
  }
}
```

The top() function invokes the lambda expression provided with an arbitrary String instance "hello" as the receiver. The nested() function does the same for its parameter with an arbitrary Int value of -2. In the call to the top() function, we pass a lambda expression that prints its receiver, this, and the length property of the receiver. That will be the String "hello" and the length of 5. Then, within that lambda expression we're calling the nested() function, again providing a lambda expression to it.

Within this nested lambda expression we print its receiver, also referenced using this and the result of call to the toDouble() method. Since the nested() function is using Int -2 as the receiver, this here refers to the Int, and toDouble() is invoked on the Int. In the next line, when we read the length property, since Int doesn't have that property, the call is quietly routed to the receiver of the parent—that is, the nesting, lambda expression. In the event of a property collision between the inner receiver and the parent's receiver or if you want to explicitly refer to the receiver of the parent, we can use the @ syntax like in the last line: this@top.

Work through the example by hand and then compare the output from your understanding to the output from execution of the following code:

```
In outer lambda hello and 5
in inner lambda -2 and -2.0
from inner through receiver of outer: 5
from inner to outer receiver hello
```

The ability to access both the inner or closest receiver and the outer or parent receiver is powerful and is consistent when working with inner classes, method extensions, and lambdas with receivers.

Wrapping Up

Fluency can make or break a language. The flexibility Kotlin provides to create fluent code is one of the reasons why programmers love the language. By using the highly contentious feature of operator overloading cautiously, we can provide concise operators for user-defined classes where it makes sense. With the ability to use extension functions, properties, and operators, we can add our own convenience members to third-party classes to make code more intuitive to use. This is possible even when those classes aren't open for inheritance. The infix notation removes the noise of dot and parenthesis. Along with implicit receivers on lambdas, these features greatly influence the power of creating internal DSLs in Kotlin.

You'll see the fluency of Kotlin shine and many of the features in this chapter come to life when you learn to create internal DSLs in the next chapter.

CHAPTER 13

Creating Internal DSLs

As humans we don't communicate the same way all the time. Sometimes we're formal, sometimes we use slang, and at times all we do is nod or grunt. And we vary between these and other forms throughout the day, depending on the situation, what we're communicating, and with whom. Programming applications is similar—we communicate with the system and fellow programmers who end up maintaining the code.

Sometimes we need the rigor and full power of general purpose programming languages. At other times we're better with highly specialized, small, and effective languages called domain-specific languages or DSLs—for a thorough discussion of DSLs see the book *Domain-Specific Languages [Fow10]*. DSLs can't be used to program an entire application, but many of them may be used in different parts of a software system.

As programmers we use a number of DSLs each day, sometimes without realizing or thinking about them as DSLs: CSS, Regular Expressions, XML configuration files, Gradle or Rake build files, React JSX, and so on. When designed well, DSLs can make programmers productive, reducing time and effort to implement parts of an application. They may also help reduce errors, while giving programmers greater flexibility.

This chapter is not about using DSLs, but how to design them so the users of your libraries can enjoy the benefits of the DSLs you create. DSLs are easy to use, but the effort to design and implement them is anything but easy, in general. A good language can alleviate some of that pain, and we'll learn how Kotlin helps.

Even when a language is flexible, we must be willing to push the boundaries to breathe fluency and ease into the mini language we're designing. "All is fair in love and war" and when creating DSLs—to achieve a certain syntax we must be willing to experiment, improvise, and adapt to different styles. That's part of what we'll explore here.

We'll start with a quick discussion about types of DSLs and their essential characteristics. Then we'll review the facilities in Kotlin that make it a suitable language to design DSLs. After that we'll look at a number of small DSLs and explore how to design and implement each one of them. The techniques you learn here will help you to create and maintain your own DSLs and also to design your APIs for more fluent use in Kotlin.

Types and Characteristics of DSLs

We'll first look at the types of DSLs and then discuss their main characteristics. Knowing these will help you make a right choice, both for the type of DSL and for the language to program them.

External vs. Internal DSLs

When designing, you have to choose between an external or an internal DSL.

You enjoy greater freedom if you opt to create an external DSL, but you're responsible for creating the parser to parse and process the DSL. That can be a lot of effort, and you have to balance that against the flexibility you get.

You design an internal or embedded DSL within the confines of a host language. The language's compilers and tools serve as the parser. The good news is you don't expend any effort to parse. However, to achieve fluency and implement certain features, you have to be very creative and apply some tricks to make that possible in the host language.

Some examples of external DSLs are CSS, the ANT build file, the good old Make build file, and so on. On the other hand, the Rake build file and the Gradle build file are good examples of internal DSLs.

In this chapter, we focus on building internal DSLs with Kotlin as the host language.

Context-Driven and Fluent

DSLs are context-driven and highly fluent. Context reduces noise in communication, it makes it succinct, concise, and expressive. It's like a smile and eye contact between friends to acknowledge hearing a favorite song. No words are spoken, but yet there's communication because they share a common context. Fluency also reduces noise and at the same time makes it easy to express ideas.

Context also can reduce possibility of errors. The same things may have different meanings in different contexts. With an implicit context, the semantics of the vocabulary falls in place, within reasonable bounds.

The fluency in Kotlin favors concise and expressive syntax. Context may be managed through parameters and receivers in Kotlin. And Kotlin also has facilities to narrow the context down further to minimize errors, as we'll see soon.

Kotlin for Internal DSLs

Kotlin is a wonderful language for creating internal DSLs. Static typing generally poses some strong limitations on a language's ability to serve as a host for internal DSLs. Surprisingly, though, some of Kotlin's unique capabilities not found in other statically typed languages push the limits to make creating internal DSLs not only possible but a pleasant experience as well. Let's quickly review some of the capabilities of Kotlin that will serve as your allies when designing DSLs.

Optional Semicolon

Kotlin doesn't insist on semicolons—see Semicolon Is Optional, on page 20. That's a clear benefit for fluency. A semicolon disrupts flow and is noise in a lot of situations. Not having to use it is especially critical for creating expressive DSL syntax.

We can compare two expressions:

```
starts.at(14.30)
ends.by(15.20)
```

The first is less noisy than this one:

```
starts.at(14.30);
ends.by(15.20);
```

That ; adds little value other than giving false comfort. Letting go of semicolons is a good first step in creating DSLs. Is it really that big a deal? one may wonder. It's a small step, but when we mix this feature with other capabilities, the difference is huge. We don't have to look far; the Kotlin feature we'll see next illustrates that sentiment.

No Dot and Parenthesis with infix

Kotlins' support for infix notation using the infix keyword—Function Fluency with infix, on page 235—is another welcome feature for DSLs. Have a look at the following code:

```
starts.at(14.30)
ends.by(15.20)
```

Using infix, we can write it as this:

```
starts at 14.30
ends by 15.20
```

The lack of dot and parenthesis, along with the absence of semicolon, makes the code almost read like English. If you're eager to see how to design for code like this, we'll cover it later in the chapter.

Get Domain Specific Using Extension Functions

Even though Kotlin is statically typed, it permits the ability to perform compile-time function injection—see Injecting Using Extension Functions and Properties, on page 226. As a result, you may design the ability for users of your library to code like the following, by injecting functions like days() into Int. Even though Int doesn't have a days() function built-in, once we inject that function into Int, we can write:

```
2.days(ago)
```

Additionally, extension functions may also be annotated with the infix keyword and then, instead of our previous example, one may write:

```
2 days ago
```

The fluency we can get for little effort in Kotlin is amazing. It's perfectly OK to take a minute to wipe away tears of joy before continuing on.

No Parenthesis Required to Pass Lambda

If the type of the last parameter of a function is a lambda expression, then you may place the lambda expression argument outside the parenthesis—see Use Lambda as the Last Parameter, on page 182. As a bonus, if a function takes only one lambda expression as its argument, then there's no need for parenthesis in the call. If the function is associated with a class, then the dot and parenthesis may be removed by using the infix keyword.

Thus, we could have written this:

```
"Release Planning".meeting({
  starts.at(14.30);
  ends.by(15.20);
})
```

But we can achieve the following fluency with Kotlin's capabilities:

```
"Release Planning" meeting {
  starts at 14.30
  ends by 15.20
}
```

That fluency lifts a heavy weight from our shoulders.

Implicit Receiver Rocks DSL Creation

One of the most significant feature of Kotlin for designing DSLs is the ability to pass implicit receivers to lambda expressions—see Implicit Receivers, on page 243. This feature singlehandedly sets Kotlin apart from other statically typed languages for the ability to attain fluency in DSLs. And the receivers are a great way to pass a context object between layers of code in DSL.

Here's a little DSL to place an order for some office supplies:

```
placeOrder {
  an item "Pencil"
  an item "Eraser"

  complete {
    this with creditcard number "1234-5678-1234-5678"
  }
}
```

In this code, there's a context of an order and a context of a payment, but the code may need both to perform the payment transaction. That's not an issue thanks to implicit receivers.

In the execution of each lambda expression, there's an implicit receiver that carries the context—a thread of conversation—forward. This makes it easy to carry the state forward for processing between the layers of code without the need to pass parameters or maintain global state. That's a breath of fresh air.

A Few More Features to Aid DSLs

We discussed some of the major features of Kotlin that influence the design of internal DSLs. When designing DSLs, you may occasionally find useful a few other minor capabilities.

The methods in the Any class that promote fluency, also(), apply(), let(), and run()—in Behavior of the Four Methods, on page 237—will serve well to invoke lambdas and to set implicit receivers. These methods can reduce the code we need to implement the DSL.

Kotlin uses this to refer to the current object and it to refer to the single parameter of a lambda expression. If you're struggling to make the syntax fluent, sometimes, you may reach for these keywords and put them to work in your favor, like in this example:

```
please add it to this cart now
```

You may also reluctantly use operator overloading in some situations, but only where it's highly intuitive and makes the DSL very fluent—don't use it otherwise; see the caution expressed in Overloading Operators, on page 222.

Challenges in Building for Fluency

Building fluency into code takes some effort. Explore if an extension function will be useful. Sometimes an infix method may help remove some clutter in code—to get rid of the dot and parenthesis. Maybe an implicit receiver will come to the rescue. You can choose from a number of techniques, and sometimes they may appear to conflict with one another. Let's look at an example of this situation.

To use the infix notation, so you can remove the dot and parenthesis, you need an object reference. For instance, a person reference is needed to use infix notation to make the following fluent: person run "fast". But by using an implicit reference to the instance of this hypothetical Person class, we can get rid of the object reference in the call and write only run("fast"). Wait, it appears that we can either get rid of the dot along with parenthesis or we can dismiss the object reference, but not both. One work-around would be to use this instead of person since the implicit reference can be explicitly referenced using this. But writing this run "fast" doesn't appeal to my fluency-demanding pallet. What gives?

It's easy to get discouraged when we run into conflicts like this. But by stepping back to the basics, we can think through ways to arrive at a working solution. Let's devise a solution: to create a fluent syntax without dots, parenthesis, and this.

Using Extension Functions

Suppose we're creating an application that will keep track of events and dates. Maybe we want to mention that some event happened 2 days ago and another event will happen maybe 3 days from_now. With some extension functions, we can make the words roll off our tongues and emerge as code—Kotlin code, that is.

We'll start with the code to extend the Int class with a days() method to facilitate the fluent domain-specific method call:

dsl/DateUtil.kt
```
package datedsl

import java.util.Calendar
import datedsl.DateUtil.Tense.*

infix fun Int.days(timing: DateUtil.Tense) = DateUtil(this, timing)
```

The newly injected days() method takes the yet-to-be-written DateUtil.Tense enum and returns an instance of the DateUtil class, also yet to be written. The import statement brings in the values of the enum into the scope for easy use with the when argument matching we'll use soon.

The DateUtil class will take the number, the Int instance on which days() was called, and the given enum and take the necessary steps to return the appropriate date for the hypothetical event. Let's take a look at the DateUtil class now.

dsl/DateUtil.kt
```
class DateUtil(val number: Int, val tense: Tense) {
  enum class Tense {
    ago, from_now
  }

  override fun toString(): String {
    val today = Calendar.getInstance()

    when (tense) {
      ago -> today.add(Calendar.DAY_OF_MONTH, -number)
      from_now -> today.add(Calendar.DAY_OF_MONTH, number)
    }

    return today.getTime().toString()
  }
}
```

The DateUtil class is nesting the enum Tense and storing the constructor parameters as immutable properties. The toString() method takes different actions for different values of the tense variable and returns the appropriate instance of time.

The easy part is exercising this code to use the domain-specific method we added to Int. Let's take a look:

```
dsl/usedatedsl.kts
import datedsl.*
import datedsl.DateUtil.Tense.*

println(2 days ago)
println(3 days from_now)
```

To run this script, we first have to compile the DateUtil class.

```
$ kotlinc-jvm DateUtil.kt -d datedsl.jar
$ kotlinc-jvm -classpath datedsl.jar -script usedatedsl.kts
```

Depending on when you run it, you'll see an output similar to the following:

```
Sun Aug 11 05:11:38 MDT 2019
Fri Aug 16 05:11:38 MDT 2019
```

Using Receiver and infix

In the previous example, the extension function did the trick, but things aren't that simple most of the time. Let's take a look at a DSL that's going to demand a lot more.

Our daily lives are filled with meetings and there seems to be no escape. Might as well make scheduling the next one a tad easier, right? Let's design a fluent syntax to make that happen:

```
dsl/meetingdsl.kts
"Release Planning" meeting {
  start at 14.30
  end by 15.20
}
```

Let's take small steps to achieve this goal. Ignore what's inside the lambda for now and focus only on the "Release Planning" meeting {} part. What do we need to make this work? Two things.

First, we need to inject a meeting() method into the String class—an extension function. Second, we need to make meeting() an infix method so we can drop the dot. The parenthesis is not an issue since the parameter is the last lambda, the only lambda.

Let's get this small part working first:

```
infix fun String.meeting(block: () -> Unit) {
  println("step 1 accomplished")
}

"Release Planning" meeting {}
```

The meeting() extension function will be called when the DSL is executed. It'll print that message we placed, and Kotlin will warn that we're not using the block variable—all good so far.

Within the lambda, we want to update the state—the details about the meeting timings. For this we may use a Meeting class that'll be the holder of the details, the state. Since the lambda will populate the state for an instance of Meeting, we might as well run it in the context of the instance. To accomplish this, we should change the lambda's signature. Let's take that next small step.

```kotlin
class Meeting

infix fun String.meeting(block: Meeting.() -> Unit) {
  val meeting = Meeting()

  meeting.block()

  println(meeting)
}

"Release Planning" meeting  {
  println("With in lambda: $this")
}
```

We have a Meeting class, but it's not much yet. The block parameter of String.meeting() now expects a receiver of type Meeting. Within the String.meeting() method we create an instance of Meeting, run the lambda in the context of that instance, and print the instance.

```
With in lambda: Meetingdsl2$Meeting@1a2e563e
Meetingdsl2$Meeting@1a2e563e
```

The output shows that the same instance created within String.meeting() is also seen as this, the receiver, inside the lambda expression.

Next step, let's create at and by methods in the Meeting class and run them both from within the lambda. That's going to grow out Meeting class from its infancy. While at it, let's also add a constructor parameter to the Meeting class to store the meeting title:

```kotlin
class Meeting(val title: String) {
  var startTime: String = ""
  var endTime: String = ""

  private fun convertToString(time: Double) = String.format("%.02f", time)
  fun at(time: Double) { startTime = convertToString(time) }
  fun by(time: Double) { endTime = convertToString(time) }

  override fun toString() = "$title Meeting starts $startTime ends $endTime"
}
```

```kotlin
infix fun String.meeting(block: Meeting.() -> Unit) {
  val meeting = Meeting(this)

  meeting.block()

  println(meeting)
}
"Release Planning" meeting  {
  at(14.30)
  by(15.20)
}
```

The at() method stores the given Double value into a property startTime after converting to a String. Likewise, the by() method stores the endTime. The toString() method reports the state of the Meeting object. The String.meeting() method is using the constructor of Meeting.

The output shows that the code is doing what's expected—the at() and by() methods are invoked in the context of a Meeting instance:

```
Release Planning Meeting starts 14.30 ends 15.20
```

We're left with good news and bad news. The good news is it worked. The bad news—the DSL is far from where we want it to be. What does at and by mean? That's not readable at all. Also, why that parenthesis? Let's first get rid of that parenthesis. For that, as you know, we'll use infix.

```kotlin
infix fun at(time: Double) { startTime = convertToString(time) }
infix fun by(time: Double) { endTime = convertToString(time) }
```

The only change we made to the Meeting class is placing the infix keyword twice, once for at() and once for by(). Now can we drop the parenthesis from the DSL? Not so fast. While infix is great, it comes with some severe limitations. To use it, you need an instance on which the method will be called, followed by a space, then the name of the method, another space, and then finally a single argument. Sadly, we can't write at 14.30 and expect that to work; an instance reference is needed before at. Let's compromise: we'll use this for the object reference, but only for a few moments.

```kotlin
"Release Planning" meeting  {
  this at 14.30
  this by 15.20
}
```

We're almost there—all we have to do is replace this with start on one line and with end on the other line. For the change to the first line, we can define start as a variable that is bound to this. That'll do the trick.

Within the lambda the receiver is implicit. We know that at(14.30) was actually this.at(14.30). If we write start at 14.30, will Kotlin see it as start.at(14.30) and then as this.start.at(14.30) and be happy to compile and produce the desired result? Let's find out right away—we're running short on nails.

dsl/meetingdsl.kts

```kotlin
class Meeting(val title: String) {
  var startTime: String = ""
  var endTime: String = ""
  val start = this
  val end = this

  private fun convertToString(time: Double) = String.format("%.02f", time)
  infix fun at(time: Double) { startTime = convertToString(time) }
  infix fun by(time: Double) { endTime = convertToString(time) }

  override fun toString() = "$title Meeting starts $startTime ends $endTime"
}

infix fun String.meeting(block: Meeting.() -> Unit) {
  val meeting = Meeting(this)

  meeting.block()

  println(meeting)
}

"Release Planning" meeting  {
  start at 14.30
  end by 15.20
}
```

That's the complete code to make the DSL work. The only changes we did in this last step are: (1) we added two properties start and end to the Meeting class, and (2) we replaced this within the DSL with start and end on the last two lines, respectively.

We achieved fluency, but there's a catch in this implementation—it doesn't prevent the users of our DSL from calling start by instead of start at, and end at instead of end by. As well, after typing start or end, the autocompletion feature of IDEs will show both at and by, thus misleading the user. This is because both start and end are properties that return the same instance and both at and by are methods on Meeting. We can prevent this potential error by moving the at and by methods to separate classes, like so:

dsl/meetingdslevolved.kts

```kotlin
open class MeetingTime(var time: String = "") {
  protected fun convertToString(time: Double) = String.format("%.02f", time)
}

class StartTime : MeetingTime() {
  infix fun at(theTime: Double) { time = convertToString(theTime) }
}
```

```kotlin
class EndTime : MeetingTime() {
  infix fun by(theTime: Double) { time = convertToString(theTime) }
}

class Meeting(val title: String) {
  val start = StartTime()
  val end = EndTime()

  override fun toString() =
    "$title Meeting starts ${start.time} ends ${end.time}"
}

infix fun String.meeting(block: Meeting.() -> Unit) {
  val meeting = Meeting(this)

  meeting.block()

  println(meeting)
}

"Release Planning" meeting  {
  start at 14.30
  end by 15.20
}
```

The MeetingTime class serves as a base class, holds a time property of type String, and contains the convertToString() function that'll be used by its derived classes. The StartTime class extends MeetingTime and contains the at() method. Likewise, the EndTime class is similar to StartTime, except it contains the by() method. Since the start time and end time are now stored in the classes StartTime and EndTime, respectively, the Meeting class doesn't need these two fields. The start property of Meeting now returns an instance of StartTime instead of this. Likewise, the end property returns an instance of EndTime.

That took some effort and trickery to get the fluent syntax working. Let's shoot for something a bit more intense next and, along the way, you can learn about the type safety Kotlin provides for internal DSLs.

Type-Safe Builders

A key benefit of using a statically typed language is verifying the soundness of code at compile time. Anytime we deviate from the syntax permitted by the language, the compiler will let us know in no uncertain terms. This prevents a variety of errors from slipping to runtime and thus saves time. When working with DSLs, however, we're inventing the syntax that's permitted. The compiler doesn't have enough details to discern if a particular property access or a method call is legitimate when used within the DSL. This is where type-safe builders come in. Using a special annotation, you can instruct the compiler to keep an eye on the scope of properties and methods. Let's explore that with a built-in example in Kotlin and then by creating our own custom builder.

HTML Builder

My wife says that I'm really good at typing…backspaces. If your typing skills are like mine, you'll appreciate finding errors sooner than later. Fail fast is a virtue, and compile-time failures can save hours of runtime debugging. We enjoy good compiler support for code we write in languages like Java and Kotlin, but what about creating HTML?

Looking at the built-in type-safe HTML builder in Kotlin is a good way to learn how type safety can be provided with DSLs in general and when working with HTML in particular. Play with the HTML builder at the online try-Kotlin site.[1]

You may create an HTML content like this:

```
<html>
  <h1>Methods' Behavior<h1>
  <p>This is a sample</p>
</html>
```

Unless you were highly observant when reading the above HTML content, you may not have noticed that there's an error in there. More complex HTML content makes finding mistakes extremely hard. Asking someone to debug, just to find a silly mistake that caused the browser to display content poorly, is time consuming, costly for the organization, frustrating, embarrassing, and a disgrace to humanity.

An HTML builder can help in two ways. First, it can help us to write code instead of plain text that'll generate the HTML content. Second, it can verify, before generation, if the syntax is sound.

Visit the site specific for the Kotlin HTML builder[2] example and replace the entire main() method with the following code:

```
fun main() {
  val result =
    html {
      h1 { +"Methods' Behavior" }
      p { "This is a sample" }
    }

  println(result)
}
```

1.　https://try.kotlinlang.org
2.　https://try.kotlinlang.org/#/Examples/Longer%20examples/HTML%20Builder/HTML%20Builder.kt

Click on the Run button on the top right. The site reports two errors: it complains that h1 and p are unresolved references. The reason is that we placed these tags at the wrong level, outside of the body tag. Let's fix that with the following code:

```
fun main() {
  val result =
    html {
      body {
        h1 { +"Methods' Behavior" }
        p { "This is a sample" }
    }
    }

  println(result)
}
```

Again, replace the entire main() method on the site with the corrected code and click on the Run button. This time the code will execute successfully and produce an HTML output.

You saw type safety in action right there. Study the code example at that site to see how it was created, and then move forward. Also take a look at Kotlinx.html,[3] an alternative HTML builder that provides greater flexibility and error handling.

An XML Builder

Inspired by the HTML builder, let's build our own XML builder now.

First, let's look at the data for which we want to create an XML representation.

```
dsl/xmlbuilder.kts
val langsAndAuthors =
  mapOf("JavaScript" to "Eich", "Java" to "Gosling", "Ruby" to "Matz")
```

The Map contains a few language names and their authors. From this data we'll create the XML representation, with names of the languages as attributes and author names as text content. Let the fun begin.

Just like HTML, XML is a hierarchical structure of elements. We'll start with a root. At each level there may be zero or more attributes and multiple child elements. Let's define some vocabulary for our DSL: xml to get the DSL in motion, element to define an element, and attributes can go within the element declaration. We may use text to represent a text content for an element. With these we can create a sample of the DSL, like so:

---

3. https://github.com/Kotlin/kotlinx.html

dsl/xmlbuilder.kts
```
val xmlString = xml {
  root("languages") {
    langsAndAuthors.forEach { name, author ->
      element("language", "name" to name) {
        element("author") { text(author) }
      }
    }
  }
}

println(xmlString)
```

Now we need to build the classes and methods that will process this and similar pieces of code that use our DSL. The first line in the DSL is xml {...}—that looks easy to implement. We can design xml as a function that takes a lambda as its parameter. From within that function we can return an object of an XMLBuilder() that will take over the building of the XML document. In other words, xml() will serve as a bootstrap function. Here's the short and succinct xml() function:

dsl/xmlbuilder.kts
```
fun xml(block: XMLBuilder.() -> Node): Node = XMLBuilder().run(block)
```

The function creates an instance of a yet-to-be-implemented XMLBuilder class. The parameter to the xml() function is a block—a lambda—with a receiver of type XMLBuilder. Within the xml() function we invoke the block with the receiver as instance of XMLBuilder that we just created. That tells us that any methods or functions called within the block passed to the xml() function will run in the context of this receiver. The reason we used run() is that it executes the given block of code in the context of the receiver and returns the result of the block—we saw this in Fluency with Any Object, on page 236. Since the lambda parameter specifies the return type to be an instance of a Node class, the result of calling the xml() function is an instance of Node. We'll soon create both the XMLBuilder class and the Node class.

The first line of code within the lambda passed to the xml() function is a call to a root() function. Since the lambda runs in the context of the instance of XMLBuilder created within the xml() function, the XMLBuilder should have this method. Whatever the root() method returns, the xml() function will return. From the details we know so far, that has to be an instance of Node. Let's define the XMLBuilder class with the root() method:

dsl/xmlbuilder.kts
```
class XMLBuilder {
  fun root(rootElementName: String, block: Node.() -> Unit): Node =
    Node(rootElementName).apply(block)
}
```

The root() method takes two parameters: rootElementName of type String to receive the name of the root element—languages in this example—and block for a lambda that will run in the context of a Node instance as receiver. The lambda won't return anything, as indicated by Unit. The root() method creates an instance of Node, passing the rootElementName as an argument to the constructor, then runs the given block, the lambda, in the context of the Node instance just created. The reason we use apply() here instead of run() is we don't care to return anything from the block passed to apply(), we merely want to run the lambda in the context of the Node instance and return that Node instance.

Within the block passed to the root() method we iterate over the Map of languages and authors, langsAndAuthors, and for each name and author we create a nested element. This element, also an instance of Node, will reside within the Node created by the root() function—that is, the receiver to the block. To achieve this behavior we can make element() a method of Node. This method will create a child Node and insert it into the current Node as its child. Each instance of Node needs to keep a collection of attributes, a collection of children nodes, and a text value.

In short, the Node should have the three properties just mentioned and two methods: element() and text(). Oh, we also need a method to create a String representation of the Node, but with proper indentation. Here's the code for the Node:

dsl/xmlbuilder.kts
```kotlin
class Node(val name: String) {
  var attributes: Map<String, String> = mutableMapOf()
  var children: List<Node> = listOf()
  var textValue: String = ""

  fun text(value: String) { textValue = value }

  fun element(childName: String,
    vararg attributeValues: Pair<String, String>,
    block: Node.() -> Unit):Node {

    val child = Node(childName)
    attributeValues.forEach { child.attributes += it }
    children += child
    return child.apply(block)
  }

  fun toString(indentation: Int):String {
    val attributesValues = if (attributes.isEmpty()) "" else
      attributes.map { "${it.key}='${it.value}'" }.joinToString(" ", " ")

    val DEPTH = 2
    val indent = " ".repeat(indentation)

    return if (!textValue.isEmpty())
        "$indent<$name$attributesValues>$textValue</$name>"
```

```
        else
            """$indent<$name$attributesValues>
            |${children.joinToString("\n") { it.toString(indentation + DEPTH) }}
            |$indent</$name>""".trimMargin()
    }

    override fun toString() = toString(0)
}
```

Take some time to walk through the call to the xml() function and how each line will result in calls to create an instance of XMLBuilder first, and then instances of Node.

Let's run the code to see the output, the result of our XML building DSL code processed by the xml() function, and the Node class:

```
<languages>
  <language name='JavaScript'>
    <author>Eich</author>
  </language>
  <language name='Java'>
    <author>Gosling</author>
  </language>
  <language name='Ruby'>
    <author>Matz</author>
  </language>
</languages>
```

The most exciting feature of Kotlin used in this design is the lambdas with receiver, both in the xml() function and in the element() method. This allows the lambdas to execute in the context of an instance of Node, thus enabling the methods of Node to be called without using this. notation in the DSL.

Narrowing Access with Scope Control

You've seen how to create internal DSLs in Kotlin. Unlike external DSLs, internal DSLs have the benefit of riding on a host language, and we don't have to implement parsers. That removes a lot of effort on our part as DSL designers. However, anything that's possible in the host language, like property access or calls to arbitrary functions and methods in scope are all permitted within the DSL code. That freedom may be too much at times. Kotlin makes an effort to narrow that access a little with a scope control annotation.

In spite of the facility Kotlin offers, there's no way to tell the compiler to reject calls to a top-level function or an access to a variable that's in lexical scope. But, with a special @DSLMarker annotation, you can tell the compiler to disallow implicit access to the members within the parent receiver of a nested lambda.

We discussed in Multiple Scopes with Receivers, on page 245, how nested lambdas have two receivers, one that's the this context object of the executing lambda and the other that's the receiver of the parent lambda. When creating a DSL, we may want to limit a lambda to accessing only the immediate implicit receiver and disallow automatic access to the members of the parent receiver. Let's take a look at an example where placing that limitation will be useful.

Let's modify the code we created previously to create the XML output for languages and authors. Previously we nested a call to element() within another element() to create a child element. But what if we add a call to root() inside the lambda passed to element(), like so:

```kotlin
val xmlString = xml {
  root("languages") {
    langsAndAuthors.forEach { name, author ->
      element("language", "name" to name) {
        element("author") { text(author) }
        root("oops") {} //This makes no sense, but we get no errors
      }
    }
  }
}

println(xmlString)
```

The Kotlin compiler won't give any errors here because the second call to root() is legal. Whereas the second call to element() is on the Node instance, which is the implicit receiver this, the call to root is on the parent receiver; that is, the call to the second call root() is routed to the same instance that handled the first call to root().

Of course, that doesn't make sense, and you can ask Kotlin to reject that call. To do that, you have to annotate either the classes or the base classes that partake in building the DSL with a custom DSL Marker annotation. Such a custom annotation itself is annotated with a @DslMarker annotation.

Let's modify the code to reject the second call to root() from within the lambda passed to element().

First, create a DSL Marker annotation:

```kotlin
@DslMarker
annotation class XMLMarker
```

The annotation class XMLMarker is considered a DSL Marker annotation since it's annotated with @DslMarker. Any class annotated with a DSL Marker annotation—XMLMarker in this example—will signal to the Kotlin compiler to restrict calls without an object reference, such as calls without a someobj. prefix, to only the immediate receiver and not the parent receiver. In other words, without a DSL Marker annotation, a call like foo() will go to the parent receiver if it's not handled by the immediate receiver. However, with the marker annotation on the processing class, a call to foo() will fail compilation if it's not handled by the immediate receiver. Thus we can get early feedback from the compiler, to verify if the DSL conforms to the intended syntax.

Let's now make use of the DSL Marker annotation XMLMarker by annotating both the XMLBuilder and Node classes:

```kotlin
@XMLMarker
class XMLBuilder {
  fun root(rootElementName: String, block: Node.() -> Unit): Node =
    Node(rootElementName).apply(block)
}

@XMLMarker
class Node(val name: String) {
  var attributes: Map<String, String> = mutableMapOf()
//...
```

After creating the XMLMarker annotation and annotating the classes XMLBuilder and Node like above, the following code will fail compilation:

```kotlin
val xmlString = xml {
  root("languages") {
    langsAndAuthors.forEach { name, author ->
      element("language", "name" to name) {
        element("author") { text(author) }
        root("oops") {} //ERROR: can't call root from here
      }
    }
  }
}

println(xmlString)
```

You see that the automatic routing of calls to the parent receiver has been removed. You may still make an explicit call to members of the parent receiver if you like, for example, with this syntax:

```kotlin
this@xml.root("oops") {}
```

When designing DSLs, most certainly use DSL Marker annotations. While the annotation won't help reject calls to top-level methods or access to variables and members in lexical scope, it will help reject automatic calls to methods that are part of the parent receivers. This is a useful feature to control scope a little within DSLs.

Wrapping Up

The fluency and the power of Kotlin makes it a great language to create internal DSLs. And the ability to assign a context object for the execution of lambdas gives Kotlin a distinctive advantage as a host language for DSLs, compared to other statically typed languages. Designing a DSL with good fluency can be challenging, but with a good understanding of the various techniques to bring forward fluency and a good dose of patience, you can find your way to design for the fluency you desire.

Since it's a statically typed language, Kotlin offers type safety when it comes to using DSLs. This has the benefit of failing fast. Also, using DSL marker annotations, you can improve error checking by restricting fluent calls to immediate receiver objects, instead of automatically routing them to the parent receiver. You can use the techniques you've learned in this chapter to design your own DSLs and also to design your APIs in a way that's fluent for users.

In the next chapter, we'll see another highly expressive power of Kotlin—the optimization it provides for tail recursions.

CHAPTER 14

Programming Recursion and Memoization

Hands down, recursion is one of the coolest programming techniques. Once we're able to formulate a solution to a problem using solutions of subproblems, we can implement that using recursion. Recursion is intriguing, a bit enigmatic, but also highly expressive.

While recursion is very powerful, it unfortunately runs into runtime stack overflow for large-size problems, making it ineffective when it's much needed. A technique called tail call optimization can solve this problem, and Kotlin provides support for that.

Recursion plays a significant role in programming, but algorithms often memoize data to achieve significant performance improvements. Kotlin doesn't provide built-in support for memoization, but, using the techniques you've learned so far, you can build it quite easily with great fluency.

In this chapter, we'll explore the power of recursion, where it falls short, and how tail call optimization can address those issues. Then we'll look at techniques to memoize the results of function calls to improve performance, while keeping the elegance of recursion.

The Power and Perils of Recursion

Using recursion we can apply the divide and conquer technique: solve a problem by implementing solutions to its subproblems. For example, here's a piece of Kotlin code to perform one implementation of the *quick sort* algorithm:

```
recursion/quicksort.kts
fun sort(numbers: List<Int>): List<Int> =
  if (numbers.isEmpty())
    numbers
```

```
  else {
    val pivot = numbers.first()
    val tail = numbers.drop(1)
    val lessOrEqual = tail.filter { e -> e <= pivot }
    val larger = tail.filter { e -> e > pivot }

    sort(lessOrEqual) + pivot + sort(larger)
  }
println(sort(listOf(12, 5, 15, 12, 8, 19))) //[5, 8, 12, 12, 15, 19]
```

The sort() function splits the given input into two parts, sorts the two parts separately, and, finally, merges the two solutions to create the overall solution. Kotlin readily supports general recursion, but it requires the return type for recursive functions—no type inference available for these.

Recursion is highly expressive, though it takes a bit more effort to arrive at recursive solutions. Programmers in general, and beginners in particular, have trouble conceptualizing solutions recursively. But once it clicks, the joy is boundless. Let's look at some very simple recursive code:

recursion/recursive.kts
```
import java.math.BigInteger

fun factorialRec(n: Int): BigInteger =
  if (n <= 0) 1.toBigInteger() else n.toBigInteger() * factorialRec(n - 1)

println(factorialRec(5)) //120
```

The factorialRec() function returns 1 if the value given is zero or less. Otherwise it returns the product of the given input and a recursive call to itself.

The factorial may be implemented using an iterative solution as well, like so:

```
fun factorialIterative(n: Int) =
  (1..n).fold(BigInteger("1")) { product, e -> product * e.toBigInteger() }
```

The fold() function is much like the reduce() function we saw in Internal Iterators, on page 206, except it takes an initial value in addition to the lambda argument. While you could use iteration, the recursive solution will help gain recognition and acceptance among programming geeks. So, let's explore that option further.

For complex problems, the recursive solution, if possible, may be more elegant and expressive than iterative solutions. Sadly, recursion runs into an issue that iterative solutions don't suffer from: recursion grows the stack, and once it reaches dangerously large levels, the program may crash.

For example, here's the iterative solution for a large value:

```
println(factorialIterative(50000))
```

The code will have no trouble running. Now try the same with the recursive solution:

```
println(factorialRec(50000))
```

Though the recursive solution is elegant, it doesn't stand up to the challenge; the code fails at runtime when the input size is large.

```
java.lang.StackOverflowError
        at java.base/java.math.BigInteger.valueOf(BigInteger.java:1182)
        at Largerecursive.factorialRec(largerecursive.kts:4)
```

Sigh, these geek cults aren't so easy to infiltrate. We need to up our skills a notch. Let's see how tail call optimization can help.

Tail Call Optimization

Consider the code you write to be a procedure and the generated bytecode that will eventually run to be a process. The factorialIterative() function is an iterative procedure and is compiled into and will run as an iterative process—no surprise there. Likewise, factorialRec() is a recursive procedure and is compiled into, and run as, a recursive process, exactly what we'd expect there as well. However, the real gain, as explained in *Structure and Interpretation of Computer Programs [AS96]*, is when a recursive procedure can be compiled into an iterative process. This approach will bring the best of both worlds—the code can be expressed as recursion, but it can enjoy the runtime behavior of iterations. So, no stack overflow errors.

That's intriguing—compiling recursion into iteration—that's exactly what the tailrec annotation will instruct the Kotlin compiler to do. Let's rewrite the factorialRec() function to make use of that technique.

As a first step, we'll annotate the function with the tailrec keyword.

```
tailrec fun factorialRec(n: Int): BigInteger =
  if (n <= 0) 1.toBigInteger() else n.toBigInteger() * factorialRec(n - 1)
```

Good try, but that doesn't work—we need to take a few more steps.

```
120
recursivetail.kts:4:1: warning: a function is marked as tail-recursive
 but no tail calls are found
tailrec fun factorialRec(n: Int): BigInteger =
^
recursivetail.kts:5:56: warning: recursive call is not a tail call
  if (n <= 0) 1.toBigInteger() else n.toBigInteger() * factorialRec(n
- 1)
                                                       ^
```

Kotlin is too polite here and gives a warning, but remember to treat warnings as errors as discussed in Sensible Warnings, on page 24. If we try to run the function for large inputs, this version's fate will be the same as the older version of factorialRec(), a runtime error. Kotlin will optimize recursion to iteration only when the call is in tail position. Let's discuss that further.

Looking at the code n.toBigInteger() * factorialRec(n - 1), we may be tempted to think that factorialRec() is executed last, but it's the multiplication operation that kicks in before the function call returns. This operation waits for a call to factorialRec() to finish, thus increasing the stack size on each recursive call. A *tail call* is where the recursive call is truly the last operation in the function. Let's rewrite the function factorialRec() and rename it as factorial() along the way.

recursion/factorial.kts
```
import java.math.BigInteger

tailrec fun factorial(n: Int,
  result: BigInteger = 1.toBigInteger()): BigInteger =
    if (n <= 0) result else factorial(n - 1, result * n.toBigInteger())

println(factorial(5)) //120
```

Running this code produces the expected result, and there are no warnings. That tells us that the Kotlin compiler was happy to optimize the function into an iteration, quietly behind the scenes.

Exercise the function for a large input value:

```
println(factorial(50000)) //No worries
```

The code will run just fine and produce, as expected, a very large output.

The successful execution is a proof of optimization, but as a curious programmer you may want to explicitly see the effect rather than assume based on empirical results. That's fair—to see the optimization at work, let's create a Factorial class and place the recursive version and the tail recursive version of factorial into it:

recursion/Factorial.kt
```
import java.math.BigInteger

object Factorial {
  fun factorialRec(n: Int): BigInteger =
    if (n <= 0) 1.toBigInteger() else n.toBigInteger() * factorialRec(n - 1)

  tailrec fun factorial(n: Int,
    result: BigInteger = 1.toBigInteger()): BigInteger =
      if (n <= 0) result else factorial(n - 1, result * n.toBigInteger())
}
```

Now compile the code and view the generated bytecode using these commands:

```
$ kotlinc-jvm Factorial.kt
$ javap -c -p Factorial.class
```

An excerpt of the generated bytecode is shown here:

```
Compiled from "Factorial.kt"
public final class Factorial {
  public final java.math.BigInteger factorialRec(int);
    Code:
              ...
      38: invokevirtual #23
                // Method factorialRec:(I)Ljava/math/BigInteger;
              ...
      44: invokevirtual #27
                // Method java/math/BigInteger.multiply:(...)
      47: dup
      48: ldc           #29                 // String this.multiply(other)
              ...

  public final java.math.BigInteger factorial(int, java.math.BigInteger);
    Code:
              ...
       7: ifgt          14
      10: aload_2
      11: goto          76
              ...
      56: invokevirtual #27
                // Method java/math/BigInteger.multiply:(...)
              ...
      73: goto          0
      76: areturn
```

In the bytecode for factorialRec(), the bytecode instruction invokevirtual is used to recursively call factorialRec(), and then a call to multiply() on BigInteger follows. That shows that the recursive procedure has been compiled into a recursive process.

On the other hand, the bytecode for factorial() doesn't have any invokevirtual recursive calls. Instead, it has calls to ifgt and goto that jump around to different parts of the function. That's evidence that the recursive procedure was compiled to an iterative process—good job, Kotlin.

The tailrec optimization works only for recursions that can be expressed as tail recursion. To use tailrec, we had to rewrite factorialRec() as factorial() so the recursion would appear as the last expression that's evaluated. If the recursion is complex, that may not be easy or even possible.

Tail call optimization keeps the number of levels in the stack under control by converting the recursion to iteration. That has an impact on efficiency, but we can make execution faster by returning a stored value rather than repetitively calling functions. That's the solution we'll explore next.

Memoization

I invite you to work with me on a small math problem. Grab a paper and pencil. All set? OK, here we go. What's 321 + 174? Without a calculator on hand it's not something I can answer spontaneously, and if you need a moment to find the answer, that's perfectly normal.

Did you find it? If you wrote down 495 you got it without any errors. Good job.

Now, one more question. What's 321 + 174? Now, you answered that in a snap, didn't you? How did you get so fast so quickly?

It's ok to admit, you looked up the result from the previous computation. That's pretty smart; you wouldn't redundantly compute the expression that you evaluated only a moment ago. That's memoization when done in code—we don't want our programs to recompute functions that were executed already for the same input, provided the output will be the same no matter how many times we call for the same input. By using saved values we can avoid recomputation and make executions faster. A caveat, though—memoization may only be used for pure functions, which are functions with no side effects.

In dynamic programming, an algorithmic technique, the problem is solved recursively using solutions to subproblems, but in a way that the results of the subproblem are memoized and reused. This technique brings the computational complexity of problems from exponential to linear and results in huge performance gains while keeping the code expressive.

Kotlin doesn't directly support memoization, but we can build it with the tools you've learned so far. We'll implement memoization in two different ways in Kotlin: one like the solution provided in the Groovy language's library and one using Kotlin delegates.

Repetitive Computation

We'll consider two problems in this chapter to illustrate memoization, a simple one first and then something a bit more complicated.

The first problem, the Fibonacci number, has been beaten to death in programming examples. One reason, and why we'll use it here, is the problem is very simple, well understood, and we can keep our eyes on the solution without getting dragged into the complexity of a problem. Once we learn how to use memoization with this simple problem, we'll apply it to the rod-cutting problem, but we'll discuss that later.

Let's implement a simple recursion in Kotlin to find the Fibonacci number.

recursion/fib.kts
```
import kotlin.system.measureTimeMillis

fun fib(n: Int) : Long = when (n) {
  0, 1 -> 1L
  else -> fib(n - 1) + fib(n - 2)
}

println(measureTimeMillis { fib(40) }) //About 3 millisconds
println(measureTimeMillis { fib(45) }) //More than 4 seconds
```

The fib() function returns 1 if the value provided is less than 2. Otherwise, it computes the result by making two recursive calls.

Call to fib(4) will invoke fib(3) and fib(2). But, when fib(3) is evaluated, it again calls fib(2). For small values of n the code will run quickly. As n increases, the computation time will increase exponentially. For instance, for n equal to 40 the code took about 3 milliseconds on my system. For 45 that jumped to well over 4 seconds. I don't dare to run it for n equals 100.

We can reduce the computation time significantly by memoizing the result of the call before returning it. Then on subsequent calls, if the value is already present, we can return it and save a slew of recursive calls.

Memoization, the Groovy Way in Kotlin

We have a few options to store the values of computations. We could create a class and put the cache of data in a field or property. Then the functions of the class can make use of the cache. That's a reasonable approach, but that would force us down the path of creating classes, which is fine if we already are heading in that direction. If we're dealing with standalone functions, we shouldn't be forced to create classes.

We need some dynamic behavior in code to handle memoization. When a function is called, we need to check the cache to see if the data exists and call the function only if it doesn't. This isn't possible with standalone functions, since the function call will bind to the function, and it's hard to replace that call dynamically to implement the conditional logic we discussed. We can work around this limitation by using lambda expressions—we'll soon see how we replace the call to lambda to include this check.

In the Groovy language, memoization is implemented as part of the library. You can call a memoize() function on any lambda expression and it will return a memoized lambda. We'll follow a similar approach here in Kotlin.

In Chapter 12, Fluency in Kotlin, on page 221, you learned to inject methods into classes and functions. That technique comes in handy here to create a memoize() method on a lambda expression.

recursion/fibmemoize.kts
```
fun <T, R> ((T) -> R).memoize(): ((T) -> R) {
  val original = this
  val cache = mutableMapOf<T, R>()

  return { n: T -> cache.getOrPut(n) { original(n) } }
}
```

In the first line we inject the memoize() method into a generic lambda expression that takes a parameter of the parametric type T and returns a result of the parametric type R. The memoize() function's return type is a lambda expression of the same type as the type of the method into which memoize() is injected. In other words, the result of calling memoize() on a function is a function with the same signature as the function.

Within the memoize() function, we save the reference to the original function by assigning this to a local variable original. Then we initialize an empty cache. Finally, we return a lambda expression that takes a parameter of type T and returns a result of type R. Within this returned function, we look up the cache, to see if the result already exists. If it doesn't exist, we compute the result, and store it before returning. If the result already exists, we skip the computation and return the stored value.

Let's use the memoize() function to memoize the computation of the Fibonacci number.

recursion/fibmemoize.kts
```
lateinit var fib: (Int) -> Long

fib = { n: Int ->
  when (n) {
    0, 1 -> 1L
    else -> fib(n - 1) + fib(n - 2)
  }
}.memoize()
```

We wrote the function as a lambda expression instead of a regular function. Since we're calling fib() within the lambda expression, we can't declare the variable fib in the same expression where we create the lambda expression. By using lateinit we're telling Kotlin that we've not forgotten to initialize the fib variable, and we plan to get to that momentarily. Without lateinit, the Kotlin compiler will give an error for unassigned variable. The fib() function returns 1 if the value provided is less than 2. Otherwise, it computes the result by making two recursive calls.

The memoize() function took the given lambda expression, stored it into the original variable inside of the memoize() function, and returned a new lambda expression. That's what's stored in the fib variable now.

Let's use this version of code to exercise the memoized version.

```
recursion/fibmemoize.kts
println(measureTimeMillis { fib(40) })
println(measureTimeMillis { fib(45) })
println(measureTimeMillis { fib(500) })
```

Let's be brave—call the function for a large value of 500. Fire away to see how this performs:

```
0
0
1
```

Those are time in milliseconds. The computation, that took well over 4 seconds for the non-memoized version, took no observable time. The execution for 500 as input took about 1 millisecond.

The memoize() function we wrote here may be used for any function that takes one parameter. The solution has pros and cons. What's nice is we can call memoize() on a lambda expression and turn it into memoized version. Also, the memoization code is concise. However, we have to first define fib and then assign the lambda expression to it. If we define the variable on the same expression as the one defining the lambda, we'll get a compilation error; Kotlin complains that fib isn't defined at the time of use.

This solution worked and it's a reasonable solution to keep, but Kotlin also has delegates. If you're curious how this solution would change if we use delegates, the answer is waiting for you next.

Memoization as Delegate

In the previous section, the code fib = {...}.memoize() replaced the variable fib with the memoized lambda expression. But you saw Kotlin's facility to intercept access to properties and local variables in Delegating Variables and Properties, on page 162. We can use that approach by writing a delegate. Instead of var, we'll use val for fib; we're going to assign to it only once. Thus, we need only a getValue() method in the delegate—no need for setValue(). Let's create the delegate.

recursion/fibdelegate.kts
```
import kotlin.reflect.*

class Memoize<T, R>(val func: (T) -> R) {
  val cache = mutableMapOf<T, R>()

  operator fun getValue(thisRef: Any?, property: KProperty<*>) = { n: T ->
    cache.getOrPut(n) { func(n) } }
}
```

The delegate holds the cache internally, keeps the original function as a property func, and the getValue() function returns a lambda expression that dispatches the call to the original function only if the value isn't in the cache.

Conceptually this solution and the previous one are similar, but this solution will be applied very differently to the fib function than the previous solution. Let's apply the delegate when creating the fib function:

recursion/fibdelegate.kts
```
val fib: (Int) -> Long by Memoize {n: Int ->
  when (n) {
    0, 1 -> 1L
    else -> fib(n - 1) + fib(n - 2)
  }
}
```

The application of memoization is a lot cleaner with delegate. Even though we're still in the middle of initializing fib, the Kotlin compiler doesn't complain about accessing fib within the lambda here. The reason is that, internally, we're using the delegate to access the variable fib and not directly accessing it.

Let's exercise this version of fib() to confirm the performance is as good as the previous version.

recursion/fibdelegate.kts
```
println(measureTimeMillis { fib(40) })
println(measureTimeMillis { fib(45) })
println(measureTimeMillis { fib(500) })
```

Here's the time the code took, in milliseconds, for each call to fib():

```
0
0
1
```

We've seen two different ways to create memoization, and both the implementations are similar; but the delegate solution is more elegant than the function call solution, due to less effort to apply memoization. Next, let's use the delegate solution further to memoize another problem that will benefit from it.

Applying Memoization to Dynamic Programming

Dynamic programming is an algorithmic technique that uses memoization to make the execution of recursive calls highly efficient. By caching and reusing the results of a function call, dynamic programming eliminates repetitive recursive calls to functions. So computations that may have exponential time complexity may execute with linear time complexity, thanks to memoization.

In the previous section, we used memoization to compute the Fibonacci number and saw how the technique greatly reduced the computation time. Let's apply the Memoize delegate we created to solve a well-known problem in dynamic programming—the rod-cutting problem.

Unlike the Fibonacci number, where there's one number for a given position, a category of problems called *optimization problems* may have multiple possible solutions. A user may pick one among the possible solutions, but we have to explore the different solutions to facilitate that. Dynamic programming is often used to recursively explore the possible solutions for optimization problems. Let's explore how our solution in the previous section applies to the rod-cutting problem, which is an optimization problem.

Given prices for different lengths of a rod, the objective of the problem is to find the maximum revenue a seller can make for a given rod length by cutting it. For example, given the prices in dollars, 2, 4, 6, 7, 10, 17, 17, for lengths of 1, 2, ..., 7 units (inches or centimeters depending on the units of measure you use), find the maximum revenue for a length of 4 units. If the seller were to sell the rod of length 4 as is, the revenue will be $7. However, if cut into four, each of length 1 unit, the revenue will be $8. Likewise, if the seller cuts it into two equal parts, the revenue will be $8. Cutting into two pieces of length 1 and 3 units, incidentally, will yield the same revenue. Thus, there are three solutions, each yielding the same maximum revenue for length of 4 units. But if further cutting the sub-length of 3 units, for example, into smaller pieces may yield a better revenue, we should explore that as well. Thus, the problem nicely fits into a recursive solution, illustrated in the following pseudocode:

```
maxPrice(length) =
  max {
              maxPrice(1) + maxPrice(length - 1),
              maxPrice(2) + maxPrice(length - 2),
              ...,
              maxPrice(length - 1) + maxPrice(1),
              price[length]
  }
```

This is a maximum of maximum computation; that is, it takes the maximum price for each combination of cuts that total the length and finds the maximum among them.

This solution can benefit from memoization. The computation of maxPrice(3), for example, involves computing maxPrice(2) and maxPrice(1). And, in turn, computing maxPrice(2) again involves computing maxPrice(1). Memoization will remove such redundancies in computation. Let's turn the above pseudocode into Kotlin code. The Memoize delegate used in the following code is the one we created in the previous section.

```
recursion/cutrod.kts
val prices = mapOf(1 to 2, 2 to 4, 3 to 6, 4 to 7, 5 to 10, 6 to 17, 7 to 17)

val maxPrice: (Int) -> Int by Memoize { length: Int ->
  val priceAtLength = prices.getOrDefault(length, 0)

  (1 until length).fold(priceAtLength) { max, cutLength ->
    val cutPrice =  maxPrice(cutLength) + maxPrice(length - cutLength)

    Math.max(cutPrice, max)
  }
}

for (i in 1..7) {
  println("For length $i max price is ${maxPrice(i)}")
}
```

The prices variable holds an immutable map of lengths and prices. The advantage of holding the prices in a Map instead of a List is that price isn't required for every single length. For a given length we can look up the price using the length as a key in a Map instead of an index in a List. That gives more flexibility. The maxPrice variable refers to a lambda that takes an Int for length and returns the maximum price for that length, as Int. The delegate that intercepts the call to the maxPrice variable computes the maximum of maximum using the fold() method of IntRange. For every value cutLength in the range from 1 to one less than the given length, we pick either the previously computed maximum value or the price we can get by cutting the rod into two pieces of cutLength and length - cutLength, whichever is higher. The iteration of fold() starts with the price for the given length, uncut, as the initial value.

We exercise the maxPrice() function for lengths from 1 to 7 to find the maximum price for each length. The output from the code is here:

```
For length 1 max price is 2
For length 2 max price is 4
For length 3 max price is 6
For length 4 max price is 8
For length 5 max price is 10
```

```
For length 6 max price is 17
For length 7 max price is 19
```

The output reflects the maximum price, which is either the same or higher than the price the seller will get if the rod of any length were sold uncut.

We've seen how the algorithm breaks the solution into recursive calls to solving the subproblems. However, the recursive calls involve repetitive invocation of functions for the same input. By using memoization, we avoid these repetitive recursive calls, thus greatly reducing the computation complexity of the code.

Wrapping Up

The power of recursion is sadly not usable for large-sized problems due to potential stack overflow error. Kotlin provides tailrec to perform tail call optimization on specially written recursions. By converting the recursion into iteration under the hood, the language provides the capability for you to enjoy the power of recursion without suffering the consequences of stack overflow. And, even though the language doesn't directly provide a memoization function, using the features of the language, we can build the ability to elegantly memoize or cache results of computations. By using this approach, we can greatly reduce the computation time of programs that make use of the algorithmic technique called dynamic programming. We've seen how to implement memoization at the function level and also how to devise a delegate-based solution.

In this chapter we've seen the elegance of recursion and memoization. In the next part, we'll explore another charming technique that also has impact on performance and ease of programming—the relatively new innovation in Kotlin—coroutines.

Part V

Programming Asynchronous Applications

Coroutines, a more recent addition to the language, are one of the most exciting features of Kotlin. Coroutines are built on the powerful concept of continuations and form the foundation for concurrent and asynchronous programming. In this part, you'll learn about suspension points and how to alter the thread and sequence of execution of code. Then you'll readily apply the techniques you learn to create high-performant asynchronous applications.

CHAPTER 15

Exploring Coroutines

No one likes to wait for a response to questions like "What's the weather like today?" You fire off that request to your smart device and continue doing your chore; and when the response arrives you take that in and move forward. The code we write should also do the same—that is, be *non-blocking*, especially when calling tasks that may take some time to run. That's where coroutines come in.

Coroutines are new in Kotlin—they're part of the standard library starting with version 1.3, and they provide a great way to create concurrent non-blocking code. Coroutines go hand in hand with suspendible functions, the execution of which may be suspended and resumed. These features are built in Kotlin using continuations, which are data structures used to preserve the internal state of a function in order to continue the function call later on.

In this chapter we'll focus on the nuts and bolts of coroutines. You'll learn how to configure code to run sequentially or concurrently, understand the relationship between threads and coroutines, control the thread of execution, and debug coroutines.

We'll also take a peek under the hood at continuations, which provide the underpinnings for coroutines, and we'll apply the knowledge to create infinite sequences and iterators that yield unbounded collections of data. The concepts you learn in this chapter will provide the foundations necessary for asynchronous programming, which we'll dig into in the next chapter.

Coroutines and Concurrency

Some tasks have to be executed sequentially, some may be performed in parallel, and yet others may be done concurrently. Most people put on the underwear before putting on the pants, though the order may be in reverse—even then, superwoman and superman don't put them on at the same time. These two tasks are inherently sequential; don't attempt an alternative.

Sequential execution is clear; we perform one task to completion before beginning the next. But some confusion exists among programmers between parallel and concurrent execution. Understanding the difference between them is critical, as multithreading on a multi-core processor generally is parallel, while coroutines are generally used more often for concurrent execution rather than parallel execution.

Parallel vs. Concurrent

Let's understand the difference between parallel and concurrent using an example. Suppose longtime friends Sara and Priya meet for dinner, and Sara is curious about Priya's recent international trip. Priya can listen to Sara while munching on food, but she'll never speak with her mouth full, as you can see in the following figure.

In the left part of the figure, we see Priya eating and listening in parallel. But when it's her turn to speak, she takes a break from eating to talk about her travel experience. She's got several things to say, but doesn't want to let the pizza go cold, so her speaking is interleaved with her eating—that's concurrency. In general, we can eat and listen in parallel, but we eat and speak concurrently.

Coroutines as Cooperating Functions

Subroutines are more common than coroutines in general-purpose programming. Subroutines are functions that run to completion before returning to the caller. Another call to the same subroutine is as good as the first call; subroutines don't maintain any state between calls. Coroutines are also functions but behave differently than subroutines. Unlike subroutines, which have a single point of entry, coroutines have multiple points of entry. Additionally, coroutines may remember state between calls. And, a call to a coroutine can jump right into the middle of the coroutine, where it left off in a previous call. Because of all this, we can implement cooperating functions—that is, functions that work in tandem—where two functions can run concurrently, with the flow of execution switching between them, like in the example shown in the figure on page 287.

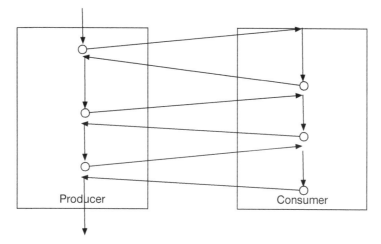

First, the Producer coroutine calls the Consumer coroutine. After executing part of its code, the Consumer saves its current state and returns or yields to the caller. The Producer performs some more steps and calls back into the Consumer. This time, however, instead of the call starting in the beginning, the call resumes from the point where the previous execution left off, with the state of the previous call restored. This appears to be magic, but let's take a closer look at one of the benefits of this capability to run coroutines as cooperating functions—the ability to run coroutines concurrently.

Running Concurrently Using Coroutines

In Kotlin coroutines are first-class citizens. They're built into the language, but the convenience functions to work with coroutines are part of a library. Coroutines offer some capabilities that aren't possible with subroutines. They're used in infinite sequences, event loops, and cooperating functions, for example. To learn about the benefits of coroutines, we'll start with an example that runs sequentially and then change the code to run concurrently with coroutines.

When executing code, you can decide if the code should run sequentially or if it should run concurrently, either within the context of the current execution or as a separate coroutine. Let's explore how we can configure these options.

Starting with Sequential Execution

Let's start with a piece of code that executes function calls sequentially—this will serve as a building block for introducing coroutines.

coroutines/sequential.kts
```
fun task1() {
  println("start task1 in Thread ${Thread.currentThread()}")
  println("end task1 in Thread ${Thread.currentThread()}")
}

fun task2() {
  println("start task2 in Thread ${Thread.currentThread()}")
  println("end task2 in Thread ${Thread.currentThread()}")
}

println("start")

run {
  task1()
  task2()

  println("called task1 and task2 from ${Thread.currentThread()}")
}

println("done")
```

Each of the two functions task1() and task2() print the details about their thread of execution upon entry and before exit. The run() function is an extension function of the Any class. We invoke run and pass a lambda expression as argument to it. Within the lambda we call the two functions and then print a message that we've invoked the functions.

Here's the output from the code:

```
start
start task1 in Thread Thread[main,5,main]
end task1 in Thread Thread[main,5,main]
start task2 in Thread Thread[main,5,main]
end task2 in Thread Thread[main,5,main]
called task1 and task2 from Thread[main,5,main]
done
```

The function calls are executing sequentially, like we expect common programs to do, with task1() completing, then task2() starting and then running to completion, and, finally, the last line within the lambda passed to run() executing. Nothing new there, but the code serves as a starting point for playing with coroutines.

Creating a Coroutine

In the previous example, the main thread executed sequentially the code within the lambda passed to run(). We'll change the program in such a way that the code in that lambda executes concurrently within a coroutine.

Before we look at the code, download the necessary coroutines extension library kotlinx-coroutines-core-1.2.2.jar file[1] and place it in an easily accessible location on your system. The library is available as a Maven package, and you may download it using Maven or Gradle, as well, instead of manually downloading it. On my machine, the library is located under the /opt/kotlin directory.

Let's change the previous code to run concurrently the code within the lambda:

```
coroutines/coroutine.kts
import kotlinx.coroutines.*

fun task1() {
  println("start task1 in Thread ${Thread.currentThread()}")
  println("end task1 in Thread ${Thread.currentThread()}")
}

fun task2() {
  println("start task2 in Thread ${Thread.currentThread()}")
  println("end task2 in Thread ${Thread.currentThread()}")
}

println("start")

runBlocking {
  task1()
  task2()

  println("called task1 and task2 from ${Thread.currentThread()}")
}

println("done")
```

You'll find only two differences between this code and the previous sequential version. First is the import from the kotlinx.coroutines.* package. Second, we replaced run() with runBlocking(), which is a function in the kotlinx.coroutines package that contains convenience functions and classes to help us program with coroutines. The runBlocking() function takes a lambda as an argument and executes that within a coroutine.

The imported package is from an extension library. While coroutines are part of the language's standard library, you'll have to download an additional library to make use of that package, which contains functions to easily create and work with coroutines.

To run the code, specify the location of that coroutines extension jar file to the kotlinc-jvm command, like so:

```
$ kotlinc-jvm -classpath /opt/kotlin/kotlinx-coroutines-core-1.2.2.jar \
  -script coroutine.kts
```

---

1. https://mvnrepository.com/artifact/org.jetbrains.kotlinx/kotlinx-coroutines-core/1.2.2

Replace /opt/kotlin/ with the correct location of where the jar file is located on your system. On Windows, use \ instead of / for path separator.

Let's take a look at the output of this code:

```
start
start task1 in Thread Thread[main,5,main]
end task1 in Thread Thread[main,5,main]
start task2 in Thread Thread[main,5,main]
end task2 in Thread Thread[main,5,main]
called task1 and task2 from Thread[main,5,main]
done
```

No, you're not reading it wrong; the output of the sequential version of code is the same as the output of the version that uses coroutines. What's the point? you may wonder. Coroutines run code concurrently—thus, the code within the lambda ran in the *main thread* interleaved between the code before the call to runBlocking() and the code after the call to that function.

Really?

That's a reasonable response to have when looking at this example. It's understandable that you want to see some action that is different from sequential execution—that's fair; we'll do that next.

Launching a Task

Let's launch the two functions, task1() and task2(), to execute in two different coroutines and then display a message that we've invoked the tasks. Let's see if that shows any difference from the execution of the sequential version. Start with the previous code and make changes only to the two function calls to task1() and task2(), within the lambda passed to runBlocking(), like so:

```
runBlocking {
  launch { task1() }
  launch { task2() }

  println("called task1 and task2 from ${Thread.currentThread()}")
}

println("done")
```

The launch() function starts a new coroutine to execute the given lambda, much like the runBlocking() function does, except the invoking code isn't blocked for the completion of the coroutine. And, unlike the runBlocking() function, the launch() function returns a job, which can be used to wait on for completion or to cancel the task. Let's take a look at the output of the above version of code:

```
start
called task1 and task2 from Thread[main,5,main]
start task1 in Thread Thread[main,5,main]
end task1 in Thread Thread[main,5,main]
start task2 in Thread Thread[main,5,main]
end task2 in Thread Thread[main,5,main]
done
```

Whew! That's different from the sequential version, albeit only slightly. The message that the two tasks were called is printed right after the line with the start message. We then see task1() run to completion and then task2(), followed by the message done at the end.

All the code still executes in the main thread, but we can see how the last line within the lambda executed before either task1() or task2(). That's at least a sign of concurrency, more than in the previous version.

Interleaving Calls with Suspension Points

More action, you demand. The previous example showed a bit of the evidence of concurrency, but let's create an example that will remove all doubt.

Kotlin coroutines library comes with suspension points—a function that will suspend execution of the current task and let another task execute. Calling such a function is like you pointing the microphone toward a colleague, in the middle of your speech, for them to say a few words. There are two functions to achieve this in the kotlinx.coroutines library: delay() and yield().

The delay() function will pause the currently executing task for the duration of milliseconds specified. The yield() method doesn't result in any explicit delays. But both these methods will give an opportunity for another pending task to execute.

The yield() function is like the nice command in Unix-like systems. By being nice you may lower your processes priority on these systems. In Kotlin, your task can be nice, using yield(), to other tasks that may have more important things to do.

Let's use yield() in both the functions task1() and task2(). Kotlin will permit the use of suspension points only in functions that are annotated with the suspend keyword. Marking a function with suspend doesn't automatically make the function run in a coroutine or concurrently, however.

Let's modify the previous code to use yield()—the changes are only to the two functions:

```
coroutines/interleave.kts
import kotlinx.coroutines.*

suspend fun task1() {
  println("start task1 in Thread ${Thread.currentThread()}")
  yield()
  println("end task1 in Thread ${Thread.currentThread()}")
}

suspend fun task2() {
  println("start task2 in Thread ${Thread.currentThread()}")
  yield()
  println("end task2 in Thread ${Thread.currentThread()}")
}

println("start")

runBlocking {
  launch { task1() }
  launch { task2() }

  println("called task1 and task2 from ${Thread.currentThread()}")
}

println("done")
```

We annotate both the functions with the keyword suspend. Then, within each of the functions, right after the first call to println(), we call yield(). Now, each of the functions will yield the flow of execution to other tasks, if any. Within the lambda passed to the runBlocking() function, we launch the two tasks, in two separate coroutines, like we did before. Let's take a look at the output after this change:

```
start
called task1 and task2 from Thread[main,5,main]
start task1 in Thread Thread[main,5,main]
start task2 in Thread Thread[main,5,main]
end task1 in Thread Thread[main,5,main]
end task2 in Thread Thread[main,5,main]
done
```

Much better—the differences between this output and the output for previous versions are vivid. We see that the task1() function executed its first line and yielded the execution flow. Then the task2() function stepped in, ran its first line, also in the main thread, and then yielded, so task1() can continue its execution. This is like working in an office where everyone is nice, highly polite, and very considerate of each other. OK, enough dreaming—let's get back to coding.

The previous example showed how the single thread main is running all that code, but the function calls aren't executed sequentially. We can clearly see the interleaving of execution—that served as a good example of concurrent execution.

The examples illustrated the behavior of coroutines, but it leaves us with the question, When will we use them? Suppose we have multiple tasks that can't be run in parallel, maybe due to potential contention of shared resources used by them. Running the tasks sequentially one after the other may end up starving all but a few tasks. Sequential execution is especially not desirable if the tasks are long running or never ending. In such cases, we may let multiple tasks run cooperatively, using coroutines, and make steady progress on all tasks. We can also use coroutines to build an unbounded stream of data—see Creating Infinite Sequences, on page 303.

In all the examples so far, the execution has been in the main thread. Let's next see how to dispatch the execution of a coroutine in a different thread.

Coroutine Context and Threads

The call to the launch() and runBlocking() functions resulted in the coroutines executing in the same thread as the caller's coroutine scope. That's the default behavior of these functions, since they carry a coroutine context from their scope. You may, however, vary the context and the thread of execution of the coroutines where you like.

Explicitly Setting a Context

You may pass a CoroutineContext to the launch() and runBlocking() functions to set the execution context of the coroutines these functions start.

The value of Dispatchers.Default for the argument of type CoroutineContext instructs the coroutine that is started to execute in a thread from a DefaultDispatcher pool. The number of threads in this pool is either 2 or equal to the number of cores on the system, whichever is higher. This pool is intended to run computationally intensive tasks.

The value of Dispatchers.IO can be used to execute coroutines in a pool that is dedicated to running IO intensive tasks. That pool may grow in size if threads are blocked on IO and more tasks are created.

Dispatchers.Main can be used on Android devices and Swing UI, for example, to run tasks that update the UI from only the main thread.

To get a feel for how to set the context for launch(), let's take the previous example and make a change to one of the launch() calls, like so:

```
runBlocking {
  launch(Dispatchers.Default) { task1() }
  launch { task2() }

  println("called task1 and task2 from ${Thread.currentThread()}")
}
```

After this change, the code in task1() will run in a different thread than the rest of the code that still runs in the main thread. We can verify this in the output—the output you see may be slightly different since the order of multiple threads running in parallel is nondeterministic:

```
start
start task1 in Thread Thread[DefaultDispatcher-worker-1,5,main]
end task1 in Thread Thread[DefaultDispatcher-worker-2,5,main]
called task1 and task2 from Thread[main,5,main]
start task2 in Thread Thread[main,5,main]
end task2 in Thread Thread[main,5,main]
done
```

In this case, the code within the lambda passes to runBlocking(), and the code within task2() runs concurrently, but the code within task1() is running in parallel. Coroutines may execute concurrently or in parallel, depending on their context.

Running in a Custom Pool

You know how to set a context explicitly, but the context we used in the previous example was the built-in DefaultDispatcher. If you'd like to run your coroutines in your own single thread pool, you can do that as well. Since you'll have a single thread in the pool, the coroutines using this context will run concurrently instead of in parallel. This is a good option if you're concerned about resource contention among the tasks executing as coroutines.

To set a single thread pool context, we first have to create a single thread executor. For this we can use the JDK Executors concurrency API from the java.util.concurrent package. Once we create an executor, using the JDK library, we can use Kotlin's extension functions to get a CoroutineContext from it using an asCoroutineDispatcher() function. Let's give that a shot.

First, import the necessary package:

coroutines/single.kts
```
import kotlinx.coroutines.*
import java.util.concurrent.Executors

//...task1 and task2 function definitions as before...
```

You may be tempted to create a dispatcher from the single thread executor and pass that directly to launch(), but there's a catch. If we don't close the executor, our program may never terminate. That's because there's an active thread in the executor's pool, in addition to main, and that will keep the JVM alive. We need to keep an eye on when all the coroutines complete and then close the executor. But that code can become hard to write and error prone. Thankfully, there's a nice use() function that will take care of those steps for us. The use() function is akin to the *try-with-resources* feature in Java. The code to use the context can then go into the lambda passed to the use() function, like so:

```
coroutines/single.kts
Executors.newSingleThreadExecutor().asCoroutineDispatcher().use { context ->
  println("start")

  runBlocking {
    launch(context) { task1() }
    launch { task2() }

    println("called task1 and task2 from ${Thread.currentThread()}")
  }

  println("done")
}
```

We first created an executor using the Executors.newSingleThreadExecutor() method of the JDK and then obtained a CoroutineContext using the asCoroutineDispatcher() extension function added by the kotlinx.coroutines library. Then we call the use() method and passed a lambda to it. Within the lambda we obtain a reference to the context, using the context variable, and pass that to the first call to launch(). The coroutines started by this call to launch()—that is, the execution of task1()—will run in the single thread pool managed by the executor we created. When we leave the lambda expression, the use() function will close the executor, knowing that all the coroutines have completed.

Let's take a look at the output and confirm that the code in task1() is running in the pool we created instead of the DefaultDispatcher pool:

```
start
start task1 in Thread Thread[pool-1-thread-1,5,main]
end task1 in Thread Thread[pool-1-thread-1,5,main]
called task1 and task2 from Thread[main,5,main]
start task2 in Thread Thread[main,5,main]
end task2 in Thread Thread[main,5,main]
done
```

If instead of using a single thread pool, you'd like to use a pool with multiple threads—say, as many threads as the number of cores on the system—you may change the line:

```
Executors.newSingleThreadExecutor().asCoroutineDispatcher().use { context ->
```

That change looks like this:

```
Executors.newFixedThreadPool(Runtime.getRuntime().availableProcessors())
  .asCoroutineDispatcher().use { context ->
```

Now the coroutines that use this context will run in this custom pool with as many threads as the number of cores on the system running this code.

Switching Threads After Suspension Points

What if you want a coroutine to start in the context of the caller but switch to a different thread after the suspension point? In other words, as long as the task involves quick computations, you may want to do that in the current thread, but in the instance we hit a time-consuming operation, we may want to delegate that to run on a different thread. We can achieve this by using the CoroutineContext argument along with a CoroutineStart argument.

To run the coroutine in the current context, you may set the value of the second optional argument of launch() to DEFAULT, which is of type CoroutineStart. Alternatively, use LAZY to defer execution until an explicit start() is called, ATOMIC to run in a non-cancellable mode, and UNDISPATCHED to run initially in the current context but switch threads after the suspension point.

Let's modify the call to the first launch() call in the previous code to use our own thread pool and also the UNDISPATCHED option for the second argument. Each of the parameters of launch() has default values, so we don't have to pass the first argument context in order to pass the second argument start. If we want to pass only the value for start, we can use the named argument feature. To illustrate this, let's use named arguments for both the first and the second argument in the code:

```
coroutines/coroutinestart.kts
import kotlinx.coroutines.*
import java.util.concurrent.Executors

suspend fun task1() {
  println("start task1 in Thread ${Thread.currentThread()}")
  yield()
  println("end task1 in Thread ${Thread.currentThread()}")
}
```

```
suspend fun task2() {
  println("start task2 in Thread ${Thread.currentThread()}")
  yield()
  println("end task2 in Thread ${Thread.currentThread()}")
}

Executors.newFixedThreadPool(Runtime.getRuntime().availableProcessors())
  .asCoroutineDispatcher().use { context ->
  println("start")

  runBlocking {
    @UseExperimental(ExperimentalCoroutinesApi::class)
    launch(context = context, start = CoroutineStart.UNDISPATCHED) { task1() }
    launch { task2() }

    println("called task1 and task2 from ${Thread.currentThread()}")
  }

  println("done")
}
```

The CoroutineStart.UNDISPATCHED option is an experimental feature in the kotlinx.coroutines library, and to use it we have to annotate the expression with @UseExperimental, as we see in the previous code. Since we're using an experimental feature, we also have to set a command-line flag when calling the -Xuse-experimental.

```
$ kotlinc-jvm  -Xuse-experimental=kotlin.Experimental \
  -classpath /opt/kotlin/kotlinx-coroutines-core-1.2.2.jar \
  -script coroutinestart.kts
```

Go ahead and execute the code and take a look at the output:

```
start
start task1 in Thread Thread[main,5,main]
end task1 in Thread Thread[pool-1-thread-1,5,main]
called task1 and task2 from Thread[main,5,main]
start task2 in Thread Thread[main,5,main]
end task2 in Thread Thread[main,5,main]
done
```

We see that the execution of task1() started in the main thread instead of in the pool-1's thread. But once the execution reached the suspension point, yield(), the execution switched over to the pool-1's thread, which is in the context specified to the launch() function.

Changing the CoroutineContext

The runBlocking() and launch() functions provide a nice way to set the context of a new coroutine, but what if you want to run a coroutine in one context and then change the context midway? Kotlin has a function for that: withContext().

Using this function you can take a part of code and run it in an entirely different context than the rest of the code in the coroutine.

Let's create an example to illustrate this:

```
coroutines/withcontext.kts
//...import, task1, and task2 functions like in previous code...

runBlocking {
  println("starting in Thread ${Thread.currentThread()}")
  withContext(Dispatchers.Default) { task1() }

  launch { task2() }

  println("ending in Thread ${Thread.currentThread()}")
}
```

Here's the output of this code:

```
starting in Thread Thread[main,5,main]
start task1 in Thread Thread[DefaultDispatcher-worker-1,5,main]
end task1 in Thread Thread[DefaultDispatcher-worker-1,5,main]
ending in Thread Thread[main,5,main]
start task2 in Thread Thread[main,5,main]
end task2 in Thread Thread[main,5,main]
```

The output shows that all code except the code within the lambda provided to withContext() is running in the main thread. The code called from within the lambda provided to withContext(), however, is running in the thread that's part of the provided context.

We see that the threads are different, but did withContext() really change the context of the currently executing coroutine or did it merely create an entirely new coroutine? It changed the context, but how can we tell? "Trust me," is not a good response for such questions—we want to see it to believe it. Time to dissect the execution.

Debugging Coroutines

"Prefer testing over debugging" is a good mantra to follow, but occasionally we have to debug code. Even when we follow good test-driven development practices, we'll have to dig into the execution to look at why things aren't working the way we expect. We'll look at testing coroutines in Chapter 18, Unit Testing with Kotlin, on page 347, but for now let's figure out a way to find out which coroutines are running our code.

Kotlin provides a command-line option -Dkotlinx.coroutines.debug to display the details of the coroutine executing a function. When you print the details of a thread, the coroutine that's running in that thread is displayed. Let's use that option on the previous code.

```
$ kotlinc-jvm -Dkotlinx.coroutines.debug \
  -classpath /opt/kotlin/kotlinx-coroutines-core-1.2.2.jar \
  -script withcontext.kts
```

When run with the command-line debug option, we see more details in the output than we have seen so far:

```
starting in Thread Thread[main @coroutine#1,5,main]
start task1 in Thread Thread[DefaultDispatcher-worker-1 @coroutine#1,5,main]
end task1 in Thread Thread[DefaultDispatcher-worker-3 @coroutine#1,5,main]
ending in Thread Thread[main @coroutine#1,5,main]
start task2 in Thread Thread[main @coroutine#2,5,main]
end task2 in Thread Thread[main @coroutine#2,5,main]
```

The output shows that withContext() didn't start a new coroutine—the code within task1() is running in the same coroutine as the code within runBlocking(). On the other hand, since we used a call to launch(), the code within task2() is running in a different coroutine.

When the debugging flag is set, Kotlin assigns consecutive identifiers for each of the coroutines it creates. This is useful for quickly looking up log messages from code running within the same coroutines. But, from the debugging point of view, instead of seeing a number like 42 for an identifier, it's better to see a logical name like searching for meaning of life for a coroutine that is executing a complex algorithm.

We can assign a name by passing an instance of CoroutineName() to runBlocking() and launch(). If we're already passing a context, we can append the name. Let's take a look at how to achieve this by changing the previous code:

```
//...import, task1, and task2 functions like in previous code...

runBlocking(CoroutineName("top")) {
  println("running in Thread ${Thread.currentThread()}")
  withContext(Dispatchers.Default) { task1() }

  launch(Dispatchers.Default + CoroutineName("task runner")) { task2() }

  println("running in Thread ${Thread.currentThread()}")
}
```

The only changes are to the runBlocking() call and the launch() call. To the runBlocking() we passed an instance of CoroutineName(). For the launch() call, we pass the name in addition to a CoroutineContext.

Let's take a look at the output of running the modified code with the command-line debug option:

```
running in Thread Thread[main @top#1,5,main]
start task1 in Thread Thread[DefaultDispatcher-worker-1 @top#1,5,main]
end task1 in Thread Thread[DefaultDispatcher-worker-3 @top#1,5,main]
start task2 in Thread Thread[DefaultDispatcher-worker-3 @task runner#2,5,main]
end task2 in Thread Thread[DefaultDispatcher-worker-3 @task runner#2,5,main]
running in Thread Thread[main @top#1,5,main]
```

In the output, the names of the coroutines are "top" and "task runner" instead of the mere "coroutine". The identifier that Kotlin creates for each coroutine is still preserved and presented in the output. Once again we can see that withContext() switched the context of the currently executing coroutine.

Not only can we use coroutines to perform actions asynchronously, but we can also perform computations and get results back on the caller side, as we'll see next.

async and await

The launch() function returns a Job object that can be used to await termination of the coroutine or to cancel. But there's no way to return a result from the coroutine that was started using launch(). If you want to execute a task asynchronously and get the response, then use async() instead of launch().

The async() function takes the same parameters as launch(), so we can configure the context and start properties of coroutines that are created using async() and launch() in the same way. The difference, though, is that async() returns a Deferred<T> future object which has an await() method, among other methods, to check the status of the coroutine, cancel, and so on. A call to await() will block the flow of execution but not the thread of execution. Thus, the code in the caller and the code within the coroutine started by async() can run concurrently. The call to await() will eventually return the result of the coroutine started using async(). If the coroutine started using async() throws an exception, then that exception will be propagated to the caller through the call to await().

We'll use async() and await() in the next chapter, but here, let's get a quick taste of these functions. In the code that follows we get the number of cores available on a system asynchronously. The Dispatchers.Default argument is optional and, if left out, the coroutine will run in the dispatcher of the scope it inherits. In this example, we have a single-threaded scope and thus the coroutine will run in the same thread as the caller. But when run in a scope of a multi-threaded dispatcher, the coroutine will execute in any of the threads of that dispatcher.

coroutines/asyncawait.kts
```
import kotlinx.coroutines.*

runBlocking {
  val count: Deferred<Int> = async(Dispatchers.Default) {
    println("fetching in ${Thread.currentThread()}")
    Runtime.getRuntime().availableProcessors()
  }

  println("Called the function in ${Thread.currentThread()}")

  println("Number of cores is ${count.await()}")
}
```

Once the request has been dispatched, the main thread will execute the print statement after the call to async(). The call to await() will wait for the coroutine started by async() to complete. The last print statement will then print the response received from the coroutine. Let's take a look at this in the output:

```
Called the function in Thread[main,5,main]
fetching in Thread[DefaultDispatcher-worker-1,5,main]
Number of cores is 8
```

The output shows the number of cores on my system; your output may vary. We see that the coroutines ran in the DefaultDispatcher pool's thread. Try removing the Dispatchers.Default argument from the call to async(), and run the code again. Notice that the coroutine, in that case, also runs in the main thread.

Coroutines run asynchronously, can switch threads, suspend and resume, and yet return the results back to where they are expected. What's the magic that makes this happen? It's time to unveil that secret.

A Peek at Continuations

Methods marked with the suspend annotation may return data. However, coroutines may suspend execution and may switch threads. How in the world does the state get preserved and propagated between threads?

To explore this further, let's take a look at an example that brings out this concern clearly. Instead of creating .kts files, we'll create .kt files so it's easy to compile to Java bytecode and examine.

coroutines/Compute.kt
```
import kotlinx.coroutines.*

class Compute {
  fun compute1(n: Long): Long = n * 2
```

```
suspend fun compute2(n: Long): Long {
  val factor = 2
  println("$n received : Thread: ${Thread.currentThread()}")
  delay(n * 1000)
  val result = n * factor
  println("$n, returning $result: Thread: ${Thread.currentThread()}")
  return result
  }
}
```

The Compute class has two methods, one marked with suspend. The compute1() method is simple; it returns the double of the given input. The compute2() method does the same thing, except it yields the flow of execution to other pending tasks and may potentially switch threads midway.

Let's create a main() function to execute the compute2() function, a couple of times, within coroutines.

coroutines/UseCompute.kt

```
import kotlinx.coroutines.*

fun main() = runBlocking<Unit> {
  val compute = Compute()

  launch(Dispatchers.Default) {
    compute.compute2(2)
  }
  launch(Dispatchers.Default) {
    compute.compute2(1)
  }
}
```

We assign a single expression function to the main() function with a call to runBlocking<Unit>. So far we used only runBlocking() without the parametric Unit, but since the return type of main() is Unit, we have to convey that the call to runBlocking() is returning the same. Otherwise we'll get a compilation error. Within the lambda passed to runBlocking<Unit>() we create two coroutines and invoke the compute2() method in each. Let's take a look at the output of this code:

```
2 received : Thread: Thread[DefaultDispatcher-worker-1,5,main]
1 received : Thread: Thread[DefaultDispatcher-worker-2,5,main]
1, returning 2: Thread: Thread[DefaultDispatcher-worker-2,5,main]
2, returning 4: Thread: Thread[DefaultDispatcher-worker-4,5,main]
```

The coroutine that's running compute2() with an input value of 2 switched threads. The first part, before the call to delay(), is executing in one thread and the second part, after the delay(), is running in a different thread. But the value of factor got passed correctly from before the delay() to after. It's not magic, it's continuations.

Using continuations, which are highly powerful data structures, programs can capture and preserve the state of execution in one thread and restore them when needed in another thread. Programming languages that support continuations generate special code to perform this seamlessly for the programmers.

At the risk of overly simplifying, think of a continuation as a closure—see Closures and Lexical Scoping, on page 188—that captures the lexical scope. We can imagine how the code after a suspension point may be wrapped into a closure and saved. Then that closure may be invoked whenever the function execution has to be resumed.

To see how this unfolds at the compilation level, we can use javap -c to explore the bytecode of the compiled Compute class. Let's take a look at the details for only the two compute... methods.

```
public final long compute1(long);
public final java.lang.Object compute2(long,
  kotlin.coroutines.Continuation<? super java.lang.Long>);
```

Looking at the source code, the signature of both compute1() and compute2() were identical except for the suspend annotation. At the bytecode level, though, they are worlds apart. The compute1() function doesn't have anything unexpected. It takes as input a long and returns a value of the same type. The compute2() function, on the other hand, looks a lot different. Even though in the source code compute2() only took one parameter, in the compiled version we see that it takes two parameters: long and Continuation<? super Long>. Furthermore, it returns Object instead of long. The Continuation encapsulates the results of the partial execution of the function so that the result can be delivered to the caller using the Continuation callback. The compiler engages continuations to implement the machinery of coroutines, to switch context between executing different tasks, to switch threads, and to restore states. The net result is that as programmers, we can focus on using continuations and leave all the heavy lifting to the compiler.

We've had a glimpse of what's going on under the hood when we use coroutines. Next let's focus on a practical application of coroutines.

Creating Infinite Sequences

Since coroutines are useful for creating cooperating tasks, we can use them to create an infinite series or unbounded values and process the generated values at the same time. A function may create a value in the series and yield it to the code that is expecting the value. Upon consuming the value, the calling code can come back asking for the next value in the series. These steps can continue in tandem until either the code that produces the series exits or the caller doesn't bother asking for another value in the series. We'll take a look at two different functions available in Kotlin to create infinite series.

Using Sequence

The Kotlin library has a sequence function that's readily available for creating a series of values. We'll use that to create an infinite series of prime numbers, starting from a given number.

Here's a primes() function that takes a starting number and returns a Sequence<Int>. The Sequence acts as a continuation, yielding values for iteration.

coroutines/primes.kts
```kotlin
fun primes(start: Int): Sequence<Int> = sequence {
  println("Starting to look")
  var index = start

  while (true) {
    if (index > 1 && (2 until index).none { i -> index % i == 0 }) {
      yield(index)
      println("Generating next after $index")
    }

    index++
  }
}
```

Within the lambda passed to the sequence() function, we look for the next prime value and yield it using a yield() method—this one is part of the standard library and is different from the yield() we used from the kotlinx.coroutines library. We can iterate over the values generated by a Sequence, much like the way we iterate over List, Set, and so on.

coroutines/primes.kts
```kotlin
for (prime in primes(start = 17)) {
  println("Received $prime")
  if (prime > 30) break
}
```

The fact that coroutines and continuations are involved here isn't visible in the code. We iterate over the values, one at a time, print a prime received from primes(), and decide to get the next element or break. At every step of the iteration, the flow of control jumps right into the primes() function, right back to where it left the last time. We can see this from the output, which has extra print messages to illustrate this behavior.

```
Starting to look
Received 17
Generating next after 17
```

```
Received 19
Generating next after 19
Received 23
Generating next after 23
Received 29
Generating next after 29
Received 31
```

The sequence() function offers three benefits. First, you don't have to create a collection of values ahead of time, so you don't have to know how many values to compute—you can create the values on the fly. Second, you can amortize the cost of creating the values over time and let the values generated so far be used. Third, since the creation of a value in the series happens only on demand—that is, lazily—we can avoid creating values that may never be used. That results in more efficient code. It's also easier to apply this technique to write custom Iterable/Iterator classes.

In addition to creating a Sequence<T>, you may also easily implement an Iterator<T> using Kotlin's iterator() function. Let's take a look at that next.

Using the iterator Function

Back in Injecting into Third-Party Classes, on page 228, we added an extension function into the ClosedRange<String> class to iterate over a range of String values. For convenience, that code is repeated here:

fluency/forstringrange.kts
```
operator fun ClosedRange<String>.iterator() =
  object: Iterator<String> {
    private val next = StringBuilder(start)
    private val last = endInclusive

    override fun hasNext() =
      last >= next.toString() && last.length >= next.length

    override fun next(): String {
      val result = next.toString()

      val lastCharacter = next.last()

      if (lastCharacter < Char.MAX_VALUE) {
        next.setCharAt(next.length - 1, lastCharacter + 1)
      } else {
        next.append(Char.MIN_VALUE)
      }

      return result
    }
  }
```

The iterator() function of ClosedRange<String> is returning an object that implements the Iterator<String> interface. The implementation has a couple of properties and two methods. The hasNext() tells us if there's another value for iteration, and the next() function returns the next value when called. If we step back from the implementation and look at the overall goal, what we want here is an iterator that *yields* one value at a time until it reaches some termination value. This fits the bill of coroutines well.

What we need is an iterator that will run as a coroutine. That's the purpose of the method iterator() in the Kotlin standard library. Let's rewrite the above function using iterator() and then call it to see its behavior.

```
coroutines/forstringrange.kts
operator fun ClosedRange<String>.iterator(): Iterator<String> = iterator {
  val next = StringBuilder(start)
  val last = endInclusive

  while (last >= next.toString() && last.length >= next.length) {
    val result = next.toString()

    val lastCharacter = next.last()

    if (lastCharacter < Char.MAX_VALUE) {
      next.setCharAt(next.length - 1, lastCharacter + 1)
    } else {
      next.append(Char.MIN_VALUE)
    }

    yield(result)
  }
}

for (word in "hell".."help") { print("$word, ") }
```

Unlike the sequence function which returned a Sequence<T>, the iterator() function returns an Iterator<T>. Within the lambda passed to the iterator() function, we loop through to generate the next String in the sequence and call the yield() function, much like the way we did in the example that used sequence(), to return a generated String to the caller. In this latest version, the hasNext() function disappeared and instead of return, which we used in the next() method, we use yield() in the iterator() function.

In the last line we exercise the ClosedRange<String>'s iterator() function using the for loop to iterate over a range of values. The output of this code is the same as the output of the other version this code replaces.

Between the sequence() function and the iterator() function, Kotlin has you covered for creating coroutines to generate unbounded values with highly expressive code.

Wrapping Up

Coroutines, built upon the concept of continuations, provide a great way to program concurrency. Coroutines are functions with multiple entry points, and they carry state between invocations. These functions can call into each other and resume execution from where they left off in the previous call. Coroutines also may yield the flow of control to other pending tasks that may need the thread and other resources to execute. You may vary the thread of execution of coroutines and, using async() and await(), perform tasks in parallel and receive the result in the future.

All these concepts nicely lay a foundation for creating powerful abstractions for concurrent programming. We can apply these to creating infinite sequences and also powerful iterators over boundless collections. We can also use coroutines to program asynchronous applications, which we'll focus on in the next chapter.

CHAPTER 16

Asynchronous Programming

Coroutines are a great way to implement non-blocking calls. You can configure coroutines to run your tasks concurrently or in parallel by using different coroutine contexts. We explored the fundamentals of coroutines in the previous chapter. In this chapter, we'll build on those concepts to create robust asynchronous programs.

We'll start by looking at how coroutines help you comprehend the complexities of asynchronous programs. Then we'll discuss that gnarly issue of exception handling and how coroutines deal with them. We'll then talk about cancelling coroutines that have been started and how cancellation and exceptions interplay. We'll also look into supervisory jobs and how they manage cancellations.

Coroutines are great for long-running tasks, but we don't want a task to unintentionally run forever. We'll use timeout to force-fail coroutines that have outrun their permissible time.

As we walk through the concepts in this chapter, along the way we'll use async() and await() functions to create practical asynchronous programs that will illustrate the power of coroutines.

Programming Asynchronously

When programming modern applications we often have to make calls to remote services, update databases, perform searches, and the list goes on. Many of these tasks aren't instantaneous. To improve program efficiency we may want to execute such operations asynchronously, in a non-blocking manner. Coroutines are intended to exactly solve that problem.

Starting Sequentially

Let's create a program to go out and get the weather details to see if there are any delays at certain airports. As a first step, we'll create an Airport class that will hold the data, along with a Weather class to hold the temperature. We'll use the Klaxon library[1] to parse the JSON response from the Federal Aviation Administration (FAA) airport status web service.

async/Airport.kt
```
import java.net.URL
import com.beust.klaxon.*

class Weather(@Json(name = "Temp") val temperature: Array<String>)

class Airport(
  @Json(name = "IATA") val code: String,
  @Json(name = "Name") val name: String,
  @Json(name = "Delay") val delay: Boolean,
  @Json(name = "Weather") val weather: Weather) {

  companion object {
    fun getAirportData(code: String): Airport? {
      val url = "https://soa.smext.faa.gov/asws/api/airport/status/$code"
      return Klaxon().parse<Airport>(URL(url).readText())
    }
  }
}
```

In the Airport class we use the @Json annotation to map the properties in the JSON response to the properties in our class. In the getAirportData() method we fetch the data, extract the text response, and parse the JSON content to create an instance of Airport.

Given a list of airport codes, let's first fetch the data sequentially using the method just described. This will soon help us compare the sequential, synchronous code for this program with the asynchronous version.

We'll loop through the list of airports and fetch the airport status information, one at a time, and print the output in a perusable format.

async/AirportInfo.kt
```
import kotlin.system.*

fun main() {
  val format = "%-10s%-20s%-10s"
  println(String.format(format, "Code", "Temperature", "Delay"))

  val time = measureTimeMillis {
    val airportCodes = listOf("LAX", "SFO", "PDX", "SEA")
```

---

1. https://mvnrepository.com/artifact/com.beust/klaxon/5.0.2

```
  val airportData: List<Airport> =
    airportCodes.mapNotNull { anAirportCode ->
      Airport.getAirportData(anAirportCode)
    }

  airportData.forEach { anAirport ->
    println(String.format(format, anAirport.code,
      anAirport.weather.temperature.get(0), anAirport.delay))
  }
}

println("Time taken $time ms")
}
```

In addition to printing the status details, we also measure the time the code takes to run, using the measureTimeMillis() function, which is a nice little convenience function in the Kotlin standard library. Let's take a look at the output of this code:

```
Code       Temperature            Delay
LAX        68.0 F (20.0 C)        false
SFO        50.0 F (10.0 C)        true
PDX        56.0 F (13.3 C)        false
SEA        55.0 F (12.8 C)        true
Time taken 2112 ms
```

Nice weather, but fifty percent of the airports queried have delays—that gives us confidence the data represents reality and is reliable. The program took a bit more than 2 seconds to run. You may observe a different speed, depending on the network performance at the time of the run.

Making Asynchronous

Each of the calls to the getAirportData() method in the previous code is blocking calls. When we make the call for "LAX" the program waits until that request is completed before making the request for the next code "SFO" to be processed. We can make those calls non-blocking; that is, we don't have to wait for the request for "LAX" to be completed before making a request for all the subsequent codes. We can fire off multiple requests and complete the first loop before any of the calls to getAirportData() have completed, or even started.

We want the main() function to block and wait for the asynchronous executions to complete. For this reason, we'll use runBlocking() around the entire code in the body of main().

To start a non-blocking call to Airport's getAirportData(), we obviously can't use runBlocking(). And launch() is intended to perform actions, not return results. So the async() function is the right choice here.

If we call async() directly within the iteration, then the coroutines will run in the currently executing coroutine context. Thus, the coroutine started will also run in the main thread. The calls to getAirportData() will be non-blocking and concurrent. In other words, the main thread won't block and wait, but the execution of the calls will be interleaved for execution in the main thread. That gives us half the benefit—the non-blocking part—but won't give us any performance advantage. Since each call will run on the same thread, the time it'll take for the code to complete will be about the same as the sequential run. We have to do better.

We can start the coroutine by telling async() to use a different context, and thus a different pool of threads. We can easily do this by passing a CoroutineContext, like Dispatchers.IO, to async(). Let's rewrite the previous code and use these ideas.

async/AirportInfoAsync.kt
```
import kotlin.system.*
import kotlinx.coroutines.*

fun main() = runBlocking {
  val format = "%-10s%-20s%-10s"
  println(String.format(format, "Code", "Temperature", "Delay"))

  val time = measureTimeMillis {
    val airportCodes = listOf("LAX", "SFO", "PDX", "SEA")

    val airportData: List<Deferred<Airport?>> =
      airportCodes.map { anAirportCode ->
        async(Dispatchers.IO) {
          Airport.getAirportData(anAirportCode)
        }
      }

    airportData
      .mapNotNull { anAirportData -> anAirportData.await() }
      .forEach { anAirport ->
        println(String.format(format, anAirport.code,
          anAirport.weather.temperature.get(0), anAirport.delay))
    }
  }

  println("Time taken $time ms")
}
```

The structure of the asynchronous code in the file AirportInfoAsync.kt is identical to the structure of the code in the file AirportInfo.kt—this is a blessing since the asynchronous code is as easy to reason and understand as the synchronous version.

While the code structures are the same between the two versions, there are some differences. First, instead of a List<Airport> we create a List<Deferred<Airport?>>, because the result of a call to async() is an instance of Deferred<T>.

Within the first iteration we called the getAirportData() method inside of the lambda passed to the async() call. The call to async() returns immediately with the result of Deferred<Airport?>, which we store in the list.

In the second iteration, we go over the Deferred<Airport?> list and invoke await() to get the data. Calls to await() will block the flow of execution but won't block the thread of execution. Had we used async() directly without the argument, the main thread would be executing the coroutines after reaching the call to await(). In our case, since we used async() with the Dispatchers.IO context, the main thread can chill, get a beverage, and stare at the stars, while the worker threads in the Dispatchers.IO pool take care of making the call to the web service.

Let's take a look at the output to see how the asynchronous program did in comparison to the sequential version.

```
Code      Temperature        Delay
LAX       68.0 F (20.0 C)    false
SFO       50.0 F (10.0 C)    true
PDX       56.0 F (13.3 C)    false
SEA       55.0 F (12.8 C)    true
Time taken 1676 ms
```

The airport data is the same between the two versions, but may be different if the two versions are run at different times. The asynchronous version took about half a second less to complete.

Use caution when you observe the time differences, however, since network speeds are often unreliable. If you see that the asynchronous version is occasionally slower than the sequential version, don't panic. Play with the asynchronous version to get a deeper understanding. Place print statements before the call to getAirportData() method to print the thread information. Notice how those calls are invoked in parallel when the program is run. Change async(Dispatchers.IO) to async() and observe how the calls run in the main thread, and the impact that has on the time the program takes.

Both the sequential and the asynchronous versions of the program focus on the happy path, assuming all things go well. Many things could go wrong, though. The web service may intermittently fail, the network may drop, the airport code the user provided may be invalid or may not be supported by the web service. The ways that Murphy's law may strike are without limit. We have to program defensively, and coroutines are exceptional on that front.

Next, let's explore how coroutines handle exceptions.

Exception Handling

Many things can go wrong when making requests to web services, updating databases, accessing a file, and so on. When delegating a task to run asynchronously, we have to be defensive and handle failures gracefully. How we deal with exceptions depends on how we start a coroutine—using launch() or async().

Be Mindful of Structured Concurrency

Unless a scope is explicitly specified, coroutines run in the context and scope of their parent coroutines—called structured concurrency, where the hierarchical structure of coroutines matches the structure of code. This is a good thing as it's easier to monitor and manage the execution of coroutines that we start. A coroutine doesn't complete until all its children complete. But this also has some ramifications on how coroutines cooperate with each other and how failures are handled.

By default, when a coroutine fails with an exception, it results in the failure of the parent coroutine as well. Later in this chapter we'll take a closer look at the behavior of coroutines in the context of structured concurrency and how we can prevent a child coroutine from cancelling a parent coroutine using a SupervisorJob context. In the examples in this section, we'll use this context to prevent a child coroutine from cancelling its parent when an exception occurs.

launch and Exceptions

If we use launch(), then the exception won't be received on the caller side—it's a fire and forget model, though you may optionally wait for the coroutine to complete. To illustrate this behavior and find a way to gracefully handle exceptions, let's query the airport status using some invalid airport codes.

```
async/LaunchErr.kt
import kotlinx.coroutines.*

fun main() = runBlocking {
  try {
    val airportCodes = listOf("LAX", "SF-", "PD-", "SEA")

    val jobs: List<Job> = airportCodes.map { anAirportCode ->
      launch(Dispatchers.IO + SupervisorJob()) {
        val airport = Airport.getAirportData(anAirportCode)
        println("${airport?.code} delay: ${airport?.delay}")
      }
    }

    jobs.forEach { it.join() }
    jobs.forEach { println("Cancelled: ${it.isCancelled}") }
```

```
  } catch(ex: Exception) {
    println("ERROR: ${ex.message}")
  }
}
```

We used two valid airport codes and two invalid codes. Instead of using async(), we're using launch() in this example to see how it deals with exceptions. The launch() function returns a Job object that represents the coroutine it starts. We use that object to wait for the coroutine to complete either successfully or with failure. Then we query the isCancelled property of Job to check if the job completed successfully or it was cancelled due to failure.

Let's take a look at the output of running this code. Note that the output you see on your system may not exactly match the one shown here:

```
LAX delay: false
SEA delay: true
Exception in thread "DefaultDispatcher-worker-1" Exception in ...
```

That's sad—the try-catch we placed around the calls to launch() and the calls to join() had no effect. Instead, we see an unpleasant termination of the program with an exception message spilled on the console. The reason for this behavior is that coroutines that are started using launch() don't propagate exceptions to their caller. That's the nature of launch(), but we gotta do better when programming with this function.

If you're using launch(), then make sure to set up an exception handler. An exception handler CoroutineExceptionHandler, if registered, will be triggered with the details of the context and the exception. Let's create a handler and register it with the launch() calls.

async/LaunchErrHandle.kt
```kotlin
import kotlinx.coroutines.*

fun main() = runBlocking {
  val handler = CoroutineExceptionHandler { context, ex ->
    println(
      "Caught: ${context[CoroutineName]} ${ex.message?.substring(0..28)}")
  }

  try {
    val airportCodes = listOf("LAX", "SF-", "PD-", "SEA")

    val jobs: List<Job> = airportCodes.map { anAirportCode ->
      launch(Dispatchers.IO + CoroutineName(anAirportCode) +
        handler + SupervisorJob()) {
        val airport = Airport.getAirportData(anAirportCode)
        println("${airport?.code} delay: ${airport?.delay}")
      }
    }
```

```
    jobs.forEach { it.join() }
    jobs.forEach { println("Cancelled: ${it.isCancelled}") }
  } catch(ex: Exception) {
    println("ERROR: ${ex.message}")
  }
}
```

This version of code has only two changes, compared to the previous version. First, we create a handler which prints the details of the context of the coroutine that failed, along with the exception details of the failure. Second, in the call to launch(), we register the handler, along with a name for the coroutine for easy identification. Let's run this version and see how the program copes with the failures.

```
Caught: CoroutineName(PD-) Unable to instantiate Airport
Caught: CoroutineName(SF-) Unable to instantiate Airport
SEA delay: true
LAX delay: false
Cancelled: false
Cancelled: true
Cancelled: true
Cancelled: false
```

That's much better. The exceptions are handled gracefully by the registered handler. Instead of printing on the console, we can choose to log the error, send a notification to the support, play sad music... the options are endless once we have a handler of the failure. And the program doesn't quit ungracefully; instead it proceeds to display the output of whether the job is completed or cancelled.

The output also shows one other behavior of coroutine we haven't discussed—if a coroutine fails with an unhandled exception, then the coroutine is cancelled. We'll discuss cancellation further in Cancellations and Timeouts, on page 318.

async and Exceptions

launch() doesn't propagate the exception to its caller, so we should register an exception handler when using launch(). The async() function, however, returns a Deferred<T> instance, which will carry the exception and deliver to the caller when await() is called. It makes no sense to register an exception handler to async() if the handler, if registered, will be ignored.

Instead of using launch() with invalid airport codes, let's use async() to see how the exceptions are handled differently by the two functions. We handle the exception using try-catch around the call to await(), using exception-handling syntax that we're all familiar with.

async/AsyncErr.kt

```kotlin
import kotlin.system.*
import kotlinx.coroutines.*

fun main() = runBlocking {
  val airportCodes = listOf("LAX", "SF-", "PD-", "SEA")

  val airportData = airportCodes.map { anAirportCode ->
    async(Dispatchers.IO + SupervisorJob()) {
      Airport.getAirportData(anAirportCode)
    }
  }

  for (anAirportData in airportData) {
    try {
      val airport = anAirportData.await()

      println("${airport?.code} ${airport?.delay}")
    } catch(ex: Exception) {
      println("Error: ${ex.message?.substring(0..28)}")
    }
  }
}
```

For the first iteration, we use map() and the functional style. But for the second iteration over the list of Deferred<T>, we use the imperative style for-loop instead of the functional style forEach(). Even though forEach() may be used for this iteration as well, the imperative style is a better choice here. If we use forEach(), then the lambda, with all the code to handle the exception, won't be concise and expressive. As we discussed in Chapter 10, Functional Programming with Lambdas, on page 175, avoid creating multiline, verbose lambdas where possible.

Let's take a look at the output to see how async() dealt with the exception.

```
LAX false
Error: Unable to instantiate Airport
Error: Unable to instantiate Airport
SEA true
```

The output shows what we expect—async() and await() not only make it easier to make asynchronous calls, they also deal well with exceptions.

When working with the previous examples, we got a hint about how unhandled exceptions cancel coroutine. A coroutine may be cancelled intentionally when we no longer care for the task, it may be cancelled due to failure, or it may be forced to cancel by a parent coroutine. We also may want to put a timeout on how long a task takes. All these sound intriguing —let's examine them next.

Cancellations and Timeouts

Coroutines can be cancelled, which will stop the code within the coroutine from further execution. Coroutine cancellations aren't related to the thread terminations that we're used to in Java. Cancellations are lightweight and have effect across the hierarchy of coroutines that share context.

Both the Job object, which is returned by launch(), and the Deferred<T> object, which is returned by async(), have a cancel() and a cancelAndJoin() method. We can use these methods to explicitly cancel a coroutine, but there's a catch. A coroutine is cancelled only if it is currently in a suspension point. If a coroutine is busy executing code, it won't receive the cancellation notice and may not bail out. Let's discuss this further and find ways to deal with this behavior.

Kotlin provides structured concurrency, where coroutines that share a context form a hierarchical relationship. Coroutines that belong to a hierarchy follow some rules and exhibit prescribed behaviors:

- A coroutine is considered to be a child of another coroutine if it shares the context of the coroutine that creates it.

- A parent coroutine completes only after all its children complete.

- Cancelling a parent cancels all its children.

- A coroutine that has entered a suspension point may receive a CancellationException thrown from the suspension point.

- A coroutine that is busy, that's not in a suspension point, may check an isActive property to see if it was cancelled when it was busy.

- If a coroutine has resources to clean up, that needs to happen within the finally block within the coroutine.

- An unhandled exception will result in the cancellation of a coroutine.

- If a child coroutine fails, it will result in the parent coroutine cancelling and thus result in cancellation of the coroutine's siblings. You can modify this behavior using supervised jobs that make cancellation unidirectional, from parent to children.

That's a lot of information in one place, but you can refer back to this when working with coroutines. Let's examine these ideas with some examples.

Cancelling Coroutines

If we don't care for the completion of a task that we started in a coroutine, we may cancel it by calling cancel() or cancelAndJoin() on the Job or the Deferred<T> instance. However, the coroutine may not budge to that command right away. If the coroutine is busy executing, the command doesn't interrupt it. On the other hand, if the coroutine is parked in a suspension point, like in a call to yeild(), delay(), or await(), then it will be interrupted with a CancellationException.

When designing a coroutine, keep the previous constraints in mind. If you're performing a long-running computation, you may want to structure it so that you take a break frequently to check if the isActive property of the coroutine is still true. If you find it to be false, you can break out of the computation, honoring the request to cancel.

Sometimes you may not have the capability to check the isActive property because the function you internally call within the coroutine is blocking and doesn't involve a suspension point. In this case, you may consider delegating that blocking call to another coroutine—a level of indirection—and await on it, thus introducing a suspension point around your blocking call.

Let's explore these options with an example. We'll verify the behavior of the code that plays nicely with cancellation and also code that doesn't. This will give us a clear view of how we should approach the design of code with a coroutine, from the cancellation point of view.

We'll first create a compute() function that runs in one of two modes: if the parameter passed in is true, it will check the isActive property in the middle of a long-running computation; if that parameter is false, it will run wild for a long time. Since we need access to the isActive property, the code needs to run in the context of a coroutine. For this, we'll wrap the code within the compute() function inside a call to coroutineScope() that carries the scope from the caller.

Here's the code for the compute() function:

async/cancelandsuspension.kts
```kotlin
import kotlinx.coroutines.*

suspend fun compute(checkActive: Boolean) = coroutineScope {
  var count = 0L
  val max = 10000000000

  while (if (checkActive) { isActive } else (count < max)) {
    count++
  }
}
```

```
  if (count == max) {
    println("compute, checkActive $checkActive ignored cancellation")
  } else {
    println("compute, checkActive $checkActive bailed out early")
  }
}
```

If the computation is long running, we may check isActive from time to time. But if in the coroutine we call a long-running function that can't be interrupted, then the coroutine won't get interrupted either. To illustrate this and to find a workaround, let's create a fetchResponse() function.

async/cancelandsuspension.kts
```
val url = "http://httpstat.us/200?sleep=2000"

fun getResponse() = java.net.URL(url).readText()

suspend fun fetchResponse(callAsync: Boolean) = coroutineScope {
  try {
    val response = if (callAsync) {
      async { getResponse() }.await()
    } else {
      getResponse()
    }

    println(response)
  } catch(ex: CancellationException) {
    println("fetchResponse called with callAsync $callAsync: ${ex.message}")
  }
}
```

The fetchResponse() function sends a request to the mentioned URL that will return the HTTP code specified, 200 in this example, after a delay provided as a value to the sleep parameter, in milliseconds. If the callAsync parameter is false, then the call to the URL is made synchronously, thus blocking the caller and disallowing cancellation. But if that parameter is true, the call to the URL is made asynchronously, thus permitting immediate cancellation of the coroutine while it awaits.

Both the compute() function and the fetchResponse() function may or may not respond to cancellation, depending on how they're called. This is true, even though the former represents a long-running computation-intensive operation while the latter is performing a long-running IO operation.

Let's use these two functions within a few coroutines, let them run for a second, and then issue a stern *cancel* command. We may either use the cancel() method and then a call to join() or we may combine the two into one call with cancelAndJoin(). Let's give that a try:

async/cancelandsuspension.kts

```
runBlocking {
  val job = launch(Dispatchers.Default) {
    launch { compute(checkActive = false) }
    launch { compute(checkActive = true) }
    launch { fetchResponse(callAsync = false) }
    launch { fetchResponse(callAsync = true) }
  }

  println("Let them run...")
  Thread.sleep(1000)
  println("OK, that's enough, cancel")
  job.cancelAndJoin()
}
```

The compute() method call started with checkActive equal to true will terminate as soon as the cancel command is issued, since it's checking the isActive property. The compute() method call with checkActive equal to false will ignore the cancel command from its parent coroutine and will behave like a typical teenager with a headset on. Likewise, the fetchResponse() function will exhibit a similar behavior. We can see this in the output:

```
Let them run...
OK, that's enough, cancel
compute, checkActive true bailed out early
fetchResponse called with callAsync true: Job was cancelled
200 OK
compute, checkActive false ignored cancellation
```

The version of the calls that saw the cancel message, either because of the exception thrown at it or by checking for isActive, quit early. The versions that had the headsets on–that is, the coroutines that ignored their cancellation message–ran to completion.

When creating coroutines, verify that the code handles cancellation correctly.

Do Not Disturb

Sometimes we don't want part of a task to be interrupted. For example, you may be performing a critical operation, and stopping it in the middle may have catastrophic consequences. To handle this, there's a special context.

If your critical task doesn't have any suspension points, you don't have to worry. When a coroutine is busy running that non-interruptible code, no cancellation command will affect it. You don't have to write any extra code to prevent cancellation in this case.

But if your critical code contains a suspension point, like a yield(), delay(), or await(), then you may want to convey that you're in the middle of a critical section and don't want to be interrupted. The withContext(NonCancellable) function call is like hanging a Do Not Disturb sign outside the door. Let's see this in action with an example:

async/donotdistrub.kts
```
import kotlinx.coroutines.*

suspend fun doWork(id: Int, sleep: Long) = coroutineScope {
  try {
    println("$id: entered $sleep")
    delay(sleep)
    println("$id: finished nap $sleep")

    withContext(NonCancellable) {
      println("$id: do not disturb, please")
      delay(5000)
      println("$id: OK, you can talk to me now")
    }

    println("$id: outside the restricted context")
    println("$id: isActive: $isActive")
  } catch(ex: CancellationException) {
    println("$id: doWork($sleep) was cancelled")
  }
}
```

The doWork() function runs in the context of the callers coroutine. First, the function delays the coroutine for the given amount of time and is cancellable during this phase. Second, it enters the NonCancellable context and the delay within this phase isn't cancellable. Any interruption during this time will be ignored, but the isActive property will be changed if a cancellation were to happen. Finally, in this code we print the isActive property.

Let's call this function a couple of times within separate coroutines, sleep for two seconds, cancel the coroutines's parent, and wait for the parent to complete.

async/donotdistrub.kts
```
runBlocking {
  val job = launch(Dispatchers.Default) {
    launch { doWork(1, 3000) }
    launch { doWork(2, 1000) }
  }

  Thread.sleep(2000)
  job.cancel()
  println("cancelling")
  job.join()
  println("done")
}
```

We can see from the output shown below that the coroutine is cancelled if the cancellation command occurs when the execution is outside of the NonCancellable context. But if the coroutine is currently inside this context, it isn't cancelled and it runs uninterrupted.

```
2: entered 1000
1: entered 3000
2: finished nap 1000
2: do not disturb, please
cancelling
1: doWork(3000) was cancelled
2: OK, you can talk to me now
2: outside the restricted context
2: isActive: false
done
```

When you leave the do-not-disturb NonCancellable context, you may check the isActive property to see if the coroutine was interrupted and decide on the course of action accordingly.

Bidirectional Cancellation

When a coroutine runs into an unhandled non-cancellation exception, it's automatically cancelled. When a coroutine cancels, its parent is cancelled. When a parent is cancelled, all its children are then cancelled. All this behavior is automatically built-in to how coroutines cooperate.

We can see this in the following example. The fetchResponse() function makes requests to the httpstat URL with the given code. Let's take a look at the code before discussing further.

```
async/cancellationbidirectional.kts
import kotlinx.coroutines.*
import java.net.URL

suspend fun fetchResponse(code: Int, delay: Int) = coroutineScope {
  try {
    val response = async {
      URL("http://httpstat.us/$code?sleep=$delay").readText()
    }.await()

    println(response)
  } catch(ex: CancellationException) {
    println("${ex.message} for fetchResponse $code")
  }
}
```

```
runBlocking {
  val handler = CoroutineExceptionHandler { _, ex ->
    println("Exception handled: ${ex.message}")
  }

  val job = launch(Dispatchers.IO + SupervisorJob() + handler) {
    launch { fetchResponse(200, 5000) }
    launch { fetchResponse(202, 1000) }
    launch { fetchResponse(404, 2000) }
  }

  job.join()
}
```

If the given code is 404, the service request will fail with an exception. Since the function doesn't handle that exception, the coroutine running the function will cancel. This will result in the eventual cancellation of all the siblings of this coroutine that haven't completed at this time.

```
202 Accepted
Parent job is Cancelling for fetchResponse 200
Exception handled: http://httpstat.us/404?sleep=2000
```

The coroutine that executes the request for code 202 finishes in about one second, before the failure of the 404 request, which will take about two seconds due to the sleep parameter passed to the URL. When the coroutine that runs the request for code 404 fails, it brings down the coroutine that is running the asynchronous request for code 200.

The default behavior is that when a coroutine cancels, it brings down the house. This may not be desirable all the time. We can alter how coroutines communicate cancellation using a supervisory job. We've seen this pop up a few times already in the code; it's time to give it a closer look.

Supervisory Job

Much like the way we passed the handler to a coroutine, we may also pass an instance, for example, supervisor, of a SupervisorJob like launch(coroutineContext + supervisor). Alternatively, we may wrap the supervised children into a supervisorScope call. In either case, the supervised children won't propagate their cancellation to their parents. But if a parent were to cancel, then its children will be cancelled.

Let's change the previous code to use a supervisor and observe the behaviors described.

```
runBlocking {
  val handler = CoroutineExceptionHandler { _, ex ->
    println("Exception handled: ${ex.message}")
  }
```

```
val job = launch(Dispatchers.IO + handler) {
  supervisorScope {
    launch { fetchResponse(200, 5000) }
    launch { fetchResponse(202, 1000) }
    launch { fetchResponse(404, 2000) }
  }
}
Thread.sleep(4000)
println("200 should still be running at this time")
println("let the parent cancel now")
job.cancel()
job.join()
}
```

We wrapped the three nested calls to launch() within a supervisorScope() call. Then we let the coroutine run for four seconds. During this time, the coroutine that's processing code 202 should complete and the coroutine that's processing code 404 should cancel. The coroutine that's processing code 200 should be unaffected during this time. If we leave it alone, it will run to completion, not affected by its siblings. But at the end of 4 seconds we cancel the parent, which causes the child coroutine to cancel. We can see this behavior in the output:

```
202 Accepted
Exception handled: http://httpstat.us/404?sleep=2000
200 should still be running at this time
let the parent cancel now
Job was cancelled for fetchResponse 200
```

Use supervised coroutines only when you want to configure a clear top-down hierarchy of independent child tasks. When one of the children fails, in this case, you still want its siblings to continue unaffected. But if the parent is cancelled, you want to shut down the tasks. On the other hand, if you want the tasks to be fully cooperative, then rely upon the default behavior of coroutines.

Programming with Timeouts

As a simple rule, both in life and programming, we should never do anything without timeouts. Coroutines are suitable for long-running cooperative tasks, but we don't want to wait an undue amount of time or forever. We can program timeouts easily when using coroutines.

If a coroutine takes more time than the given allowance to complete, it'll receive a TimeoutCancellationException, which is a subclass of CancellationException. In effect, the task that takes longer than the permitted time to complete will be cancelled due to timeout, and all the rules we discussed about cancellation apply to this type of cancellation also.

Let's replace the code within runBlocking() in the previous example with the following. We wrap the inner calls to launch() with a call to withTimeout() and specify a time allowance of 3000 milliseconds. Then we wait for the coroutines to finish.

```
runBlocking {
  val handler = CoroutineExceptionHandler { _, ex ->
    println("Exception handled: ${ex.message}")
  }

  val job = launch(Dispatchers.IO + handler) {
    withTimeout(3000) {
      launch { fetchResponse(200, 5000) }
      launch { fetchResponse(201, 1000) }
      launch { fetchResponse(202, 2000) }
    }
  }

  job.join()
}
```

Let's run the code and take a look at the output:

```
201 Created
202 Accepted
Timed out waiting for 3000 ms for fetchResponse 200
```

The coroutines that took shorter than the given 3 seconds (and thankfully didn't run into any network errors) completed successfully. The coroutine that took its sweet time got cancelled.

Wrapping Up

Coroutines not only provide a great way to program asynchronous execution, but they also offer a sensible and easy way to deal with exceptions. Coroutines nicely help keep the code structure of synchronous, sequential code similar to concurrent and asynchronous code. This reduces the cost of making code change when concurrency and asynchronous operations are necessary, and also makes it easier to reason, debug, and maintain code. In addition to paving the way for efficient execution, mapping a complex network of tasks onto a hierarchy of coroutines makes it easier to manage the lifecycle of execution. You can control the duration of execution using timeouts and also set up supervisory jobs to control the interaction between the coroutines in the hierarchy.

In this chapter, in addition to learning these nuances of coroutines, you've also seen how to asynchronously fetch data from a remote service. Next, we'll focus on integrating Kotlin with Java and apply the language capabilities to build Spring and Android applications.

Part VI

Interop and Testing

Having looked at the core capabilities of the language, let's now turn our attention to applying Kotlin. In this part, you'll learn how to use Kotlin with Spring and to create Android applications. You'll also learn how to use Kotlin with Gradle and Maven and, along the way, pick up some techniques for unit testing Kotlin code with tools like KotlinTest and Mockk. We'll also explore the options to interoperate between Java and Kotlin code running side by side.

CHAPTER 17

Intermixing Java and Kotlin

The focus of this book is Kotlin for developers familiar with Java, and in this chapter, we'll take a look at intermixing Kotlin and Java code. We'll first look at calling Java code from Kotlin. Then we'll dive into the intricacies of calling Kotlin code from Java.

If your application is being developed predominantly using Kotlin, you may use Java libraries in your projects as much as you want. You may even intermix Kotlin source files and Java source files in your projects, if you like. You'll see in this chapter that calling Java code from within Kotlin is straightforward, and the issues you'll run into are minimal and easy to resolve.

If your application is mostly written in Java, you may use Kotlin libraries or even intermix Kotlin source files in your projects. Since Kotlin has special features that are not available in Java—default arguments, to mention one example—the authors of the Kotlin code have to take extra measures if they intend to make the code properly available for calls from Java. While calling code written in Kotlin from other Kotlin code is natural and effortless, calling the code from Java takes effort. In this chapter, we'll discuss various measures you have to take to make your Kotlin code available for practical use from Java.

We'll first look at why and how to mix Kotlin and Java source files in the same project. Then we'll explore calling Java code from within Kotlin and how to resolve some minor glitches you may run into. After that, for most of this chapter we'll focus on how to prepare Kotlin code for use from Java.

Joint Compilation

You can intermix code written using Java and Kotlin two different ways:

- Bring code written in either of those languages into a Java or Kotlin project as a JAR file dependency.

- Have source files written in the two languages, side by side, in a project.

The first approach is the most common. Currently you bring dependencies from Maven or JCenter into your Java projects using a build tool like Maven or Gradle. Likewise, you can bring dependencies into your Kotlin projects. The JAR files your code depends on may be created from Java, Kotlin, or both. If there are no compatibility issues, using these JAR files written in Kotlin or Java feels natural, just like using Java JAR files in Java projects. Any compatibility issues that may surface will be due to the language differences and not due to the JAR file integration. The techniques discussed later in this chapter will help resolve those issues.

The second approach, of mixing both Java and Kotlin source code in one project, is an option if you're introducing Kotlin into legacy Java projects and you want to make use of the power of Kotlin in some areas of the application.

Obviously, to compile the code written in the two different languages, you'll have to use the compilers of the respective languages. However, complications will arise from interdependencies.

Suppose your Kotlin code is calling some of your Java code, and some of your Java code is calling your Kotlin code. Compiling Java code first will fail since the Kotlin code it depends on hasn't been compiled yet into bytecode. Thankfully, this situation can be resolved by running the Kotlin compiler first and then the Java compiler. For this method to work, you must provide both the Kotlin source files and the Java source files to the Kotlin compiler. Upon seeing the Java source files, the Kotlin compiler will create stubs for the classes and methods in the given Java source files so that the dependencies of the Kotlin code are satisfied. Once the bytecode from the Kotlin code is generated, when you run the Java compiler, it will find the necessary Kotlin code dependencies for the Java code.

If you're using Maven or Gradle to run your build, then refer to the documentation[1] to set up the project for joint compilation.

---

1. https://kotlinlang.org/docs/tutorials/build-tools.html

Irrespective of the tools you use to build, running the compilations from the command line will give a clear view of the underlying mechanism. For that reason, let's explore compiling code for a small sample project that mixes source files from both Java and Kotlin.

The following project contains two Kotlin source files under the directory jointcompilation/src/main/kotlin/com/agiledeveloper/joint and one Java source file under the directory jointcompilation/src/main/java/com/agiledeveloper/joint. The Constants class written in Kotlin doesn't have any dependencies, and we'll take a look at that first:

intermixing/jointcompilation/src/main/kotlin/com/agiledeveloper/joint/Constants.kt
```kotlin
package com.agiledeveloper.joint

class Constants {
  val freezingPointInF = 32.0
}
```

The Constants class has a property named freezingPointInF, which has been initialized to the expected value. Let's take a look at the Java class that will use this class:

intermixing/jointcompilation/src/main/java/com/agiledeveloper/joint/Util.java
```java
package com.agiledeveloper.joint;

public class Util {
  public double f2c(double fahrenheit) {
    return (fahrenheit - new Constants().getFreezingPointInF()) * 5 / 9.0;
  }
}
```

The Util Java class has a f2c() method that uses the Constants Kotlin class, but the syntax is no different from the way a Java class will use another Java class. The property in the Constants Kotlin class is accessed using a getter from Java, much like the way properties are accessed in Java. The Kotlin compiler creates getters for val properties and both getters and setters for var properties. Whereas we use the property name directly in Kotlin to access the properties of a class, from within Java we use the getters/setters. Let's look at some other Kotlin code that will make use of the Util Java class:

intermixing/jointcompilation/src/main/kotlin/com/agiledeveloper/joint/App.kt
```kotlin
package com.agiledeveloper.joint

import kotlin.jvm.JvmStatic

object App {
  @JvmStatic
  fun main(@Suppress("UNUSED_PARAMETER") args: Array<String>) {
    println("Running App...")

    println(Util().f2c(50.0))
  }
}
```

The App object, a singleton, has a main() method that has been marked with the JvmStatic annotation so the compiler will generate the method as a static method—we'll take a look at this annotation later in this chapter. Within the main() method, we use the Java class much like how we use any Kotlin class from within Kotlin.

To compile this code, we have to first run the Kotlin compiler, but include both the Kotlin source files and the Java source file, like so:

```
$ kotlinc-jvm -d classes \
  src/main/kotlin/com/agiledeveloper/joint/*.kt \
  src/main/java/com/agiledeveloper/joint/*.java
```

The command instructs the compiler to place the generated class files in the classes directory. If you take a peek into the classes/com/agiledeveloper/joint directory after running the above command, you'll see the files App.class and Constants.class. The compiler generated a stub for the Util Java class, but didn't save it into the destination directory. However, the compiler was able to use the stub to verify proper dependency of App on the Util class. And since the Constants.class file has been generated, the Java compiler should be able to verify the needs of the Util class. Let's now compile the Util Java class, using the Java compiler:

```
$ javac -d classes -classpath classes \
  src/main/java/com/agiledeveloper/joint/*.java
```

We provided the path to the classes directory as the classpath compile-time argument to the Java compiler. We specified the same directory as the destination directory for the generated .class file. After running the command, take a look at the classes/com/agiledeveloper/joint directory to confirm that the .class file exists for all the three files, two generated earlier by the Kotlin compiler and now the new one by the Java compiler.

You may run the code using the kotlin command or the java command. Let's run it using the kotlin command:

```
$ kotlin -classpath classes com.agiledeveloper.joint.App
```

All it needed was a reference to the classpath, to where the .class files are located.

To run it using the java command, include the path to the Kotlin standard library, like so:

```
$ java -classpath classes:$KOTLIN_PATH/lib/kotlin-stdlib.jar \
  com.agiledeveloper.joint.App
```

On Windows, use ; instead of : to separate the paths in the classpath and also %KOTLIN_PATH% for the environment variable that specifies the path to where Kotlin is installed on the system.

Whether you run the compiled code using kotlin or java, the output will be:

```
Running App...
10.0
```

If you're programming with modules for Java 9 or later, then place your code in the modulepath instead of the classpath.

In short, run the Kotlin compiler first and then the Java compiler. Also, remember to provide both Kotlin source files and Java source files to the Kotlin compiler so it can create the necessary stubs for Java code and verify that the Kotlin code's dependencies are correct.

The flexibility offered by the Kotlin compiler to create a stub for the Java code makes it possible to intermix Java and Kotlin source files in the same project. But that doesn't solve all the integration woes that may arise. Let's dive in to see some of the challenges that may arise when we use code written in one language in the other, irrespective of whether we use JAR dependencies or intermix source files from the two languages in the same project.

Calling Java from Kotlin

Calling code written in Java from within Kotlin .kt files and .kts scripts is straightforward for most part. Kotlin naturally integrates with Java, and we can use properties and methods without thinking twice—it almost always just works.

To see this in action, and learn ways to work around occasional glitches you may run into, let's write a Java class that we will then use from Kotlin.

```
intermixing/javafromkotlin/src/main/java/com/agiledeveloper/JavaClass.java
package com.agiledeveloper;

import java.util.List;
import static java.util.stream.Collectors.toList;

public class JavaClass {
  public int getZero() { return 0; }

  public List<String> convertToUpper(List<String> names) {
    return names.stream()
      .map(String::toUpperCase)
      .collect(toList());
  }
```

```java
  public void suspend() {
    System.out.println("suspending...");
  }
  public String when() {
    return "Now!";
  }
}
```

The class JavaClass has a getter method, a convertToUpper() method, a method named suspend(), and another method named when(). The purpose of the first two methods is to illustrate how Kotlin works well with Java. The last two methods will help to see how Kotlin deals with Java method names that conflict with keywords in Kotlin.

In this example, the Kotlin code we'll soon write will depend on Java code, but no Java code depends on Kotlin code. So we can straightaway compile the Java code using the Java compiler, instead of having to run the Kotlin compiler first. Here's the command to compile the Java code:

```
$ javac -d classes src/main/java/com/agiledeveloper/*
```

This command places the generated .class file under the classes subdirectory. We can use this from Kotlin code written in a .kt file or script written in a .kts file. Let's write a script in a file named sample.kts, which we will run using the followng command:

```
$ kotlinc-jvm -classpath classes -script sample.kts
```

Let's exercise the getZero() method of the JavaClass from within a Kotlin script written in a file named sample.kts.

intermixing/javafromkotlin/sample.kts
```kotlin
import com.agiledeveloper.JavaClass

val javaObject = JavaClass()

println(javaObject.zero) // 0
```

We imported the Java class, created an instance of the class, and accessed the property zero. The fact that the class was written using Java didn't matter, and we used the class using the natural Kotlin syntax. Even though the Java class has a getter, we access the property from Kotlin using the name of the property instead of the getter. Run the script using the command mentioned previously to see the result 0 printed on the console.

It was easy to call the property on the instance of JavaClass. Calling the convert-ToUpper() method from Kotlin shouldn't pose any challenges either.

Let's add a call to the convertToUpper() method to the sample.kts file.

intermixing/javafromkotlin/sample.kts
```
println(javaObject.convertToUpper(listOf("Jack", "Jill"))) //[JACK, JILL]
```

To the convertToUpper() method we passed an instance of List<String>, created using the Kotlin's listOf() method. Since Kotlin's collections are compile-time views and map directly to JDK collections, there's no runtime overhead or compile-time stunts to use the Kotlin collections API to interact with Java code that uses the JDK collections. Run the script to verify that the output shows the list returned by the method call.

Let's step it up a notch to see how Kotlin handles a call to the suspend() method of the JavaClass. Kotlin's suspend keyword is used to mark functions as suspendible, but will the Kotlin compiler choke up on a call to a method named suspend? Let's address that question straight on to put an end to the suspense.

To the sample.kts file add a call to the suspend() method, like so:

intermixing/javafromkotlin/sample.kts
```
javaObject.suspend() //suspending...
```

Execute the script to see if the compiler had any issues with the call. You'll see the output of the suspend() method on the console. Phew.

Kotlin handled that gracefully, even though suspend is a keyword. The compiler doesn't flinch, and the program executes the call to the suspend() method of the JavaClass just fine.

With the encouragement from the previous result, let's move ahead to calling the when() method of the JavaClass. In Kotlin, when is both an expression and a statement. Let's see if Kotlin is able to handle a call to a method named when(), much like how it was able to deal with suspend().

intermixing/javafromkotlin/sample.kts
```
println(javaObject.when()) //error: expecting an expression
```

As an experienced programmer, you know it's not a question of *if*, but of *when* things fall apart. The Kotlin compiler chokes up when it sees the call to when(), and complains that it is expecting to see a when expression of Kotlin. A rogue developer who may be opposed to using Kotlin may now name methods when() just to make our lives difficult. Should we keep this quiet—what gives?

Thankfully, this isn't a showstopper to calling Java code from Kotlin. The language provides an escape facility, a work-around, for situations like this—the backtick.

When there's a keyword conflict between Java code and Kotlin, use the backtick operator to escape the method or property name:

intermixing/javafromkotlin/sample.kts
```
println(javaObject.`when`()) //Now!
```

When there's a conflict with a Kotlin keyword, we merely wrap the property or method name within a pair of backtick symbols, and off we go.

Kotlin was designed with interoperating with Java code and libraries in mind. Thus, calling Java code from Kotlin isn't an issue, and any minor glitches have an easy work-around. Let's next take a look at calling Kotlin code from within Java.

Calling Kotlin from Java

Once you compile Kotlin code to bytecode, you can use the .class files and JAR files created from Kotlin source files in Java projects. Alternatively, you may also intermix Kotlin source files, side by side, with Java source files and call Kotlin code from within Java code. We've already seen the mechanics to make this work. Let's now focus on the issues with source code we may run into with such integration efforts.

Kotlin has a number of features that don't exist in Java. Also, Kotlin is idiomatically different from Java in many ways. Thus, the Kotlin way of doing things that work elegantly and expressively when writing code in Kotlin won't work when calling Kotlin code from Java.

If the Kotlin code you're creating is for exclusive use with other Kotlin code, then don't worry about calling from Java—for example, with code related to UI or controllers and services written to run within a framework. Since no Java code will directly call such code, there's no reason to spend time and effort to make the code accessible from Java.

If you intend your Kotlin code to be used from Java code, then you have to take some extra steps for a smoother integration. If you're working on a project where such integration is needed, then integrate early and often to make sure that the Kotlin compiler is generating bytecode that's compatible with the needs of programmers using the code from Java. If you're creating a library in Kotlin for third-party programmers to use from Java, then create test code in Java, in addition to creating test code in Kotlin, and run those tests using continuous integration. This will help you to both verify that your code works as intended, whether it's called from Java or Kotlin, and also verify that your code integrates well when called from Java.

In spite of the idiomatic differences, the designers of the Kotlin language and the Kotlin standard library have provided many things to make the integration of Java code with Kotlin code as smooth as possible. When programming in Kotlin, we have to make use of some of these integration-related features so that our Kotlin code can be properly used from Java. Let's take a look at various features that are geared toward Java to Kotlin integration.

We'll create a Counter class in Kotlin, use it from a Kotlin script usecounter.kts and also from a UseCounter class written in Java. Using the Counter class from both Kotlin and Java will help us clearly see the extra steps we have to take for Java integration.

To practice along with the following examples, you'll have to compile the Kotlin code and the Java code separately. Take note of the following commands. As we incrementally develop the code, you can use these commands to compile and run the code, to see the outputs.

To compile the Kotlin code, use the following command:

```
$ kotlinc-jvm -d classes src/main/kotlin/com/agiledeveloper/Counter.kt
```

When you're ready to execute the Kotlin script usecounter.kts, use this command:

```
$ kotlinc-jvm -classpath classes -script usecounter.kts
```

You can compile the Java code with this command:

```
$ javac -d classes -classpath classes:$KOTLIN_PATH/lib/kotlin-stdlib.jar \
  src/main/java/com/agiledeveloper/UseCounter.java
```

In addition to including the path to where the bytecode generated from Kotlin source is located, we also add the Kotlin standard library to the classpath. Later, as we work on the examples, we'll see why the Kotlin standard library is needed during compilation.

Finally, to run the Java class UseCounter, use the following command:

```
$ java -classpath classes:$KOTLIN_PATH/lib/kotlin-stdlib.jar \
  com.agiledeveloper.UseCounter
```

Now that we've seen the commands to compile, let's get down to the code. We'll walk through several integration issues and find ways to resolve each one of them.

Using Overloaded Operators from Java

When programming in Kotlin we can make use of operator overloading to create concise and expressive code. Operator-overloaded functions are created using well-defined method-naming conventions, as we saw in Overloading Operators, on page 222. Let's create a Counter Kotlin data class with a plus() function to overload the + operator on instances of the class.

intermixing/kotlinfromjava/src/main/kotlin/com/agiledeveloper/Counter.kt
```kotlin
package com.agiledeveloper

data class Counter(val value: Int) {
  operator fun plus(other: Counter) = Counter(value + other.value)
}
```

The Counter class's constructor takes an initial value of type Int for the value property. The class also has one method that will return a new Counter instance whose value is the sum of two Counter instances used as operands for the + operator.

Before we look at using this class from Java, let's use it from within a Kotlin script:

intermixing/kotlinfromjava/usecounter.kts
```kotlin
import com.agiledeveloper.*

val counter = Counter(1)
println(counter + counter)
```

We used the + operator to sum up the values in the two operands. This fluency of Kotlin isn't possible in Java, since Java doesn't permit operator overloading. Not all is lost, though. The method-naming convention used in Kotlin for operators was chosen carefully to promote interoperability with Java. From within Java, instead of using + we can use the plus() function, like so:

intermixing/kotlinfromjava/src/main/java/com/agiledeveloper/UseCounter.java
```java
package com.agiledeveloper;

import kotlin.jvm.functions.Function1;

public class UseCounter {
  public static void main(String[] args) {
    Counter counter = new Counter(1);

    System.out.println(counter.plus(counter)); //Counter(value=2)
  }
}
```

Within the main() method of UseCounter Java class, we create an instance of Counter and invoke the plus() method on it. Compile the Kotlin code and then the Java code, using the commands mentioned previously, and execute the Java code. The output will display the class name, along with the value of the value property, as shown in the comment on the line with the call to plus() in the example code.

When programming in Kotlin, we don't have to do anything special to permit Java code to make use of operator overloading. Whereas the Kotlin code will use the operators, the Java code will use the corresponding methods.

Creating static Methods

Kotlin doesn't have static methods. The closest to static methods in Kotlin are methods we create in singletons (Singleton with Object Declaration, on page 110) and companion objects (Companion Objects and Class Members, on page 124). We can call the methods in singleton objects and companion objects without creating an instance of a class in Kotlin. But to easily call these methods from Java, we have to instruct the Kotlin compiler to mark these methods as static in the bytecode. That can be achieved using the JvmStatic annotation. Let's add a companion object to the Counter class and mark a create() method in it with that annotation.

intermixing/kotlinfromjava/src/main/kotlin/com/agiledeveloper/Counter.kt
```kotlin
//within the Counter class...
companion object {
  @JvmStatic
  fun create() = Counter(0)
}
```

For this code to compile correctly, we have to import the JvmStatic class in the top of the Counter.kt file, right after the package declaration line:

intermixing/kotlinfromjava/src/main/kotlin/com/agiledeveloper/Counter.kt
```kotlin
import kotlin.jvm.JvmStatic
```

Irrespective of whether we mark the methods in singletons or companion objects with the JvmStatic annotation, we can call the methods from Kotlin without explicitly creating an instance, as you can see in the following code to call the create() method of the Counter companion object:

intermixing/kotlinfromjava/usecounter.kts
```kotlin
println(Counter.create())
```

However, since the create() method is marked with the annotation, we can call that method from Java as well, much like how we would call static methods in Java. Let's add the following code to the main() method of the UseCounter Java class.

intermixing/kotlinfromjava/src/main/java/com/agiledeveloper/UseCounter.java
```java
//within the main method of UseCounter...
Counter counter0 = Counter.create();
System.out.println(counter0); //Counter(value=0)
```

Try removing the JvmStatic annotation in the Kotlin code and notice how the Java code no longer compiles. When creating methods that belong to a singleton or a companion object, ask if you intend each one of those methods to be easily accessible as a static method from Java. If the answer to that question for a method is yes, then annotate it; otherwise leave out the annotation.

Passing Lambdas

In addition to receiving objects, both in Kotlin and in Java, functions may receive other functions as arguments. On the receiving end, the parameters for the lambda expressions are backed by functional interfaces in Java, like Runnable, Consumer<T>, Function<T, R>, or your own homegrown interfaces with exactly one abstract method. In the case of Kotlin, functions that receive lambda expressions are defined using a different syntax when compared to how such functions are defined in Java—see Receiving Lambdas, on page 181. But, internally, Kotlin also uses functional interfaces to represent lambda expressions. Let's create a function in Kotlin that receives a lambda expression and see how we can make use of it in Java.

Let's add a method named map() to the Counter class in Kotlin. This method will receive a lambda expression as its parameter.

intermixing/kotlinfromjava/src/main/kotlin/com/agiledeveloper/Counter.kt
```
fun map(mapper: (Counter) -> Counter) = mapper(this)
```

The type of the mapper parameter of the map() function is a lambda expression—an anonymous function—that takes a Counter instance as its parameter and returns a Counter instance as its result. In the implementation of the map() function, we invoke the lambda expression referenced by the mapper parameter and pass the current object this as argument. The instance returned by the lambda expression is in turn returned by the map() function.

In Chapter 10, Functional Programming with Lambdas, on page 175, we saw how to invoke higher-order functions—that is, functions that take lambda expressions. Let's call the above map() function from within Kotlin code and then compare that call to a call from Java.

intermixing/kotlinfromjava/usecounter.kts
```
println(counter.map { ctr -> ctr + ctr })
```

Since the map() function takes only one parameter, and that happens to be a lambda expression, we can use the flexible Kotlin syntax with {} to pass the lambda expression. Java doesn't permit the use of {}, and lambdas are placed within (). Here's the Java code to call the map() method:

intermixing/kotlinfromjava/src/main/java/com/agiledeveloper/UseCounter.java

```
System.out.println(counter.map(ctr -> ctr.plus(ctr))); //Counter(value=2)
```

If that works, then that syntax is pretty good—it means that we're able to pass a lambda expression written in Java to a function written in Kotlin that takes a lambda expression. But if you try to compile that Java code, you'll get an error saying kotlin.jvm.functions.Function1 is not found. The reason for that error is, internally, the bytecode generated for the map() function references a functional interface defined in the Kotlin standard library. The Java compiler tries to bind the lambda expression to that interface and complains that it has no knowledge of that interface. We can fix that easily by adding an import.

intermixing/kotlinfromjava/src/main/java/com/agiledeveloper/UseCounter.java

```
import kotlin.jvm.functions.Function1;
```

The compiler needs access to the Kotlin standard library which contains the definition of the Function1 interface. That's the reason—earlier, when we looked at the compilation commands—we included the Kotlin standard library in the classpath during compilation.

With the import in place, we can pass a lambda expression written in Java to the map() function. Depending on the number of arguments the lambda expressions take, we have to import interfaces like Function0, Function1, Function2, and so on, from the Kotlin standard library. A quick look at the error message from the Java compiler will reveal the details of what we need to import.

Adding throws Clause

Unlike the Java compiler which distinguishes between checked exceptions and unchecked exceptions, the Kotlin compiler treats them as one. We saw in try-catch Is Optional, on page 24, how the Kotlin compiler doesn't force you to handle exceptions. You may choose to handle an exception in a particular function or let the exception propagate to the caller. The low ceremony, flexible nature of Kotlin allows us to evolve code more freely, as our understanding of the requirements improves. However, that flexibility will get in the way if we intend to access the functions written in Kotlin from Java. The reason is that the Java compiler won't allow you to place a catch for a checked exception unless the signature of the method being called has a throws clause. To illustrate this issue, and find a solution, let's write a function in Kotlin that may potentially result in an exception.

Add a readFile() method to the Counter class that will return the contents of a file whose path is given as the parameter.

intermixing/kotlinfromjava/src/main/kotlin/com/agiledeveloper/Counter.kt
```
fun readFile(path: String) = java.io.File(path).readLines()
```

The readFile() function is using the java.io.File class which may blow up with a checked exception java.io.FileNotFoundException if the given path is invalid. The Kotlin compiler doesn't force us to deal with the exception on the spot, just like the Java compiler doesn't force us to deal with unchecked exceptions.

When calling the readFile() function from within Kotlin, we may decide to play it safe and handle the exception, in case the call results in an exception. Let's make a call to the readFile() function but wrap it within a try-catch:

intermixing/kotlinfromjava/usecounter.kts
```
try {
  counter.readFile("blah")
} catch(ex: java.io.FileNotFoundException) {
  println("File not found")
}
```

Execute the Kotlin script and you'll notice the code reports a File not found error message since a file named blah doesn't exist in the current directory. If you don't handle the exception, the script will blow up.

Now let's turn our attention to calling the readFile() function from Java.

intermixing/kotlinfromjava/src/main/java/com/agiledeveloper/UseCounter.java
```
try {
  counter.readFile("blah");
} catch(java.io.FileNotFoundException ex) {
  System.out.println("File not found");
}
```

The above Java code is the syntactical equivalent of the code we wrote in Kotlin to call the readFile() function. But when we compile the Java code, we'll get an error:

```
exception FileNotFoundException is never thrown in body of corresponding try
  statement
```

The Java compiler notices that the catch targets a checked exception, but the readFile() function, in the generated bytecode, isn't marked with the throws clause. To place the call to readFile() in Java within a try block and to handle a checked exception, we'll have to tell the Kotlin compiler to generate the appropriate throws clause. This is done using the Throws annotation.

Revisit the Counter class and update the readFile() method definition to add the annotation.

intermixing/kotlinfromjava/src/main/kotlin/com/agiledeveloper/Counter.kt
```
@Throws(java.io.FileNotFoundException::class)
fun readFile(path: String) = java.io.File(path).readLines()
```

The annotation tells the Kotlin compiler to add a throws java.io.FileNotFoundException clause in the bytecode as part of the signature of the readFile() method.

After making the above change and recompiling the file Counter.kt, recompile the Java file UseCounter.java with the call to readFile() wrapped within the try-catch block. The code will compile with no errors this time, and when run, the Java code will print the same error message as the Kotlin version did.

Using Functions with Default Arguments

Kotlin's default arguments feature that we saw in Default and Named Arguments, on page 43, allows us to omit some arguments when making function calls. Let's explore how this feature pans out when we call functions with default arguments from Java.

Open the Counter class and add a new function add() that takes one parameter with a default argument value.

intermixing/kotlinfromjava/src/main/kotlin/com/agiledeveloper/Counter.kt
```
fun add(n: Int = 1) = Counter(value + n)
```

From within the Kotlin code, we can call the add() function, either with one argument of type Int or without any arguments. When called with no arguments, the Kotlin compiler will pass the default value of 1 to the add() function.

intermixing/kotlinfromjava/usecounter.kts
```
println(counter.add(3))
println(counter.add())
```

That flexibility is nice. Let's try to make use of that from Java code.

intermixing/kotlinfromjava/src/main/java/com/agiledeveloper/UseCounter.java
```
System.out.println(counter.add(3));
System.out.println(counter.add());
```

In the first line, we call the add() function with one argument, 3. That's not a problem. If you want to call from Java a function with values for all the arguments, there's no issue. But if you like to take advantage of the default arguments and call, as in this example, the add() function without all the arguments, the compiler will choke up. The call to add() with no arguments will result in the following error:

```
error: method add in class Counter cannot be applied to given types;
```

The reason for this failure is that the Java compiler is complaining that it couldn't find a function add() that doesn't take any arguments.

If you'd like Java programmers to be able to call your functions with default arguments with fewer than all the possible arguments, then you can instruct the Kotlin compiler to generate overloaded functions using the JvmOverloads annotation. Upon seeing this annotation, the Kotlin compiler will generate multiple overloaded functions, as necessary, and provide a thin implementation in each to route the call to the version that takes all the parameters.

Let's modify the add() function in the Counter class to add the annotation.

intermixing/kotlinfromjava/src/main/kotlin/com/agiledeveloper/Counter.kt
```
@JvmOverloads
fun add(n: Int = 1) = Counter(value + n)
```

After this change, compile the Kotlin code and then the Java code. Both the calls to add(3) and add() will now compile.

Accessing Top-Level Functions

Functions aren't required to belong to a class or a singleton in Kotlin. We saw in Chapter 3, Working with Functions, on page 37, that top-level functions belong to packages. We can directly import the functions, from their respective packages, into Kotlin and use them without much fanfare. Let's see how to use the top-level functions from within Java code.

First, we'll create a top-level function in the com.agiledeveloper package, right above the Counter class in the file Counter.kt.

intermixing/kotlinfromjava/src/main/kotlin/com/agiledeveloper/Counter.kt
```
//place this after the import and before the data class Counter
fun createCounter() = Counter(0)
```

Using this createCounter() top-level function is easy. We already have the line import com.agiledeveloper.* in the script file usecounter.kts. So we can readily refer to the top-level function in the script:

intermixing/kotlinfromjava/usecounter.kts
```
println(createCounter())
```

It'll take a bit more effort to access this top-level function from within Java. In the bytecode, top-level functions aren't permitted, and Kotlin's top-level functions have to be sheltered in a class. By default, Kotlin chooses to place the top-level functions in a class that's derived from the name of the file that contains the code.

In this example, the top-level function createCounter() is in the file Counter.kt. The Kotlin compiler decided to place that file in a class named CounterKt. Once you create a top-level function, you can see the CounterKt.class file being created in the classes/com/agiledeveloper directory when you compile the Counter.kt file using the Kotlin compiler command.

To access the top-level function, prefix the name of the function with the fully qualified class name, like so:

intermixing/kotlinfromjava/src/main/java/com/agiledeveloper/UseCounter.java
```
System.out.println(com.agiledeveloper.CounterKt.createCounter());
```

If the generated class name doesn't please you, you can change the name of the class that will hold the top-level functions of your package using the Jvm-Name annotation. You may use this annotation to resolve function signature collisions, to change the names of getters or setters, and so on. In this example, we'll use the annotation to define the class name that this file will map to.

intermixing/kotlinfromjava/src/main/kotlin/com/agiledeveloper/Counter.kt
```
@file:JvmName("CounterTop")
package com.agiledeveloper
```

With the @file:JvmName annotation, placed before the package declaration, we tell the Kotlin compiler that the top-level function in this file—Counter.kt—should be in a class file CounterTop.class instead of in CounterKt.class. Compile the code and take a peek at the generated bytecode to confirm the new name of the .class file.

Now we can change the Java code to use the new name we gave for the host of the top-level function in our package.

intermixing/kotlinfromjava/src/main/java/com/agiledeveloper/UseCounter.java
```
System.out.println(com.agiledeveloper.CounterTop.createCounter());
```

Compile the code and execute it to confirm that the Java to Kotlin integration works as expected.

More Annotations

The annotations we've seen so far are useful for telling the Kotlin compiler to generate bytecode that allows the Java code to seamlessly interact with Kotlin code. The kotlin.jvm package has many more annotations to tailor different aspects of bytecode generation. For example, you can instruct the Kotlin compiler to mark a method as synchronized using the Synchronized annotation. You can instruct it to mark a method in an interface as a default method using the JvmDefault annotation. You can customize backing fields generated by the

Kotlin compiler to be volatile by using the Volatile annotation or transient by using the Transient annotation.

Explore the different annotations[2] available in the kotlin.jvm package, but don't go overboard with them. Use only annotations that are absolutely necessary, based on real use, and not for hypothetical extensibility.

Wrapping Up

It's highly likely that you'll have a need to intermix Kotlin and Java code on your projects. In this chapter we've seen how easy it is to use Java from Kotlin, but the other way around requires some effort and planning.

You may use any Java library from your Kotlin applications and also use Kotlin libraries from within Java applications. You may also use both Java and Kotlin source files side by side in your projects. The Kotlin compiler has facilities to enable joint compilation of source files written in Java and Kotlin.

Calling into Java code from Kotlin is fairly straightforward and mostly works without any effort. You may use a pair of backticks to escape any keyword conflicts that may arise. Calling from Java to Kotlin requires planning and effort. The reason for this stems from the differences between Kotlin and Java; in particular, the enhanced features are available only in Kotlin. Using annotations that are part of the Kotlin standard library, you can customize the bytecode generated by the Kotlin compiler so you can more easily call it from Java.

Creating automated tests is a great way to make sure that integration efforts are successful. And tests can provide fast feedback that code continues to work as expected as it evolves. In the next chapter, we'll take a look at writing unit tests for code written in Kotlin.

---

2. https://kotlinlang.org/api/latest/jvm/stdlib/kotlin.jvm/index.html

CHAPTER 18

Unit Testing with Kotlin

Code always does what we type and not what we meant, and that's true in statically typed languages as much as in dynamically typed languages. The Kotlin compiler's rigorous verification will substantially reduce errors that may occur in code. But, as the application evolves, it's our responsibility to verify that code continues to work as intended.

Manually running the code to verify if everything works as expected is expensive, time consuming, and in itself error prone. Automated testing is one of those steps that takes time but, in turn, results in saving significant time in the long run. Unit testing is a part of automated testing and, in this chapter, we'll look at how to write unit tests for code written using Kotlin.

We'll first look at how to write empirical tests for functions with no side effects—functions that will result in fast, predictable, deterministic results. Then we'll explore writing interaction tests for code with dependencies—that is, code that isn't idempotent and, depending on the state of the dependencies, may yield different results for each call. Finally, we'll look at writing tests for code that uses coroutines to make asynchronous calls.

You may pick from a variety of tools to unit test Kotlin code. In this chapter, we'll use KotlinTest for running the tests and Mockk for mocking out dependencies. We'll also measure the code coverage using Jacoco. Along the way, we'll discuss the reasons for choosing these tools.

At the end of this chapter, you'll know how to write automated tests for classes written in Kotlin and for top-level functions, how to mock out classes and extension functions, how to write tests for coroutines/asynchronous calls, and how to measure code coverage.

Let's get started with writing automated tests.

The Code Under Test

To practice writing automated tests for Kotlin code, we'll pick a sample application. We'll create an asynchronous program that will print, in sorted order of name, the status of different airports. The program will fetch the necessary data from a remote web service, like we saw in Chapter 16, Asynchronous Programming, on page 309. The overall design of the application that we'll create is shown in the following figure.

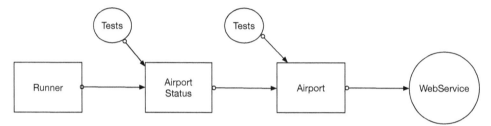

The AirportApp.kt file will hold the main() function to invoke a top-level function, written in the AirportStatus.kt file, within a com.agiledeveloper.airportstatus package. That function will use an Airport data class to hold the data for each airport of interest and to fetch the data from the remote web service.

The design will be implemented from right to left. The WebService, thankfully, already exists—we'll use the FAA website for airport information. We'll create, using tests, the Airport class first with methods to sort a list of airports, to get the data from the remote service, and to parse the JSON data. Then we'll implement, again with tests, the function in the AirportStatus.kt file. Finally, we'll write the main() function in AirportApp.kt.

We'll take the test-first approach—that is, we'll follow short cycles: write a small useful test first and then minimum code to make the test pass. At any time we'll be a maximum of one step away from code that passes all the tests.

Before we write any code, we have to make sure the necessary automated testing tool is set up properly. To test code written in Kotlin, you may use the traditional Java unit-testing tools: the good old JUnit 4 or the much newer JUnit 5. In this chapter, though, we'll use KotlinTest,[1] a unit testing tool targeted at unit testing Kotlin code. The benefit of using KotlinTest over JUnit is that the tests can follow the Kotlin idiomatic style. KotlinTest also provides facilities to create property-based tests and also data-driven tests. The first step should be to set up a project with the necessary tools. Let's do that next.

---

1.   https://github.com/kotlintest/kotlintest

Getting the Project Files

We'll write code in the unittests/airportapp directory—our project location for this example. Since setting up the build files often takes effort, we can save significant time by using a pre-created project structure. Download the source code zip file from the book's website,[2] unzip the file, and cd to the unittests/airportapp directory. Take a few minutes to study the project structure.

You'll find the following empty directories: src/main/kotlin/com/agiledeveloper/airportstatus and src/test/kotlin/com/agiledeveloper/airportstatus. These are the default directory structures, for source files and test files, used by both Gradle and Maven build tools. So we can use this structure irrespective of which build tool we pick from those two.

In addition to the two empty directories, in the project directory you'll also find files related to Gradle build and Maven build.

First, we have to pick either Gradle or Maven for the build tool. Maven is the more popular tool, while Gradle is the more pragmatic and lightweight tool. Depending on what you're comfortable with or what's used in projects you work on, feel free to make the appropriate choice.

If you choose to use Maven, skip the next subsection and proceed to Setting Up Maven, on page 351. If you opt to use Gradle, read along.

Setting Up Gradle

With Gradle[3] you may either use Groovy DSL to create a build.gradle build file or the Kotlin DSL to create a build.gradle.kts build file. As you may guess, we'll use the Kotlin DSL for Gradle in this chapter. You can use the readily provided build file from the airportapp project directory:

```
unittest/airportapp/build.gradle.kts
plugins {
  kotlin("jvm") version "1.3.41"
  application
  jacoco
}

repositories {
  mavenCentral()
  jcenter()
}
```

---

2. https://pragprog.com/titles/vskotlin/source_code
3. https://gradle.org/

```
val test by tasks.getting(Test::class) {
  useJUnitPlatform {}

  testLogging.showStandardStreams = true
}

dependencies {
  implementation(kotlin("stdlib"))
  implementation(kotlin("reflect:1.3.41"))
  implementation("org.jetbrains.kotlinx:kotlinx-coroutines-core:1.2.2")
  implementation("com.beust:klaxon:5.0.2")

  testImplementation("io.kotlintest:kotlintest-runner-junit5:3.3.1")
  testImplementation("io.mockk:mockk:1.9")
}

tasks {
  getByName<JacocoReport>("jacocoTestReport") {
      afterEvaluate {
          setClassDirectories(files(classDirectories.files.map {
              fileTree(it) { exclude("**/ui/**") }
          }))
      }
  }
}

jacoco {
  toolVersion = "0.8.3"
}

application {
  mainClassName = "com.agiledeveloper.ui.AirportAppKt"
}

defaultTasks("clean", "test", "jacocoTestReport")
```

We use the kotlin plugin to bring in the dependencies for Kotlin-related Gradle tasks to compile and test, the application plugin to be able to easily run the main() function through Gradle, and finally the jacoco plugin for the code coverage tool. The build file specifies both the mavenCentral repository, from which most necessary dependencies will be downloaded, and also the jcenter repository from which the JSON parser will be downloaded by Gradle.

The useJunitPlatform {} function is used to configure KotlinTest to run on top of the JUnit execution platform, a step needed by the KotlinTest tool. In the dependencies section, we have listed all the dependencies needed for this project: the Kotlin standard library, the reflection API, the coroutines library, the Klaxon JSON parser, the KotlinTest library, and the Mockk library. The application {} function is used to run the main() function from the AirportAppKt class, which we'll eventually write. Finally, the defaultTask specifies the build steps Gradle will follow by default, to clean up the project build directory, to compile and run the tests, and to measure code coverage.

To run the build file build.gradle.kts, we need the Gradle tool. The easiest way to download the desired version of Gradle is using the Gradle wrapper. It's already provided in the airportapp project directory for your convenience. To install Gradle and to run the tests, type the following command:

```
$ gradlew
```

On Windows, the command will execute the gradlew.bat file. On some Unix-like systems you may have to prefix the command with a dot-slash, like so, ./gradlew to run the command tool from the current directory.

Even though we don't have any tests or code yet, the build command should download the specified dependencies and print a message on the console that the build was successful.

It's time to write our first test. Since you're using Gradle, skip the next sub-section and proceed to Starting with a Canary Test, on page 352.

Setting Up Maven

You can use the readily provided Maven build file from the airportapp project directory. The pom.xml file contains the configurations for the necessary dependencies:

- The repositories include mavenCentral by default, but we've also added jcenter repository to download the JSON parser. The build file also shows configuration for the kotlin-maven-plugin and the maven-compiler-plugin, among other things.

- The build file also brings in the following dependencies: the Kotlin standard library, the reflection API, the coroutines library, the Klaxon JSON parser, the KotlinTest library, and the Mockk library.

- The build file is configured to create an archive, a jar file, with the necessary manifest entry to easily run the main() function from AirportAppKt, which we'll write eventually.

To use the build file, first download Maven[4] if you don't already have it on your system. Once you have Maven installed, run the build and test using the command:

```
$ mvn package
```

---

4. https://maven.apache.org/

Even though we don't have any tests or code yet, the build command should download the specified dependencies and print a message on the console that the build was successful.

It's time to write our first test.

Starting with a Canary Test

A canary test is a test that asserts that true is equal to true. That sounds silly, as it appears that such a test isn't doing much, but starting with a canary test is a good way to verify that the project is set up properly with the necessary tools. If we run into any errors at this stage, it's easier to ask for help, in a team setting, from just about anyone who knows the tools.

From the design diagram we saw in The Code Under Test, on page 348, the AirportTest is a good starting point. Let's create a test suite, using KotlinTest, with just one test in it.

Practice Along by Starting with a Sample Project

The best way to gain a deeper understanding of writing tests is to practice. To make it easier for you, the source code repository contains an airportapp directory that has both the Gradle and Maven build files. On your system, change to the airportapp directory and create your files there, using the subdirectory names and files specified in the text in this chapter. Since we'll be evolving code incrementally using tests, if you click on the links above the code listings in this chapter, you'll see the partial code instead of the complete code.

Create a file named AirportTest.kt under the src/test/kotlin/com/agiledeveloper/airportstatus directory.

unittest/steps/canary/src/test/kotlin/com/agiledeveloper/airportstatus/AirportTest.kt
```kotlin
package com.agiledeveloper.airportstatus

import io.kotlintest.specs.StringSpec
import io.kotlintest.shouldBe

class AirportTest : StringSpec() {
  init {
    "canary test should pass" {
      true shouldBe true
    }
  }
}
```

The KotlinTest library comes with a few different assertion options, and in the code we use the shouldBe function to assert. Test suites written using KotlinTest inherit from one of the base classes from the KotlinTest library, the simplest of which is a StringSpec, which provides a nice way to describe the specifications—that is, the tests. We inherit the AirportTest class from Kotlin-Test's StringSpec class. Within the class, we write tests inside a lambda passed to the init() method, using a very flexible syntax—a string to represent a test method name and a lambda to hold the body of the test. The KotlinTest library provides a few variations in syntax to define tests, but the structure we're using is useful, as we'll see soon, to define pre- and post-operations to run before and after each test.

The Kotlin idiomatic style shines here. KotlinTest has injected the String class with an extension function, invoke(). This allows us to treat an arbitrary String like it's a function name. So to define a test, we merely key in a string to describe the test, and pass a lambda with the test body as argument to that string—nice syntax.

Also, the shouldBe assert function is declared in KotlinTest as an infix function, so we can omit the dot and parenthesis when invoking that function.

Once you save the file, either run the Gradle build file like you saw in Setting Up Gradle, on page 349, or the Maven build file like you saw in Setting Up Maven, on page 351. Irrespective of which build tool you used, you should see a build success message, indicating that the canary test passed.

To verify things are really working well, change the first true in the expression true shouldBe true to false, like so: false shouldBe true. Run the test again and watch it fail—that confirms the tool is set up properly and doing its job. Change false to true again, and verify the test is passing.

Now that we know the environment is set up properly, let's move forward to write some real tests.

Writing Empirical Tests

Empirical tests are common in unit testing—you call a method and verify that it did what you expected. Such tests help us to verify that, as code evolves, the expectations are still met and the code continues to work as intended.

Empirical tests are useful for functions and methods that are deterministic and don't have any dependencies that hold state. We'll create a few empirical tests for the Airport class now.

First, let's create some properties in the test suite using the yet-to-be-written Airport class. For this, within the AirportTest class, let's define a few sample properties before the init() function:

unittest/steps/empirical/src/test/kotlin/com/agiledeveloper/airportstatus/AirportTest.kt
```
val iah = Airport("IAH", "Houston", true)
val iad = Airport("IAD", "Dulles", false)
val ord = Airport("ORD", "Chicago O'Hare", true)
```

We can write a new test, right after the canary test, to exercise the properties of Airport, like so:

unittest/steps/empirical/src/test/kotlin/com/agiledeveloper/airportstatus/AirportTest.kt
```
"create Airport" {
  iah.code shouldBe "IAH"
  iad.name shouldBe "Dulles"
  ord.delay shouldBe true
}
```

Try running the build, and you'll notice it fails because the Airport class doesn't exist yet. Let's define the Airport class, in the file Airport.kt, under the directory src/main/kotlin/com/agiledeveloper/airportstatus:

unittest/steps/empirical/src/main/kotlin/com/agiledeveloper/airportstatus/Airport.kt
```
package com.agiledeveloper.airportstatus

data class Airport(val code: String, val name: String, val delay: Boolean)
```

We defined the Airport class as a data class with three properties. No further code is needed for the class at this time. Run the build and verify that it passes.

The previous test was trivial, but it helped us to get the properties in place. Let's write a test for a sort() method that will take a list of airports and return them sorted by their names.

When driving the design of code using tests, we use the first few tests to help define the interface of methods and then a few more tests to bring in the necessary implementation. In that spirit, let's start with a small test that passes an empty list to the sort() method and expects an empty list as the result:

unittest/steps/empirical/src/test/kotlin/com/agiledeveloper/airportstatus/AirportTest.kt
```
"sort empty list should return an empty list" {
  Airport.sort(listOf<Airport>()) shouldBe listOf<Airport>()
}
```

This test will fail since the sort() method doesn't exist in the Airport class. Let's create that method now. In the test, we invoked the sort() method directly on

Airport, instead of on an instance of Airport. Thus, sort() has to be a method in a companion object of Airport, like so:

unittest/steps/empirical/src/main/kotlin/com/agiledeveloper/airportstatus/Airport.kt

```kotlin
data class Airport(val code: String, val name: String, val delay: Boolean) {
  companion object {
    fun sort(airports: List<Airport>) : List<Airport> {
      return airports
    }
  }
}
```

To satisfy the new test, which passes in an empty list to sort(), we merely have to return the given list—that's exactly what we did in sort(), in the spirit of writing the minimum code to make the tests pass. Run the build, and verify that all three tests we have so far pass.

This test helped us to focus on the method name, the parameter type, and the return type; that is, it drove the design of the method signature. Let's write another test for the sort() method, this time passing in a list with one element.

unittest/steps/empirical/src/test/kotlin/com/agiledeveloper/airportstatus/AirportTest.kt

```kotlin
"sort list with one Airport should return the given Airport" {
  Airport.sort(listOf(iad)) shouldBe listOf(iad)
}
```

After writing this test, run the build. All tests, including the new one, should pass. That tells us that the current implementation suffices for the tests we have in place so far.

Next let's write a test that takes two airports, but already in sorted order:

unittest/steps/empirical/src/test/kotlin/com/agiledeveloper/airportstatus/AirportTest.kt

```kotlin
"sort pre-sorted list should return the given list" {
  Airport.sort(listOf(iad, iah)) shouldBe listOf(iad, iah)
}
```

There should be no issues with the build passing to run this and all the other tests we wrote previously. It's time to take the leap for the sort to actually have the necessary implementation.

unittest/steps/empirical/src/test/kotlin/com/agiledeveloper/airportstatus/AirportTest.kt

```kotlin
"sort airports should return airports in sorted order of name" {
  Airport.sort(listOf(iah, iad, ord)) shouldBe listOf(ord, iad, iah)
}
```

The output of the sort() method should be in sorted order of the airports, based on the name of the airports. If we run the build now the new test will fail. Let's modify the sort() function to make all the tests we have so far pass.

```kotlin
fun sort(airports: List<Airport>) : List<Airport> {
    return airports.sortedBy { airport -> airport.name }
}
```

Run the build and verify all tests pass. When writing automated tests, we should explore different reasonable edge cases and verify that the code behaves appropriately. As an exercise, write a few more tests for the sort() method. For example, what if two airport names start with the same substring? After all, some cities have multiple airports and we want to make sure the sorting works according to the specifications. Tests represent specifications—if our code has to handle edge cases, it's a good practice to express the behavior for such situations in tests first, and then implement the necessary minimum code.

When developing code using tests, we'll want to verify multiple scenarios or combinations of input to functions. However, if we write one test for each combination, the test file can get long and verbose. This is where data-driven tests come in, to reduce the noise and make tests concise, as we'll see next.

Writing Data-Driven Tests

Good tests are FAIR—fast, automated, independent, and repeatable. If tests aren't independent of each other, then they have to run in a specific order. And by adding or removing a test, we may break the order and the tests may fail. Such tests will become expensive and hard to maintain.

One way to guarantee independence of tests is to never place multiple asserts in the same test for verifications that are independent of each other. The obvious benefit of this approach is that tests can evolve without affecting and without being affected by existing tests. The downside, though, is that we end up with too many tests—verbose, hard to understand, and tiring to write.

KotlinTest provides data-driven tests to solve this issue. We can provide a table of data and KotlinTest will take input parameters from the table and verify that the output of a function under test is equal to the output expressed in the table. The benefit of this approach is that the asserts are run for each row. If the asserts for one row fail, it doesn't stop the execution of that test; instead it separately verifies each given row.

An example will help to see data-driven tests in action. First, let's bring in some necessary imports to the top of the AirportTest.kt file:

unittest/steps/datadriven/src/test/kotlin/com/agiledeveloper/airportstatus/AirportTest.kt
```
import io.kotlintest.data.forall
import io.kotlintest.tables.row
```

Now, replace all the tests we've written for the sort() function with just one test, like so:

unittest/steps/datadriven/src/test/kotlin/com/agiledeveloper/airportstatus/AirportTest.kt
```
"sort airports by name" {
  forall(
    row(listOf(), listOf()),
    row(listOf(iad), listOf(iad)),
    row(listOf(iad, iah), listOf(iad, iah)),
    row(listOf(iad, iah, ord), listOf(ord, iad, iah))) { input, result ->
      Airport.sort(input) shouldBe result
  }
}
```

Within the test body we call a forall() method and pass two arguments to it—a table of rows and a lambda expression that contains the method invocation with assert. In the first parameter, each row() represents a row of data in a table. In this example, our table has two columns, one for the input to sort() and the other for the expected result from the call. The lambda expression provided is invoked by KotlinTest for each row, passing the value associated with the first and second column as input and result, the first and second parameter of the lambda, respectively.

Run the build and verify all tests pass. If you change the expectations for a couple of rows and then run the build, you'll notice that KotlinTest reports multiple errors instead of one error. In other words, even though only one test is failing, it reports the failure of each row. Thus we get good visibility of regression, if and when it happens. If you're using Gradle, add a -i option to the command line to see the detailed failure message.

The sort() function was simple: it took a parameter, did its computation, and returned a result. We were able to write empirical tests to easily verify the behavior of that function. Things get more complicated when dependencies step in. Let's see how to deal with that next.

Mocking Out Dependencies

Dependencies often make testing hard. Our code needs to get the status of airports from a remote web service. The response from the service will be different at different times due to the nature of the data. The web service may fail intermittently, the program may run into a network failure, and so on. All these situations make it hard to write unit tests, which should be FAIR, for a piece of code that has to talk to such non-deterministic, and by their nature, unreliable external dependencies. This is where mocks come in.

A mock is an object that stands in for the real object, much like how a stunt person, instead of your favorite high-paid actor, stands in or jumps off a cliff in an action thriller. During normal execution the code under test will use the real dependency. During automated testing, however, the mock will replace the real dependency so the test can be run FAIRly.

To facilitate unit testing of code with dependencies, the test will prepare a mock to return a canned response, attach the mock to the code under test, run the test, verify the result is as expected, and, finally, verify with the mock that the code under test interacted with its dependency as expected.

To learn how to create and use mocks, let's turn our attention to the method that will get data from the remote FAA web service. Given an airport code, the web service returns a JSON response with the airport status data. Getting this data involves two actions: first, we have to send a request to the service URL and, second, we have to parse the response and deal with any possible errors.

Parsing data is straightforward; given a string containing JSON data, extract the necessary details from it. If there was an error, deal with it appropriately. We can easily write tests for that. It's getting the data from the URL that makes this feature unpredictable and hard to test. We can mock that part out by using a level of indirection.

We can devise the solution using two methods instead of one. A getAirportData() function can rely upon a fetchData() function. We'll write the fetchData() function, to get the real data from the FAA web service, later . For now, we'll leave it with a TODO implementation, by throwing an exception if it's called. The getAirportData() function can then call fetchData() and parse the response JSON string to extract the data. In the test, we'll mock out the fetchData() function; when getAirportData() calls fetchData(), the call will go to the mock function instead of calling the real implementation. We'll program the mock function to return a desired canned response.

Many mocking tools are available on the JVM. For example, Mockito is one of the more popular mocking tools for Java. You can use that for mocking dependencies in Kotlin code as well. However, in this chapter we'll use Mockk[5] for a few good reasons. First, Mockk is capable of easily mocking final classes, and that goes in hand with the fact that in Kotlin classes are final by default.

---

5.   https://mockk.io

Second, Mockk offers nice capabilities to mock dependencies on singleton objects/companion objects and also to mock extension functions. Mockk also provides facilities to test coroutines. In short, when we use features that are specific to Kotlin, we can benefit from a tool that was created to deal with those.

Creating an Interaction Test

Let's start with a test for the getAirportData() method of Airport, where we'll mock fetchData() to return a canned JSON response. In the test, we'll verify that getAirportData() called the fetchData() function. This is an interaction test as opposed to an empirical test.

Before we can dive into the test, we have to prepare to mock the fetchData() function. For this, we first need to import the functions from the Mockk library. While at it, let's also bring along a few more imports we'll need to create the pre- and post-listeners to run code before and after each test.

In the top of the AirportTest.kt file, after the current imports, add the following import statements:

unittest/steps/mocking/src/test/kotlin/com/agiledeveloper/airportstatus/AirportTest.kt
```
import io.kotlintest.TestCase
import io.kotlintest.TestResult
import io.mockk.*
```

We'll design the fetchData() function to be part of the Airport's companion object. To mock that function, we'll have to create a mock of the Airport singleton companion object. We can achieve this in a special beforeTest() function. The pair of functions beforeTest() and afterTest() sandwich each test, so that the code within beforeTest() runs before each test and the code within afterTest() runs after each test. In the AirportTest class, right after the fields and before the init() function, add the following two functions:

unittest/steps/mocking/src/test/kotlin/com/agiledeveloper/airportstatus/AirportTest.kt
```
override fun beforeTest(testCase: TestCase) {
  mockkObject(Airport)
}

override fun afterTest(testCase: TestCase, result: TestResult) {
  clearAllMocks()
}
```

In the beforeTest() function, we've created a mock of the Airport singleton using the mockkObject() function of the Mockk library. In the afterTest() function, at the end of each test, we clear all the mocks that were created and used. Thus, each test can be isolated and independent of each other.

Now we can focus on the test for the getAirportData() function. In the AirportTest class, let's add a new test after the previous data-driven test for the sort() method:

```
unittest/steps/mocking/src/test/kotlin/com/agiledeveloper/airportstatus/AirportTest.kt
"getAirportData invokes fetchData" {
  every { Airport.fetchData("IAD") } returns
    """{"IATA":"IAD", "Name": "Dulles", "Delay": false}"""

  Airport.getAirportData("IAD")

  verify { Airport.fetchData("IAD") }
}
```

In the test to verify that getAirportData() invokes fetchData(), we first mock—using the every() function of Mockk—the fetchData() of the Airport companion object, so that it returns a canned JSON response if the given airport code is "IAD". The format of the canned response is an excerpt from the actual response the web service returns—we can find this by visiting the FAA website,[6] using a browser, with IAD as the airport code.

Once the every() function is executed, any calls, direct or indirect from within the test, to the fetchData() function of Airport with argument "IAD" won't go to the real implementation. Instead, such a call will result in the canned response that follows the returns part attached to the every() expression.

In the test, after the call to every() to set up the mock behavior, we call the yet-to- be-implemented getAirportData() function. Then we verify that the fetchData() function was called, using Mockk's verify() function. The success of this call to verify() will imply that the call to getAirportData() resulted in a call to the fetch-Data() function.

Running the build right now will fail, since the methods getAirportData() and fetchData() don't exist in the Airport companion object. Let's implement minimally those two functions to satisfy the test.

```
unittest/steps/mocking/src/main/kotlin/com/agiledeveloper/airportstatus/Airport.kt
package com.agiledeveloper.airportstatus

data class Airport(val code: String, val name: String, val delay: Boolean) {
  companion object {
    fun sort(airports: List<Airport>) : List<Airport> {
      return airports.sortedBy { airport -> airport.name }
    }
```

---

6.   https://soa.smext.faa.gov/asws/api/airport/status/IAD

```kotlin
    fun getAirportData(code: String) = fetchData(code)

    fun fetchData(code: String): String {
      throw RuntimeException("Not Implemented Yet for $code")
    }
  }
}
```

The getAirportData() function simply calls fetchData(), as that's the current expectation we have for this function. Since our focus is on getAirportData(), we shouldn't care about the implementation of fetchData() at this time. Thus, within fetchData() we merely throw an exception that it hasn't been implemented yet.

Run the build and verify that all tests pass.

That worked, but we have to get to a more useful implementation for getAirport-Data().

Test for Parsing Data

The getAirportData() function at this point merely calls the fetchData() function. We have to implement code to parse the response from fetchData() to create an Airport instance. We'll drive that using the next test.

unittest/steps/mocking/src/test/kotlin/com/agiledeveloper/airportstatus/AirportTest.kt
```kotlin
"getAirportData extracts Airport from JSON returned by fetchData" {
  every { Airport.fetchData("IAD") } returns
    """{"IATA":"IAD", "Name": "Dulles", "Delay": false}"""

  Airport.getAirportData("IAD") shouldBe iad

  verify { Airport.fetchData("IAD") }
}
```

The only difference between this test and the previous one is that we verify that getAirportData() returns the expected instance of Airport.

Running the build now will fail, since the method getAirportData() isn't currently returning an instance of Airport. Let's implement the code for getAirportData() to use the Klaxon parser—we saw this in Chapter 16, Asynchronous Programming, on page 309—to create an instance of Airport from the JSON response that getAirportData() receives from fetchData(). To help Klaxon easily parse the JSON data and create an instance of Airport, we'll annotate the properties of the class with @Json. This will help the Klaxon parser to map the values in the JSON response to the appropriate properties in the object. This annotation is necessary only if the property names within the object are different from the property names in the JSON data.

```kotlin
package com.agiledeveloper.airportstatus

import com.beust.klaxon.*

data class Airport(
  @Json(name = "IATA") val code: String,
  @Json(name = "Name") val name: String,
  @Json(name = "Delay") val delay: Boolean) {

  companion object {
    fun sort(airports: List<Airport>) : List<Airport> {
      return airports.sortedBy { airport -> airport.name }
    }

    fun getAirportData(code: String) =
      Klaxon().parse<Airport>(fetchData(code)) as Airport

    fun fetchData(code: String): String {
      throw RuntimeException("Not Implemented Yet for $code")
    }
  }
}
```

The properties have been annotated so the Klaxon JSON parser can perform the mapping of JSON properties to the corresponding object properties. The getAirportData() function invokes the fetchData() function, and passes the result of that call to the parse() method of Klaxon. The parse() method's return type is a nullable type, Airport? in this example. This method will either return an instance that it has created using the given JSON data or it will throw an exception—it never really returns a null. So we can convert the returned value of parse() from type Airport? to Airport, using the explicit type-casting operator we saw in Explicit Type Casting, on page 91.

Run the build and verify that all the tests pass.

The test we wrote for getAirportData() assumes that fetchData() returned a valid JSON object. But the fetchData() method may not always behave that way. If the airport code is invalid, if an airport isn't supported by the web service, if there's a network error, or if Murphy's Law decides to strike in any other way, then the fetchData() method won't return valid JSON data. It may return a JSON data which contains some error information instead of airport data, or the method may simply blow up with an exception. If the method returns JSON data with an error, the Klaxon parser will blow up with an exception. Irrespective of whether the parsing results in an exception or we receive an exception from the call to fetchData(), our getAirportData() method needs to handle the situation gracefully. We'll design our method in such a way that if there's an exception, it will return an Airport with the given code but with "Invalid Airport" as the name. Let's write a test for this scenario.

unittest/steps/mockingerr/src/test/kotlin/com/agiledeveloper/airportstatus/AirportTest.kt
```kotlin
"getAirportData handles error fetching data" {
  every { Airport.fetchData("ERR") } returns "{}"

  Airport.getAirportData("ERR") shouldBe
    Airport("ERR", "Invalid Airport", false)

  verify { Airport.fetchData("ERR") }
}
```

If the given airport code is "ERR", the mocked-out fetchData() in this test will return a JSON response without any valid airport data (for the purpose of this test, we'll assume that "ERR" is an invalid airport code—no one would dare fly in to an airport with such a code anyway). Upon seeing the response JSON, the Klaxon parser will blow up with an exception. The test sets the expectation that our getAirportData() method, which internally calls the parser, should return an Airport instance with the given code and an invalid name.

To make this test pass we have to modify the getAirportData() method, like so:

unittest/steps/mockingerr/src/main/kotlin/com/agiledeveloper/airportstatus/Airport.kt
```kotlin
fun getAirportData(code: String) =
  try {
    Klaxon().parse<Airport>(fetchData(code)) as Airport
  } catch(ex: Exception) {
    Airport(code, "Invalid Airport", false)
  }
```

The method wraps the call to parse() and fetchData() in a try block, and in the catch block it returns the expected Airport instance that indicates a failure.

Run the tests and verify all the tests are passing.

With the aid of a few tests, we designed the getAirportData() method, but the implementation of the fetchData() method is incomplete. The fetchData() method has to make a network call, and the test for that will be an integration test rather than a unit test. We'll visit that later, but let's continue on with our focus on unit testing. Let's leave the Airport class for now and look at the code for the class just to the left of it in the design diagram in The Code Under Test, on page 348: the AirportStatus.

Testing Top-Level Functions

The Airport class we designed using tests has the facility to return the information about a single airport and to sort a list of airports by name. We need a function that will take a list of airport codes and return a sorted list of airport information. We'll implement that function in a new AirportStatus.kt file, as a top-level function rather than as a method of a class. It turns out testing a top-level function isn't any different than testing a method of a class, as we'll see soon.

In the spirit of growing code incrementally using tests, let's first implement a simple, synchronous version of a getAirportStatus() function that takes a list of airport codes and returns a sorted list of Airport instances filled with information about each relevant airport. Let's look at the test first.

We'll use the first test to tease out the signature of the method getAirportStatus()—it should take a list of airport codes and return a list of Airports. Very quickly we'll need a few more tests for different combinations of airport codes. When writing the first test, we'll prepare for that by writing a data-driven test. Let's create a file named AirportStatusTest.kt under the src/test/kotlin/com/agiledeveloper/airportstatus directory with the following code:

unittest/steps/sychnornous1/src/test/kotlin/com/agiledeveloper/airportstatus/AirportStatusTest.kt
```
package com.agiledeveloper.airportstatus

import io.kotlintest.specs.StringSpec
import io.kotlintest.shouldBe
import io.kotlintest.data.forall
import io.kotlintest.tables.row
import io.kotlintest.TestCase
import io.kotlintest.TestResult
import io.mockk.*

class AirportStatusTest : StringSpec() {
  init {
    "getAirportStatus returns status for airports in sorted order" {
      forall(
        row(listOf<String>(), listOf<Airport>())
      ) { input, result ->
          getAirportStatus(input) shouldBe result
        }
    }
  }
}
```

In the test, within the argument passed to the forall function, we define a pair of input and expected output using the row() function. Then in the lambda attached to forall we invoke the function under test, pass the first value from the row, and expect the result to be the second value from the row. Right now, the only expectation we have for the getAirportStatus() function is that it takes a list of String and returns an empty list of Airports. Let's get that implementation in place. To pass this test, create a file named AirportStatus.kt under the directory src/main/kotlin/com/agiledeveloper/airportstatus and add the following code:

unittest/steps/sychnornous1/src/main/kotlin/com/agiledeveloper/airportstatus/AirportStatus.kt

```kotlin
package com.agiledeveloper.airportstatus

fun getAirportStatus(airportCodes: List<String>): List<Airport> = listOf()
```

Next, we'll add another row to the test, with one airport code in the input list of airport codes and an expected Airport information.

unittest/steps/sychnornous2/src/test/kotlin/com/agiledeveloper/airportstatus/AirportStatusTest.kt

```kotlin
forall(
  row(listOf<String>(), listOf<Airport>()),
  row(listOf("IAD"), listOf(iad)),
) { input, result ->
    getAirportStatus(input) shouldBe result
  }
```

Two issues arise in running this test. First, we need to define the reference iad provided in the second row. Second, to make this test to pass, if we change getAirportStatus() so that it calls Airport.getAirportData(), the test will fail since the latter function calls fetchData(), which isn't implemented yet. To keep our focus on the design and implementation of getAirportStatus() we'll mock the Airport.getAirportData() function, in the AirportStatusTest class, like so:

unittest/steps/sychnornous2/src/test/kotlin/com/agiledeveloper/airportstatus/AirportStatusTest.kt

```kotlin
val iad = Airport("IAD", "Dulles", true)
val iah = Airport("IAH", "Houston", false)
val inv = Airport("inv", "Invalid Airport", false)

override fun beforeTest(testCase: TestCase) {
  mockkObject(Airport)
  every { Airport.getAirportData("IAD") } returns iad
  every { Airport.getAirportData("IAH") } returns iah
  every { Airport.getAirportData("inv") } returns inv
}

override fun afterTest(testCase: TestCase, result: TestResult) {
  clearAllMocks()
}
```

We've defined three fields in the test, each referring to canned airport information. Within the every() functions, we instruct the mock for Airport to return the appropriate canned value based on the airport code passed to the Airport.getAirportData() function.

To make the test pass, edit the getAirportStatus() function to return a list of Airport for the given list of airport codes.

unittest/steps/sychnornous2/src/main/kotlin/com/agiledeveloper/airportstatus/AirportStatus.kt

```kotlin
fun getAirportStatus(airportCodes: List<String>): List<Airport> =
  airportCodes.map { code -> Airport.getAirportData(code) }
```

Using the map() function, we iterate over each element in the input airportCodes collection and create a list of Airport instances returned by the getAirportData() function.

Let's add a few more rows of test data, where the rows we'll add will expect the result from getAirportStatus() to be in sorted order by name of the airport.

```
unittest/steps/sychnornous3/src/test/kotlin/com/agiledeveloper/airportstatus/AirportStatusTest.kt
forall(
  row(listOf<String>(), listOf<Airport>()),
  row(listOf("IAD"), listOf(iad)),
  row(listOf("IAD", "IAH"), listOf(iad, iah)),
  row(listOf("IAH", "IAD"), listOf(iad, iah)),
  row(listOf("inv", "IAD", "IAH"), listOf(iad, iah, inv))
) { input, result ->
    getAirportStatus(input) shouldBe result
  }
```

To make the modified test pass, we'll pass the result of the call to map() through the Airport.sort() function.

```
unittest/steps/sychnornous3/src/main/kotlin/com/agiledeveloper/airportstatus/AirportStatus.kt
fun getAirportStatus(airportCodes: List<String>): List<Airport> =
  Airport.sort(
    airportCodes.map { code -> Airport.getAirportData(code) })
```

Run the tests and verify that all tests pass.

Testing Coroutines and Asynchronous Calls

The getAirportStatus() function is making synchronous calls, one at a time, to the getAirportData() function. If we receive a large number of airport codes, then making blocking calls, one by one, won't be efficient. If we make the calls to getAirportData() asynchronous, using coroutines, then we can get a better throughput. Of course, we'll have to test first and then write the code for asynchronous execution.

For getAirportStatus() to make asynchronous calls, we have to do three things. First, mark the function with the suspend keyword. Then execute the body of the function in the context of a Dispatchers.IO thread pool. Finally, embed the calls to getAirportData() within async calls and await for the results by applying the techniques we saw in Chapter 16, Asynchronous Programming, on page 309. We'll write a test for each of these three steps and then implement the code.

The instant we mark the getAirportStatus() function with suspend, the previous test will fail compilation with the error "Suspension functions can be called only within the coroutine body." To address this, let's go back to the previous test and embed the call to getAirportStatus() within a call to runBlocking(), like so:

unittest/steps/coroutines1/src/test/kotlin/com/agiledeveloper/airportstatus/AirportStatusTest.kt

```
runBlocking { getAirportStatus(input) shouldBe result }
```

Remember to import the necessary coroutines library for this code to compile:

unittest/steps/coroutines1/src/test/kotlin/com/agiledeveloper/airportstatus/AirportStatusTest.kt

```
import kotlinx.coroutines.*
```

Now we can mark the function getAirportStatus() with the suspend keyword.

unittest/steps/coroutines1/src/main/kotlin/com/agiledeveloper/airportstatus/AirportStatus.kt

```
suspend fun getAirportStatus(airportCodes: List<String>): List<Airport> =
  Airport.sort(
    airportCodes.map { code -> Airport.getAirportData(code) })
```

Run the tests and make sure they pass.

Before we can make an asynchronous call, we have to decide which thread pool to run the request in. Since getAirportData() will be making a call to a remote web service, it's appropriate to run the request in an IO thread pool. For this reason, we'll embed the body of getAirportStatus() within a call to withContext() so the code will run in the coroutine context we provide to that function. In short, our test needs to verify that getAirportStatus() makes a call to withContext(). How in the world can we do that?

We can write an interaction test by mocking the withContext() function. But that requires a bit of digging in. The withContext() function is a top-level function defined in the kotlinx.coroutines package. Sadly, we can't simply tell the Mockk library to mock the withContext function, as it won't know which function we're referring to. Even though Kotlin has top-level functions, at the bytecode level they don't reside directly in the package, but within a class. We have to track down which class, in the bytecode, the top-level function withContext() has been compiled into and ask Mockk to mock that class—yikes, that's going to take some effort.

Visit the documentation[7] for the withContext() function, and click the *source* link that is next to the return type T of the function. You'll notice that the file that has this function is Builders.common.kt, and in that file withContext() is defined as a top-level function. Now we have to find what class this code is compiled into. For this, you'll need the super-investigative skills of Sherlock Holmes and the jar tool that is part of the JDK. Download the jar file kotlinx-coroutines-core-1.2.2.jar by clicking the *jar* link in the Maven repository page,[8] and use

---

7.   https://kotlin.github.io/kotlinx.coroutines/kotlinx-coroutines-core/kotlinx.coroutines/with-context.html
8.   https://mvnrepository.com/artifact/org.jetbrains.kotlinx/kotlinx-coroutines-core/1.2.2

the jar -tf command, on the command line, to find the class name. If you're on a Unix-like system, use this command:

```
$ jar -tf kotlinx-coroutines-core-1.2.2.jar | grep Builders | grep common
```

If you're on Windows, then use the the following command:

```
$ jar -tf kotlinx-coroutines-core-1.2.2.jar | Find "Builders" | Find "common"
```

The fruit of the that effort is the output:

```
kotlinx/coroutines/BuildersKt__Builders_commonKt.class
```

This tells us the code in the file Builders.common.kt is compiled into the class named BuildersKt__Builders_commonKt. That's the class we should mock to replace the withContext() method with the fake implementation in test.

Let's write the test for verifying that getAirportStatus() is calling withContext() with the appropriate arguments.

unittest/steps/coroutines2/src/test/kotlin/com/agiledeveloper/airportstatus/AirportStatusTest.kt

```kotlin
"getAirportStatus runs in the Dispatcher.IO context" {

  mockkStatic("kotlinx.coroutines.BuildersKt__Builders_commonKt")

  coEvery {
    withContext<List<Airport>>(
      context = Dispatchers.IO, block = captureCoroutine())
  } answers {
    listOf(iah)
  }

  getAirportStatus(listOf("IAH")) shouldBe listOf(iah)

  coVerify {
    withContext<List<Airport>>(Dispatchers.IO, block = any())
  }
}
```

Since the top-level function withContext() is compiled as a static method in the bytecode within the class BuildersKt__Builders_commonKt, we ask Mockk to mock that class. Then, using Mockk's coEvery function, which is like the every() function but for mocking functions that use coroutines, we mock the withContext() function. The withContext() function takes two parameters: CoroutineContext and a lambda to be executed as a coroutine. We pass Dispatchers.IO for the first argument context and Mockk's special captureCoroutine() as the second argument block. As the name alludes to, captureCoroutine() serves as a place holder for the coroutine that is passed to withContext() by the caller—that is, the code being tested. In response to the call to withContext(), our fake implementation will return a canned response of a list with iah Airport.

After the coEvery() call, we call the code under test and verify that the result of the call is the expected list. Finally, we verify, using coVerify(), that the with-Context() function was in fact called by the code being tested.

Running the tests now will fail because our getAirportStatus() function isn't calling the withContext() function. Let's change the function to make the test pass.

unittest/steps/coroutines2/src/main/kotlin/com/agiledeveloper/airportstatus/AirportStatus.kt

```kotlin
package com.agiledeveloper.airportstatus

import kotlinx.coroutines.*

suspend fun getAirportStatus(airportCodes: List<String>): List<Airport> =
  withContext(Dispatchers.IO) {
    Airport.sort(
      airportCodes.map { code -> Airport.getAirportData(code) })
  }
```

With this change, the test will pass. We're now ready to make asynchronous the call to getAirportData() within getAirportStatus(). Test first, of course.

unittest/steps/coroutines3/src/test/kotlin/com/agiledeveloper/airportstatus/AirportStatusTest.kt

```kotlin
"getAirportStatus calls getAirportData asynchronously" {

  mockkStatic("kotlinx.coroutines.BuildersKt__Builders_commonKt")

  coEvery {
    any<CoroutineScope>().async<Airport>(
      context = any(), block = captureCoroutine())
  } answers {
    CompletableDeferred(iad)
  }

  getAirportStatus(listOf("IAD")) shouldBe listOf(iad)

  coVerify {
    any<CoroutineScope>().async<Airport>(context = any(), block = any())
  }
}
```

In this test we again mock the BuildersKt_Builders_commonKt class, but this time we mock the async() function to receive any object for context and a coroutine for the second argument named block. In response to the call, we return a Deferred<Airport> object that holds the iad mock instance. After the mock is arranged, we call the function under test and verify the result is what we expected. Finally, we verify that the async() function was called by the code under test.

To make the above test pass, let's modify the getAirportStatus() function.

unittest/steps/coroutines3/src/main/kotlin/com/agiledeveloper/airportstatus/AirportStatus.kt

```
package com.agiledeveloper.airportstatus

import kotlinx.coroutines.*

suspend fun getAirportStatus(airportCodes: List<String>): List<Airport> =
  withContext(Dispatchers.IO) {
    Airport.sort(
      airportCodes.map { code -> async { Airport.getAirportData(code) } }
        .map { response -> response.await() })
  }
```

Instead of making a synchronous call to getAirportData(), the getAirportStatus() now wraps the call within async(). The call will now run in the Dispatchers.IO thread pool. After dispatching the calls to getAirportData() for each airport code in the given list airportCodes, the getAirportStatus() awaits the response using the await() function call on the response returned by async(), the Deferred<Airport> object.

Run the test and make sure it passes.

Let's revisit the two tests we just wrote, to reflect on the efforts and the benefits. The nice part of the tests is that by mocking the functions withContext() and async(), we were able to perform interaction tests and didn't have to worry about actually running asynchronous operations and waiting for results in the tests. This makes the tests fast and deterministic. The biggest downside to this approach is figuring out which class to mock in order to reach in and replace the functions like withContext(). To say the least, this isn't easy, and it can be frustrating to find the correct class to mock. But the fast feedback we get from the tests is worth the effort.

Integrating with the Service

We have one unfinished piece of work in the Airport class—the fetchData() function is pending implementation. We need to replace the exception in that function with code to talk to the web service. Since it needs a network connection to talk to an external service, the test for fetchData() will be an integration test and not a unit test. We can't get too specific about what to expect from the call, as details like delay will change frequently. Let's write the integration test in a separate test class. Create a file named AirportIntegrationTest.kt in the directory src/test/kotlin/com/agiledeveloper/airportstatus and key in the following code:

unittest/steps/integration/src/test/kotlin/com/ ... eveloper/airportstatus/AirportIntegrationTest.kt

```
package com.agiledeveloper.airportstatus

import io.kotlintest.specs.StringSpec
import io.kotlintest.data.forall
import io.kotlintest.tables.row
import io.kotlintest.matchers.string.shouldContain
```

```
class AirportIntegrationTest : StringSpec() {
  init {
    "fetchData returns response from URL" {
      forall(
        row("IAD", "Dulles"),
        row("SFO", "San Francisco"),
        row("ORD", "Chicago")
      ) { code, partialName ->
          Airport.fetchData(code) shouldContain partialName
      }
    }
  }
}
```

We test the fetchData() function for three different airport codes, to verify that the function returns a response that contains the partial name of the airport. Let's replace the call to throw in the fetchData() function of the Airport class with the code to talk to the web service.

unittest/steps/integration/src/main/kotlin/com/agiledeveloper/airportstatus/Airport.kt
```
fun fetchData(code: String) =
  java.net.URL("https://soa.smext.faa.gov/asws/api/airport/status/$code")
    .readText()
```

If the network connection doesn't fail, then as long as the web service at the URL is available and the airports don't change their names, the integration test we wrote should pass. Run the tests to verify that all the tests are passing.

Viewing the Code Coverage

"What's a good coverage number?" is a question that can start a bar fight among drunken developers: "If we write a test and then write the minimum code necessary to make the test pass…" Irrespective of what your team believes to be the appropriate coverage percentage, you'll need a way to view the coverage. Jacoco, which is a coverage tool that works for Java, works nicely with Kotlin as well. Let's see how we did with code coverage so far in the sample we created in this chapter.

Whether you've been using Gradle or Maven to build the examples so far, you've been generating the code coverage all along. If you're using Gradle, take a look at the configuration for Jacoco in the build.gradle.kts file and take note of the version number of the library in particular. Likewise, if you're using Maven, take a look at the pom.xml file and look for the configuration of the Jacoco plugin. After running the build, using Gradle or Maven, take a peek at the Jacoco report file. If you're using Gradle, you'll find the report index.html under build/reports/jacoco/test/html, and if you're using Maven look for it under target/site/jacoco.

Here's the coverage report generated by Jacoco for the Kotlin code we've created so far in this chapter.

airportapp > com.agiledeveloper.airportstatus

com.agiledeveloper.airportstatus

Element	Missed Instructions	Cov.	Missed Branches
AirportStatusKt.getAirportStatus.new Function2() {...}		100%	
Airport.Companion		100%	
Airport		100%	
AirportStatusKt		100%	
AirportStatusKt.getAirportStatus.2.1.new Function2() {...}		100%	
Airport.Companion.sort..inlined.sortedBy.new Comparator() {...}		100%	
Total	0 of 166	100%	0 of 0

We've driven the design and implementation of the code using tests; as a last step, we'll write a driver program to run the code.

Taking the App for a Drive

Let's write a main() function to call the getAirportStatus() function with a few different airport codes and print the status of the airports with those codes to the console. Create a file named AirportApp.kt in the directory src/main/kotlin/com/agiledeveloper/ui and key in the following code:

```
unittest/steps/app/src/main/kotlin/com/agiledeveloper/ui/AirportApp.kt
package com.agiledeveloper.ui

import kotlinx.coroutines.*
import com.agiledeveloper.airportstatus.*

fun main() = runBlocking {
  getAirportStatus(listOf("SFO", "IAD", "IAH", "ORD", "LAX"))
    .forEach { println(it) }
}
```

Since getAirportStatus() is a function that may be suspended, it can only be called within a coroutine. So we invoke it from within the block passed to the run-Blocking() function. Whatever data is returned for each airport is printed in the lambda provided to the forEach() function. Since the data obtained by this program is real, the output will be different for each run.

The Gradle build file uses the application plugin to specify the main class. The Maven build file creates the manifest information with the main class. We can easily run the program:

If using Gradle, run this command:

```
$ gradlew run
```

If using Maven, run the following command:

```
$ java -jar target/airportapp-1.0-jar-with-dependencies.jar
```

Here's one sample output from the program execution:

```
Airport(code=ORD, name=Chicago O'hare Intl, delay=true)
Airport(code=IAH, name=George Bush Intercontinental/houston, delay=true)
Airport(code=LAX, name=Los Angeles Intl, delay=false)
Airport(code=SFO, name=San Francisco Intl, delay=true)
Airport(code=IAD, name=Washington Dulles Intl, delay=false)
```

Try including other airports, along with invalid airports or airports not supported by the web service, to see how the program behaves. Also, see if the program fails gracefully if there's no network connection.

You can find the final code, including the tests and the build files in the unittest/final/airportapp directory.

Wrapping Up

Automated testing is a key technical practice for sustainable agile development. You may use tools that you're used to in Java to write automated tests for Kotlin. Alternatively, you may use tools that are targeted specifically for Kotlin, to enjoy fluency and to be able to use idiomatic Kotlin style. In this chapter, we used KotlinTest, Mockk, and Jacoco to write tests, to mock dependencies, and create the code coverage report. In addition, we used Gradle and Maven to run the builds.

KotlinTest provides elegant syntax and fluent asserts, along with many different options to write tests. Mockk is a powerful mocking tool that can be used to stub and mock classes, singletons, companion objects, and top-level functions. Mockk also has facilities to test code that makes use of coroutines.

In this chapter we've explored, step by step, how to unit test a small program that makes asynchronous calls, using coroutines, to an external web service. We've written unit tests, mocked the dependencies, written integration tests, and finished by writing a driver program to exercise the code created using automated tests.

In the next chapter, we'll take a quick look at using Spring Boot with Kotlin.

CHAPTER 19

Programming Spring Applications with Kotlin

Both Kotlin and Spring are favored for their high essence and low ceremony. Programming Spring applications with Kotlin feels like a marriage made in heaven. Spring applications created using Kotlin, when compared to those created using Java, are concise and easier to maintain.

The concise and expressive nature of Kotlin is alluring. So far in this book, we've seen how it takes only a few lines of code to get things done in Kotlin and how each line is succinct as well. Spring predominantly favors three different languages: Java, Groovy, and Kotlin. The developers of Spring recognized the benefits of Kotlin and decided to provide superb support for programming Spring applications with Kotlin. Several Kotlin features, among them null safety and fluent, elegant DSL syntax, convinced the Spring team to recognize[1] Kotlin as a first-class language for programming Spring applications.

This chapter assumes that you're familiar with creating Spring and Spring Boot applications with Java. We'll see how Spring code written using Kotlin shines in comparison with similar code written using Java.

We'll begin with a starter Spring Boot project and develop a small RESTful service that manages a TODO list. We'll develop this program using Kotlin, and along the way, we'll see what the code would look like if developed in Java. That way you'll be able to compare the familiar Java code with the concise Kotlin code, and appreciate the elegance of Kotlin in the context of Spring. Let's get started with Spring Boot.

---

1. https://spring.io/blog/2017/01/04/introducing-kotlin-support-in-spring-framework-5-0

Creating a Starter Project

The easiest way to get started is using the Spring Initializr[2] website. We'll create a Spring Boot RESTful web service that stores data in the in-memory H2 database.

Once you visit the Spring Initializr website, choose either Maven Project or Gradle Project. For language, select Kotlin, of course. Then choose the desired version of Spring Boot—for the examples in this chapter, we use version 2.1.2. For the Group text box, type a desired top-level package name—for example, com.agiledeveloper. For the Artifact, type todo. In the text box next to Search for Dependencies, type "Web" and select it from the drop-down list that appears. Also, type "H2" and select it from the drop-down. As a final dependency, type "JPA" and select it from the drop-down. Finally, click the Generate Project button and save the generated zip file to your system.

Unzip the todo.zip file on your system and, using the command-line tool, cd to the todo directory.

Examine the pom.xml file if you selected a Maven project, or the build.gradle file if you selected Gradle instead. Take note of the dependencies. You'll see dependencies on the H2 library, the Jackson-kotlin library, which will be used to create a JSON response, the JPA library, and the Kotlin-stdlib library compatible with JDK 8.

Spring Boot uses a special Kotlin-Spring compiler plugin to deal with a few things that conflict with the default Kotlin way and the Spring way. In Kotlin, classes are final by default. But Spring expects classes to be open. Without the Kotlin-Spring compiler plugin integration, each class written using Kotlin, like a controller, for example, will have to be explicitly marked open. Thanks to the plugin, we can write the classes without the open keyword. The plugin will inspect a class to see if it has some Spring-related meta-annotations, like @Component, @Async, @Transactional, and so on, and if it does, it'll automatically open those classes during compilation. Since these are meta-annotations, in addition to opening classes that are decorated with these annotations, the plugin also opens classes that are decorated with derived annotations like @Component.

The entry point for a Spring Boot application is the class containing the main() method. If we were to create the Spring Boot application using Java, we'd have something like this:

---

2.   https://start.spring.io/

```
//Java code only for comparison purpose
package com.agiledeveloper.todo;

import org.springframework.boot.SpringApplication;
import org.springframework.boot.autoconfigure.SpringBootApplication;

@SpringBootApplication
public class TodoApplication {

        public static void main(String[] args) {
                SpringApplication.run(TodoApplication.class, args);
        }
}
```

You know that Kotlin is a language of low ceremony, and we don't need a class to create the main() function in Kotlin. The Spring Initializr tool created a much simpler file for our Kotlin version of the application:

spring/kotlin/todo/src/main/kotlin/com/agiledeveloper/todo/TodoApplication.kt
```
package com.agiledeveloper.todo

import org.springframework.boot.autoconfigure.SpringBootApplication
import org.springframework.boot.runApplication

@SpringBootApplication
class TodoApplication

fun main(args: Array<String>) {
        runApplication<TodoApplication>(*args)
}
```

The Java version and the Kotlin version of TodoApplication have three differences between them: First, the main() function in the Kotlin version is a standalone top-level function, instead of being a member of the class. Second, the bootstrap call to SpringApplication.run() in the Java version has been replaced with a more concise, less cluttered call to runApplication()—thanks to the powerful generics facility of Kotlin, we're able to infer the class details from the parametric type provided. The third difference is the lack of semicolon—let's not forget that.

We've not written any code yet, but before we make any changes, let's compile the downloaded starter project code and make sure it builds successfully.

If you choose to use Maven, run the following commands to build the code and to start the application:

```
$ ./mvnw clean install
$ java -jar target/todo-0.0.1-SNAPSHOT.jar
```

If you choose Gradle instead, then run the following commands to build the code and to start the application:

```
$ ./gradlew build
$ java -jar build/libs/todo-0.0.1-SNAPSHOT.jar
```

Refer back to the above commands anytime you want to build the application.

We have the starter code in place. Our application will manage tasks where each task has a description. We'll have three routes, all through the endpoint task, but with three different HTTP methods:

- GET method to list all available tasks.
- POST method to add a new task.
- DELETE method to remove an existing task.

Let's now move on and write some code for the application at hand.

Creating a Controller

One of the core capabilities of Spring Boot is to auto-discover application components based on what it finds in the classpath. Among those components are controllers, which provide the routes for a web application. In the examples in this chapter, we'll use this facility.

Use Kofu to Explicitly Configure Applications

If you'd like to explicitly configure the application, refer to the Spring-fu[a] initiative and the Kofu DSL[b] that provide a fluent syntax to configure various properties. In addition to benefiting from a fluent Kotlin API, Kofu-based applications benefit from a significantly less startup time compared to auto-configured applications.

---

a. https://github.com/spring-projects/spring-fu
b. https://github.com/spring-projects/spring-fu/blob/master/kofu/README.adoc

Our controller needs to support three different routes/operations. Let's start with one route. The first route we'll create has an endpoint task, supports the GET HTTP method, and simply returns a message "to be implemented" as a starting point.

We'll name our controller TaskController. If we were writing this application in Java, our controller would look like this:

```
//Java code only for comparison purpose
package com.agiledeveloper.todo;

import org.springframework.stereotype.Controller;
```

```
import org.springframework.web.bind.annotation.*;
import org.springframework.http.ResponseEntity;

@RestController
@RequestMapping("/task")
class TaskController {

  @GetMapping
  String tasks() {
    return "to be implemented";
  }
}
```

Since we're using Kotlin, we can hope for less clutter than that. Create a file named TaskController.kt under the directory todo/src/main/kotlin/com/agiledeveloper/todo/ and add the following code to that file:

spring/kotlin/todo/src/main/kotlin/com/agiledeveloper/todo/TaskController.kt
```
package com.agiledeveloper.todo

import org.springframework.web.bind.annotation.*
import org.springframework.http.ResponseEntity

@RestController
@RequestMapping("/task")
class TaskController {

  @GetMapping
  fun tasks() = "to be implemented"
}
```

The TaskController class belongs to the com.agiledeveloper.todo package. The class is first annotated with the Spring Boot annotation @RestController, to declare that this class will serve as a controller and will support REST endpoints. The @RequestMapping annotation defines the endpoint supported by this controller. The tasks() method of the TaskController class is annotated with the @GetMapping annotation, and it returns a sample string.

We're ready to build the code and exercise this controller's route. Using the commands we saw in Creating a Starter Project, on page 376, build the project and execute the java command to run the program.

We'll use curl to verify that the endpoint works as expected. If you don't have curl already, you may download it for your operating system. Alternatively, you may use other tools like Advanced REST Client extension for Chrome, for example, that you typically use to interact with REST APIs.

Here's the curl command:

```
$ curl -w "\n" http://localhost:8080/task
```

This command sends a GET request to the mentioned URL, and the response should be the string returned by the tasks() method of TaskController.

These steps show that the controller we wrote using Kotlin works. That's a good first step. Next, let's create an entity class to represent persistent data.

Creating an Entity Class

Seeing the H2 library in the classpath, Spring has already configured the database. We need to define an entity class that represents data that will be stored in a table in the database.

Again, if we were using Java, we'd write the Task entity class like so:

```java
//Java code only for comparison purpose
package com.agiledeveloper.todo;

import javax.persistence.*;

@Entity
public class Task {
  @Id @GeneratedValue private Long id;
  private String description;

  public Long getId() { return id; }

  public String getDescription() { return description; }
}
```

Instead, we'll write that code using Kotlin. Create a new file todo/src/main/kotlin/com/agiledeveloper/todo/Task.kt and add the following content in it:

```kotlin
spring/kotlin/todo/src/main/kotlin/com/agiledeveloper/todo/Task.kt
package com.agiledeveloper.todo

import javax.persistence.*

@Entity
data class Task(@Id @GeneratedValue val id: Long, val description: String)
```

The class Task has been annotated with @Entity. Also, the first property id has been annotated with @Id and @GeneratedValue. These annotations indicate that the property is a primary key and the unique values are generated by the database. The Task entity, in addition to an id, also has a description of type String. Since Kotlin generates the getters automatically, we don't have to write anything more. And, since we created Task as a data class, we get all the goodies like equals(), hashCode(), and toString() methods for free.

We have the entity class, but we need a way to store instances of that into the database. Spring makes that easy, and we only have to write the minimum code necessary for that step using Kotlin, as we'll see next.

Creating a Repository Interface

Spring's CrudRepository interface provides all the methods like findById() and save() to fetch from the database or to update the database. All we need to do is define a specialized interface to extend the CrudRepository. Spring Data will generate implementations for interfaces that extend CrudRepository.

If we were writing in Java, we'd write something like:

```java
//Java code only for comparison purpose
package com.agiledeveloper.todo;

import org.springframework.data.repository.CrudRepository;

interface TaskRepository extends CrudRepository<Task, Long> {
}
```

The Kotlin code isn't too different from that: there's no need for ; or {}, and we replaced extends with :. Let's write the Kotlin equivalent of the interface by creating a file, todo/src/main/kotlin/com/agiledeveloper/todo/TaskRepository.kt, with the following content:

spring/kotlin/todo/src/main/kotlin/com/agiledeveloper/todo/TaskRepository.kt

```kotlin
package com.agiledeveloper.todo

import org.springframework.data.repository.CrudRepository

interface TaskRepository : CrudRepository<Task, Long>
```

The interface TaskRepository extends from CrudRepository<Task, Long>, where the first parametric type Task specifies the type of the entity, and the second parametric type Long specifies the type of the primary key.

We're all set to perform CRUD operations, but we need a service to make the calls from. Let's write that next.

Creating a Service

In a simple example such as the one we're looking at, we may skip the service and directly let the controller talk to the repository. However, introducing a service will help us see how Kotlin can be used to create a service. And if we decide to expand the example, to add more behavior, then that can readily go into the service.

The service will sit in between the controller and the database and take care of making all the calls necessary to manipulate the persistent data. The service needs to talk to the repository; but no worries, Spring can auto-wire that dependency in a blink. We need a method to get all the tasks—one to save a new task, and one to delete a task with a given id. Given all that, the Java version is sure to be more verbose than the Kotlin version. If we were to write in Java, we'd end up with something like this:

```java
//Java code only for comparison purpose
package com.agiledeveloper.todo;

import java.util.Optional;
import org.springframework.stereotype.Service;
import org.springframework.transaction.annotation.Transactional;

@Service
@Transactional
class TaskService {
  private final TaskRepository repository;

  public TaskService(TaskRepository repository) {
    this.repository = repository;
  }

  Iterable<Task> getAll() {
    return repository.findAll();
  }

  Task save(Task task) {
    return repository.save(task);
  }

  boolean delete(Long id) {
    boolean found = repository.existsById(id);

    if (found) {
      repository.deleteById(id);
    }

    return found;
  }
}
```

Using Kotlin we can shave off some noise. Let's start by creating the file todo/src/main/kotlin/com/agiledeveloper/todo/TaskService.kt and update the code to:

```kotlin
spring/kotlin/todo/src/main/kotlin/com/agiledeveloper/todo/TaskService.kt
package com.agiledeveloper.todo

import org.springframework.stereotype.Service
import org.springframework.transaction.annotation.Transactional

@Service
@Transactional
class TaskService(val repository: TaskRepository) {
  fun getAll() = repository.findAll()

  fun save(task: Task) = repository.save(task)

  fun delete(id: Long): Boolean {
    val found = repository.existsById(id)
```

```
    if (found) {
      repository.deleteById(id)
    }

    return found
  }
}
```

The TaskService class is annotated with @Service and @Transactional. In the class, the getAll() method returns the result of the synthesized method findAll() of the TaskRepository. The save() method takes an instance of the entity Task and sends it off to the TaskRepository's save() method so it's inserted into the database. Finally, the delete() method looks up the given id. If an object with that id exists, then it's removed from the database, using the TaskRepository's deleteById() method, and true is returned as the result of this call. If an object with that id wasn't found, then false is returned.

As a last step, we need to integrate the service with the controller.

Integrating the Service with Controller

It's time to modify the TaskController we wrote earlier, to add two new methods and to modify the existing tasks() method—that is, the GET operation.

Once again, if we were to write in Java, here's what the modified controller would look like:

```java
//Java code only for comparison purpose
package com.agiledeveloper.todo;

import org.springframework.stereotype.Controller;
import org.springframework.web.bind.annotation.*;
import org.springframework.http.ResponseEntity;

@RestController
@RequestMapping("/task")
class TaskController {

  private final TaskService service;

  public TaskController(TaskService service) {
    this.service = service;
  }

  @GetMapping
  ResponseEntity<Iterable<Task>> tasks() {
    return ResponseEntity.ok(service.getAll());
  }

  @PostMapping
  ResponseEntity<String> create(@RequestBody Task task) {
    Task result = service.save(task);
```

```
  return ResponseEntity.ok(
    "added task with description " + result.getDescription());
}

@DeleteMapping("/{id}")
ResponseEntity<String> delete(@PathVariable Long id) {
  if (service.delete(id)) {
    return ResponseEntity.ok("Task with id " + id + " deleted");
  }

  return ResponseEntity.status(404)
    .body("Task with id " + id + " not found");
}

}
```

Let's change the Kotlin version of the TaskController to add the necessary operations:

spring/kotlin/todo/src/main/kotlin/com/agiledeveloper/todo/TaskController.kt

```kotlin
package com.agiledeveloper.todo

import org.springframework.web.bind.annotation.*
import org.springframework.http.ResponseEntity

@RestController
@RequestMapping("/task")
class TaskController(val service: TaskService) {

  @GetMapping
  fun tasks() = ResponseEntity.ok(service.getAll())

  @PostMapping
  fun create(@RequestBody task: Task): ResponseEntity<String> {
    val result = service.save(task)

    return ResponseEntity.ok(
      "added task with description ${result.description}")
  }

  @DeleteMapping("/{id}")
  fun delete(@PathVariable id: Long) = if (service.delete(id)) {
    ResponseEntity.ok("Task with id $id deleted")
  } else {
    ResponseEntity.status(404).body("Task with id $id not found")
  }

}
```

First, we modified the class to add a property service of type TaskService. Spring will automatically inject a reference to that dependency when the instance of TaskController is created. Next, we modified the tasks() method to return the result of the getAll() method of the service. We also added two more methods, create() and delete().

The create() method has been annotated to specify that it supports the POST HTTP method, and it accepts a Task as post data through the body of the incoming request. The method invokes the service's save() method to save the given object to the database.

The delete() method supports the DELETE HTTP method and the annotation also specifies that the request should include the id of the task to be deleted. The method forwards the request to the service's delete() method and returns an appropriate HTTP response.

Taking It for a Ride

Let's verify that all that code works well together. Once again, build the application and run the service. Use curl or any tool of your choice to exercise the application. Here's a series of curl calls to exercise the service.

```
$ curl -w "\n" -X GET http://localhost:8080/task
$ echo ""
$ curl -w "\n" -X POST \
  -H "Content-Type: application/json" \
  -d '{"description": "write code"}' http://localhost:8080/task
$ curl -w "\n" -X POST \
  -H "Content-Type: application/json" \
  -d '{"description": "test"}' http://localhost:8080/task
$ echo ""
$ curl -w "\n" -X GET http://localhost:8080/task
$ echo ""
$ curl -w "\n" -X DELETE http://localhost:8080/task/1
$ curl -w "\n" -X DELETE http://localhost:8080/task/10
$ echo ""
$ curl -w "\n" -X GET http://localhost:8080/task
```

First, we perform a GET operation on the task endpoint. Since we've not created any tasks yet, this should return an empty collection. Then we make two calls to add two tasks, with descriptions "write code" and "test," using the POST method to the same endpoint. We then query to verify the tasks have been added. Finally, we delete two tasks with one valid id and one nonexistent id and query the tasks list again. Here's the output of all these calls to the web service we wrote:

```
[]

added task with description write code
added task with description test

[{"id":1,"description":"write code"},{"id":2,"description":"test"}]

Task with id 1 deleted
Task with id 10 not found

[{"id":2,"description":"test"}]
```

The output shows all went well. The Kotlin version of code has twenty-five to forty percent less code compared to the Java version. And the low ceremony and expressive nature of Kotlin shines throughout the code. The more complex operations we have to perform in the services and controllers, the bigger gain we'll see when using Kotlin compared to using Java.

Wrapping Up

Using Kotlin with Spring is a marriage made in heaven, since both promote low ceremony and high essence. Kotlin code is highly concise, expressive, and less error prone. The developers behind Spring chose to support Kotlin as a first-class citizen because of several benefits the language offers. Kotlin classes are final by default, but a special Kotlin-Spring plugin takes care of opening classes at compile time, based on Spring annotations. The fluency of Kotlin shines when we create Spring controllers and services. With Kotlin, you can deliver the same features you expect from your Spring applications, but with fewer lines of highly elegant, type-safe code.

In the next chapter, we'll see how to create Android applications using Kotlin, a language that's now preferred by Google for Android development.

CHAPTER 20

Writing Android Applications with Kotlin

Since Google announced that Kotlin will be a first-class language for Android development, Kotlin has rapidly grown and surpassed Java as the language of choice for creating Android apps. Google has invested efforts into making Android applications faster, efficient, expressive, and easy to develop using Kotlin.[1]

The Android Studio IDE provides full support for writing code in Kotlin. It also provides facilities to convert Java code to Kotlin syntax, in case you want to transition from existing Java code or bring over code snippets written in Java into your Kotlin code. When programming Android applications, you can benefit from the rich Android SDK, the Kotlin idiomatic style, Kotlin standard library, the Java JDK, and also advanced facilities like Coroutines.

In this chapter, we'll implement the airport status example we saw in the previous chapters as an Android app. The application will ask the user to enter airport IATA codes. For each of the airport codes the user enters, the app will make asynchronous calls, using coroutines, to a remote web service to fetch the name of the airport, current temperature at that airport, and whether there's a delay. The app will display these details in a table, in sorted order of airport names.

Even though the example we create in this chapter is relatively small, it'll give you a pretty good idea of how to create Android apps using Kotlin and how to use coroutines to make asynchronous calls on Android devices. Get settled at your comfortable location—we're ready to fire up the IDE and create an Android app.

---

1. https://developer.android.com/kotlin

Creating a Project

The Android Studio is a pretty good IDE to create Android applications. Download the latest version of the IDE[2] if you don't have that already on your system. Fire up the IDE to create a new project. If the IDE doesn't open an existing project, click on the link "Start a new Android Studio project." If you already have a project open, then click on the File | New | New Project... menu items. Irrespective of the path you take to create a new project, in the next step, in the Choose your Project dialog select Phone and Tablet, and then select Empty Activity. Finally, click the Next button.

Name the project "Airports" and the package name com.agiledeveloper.airports. Provide an appropriate location to save your project. Make sure to select Kotlin as the language in the list box under the Language label. For the Minimum API Level, select API 28: Android 9.0 (Pie). Click on Finish to create the project.

Let's review the interesting parts of the project from within Android Studio.

In the Project pane on the left, in the Android section, take note of the contents under app.

- The manifests folder contains the file AndroidManifest.xml, which we'll edit soon to enable network access from within the Android emulator.

- Even though we're using Kotlin, the IDE is storing the source files under java but within the package name we provided.

---

2.   https://developer.android.com/studio

- Under layout there is currently one layout file activity_main.xml for the empty activity we created—we'll edit this file later.

- Under values are some files that can be used to tailor settings for internationalization. The strings.xml file contains the name of the application, Airports, that will be displayed at the top of the application.

- Under Gradle Scripts are two build.gradle files. The one annotated with "(Project: Airports)" is the top-level build file, and the one with the words "(Module: app)" is the subproject-level build file. Soon we'll edit the latter to add dependencies needed for the application.

Before going any further, let's update a few dependencies we'll need as soon as we start coding the app.

First, add dependency to the Klaxon library that will be used to parse the JSON response from the web service. For this, double click the file build.gradle (Module: app). Scroll down in the file to the dependencies section, and right after the other lines that start with implementation, add the following line:

```
implementation "com.beust:klaxon:5.0.2"
```

In addition to using the Klaxon library, our app will also use Kotlin coroutines. To facilitate that, add these two lines right after the line that specifies the Klaxon dependency:

```
implementation "org.jetbrains.kotlinx:kotlinx-coroutines-core:1.2.2"
implementation "org.jetbrains.kotlinx:kotlinx-coroutines-android:1.2.2"
```

The first is for the Kotlin's coroutines library, and the second is for Android-specific coroutines integration that's needed to support coroutines in Android.

After making these changes, we need to tell the IDE to refresh the Gradle build file and download the dependencies. For this, in the IDE, click the File menu and select Sync Project with Gradle Files. Wait a moment for the IDE to refresh the project, and download the dependencies we've introduced.

One final configuration before we can move on to the coding—we'll be running the app within an Android emulator. By default, the code running within the emulator doesn't have unrestricted access to the network. For the app to be able to get data from the remote web service, we have to modify the file Android-Manifest.xml, which you can find in the Project pane under app/manifest. Open that file, and add the following line right before the </manifest> closing tag:

```
<uses-permission android:name="android.permission.INTERNET" />
```

Now that the project is set up and the necessary dependencies and configurations are in place, let's move on to the code.

Defining Domain Objects

Our app will make requests to the FAA web service to fetch the airport data. For this, we'll need a variation of the Airport class we created in Chapter 18, Unit Testing with Kotlin, on page 347. In Android Studio, in the Project pane, right click the package name com.agiledeveloper.airports under app/java and select New, and Kotlin File/Class. Change the value for Kind to Class and key in the name "Airport" in the text box next to the Name label.

Edit the generated file to create the Airport class, like so:

```
android/Airports/app/src/main/java/com/agiledeveloper/airports/Airport.kt
package com.agiledeveloper.airports

import com.beust.klaxon.*

class Weather(@Json(name = "Temp") val temperature: Array<String>)

data class Airport(
  @Json(name = "IATA") val code: String,
  @Json(name = "Name") val name: String,
  @Json(name = "Delay") val delay: Boolean,
  @Json(name = "Weather") val weather: Weather = Weather(arrayOf(""))) {

  companion object {
    fun sort(airports: List<Airport>) : List<Airport> {
      return airports.sortedBy { airport -> airport.name }
    }

    fun getAirportData(code: String) =
      try {
        Klaxon().parse<Airport>(fetchData(code)) as Airport
      } catch(ex: Exception) {
        Airport(code, "Invalid Airport", false)
      }

    private fun fetchData(code: String) =
      java.net.URL("https://soa.smext.faa.gov/asws/api/airport/status/$code")
        .readText()
  }
}
```

The Weather class is used to store the temperature at an airport. An instance of this class is used within the Airport class, which comes next. The Airport class isn't much different from the one we created in previous chapters. The getAirportData() function uses the Klaxon parser to create an Airport instance from the data received from the FAA web service. If there's an error, it returns an Airport instance with the name Invalid Airport.

Let's now create the AirportStatus file that will contain the function to make asynchronous calls to the Airport's getAirportData() function. Create a file named AirportStatus.kt, following the steps that we used to create the Airport class. Change the contents of the generated file, like so:

android/Airports/app/src/main/java/com/agiledeveloper/airports/AirportStatus.kt

```
package com.agiledeveloper.airports

import kotlinx.coroutines.*

suspend fun getAirportStatus(airportCodes: List<String>): List<Airport> =
  withContext(Dispatchers.IO) {
    val airports = airportCodes
      .map { code -> async { Airport.getAirportData(code) } }
      .map { response -> response.await() }

    Airport.sort(airports)
  }
```

The getAirportStatus() function is the same as the one we implemented in the previous chapters. It makes the calls to getAirportData() asynchronously, from a thread within the Dispatchers.IO thread pool, instead of from the Main thread. Thus the UI thread won't block when the code makes network calls. Since we already added the dependency to the kotlinx.coroutines library, we should have no trouble compiling this code.

We're done with coding the part that gets data from the web service. Next, we'll turn our attention to the UI.

Creating Layouts

We'll use two layouts in this app, one for the main landing page and the other for each of the rows to display airport status information. Let's start with the design of the first one.

In the Project pane, under app/res/layout, you'll see the file activity_main.xml—it was created by the IDE when the project was created. Double click this file name and take a look at the layout. You can view and edit the layout using the Design view, or directly view and edit the XML document using the Text view. Let's edit the layout from the Design view.

The Android Studio provides powerful ways to add various widgets to the layout. Start by deleting the TextView with the words Hello World from the middle of the layout. Then from the Text section under the Palette, drag and drop a TextView onto the layout. On the right pane, change the text value for the newly placed widget from TextView to Airport Code. In the right pane, above the text box that you changed, take note of a rectangle with four + symbols around it.

Click the top + and change the number that appears to 48. Likewise, click the left + and change the number to 16. These changes tell the newly added widget to be placed at 16dp from the left and 48dp from the top.

Next, drag and drop Plain Text from the Text section of Palette to the right of the previously placed TextView. This new widget is an object of an EditText. Change the ID to airportCode. Provide a three-letter code for the text box next to Hint. Click + in the sequence left, top, and right, and enter the values 8, 32, and 88, respectively. In the Attributes pane, scroll down to find the text label and remove the Name value in the text box next to the label.

Now, click the Buttons section in the palette and place a Button next to EditText. Change the ID to addAirportCode, the value for text from Button to Add. Click the + symbols on the left, top, and right, and change the values to 8, 32, and 8, respectively.

We'll use a RecyclerView to display the status of the airports. Under Palette, click Common, and drag and drop RecyclerView to right below the TextView we placed before. Enter airportStatus for the ID, and change the layout_width value to match_parent. Click the + symbols at the left, top, and right, and key in the number 8 for each.

Once you place the four components, the design view of the layout in activity_main.xml will look like this:

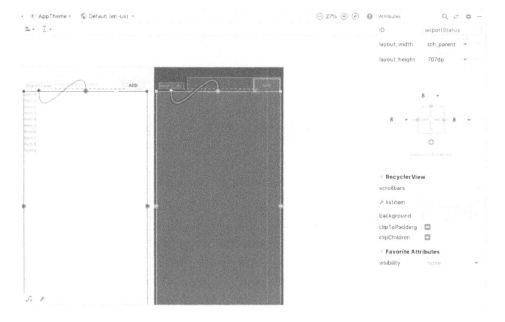

Next, let's create a layout for a row to represent an airport's status. The number of rows in the RecyclerView will change dynamically based on the number of airports the user is interested in. But each row should conform to the same structure, even though each will display different airport information. To make this easy, we'll create a template layout for the row.

In the Project pane, under app/res, right click layout, which is the parent node of activity_main.xml. Select New, and select Layout resource file. Key in "airport_info" for File name: and click the OK button. In this layout, we'll create a TableRow that contains four TextViews to hold the details about an airport.

Before adding any widgets to this layout, change the value for the android:layout_height attribute (in the android.support.constraint.ConstraintLayout element) to wrap_content. This ensures that a row doesn't occupy the entire RecyclerView and provides space for multiple rows to be visible.

In the Design view, drag and drop a TableRow from the Layouts section under Palette to the airport_info layout. Change the value for layout_width to 400dp and the value for layout_height to match_parent. Click the left and the right + symbols, and change both the values to 0.

We'll next place four TextViews into the TableRow, one at a time. Let's start with the first one.

Drag and drop a TextView into the TableRow. Change the ID of the newly placed TextView to airportCode. Set the value to Code for the text property. Change the layout_width to 0dp and the value for layout_weight to 5.

Create a second TextView with ID set to airportName, value for the text property set to Name, layout_width to 0dp, and layout_weight to 20.

For the third TextView, set ID to airportTemperature, text to Temp, layout_width to 0dp, and layout_weight to 10.

Finally, for the fourth TextView, set ID to airportDelay, text to \u23F3, layout_width to 0dp, and layout_weight to 2. The value for the text is unicode for an hour-glass icon to represent a delay.

The layout_weight properties instruct that the TextView components be arranged within the row so that the name gets the lion's share of space, the temperature data gets the next maximum space, the code occupies less, and the delay take up the least amount of relative space.

When you're done, the file airport_info.xml should look like this:

android/Airports/app/src/main/res/layout/airport_info.xml

```xml
<?xml version="1.0" encoding="utf-8"?>
<android.support.constraint.ConstraintLayout
  xmlns:android="http://schemas.android.com/apk/res/android"
  xmlns:app="http://schemas.android.com/apk/res-auto"
  xmlns:tools="http://schemas.android.com/tools"
  android:layout_width="match_parent"
  android:layout_height="wrap_content">

  <TableRow
    android:layout_width="400dp"
    android:layout_height="match_parent"
    tools:layout_editor_absoluteY="8dp"
    app:layout_constraintStart_toStartOf="parent"
    app:layout_constraintEnd_toEndOf="parent">

    <TextView
      android:text="Code"
      android:layout_width="0dp"
      android:layout_height="wrap_content"
      android:id="@+id/airportCode"
      android:layout_weight="5"/>

    <TextView
      android:text="Name"
      android:layout_width="0dp"
      android:layout_height="wrap_content"
      tools:layout_editor_absoluteY="0dp"
      tools:layout_editor_absoluteX="134dp"
      android:id="@+id/airportName"
      android:layout_weight="20"/>

    <TextView
      android:text="Temp"
      android:layout_width="0dp"
      android:layout_height="wrap_content"
      tools:layout_editor_absoluteY="0dp"
      tools:layout_editor_absoluteX="134dp"
      android:id="@+id/airportTemperature"
      android:layout_weight="10"/>

    <TextView
      android:text="\u23F3"
      android:layout_width="0dp"
      android:layout_height="wrap_content"
      tools:layout_editor_absoluteY="0dp"
      tools:layout_editor_absoluteX="134dp"
      android:id="@+id/airportDelay"
      android:layout_weight="2"/>
  </TableRow>
</android.support.constraint.ConstraintLayout>
```

Save the changes and get ready to write the code for the UI activity.

Implementing the Activity

It's time to implement the code for the UI, starting with the landing page, which is the main activity. We'll first write the code to handle the airport code that the user enters into the text box and the button click. Then we'll write the code to populate the RecyclerView with data obtained from the web service. That appears like a lot of work, but, surprisingly, we won't need too much code to implement these actions. Let's get started, one step at a time.

As the first step, let's address head-on the need for coroutines in the UI. The UI will have to fetch the airport status from the web service, but we don't want the UI to block and become inactive when the application is in the middle of network calls. To address this, we've already designed the getAirport-Status() top-level function in AirportStatus to be non-blocking, using the suspend keyword. From Chapter 15, Exploring Coroutines, on page 285, we know that functions marked with suspend can't be called from within arbitrary functions—they have to be called from within coroutines. There's a catch, however—the UI code created by the Android Studio doesn't use coroutines. So if we invoke getAirportStatus() from an event handler, the code will fail compilation. In short, we have to run the UI code in a coroutine context so that the event handlers can call functions that are marked with suspend.

We can easily run the UI code as a coroutine by making a small change to the generated MainActivity class—we'll implement Kotlin's CoroutineScope and override the coroutineContext property. With this change, the activity class can provide a coroutine scope for the execution of coroutines. Let's make this change in the MainActivity.kt file:

android/Airports/app/src/main/java/com/agiledeveloper/airports/MainActivity.kt
```
package com.agiledeveloper.airports

class MainActivity : AppCompatActivity(), CoroutineScope {
  override val coroutineContext: CoroutineContext
    get() = Dispatchers.Main

  override fun onCreate(savedInstanceState: Bundle?) {
    super.onCreate(savedInstanceState)
    setContentView(R.layout.activity_main)
  }
}
```

The onCreate() function shown in the code was generated by the IDE when the project was created. The only changes we made to the class are the addition of the CoroutineScope implementation and the coroutineContext property. Note the fact that the coroutineContext property's get() is returning a reference to Dispatchers.Main—we'll discuss this further when we're ready to make an asynchronous call.

As you key in the code, the IDE will prompt you for the necessary imports. Accept the appropriate choice the IDE gives, and move forward.

Next, we'll define a field in the MainActivity class:

android/Airports/app/src/main/java/com/agiledeveloper/airports/MainActivity.kt
```
private val airportCodes = mutableListOf<String>()
```

The airportCodes field will hold a list of airport IATA codes the user will provide at runtime.

Next, we'll edit the onCreate() function, which currently has two lines of code.

As a first step, we want to disable the Add button so the user won't be able to click it until an airport code is entered. To disable the button, we need a reference to the button widget from the layout. The Kotlin Android integration makes this effortless by synthesizing the UI widgets as properties with the activity class. To enable this facility, in the top of the MainActivity.kt file, import the following:

android/Airports/app/src/main/java/com/agiledeveloper/airports/MainActivity.kt
```
import kotlinx.android.synthetic.main.activity_main.*
```

Now, in the onCreate() function, we can refer to the button from the layout using the id we provided for the button, namely addAirportCode, like so:

android/Airports/app/src/main/java/com/agiledeveloper/airports/MainActivity.kt
```
addAirportCode.isEnabled = false
```

We set the isEnabled property of the addAirportCode button to true if the airportCode text box has some text; otherwise we set it to false, disabling the button.

As soon as the user starts typing in the text box, we'll want to enable the button. To achieve this, we'll handle the text change event on the EditText by calling the addTextChangedListener() function.

android/Airports/app/src/main/java/com/agiledeveloper/airports/MainActivity.kt
```
airportCode.addTextChangedListener(object: TextWatcher {
  override fun afterTextChanged(s: Editable) {
    addAirportCode.isEnabled = airportCode.text.isNotBlank()
  }

  override fun beforeTextChanged(
    s: CharSequence, start: Int, count: Int, after: Int) { /* no-op */ }

  override fun onTextChanged(
    s: CharSequence, start: Int, before: Int, count: Int) { /* no-op */ }
})
```

The addTextChangedListener() function takes an object of TextWatcher as argument. We use the concise Kotlin syntax to create an anonymous instance of TextWatcher. In this object's afterTextChanged() callback event we enable the button, using the handle in the addAirportCode field, if the airportCode EditText's text box is non-empty. The other two callback methods of TextWatcher are intentionally left blank since we have no use for them.

As the next step within onCreate(), we need to register an event handler for the button click event. In the callback for the button click, we'll take the airport code entered by the user and add it to the list airportCodes, which resides in the first field we created in the MainActivity class. Let's add the following code to the bottom of the onCreate() function.

android/Airports/app/src/main/java/com/agiledeveloper/airports/MainActivity.kt

```
addAirportCode.setOnClickListener {
  airportCodes.add(airportCode.text.toString())
  airportCode.setText("")

  launch {
    updateAirportStatus()
  }
}
```

After adding the airport code to the list, we clear the EditText's text box. If the newly added airport code is the first, we need to populate the RecyclerView with status for that airport. If airport codes already are in the list, then at this time, we can update the status for all the airports the user has requested information for. We'll use a yet-to-be-written function, updateAirportStatus(), to get the data from the AirportStatus's getAirportStatus() function. Since the call to that function will be asynchronous, we'll have to mark updateAirportStatus() with suspend. That, in turn, will demand that the call to updateAirportStatus() be made from a coroutine from within that callback. But, there's a catch—let's dig in.

If you take a look at the getAirportStatus() function in AirportStatus.kt, that function runs the asynchronous calls in the Dispatchers.IO thread. This makes good sense since calls to the web service are IO operations. However, when the response comes back from the calls, the UI code can't directly add the result to the UI components. The reason for this is the UI components aren't thread-safe, and accessing UI components from within arbitrary threads will result in an exception. In short, whereas the asynchronous calls run in the IO thread pool, we should run the UI updates in the Main thread. Thankfully, that's really easy to achieve, and in fact, we've already taken care of it.

When we call launch() in the callback, that coroutine will run in the CoroutineScope defined in MainActivity. Take a look at the definition of the MainActivity class—it implements CoroutineScope. The coroutineContext property is returning a Dispatchers.Main as the coroutine context. This option Main is only available in the Android API—we discussed this in Explicitly Setting a Context, on page 293. As a result, the code directly invoked within launch() will run concurrently in the UI's main thread—see Parallel vs. Concurrent, on page 286. The calls to the web service, though, will run in parallel in the IO threads. Thus, the data fetch will happen in parallel from the IO threads, but the update of the UI will happen in the main threads concurrently with the user's interaction.

As a final step within the onCreate() function, we need to get the RecyclerView ready to display the statuses of the airports:

android/Airports/app/src/main/java/com/agiledeveloper/airports/MainActivity.kt
```
airportStatus.apply {
  setHasFixedSize(true)
  layoutManager = LinearLayoutManager(this@MainActivity)
  adapter = AirportAdapter()
}
```

We configure the RecyclerView widget (connected to the id airportStatus) to have a fixed size, assign a layout manager to manage the child widgets, and connect an adapter (a yet-to-be-written AirportAdapter) to manage the display of the airport statuses.

We have one final task to complete in the MainActivity class—we need to implement the updateAirportStatus() function, which will trigger the redisplay of the RecyclerView when new airport statuses are received from getAirportStatus().

We can obtain the airport status information from the AirportStatus's top-level getAirportStatus() function. Once the data arrives within the updateAirportStatus() function, we can pass that to the adapter of the RecyclerView so it can take up the task of displaying the airport statuses. Here's the code to accomplish that:

android/Airports/app/src/main/java/com/agiledeveloper/airports/MainActivity.kt
```
private suspend fun updateAirportStatus() {
  val airports = getAirportStatus(airportCodes)
  val airportAdapter = airportStatus.adapter as AirportAdapter
  airportAdapter.updateAirportsStatus(airports)
}
```

We obtain a sorted list of Airports by calling the getAirportStatus() top-level function from the com.agiledeveloper.airport package—this is the function we wrote in the AirportStatus file. The list of Airports is passed to the adapter using the updateAirportStatus(). It's time to implement the adapter.

Updating the RecyclerView

The RecyclerView uses an adapter to display each row of data. We'll use a new AirportAdapter class for this purpose, to display the status of each airport.

Create a new Kotlin class file named AirportAdapter.kt that will hold the class AirportAdapter. Let's start with this initial code for the class in this file:

android/Airports/app/src/main/java/com/agiledeveloper/airports/AirportAdapter.kt

```
package com.agiledeveloper.airports

import android.support.v7.widget.RecyclerView
import android.view.LayoutInflater
import android.view.View
import android.view.ViewGroup
import kotlinx.android.synthetic.main.airport_info.view.*

class AirportAdapter : RecyclerView.Adapter<AirportViewHolder>() {
}

class AirportViewHolder(itemView: View) : RecyclerView.ViewHolder(itemView) {
}
```

An adapter inherits from RecyclerView.Adapter<T>, where the parametric type T represents a holder of a view for the data to be displayed. In our implementation, we specialize the parametric type to an AirportViewHolder. The AirportViewHolder class, in turn, inherits from RecyclerView.ViewHolder, which expects an instance of View into which the data will be displayed. The central approach is RecyclerView will call upon an adapter to create a view holder for each row. The view holder will take on the responsibility to appropriately display the data for each row. Let's focus on the implementation of the adapter and then take a look at the view holder.

In the AirportAdapter class, let's first define a field to store the list of airports:

android/Airports/app/src/main/java/com/agiledeveloper/airports/AirportAdapter.kt

```
private val airports = mutableListOf<Airport>()
```

The airports field is initialized to an empty mutable list of Airports. We'll soon implement the updateAirportsStatus() function to modify the values in this list. The RecyclerView needs to know how many rows it should create. For this, we'll override the getItemCount() function of the base class:

android/Airports/app/src/main/java/com/agiledeveloper/airports/AirportAdapter.kt

```
override fun getItemCount() = airports.size + 1
```

In addition to displaying the status of each airport, we also want to display a header row. For this reason, we return the size of the collection of Airports plus one. Next, the adapter needs to produce a view holder for each row. This is done by overriding the onCreateViewHolder() function:

android/Airports/app/src/main/java/com/agiledeveloper/airports/AirportAdapter.kt

```kotlin
override fun onCreateViewHolder(
  parent: ViewGroup, position: Int): AirportViewHolder {

  val view = LayoutInflater.from(parent.context)
    .inflate(R.layout.airport_info, parent, false)

  return AirportViewHolder(view)
}
```

We create a view using the layout we created earlier in the file air-port_info.xml—the TableRow with TextViews for code, name, and so on. We then attach that view to a new instance of AirportViewHolder and return that instance.

The RecyclerView will use the view holder created by the onCreateViewHolder() function to display the data for each row. But it has to map or bind the data to be displayed with the view holder. We achieve this by overriding the onBindViewHolder() function:

android/Airports/app/src/main/java/com/agiledeveloper/airports/AirportAdapter.kt

```kotlin
override fun onBindViewHolder(viewHolder: AirportViewHolder, position: Int) {
  if (position > 0) viewHolder.bind(airports[position - 1])
}
```

If the value of position is equal to 0, then the default text we hard-coded in the layout—Code, Name, Temp, and Delay—should be displayed as the header. Otherwise, we need to bind the data in an Airport instance at that position in the list to the view holder. We delegate that responsibility to the bind() function of the view holder.

The last function we need in the AirportAdapter class is updateAirportsStatus(), which is responsible for taking the updated/new airport statuses and modifying the mutable list stored as a field within the adapter.

android/Airports/app/src/main/java/com/agiledeveloper/airports/AirportAdapter.kt

```kotlin
fun updateAirportsStatus(updatedAirports: List<Airport>) {
  airports.apply {
    clear()
    addAll(updatedAirports)
  }

  notifyDataSetChanged()
}
```

In the updateAirportsStatus() function, we clear the existing list of Airports, add all the airports from the provided updatedAirports, and trigger a refresh of the RecyclerView by calling the notifyDataSetChanged() function. This function will result in the RecyclerView calling the getItemCount() to find the number of airports, then calling onCreateViewHolder() that many times to create as many view holders, then bind the view to the data using onBindViewHolder() for each row of data.

The only piece of code left unfinished is the bind() function of the view holder. Let's implement that now.

```
android/Airports/app/src/main/java/com/agiledeveloper/airports/AirportAdapter.kt
class AirportViewHolder(itemView: View) : RecyclerView.ViewHolder(itemView) {
  fun bind(airport: Airport) {
    val (code, name, delay, weather) = airport
    val clock = if (delay) "\uD83D\uDD52" else ""

    itemView.apply {
      airportCode.text = code
      airportName.text = name
      airportTemperature.text = weather.temperature.firstOrNull()
      airportDelay.text = clock
    }
  }
}
```

The bind() function uses the destructuring syntax to fetch the four properties from the given instance of Airport. If the delay is true, then the variable clock is set to an ASCII value that represents a clock; otherwise, it's set to an empty string. Finally, we update each widget in the view, to display the code, name, temperature value, and delay, respectively.

That completes all the code necessary for the view. Compile the code and make sure there are no errors. If you run into any errors, refer to the code from the book's source code to find the differences and resolve.

Seeing the App in Action

We're ready to take the application for a ride. We'll use an Android emulator to run the application and interact with it.

Click the Run menu in the IDE and select the Run App menu item. In the dialog that opens, click the Create New Virtual Device button. Select Pixel 2 XL in the Phone tab. Click the x86 Images tab and click the Download link next to Pie on the line for x86_64 (or select the one that is appropriate for your system). Once you have the system image installed on your system, select it and press the Next button. Click the Finish button. Now select the device Pixel 2 XL API 28 and click OK.

Once the app launches in the emulator, enter a few airport codes, for example, "IAD", "SFO", "AUS", "PDX", one at a time, and click the ADD button. As you click the button, you'll see the details of the airport emerge in the RecyclerView, like in the following figure:

The output shows the status of the airports that we entered, with only the San Francisco airport showing delays at the time of the run. The temperature is displayed both in Fahrenheit and Celsius.

Wrapping Up

Creating Android apps using Kotlin has many benefits. The language is supported as a first-class citizen by Google for programming Android devices. By using Kotlin for Android development, you can access all the benefits of Kotlin when programming on the Android platform—the code is concise and expressive, it's less error prone, it boosts productivity, and the list goes on. In addition, the Android Studio IDE provides features to convert Java code and code snippets to Kotlin syntax for easy porting.

In this chapter we created a small app to illustrate the power of Kotlin for programming Android apps. The application fetches data from the web and displays airport status information in a RecyclerView. Throughout the code, we can see the Kotlin idioms and capabilities shine. Since fetching data from a remote service can take some time, to speed up access we used coroutines to make parallel calls to the service. Whereas parallel execution can improve performance, we can't update the UI from arbitrary threads. This is because

UI components are not thread safe and can be updated only from the main thread. Again, using the coroutines's capabilities we direct the update of the UI components to happen in the main thread, concurrent with the user interactions.

The app we created nicely illustrates the different capabilities of Kotlin and also shows the ease with which we're able to use coroutines to create apps that can provide good performance and, at the same time, be responsive to user interactions.

Throughout the book, we've seen the capabilities of Kotlin as a highly expressive, concise, safe, and powerful statically typed language. We've seen the various capabilities of the language, from the ability to program object-oriented code to writing both imperative and functional-style code. We've seen the facilities to create internal DSLs, thanks to Kotlin fluency, and the ease with which we can create both parallel and concurrent code with coroutines. With all this power packed into the language, Kotlin has emerged as one of the few multi-platform languages where the code can be targeted to different runtime environments. I hope this book has stimulated your creativity and given you some good ideas of how you can apply this wonderful language to your projects. Thank you for reading.

Transpiling to JavaScript

Front-end development is gaining momentum, and there's an increasing demand for full-stack developers. JavaScript has evolved significantly in recent years, but it's a dynamically typed language and also a weakly typed language—see *Rediscovering JavaScript [Sub18]*. In recent years, some programmers have gravitated toward statically typed languages, for example TypeScript, that will transpile to JavaScript. Statically typed languages can help find errors early, during compile time, and remove certain problems that may creep up during runtime if the code was written directly in JavaScript.

Languages like TypeScript offer static typing, but languages like Kotlin bring in that and a lot more. If you're going to choose static typing for front-end development, why stop at languages like TypeScript, when you could go all the way and benefit from the wealth of features of a powerful language like Kotlin? Kotlin makes it easier to create common code and to reuse code between platforms. You can also use Kotlin DSLs for HTML and CSS and thus use Kotlin for the entire front-end development.

Though the focus of this book isn't on creating front-end applications with Kotlin, let's explore this idea of Kotlin to JavaScript a bit here. If you're using IntelliJ IDEA, it'll extract the necessary Kotlin JavaScript[1] runtime library for you automatically when you compile to JavaScript. If you're using other IDEs or a build tool, you have to do some extra steps. Here, you'll see how to use the command line to compile and run the generated JavaScript code both in Node and within a browser.

---

1. https://kotlinlang.org/docs/tutorials/javascript/kotlin-to-javascript/kotlin-to-javascript.html

Compiling in Command Line

We'll write a Kotlin source file, transpile it to JavaScript, and also extract the necessary Kotlin JavaScript runtime library files from the Kotlin distribution.

Let's start with a Kotlin file first.

```
running/js/greetnames.kt
package com.agiledeveloper.jsexample

fun greetNames(names: List<String>) = "hello ${names.joinToString(", ")}"

fun main() {
  println(greetNames(listOf("Jack", "Jill")))
}
```

There's no sign of JavaScript here. If you like, you may compile the file greetnames.kt using kotlinc-jvm and run it within the JVM. But here, we'll transpile that into JavaScript instead.

To transpile to JavaScript, we have to use kotlinc-js instead of kotlinc-jvm. The -help option will give you all the available command-line options. We'll use the -output option to specify the JavaScript file to place the transpiled JavaScript code in.

Also, we need to extract the Kotlin JavaScript runtime library from the file kotlin-stdlib-js.jar, which is present in the Kotlin distribution under the lib directory.

Here are the commands for those two steps:

```
$ kotlinc-js -output greet.js greetnames.kt
$ unzip $KOTLIN_PATH/lib/kotlin-stdlib-js.jar -d lib
```

For Windows, remember to use %KOTLIN_PATH% instead of $KOTLIN_PATH. Also, you may use jar with xf option to extract the files from kotlin-stdlib-js.jar or use any program that will allow you to unzip the contents of that jar file. If you're using jar, then create a lib directory, cd into that directory, and then use the jar command to extract into that directory.

After running the above two commands, in addition to greetnames.kt, you'll find the greet.js file and a lib directory. Within the lib directory, among other files, you'll find kotlin.js and kotlin.meta.js.

We're all set to run the transpiled JavaScript. You may run it within Node.js for server-side JavaScript or within a browser, like Chrome, Firefox, and so on, for client-side JavaScript.

Running in Node

For this section, you'll need Node.js, or Node for short, installed on your system. If you don't already have it, download it from the Node website[2] and verify that it's in your system path by running the command node --version on the command line.

The transpiled JavaScript code needs the content of the Kotlin JavaScript library that we extracted into the lib directory. Thus, we have to require that first. Then we can load and execute the transpiled file. To make these steps easy, let's create a JavaScript file:

running/js/run-in-node.js
```
kotlin = require('./lib/kotlin');

require('./greet')
```

To run this code, use the command:

```
$ node run-in-node.js
```

Node will load the Kotlin JavaScript runtime file kotlin.js from within the lib directory, and also the transpiled file greet.js, and display the following output on the console:

```
hello Jack, Jill
```

The Kotlin-to-JavaScript transpiler converted the call to println() to console.log();, and thus the output appears on the console when JavaScript is executed.

Running in Browsers

To compile and merge scripts, to eliminate unused code, and to generate smaller JavaScript files, we typically use tools like WebPack. It's common to use such tools when using Kotlin for the front end as well. Since we're creating a very small example and our focus isn't on the front-end development, we won't delve into that here. Let's focus on running the greet.js file that we compiled from Kotlin in a browser.

To see the file greet.js run within a browser, we will first need to create an index.html file:

---

2.   https://nodejs.org/en/

running/js/index.html

```
<!DOCTYPE html>
<html>
  <body>
    <p>Please see the output in the browser console</p>
  </body>
  <script src="./lib/kotlin.js"></script>
  <script src="greet.js"></script>
</html>
```

In the HTML file, remember to load the kotlin.js script first, before loading the greet.js file.

Then open the file index.html within your favorite browser and take a peek at the browser's console. Here's an excerpt of the file being executed within Chrome.

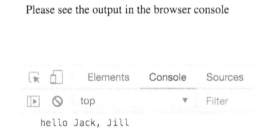

Kotlin/Native

In addition to JVM, JavaScript, Android devices, iOS, and Raspberry Pi, you can target your Kotlin code to native platforms like Windows, Mac OS, and Linux. The Kotlin compiler's front end compiles your Kotlin code to an intermediate representation. Kotlin/Native is an LLVM-based back end of the compiler that targets the intermediate representation to self-contained programs that can run natively without a virtual machine. Your Kotlin code can interoperate with native libraries—for example, code written using the C language, Objective-C, and Swift. You can use this option to create fast running native applications and to interoperate with native libraries.

In this appendix, we'll take a look at a small example that illustrates compiling Kotlin code to target MacOS. To target the example to other operating systems, refer to the toolchain requirements on the Kotlin/Native[1] website.

To compile Kotlin code to native platform, you need the Kotlin/Native compiler. Download it from the binary distribution[2] website. Once you install it, add the bin directory that contains the tools like cinterop and kotlinc-native to the path.

To get a glimpse of the power of Kotlin/Native, let's create a small function in C and then call it from within Kotlin code. As a first step, let's create a C header file named fib.h under a c directory.

native/c/fib.h
```
int fib(int n);
```

The header file declares a function named fib() that takes an integer value and returns an integer value.

---

1. https://kotlinlang.org/docs/reference/native-overview.html
2. https://github.com/JetBrains/kotlin/releases/tag/v1.3.31

Next, let's implement this function in a file named fib.c, also placed in the c directory:

```
native/c/fib.c
#include "fib.h"

int fib(int n) {
  return n < 2 ? 1 : fib(n - 1) + fib(n - 2);
}
```

The function computes, using recursion, the Fibonacci number for the given parameter. We'll need a C compiler to compile this code and create a library. You may use any C compiler that you're familiar with. Here, we'll use the GCC[3] GNU compiler and then the ar archival tool to bundle the object file created by the compiler into a library archive file.

```
$ gcc -c c/fib.c
$ ar crv libfib.a fib.o
```

The gcc command as shown above will compile the C code that is in the file fib.c into an object file named fib.o. Then the ar command will bundle that file into an archive file named libfib.a.

Next, we'll use this library from within Kotlin code. To invoke the int fib(int); C function from within Kotlin, we need a Kotlin representation fun fib(n: Int): Int. Creating this manually can be tedious and error prone when working with any nontrivial libraries. The cinterop tool, which is part of the Kotlin/Native distribution, removes that burden by autogenerating the function signature from the C header files.

To assist the cinterop tool, we need to create an interop def that provides the necessary information, like the name and location of the header files, library file to link with, and so on. You may also include declarations and implementations of C functions directly in the def file after a triple dash separator line (—). That's a way to try interop without the need to have a C compiler.

Let's create the def file, also under the c directory:

```
native/c/interop.def
headers = fib.h
linkerOpts.osx = -L. -lfib
```

The headers property lists the header files for the cinterop tool to process. The linkerOpts property lists the location and the name of the archive file—the -l option mentions the archive file name without the lib prefix and the .a suffix.

---

3.   https://gcc.gnu.org/

Let's run the cinterop tool to generate the Kotlin signature for the C function:

```
$ cinterop -def c/interop.def -compilerOpts -I./c -o libfib
```

This command instructs the cinterop tool to process the interop.def file. The -I option provides the location of the header file mentioned within the def file. The -o option specifies the name of the Kotlin linking file to generate.

After running the command, examine the files generated. The Kotlin signature file for the function resides in the generated file libfib-build/kotlin/interop/interop.kt. We'll import this file from within our Kotlin code to call the fib() C function.

Here's the sample Kotlin code to call the fib() function, written in a file named sample.kt under a new kotlin directory.

native/kotlin/sample.kt
```
import interop.*

fun main() {
  println("fib(10) is ${fib(10)}")
}
```

We'll use the kotlinc-native compiler to compile this Kotlin source code to a native target.

```
$ kotlinc-native kotlin/sample.kt -library libfib -o sample
```

The previous command generates a native executable file named sample.kexe. Run the executable to watch Kotlin code call the C function:

```
$ ./sample.kexe
fib(10) is 89
```

This example illustrates both the Kotlin-C interop and how Kotlin code can be targeted to a native platform and can be run as a native executable.

Kotlin to WebAssembly

WebAssembly (WASM) is poised to be the next major disruptive technology. In the past, JavaScript was the only predominant viable option for executing code within browsers. With WebAssembly, you can compile code written in many different languages—including C, C++, Rust, Go, C#, Python, Java, and Kotlin—to the WASM[1] binary instruction format, for a stack-based virtual machine that runs within modern browsers. WASM brings many benefits, including speed of development using higher-level languages, high runtime performance, enhanced safety, and code that's easier to test and debug and that interoperates with code written in different languages.

Kotlin to WebAssembly is currently in initial stages at the time of this writing. Treat the material in this appendix as experimental.

To target Kotlin to WASM, use the Kotlin/Native compiler with the -target wasm32 command-line option. If you've not had a chance to install the Kotlin/Native distribution in Appendix 2, Kotlin/Native, on page 409, do so before you continue.

In this appendix, we'll create a small example to draw on an HTML5 canvas, using Kotlin code to illustrate Kotlin to WASM targeting. We'll need an HTML file to fire up a page in the browser. We'll also need Kotlin source code to draw on the canvas that will be defined within the HTML file. In addition to using Kotlin/Native, we also need a minimal lightweight web server to serve the files into a browser. Let's get these things set up, one step at a time.

In an empty directory named wasm, run the command npm init and accept the defaults—for this step you'll need to have Node.js[2] installed on your system. When done, install the lite-server using the command npm install lite-server --save.

---

1. https://webassembly.org
2. https://nodejs.org/en/

After the installation completes, open the file package.json and edit it to add a start command to start the lite-server. The file should look like the following when you're done with these steps—the version of lite-server that you see may be different.

wasm/package.json
```json
{
  "name": "wasm",
  "version": "1.0.0",
  "description": "",
  "main": "index.js",
  "scripts": {
    "start": "lite-server"
  },
  "author": "",
  "license": "ISC",
  "dependencies": {
    "lite-server": "^2.4.0"
  }
}
```

Create an index.html file with the following content:

wasm/index.html
```html
<!DOCTYPE html>
<html>
  <head>
    <title>Kotlin to WebAssembly</title>
  </head>
  <body>
    <h1>Drawing into HTML 5 Canvas using Kotlin</h1>
    <canvas id="display" width="300" height="300"></canvas>
  </body>
  <script wasm="check.wasm" src="check.wasm.js"></script>
</html>
```

In the HTML file, we've defined an HTML5 canvas into which we'll render from within the Kotlin code we'll write soon. We've also included, using the script tag, a check.wasm file that uses the wasm attribute and a check.wasm.js file that uses the src attribute. Modern browsers that support WASM will recognize the wasm attribute and load the code within the embedded WASM virtual machine.

As a next step, let's create the Kotlin code to render into the canvas:

wasm/check.kt
```kotlin
import kotlinx.interop.wasm.dom.*

fun main() {
  val canvas = document.getElementById("display").asCanvas

  val context = canvas.getContext("2d")

  val rect = canvas.getBoundingClientRect()
  val offsetX = (rect.right - rect.left) / 4
  val offsetY = (rect.bottom - rect.top) / 4

  context.apply {
    fillStyle = "green"
    strokeStyle = "white"
    lineWidth = 10

    fillRect(rect.left, rect.top, rect.right, rect.bottom)
    beginPath()
    moveTo(rect.left + offsetX / 2, rect.bottom - 3 * offsetY)
    lineTo(rect.left + offsetX, rect.bottom - 2 * offsetY)
    lineTo(rect.right - offsetX, rect.top + offsetY)
    stroke()
  }
}
```

We first import the contents of the kotlinx.interop.wasm.dom package—we'll see soon where this dependency comes from. In the main() function we get a reference to the canvas object from the HTML file's DOM document object. Then we obtain a reference to the "2D" context object of the canvas. Then using the canvas API, we fill the rectangle of the canvas with green color and draw white color lines to represent a check mark. Even though we're writing this code in Kotlin, the API is pretty much the HTML5 canvas API—refer to the W3C standard API[3] documentation.

It's time to compile the code and see it in action. First we need to create the JavaScript interop functions to talk to the canvas API from our Kotlin code. In that vein, the jsinterop tool is like the cinterop tool we saw in Appendix 2, Kotlin/Native, on page 409. At the time of this writing, the jsinterop tool is limited to creating interop functions only for two libraries, and it also has limitations to the functions it maps to Kotlin signature. Over time, as development continues, these limitations will disappear, and the tool will become versatile so we can easily interact from Kotlin with different libraries written in JavaScript and other languages.

---

3.   https://www.w3schools.com/tags/ref_canvas.asp

Run the jsinterop tool and specify the necessary target and the pkg command-line options:

```
$ jsinterop -target wasm32 -pkg kotlinx.interop.wasm.dom
```

This command will generate the Kotlin signatures for the DOM API and thus the files necessary to satisfy the import we saw at the top of our Kotlin code. Take note of the generated files and the nativelib library—we'll use this library in the next step.

Next, run the kotlinc-native compiler to compile the Kotlin source code to WASM:

```
$ kotlinc-native -target wasm32 check.kt -library nativelib -o check
```

This command will result in the creation of the check.wasm and check.wasm.js files. We've already referenced these two files in the index.html file, and we're ready to take the WASM code compiled from Kotlin for a ride.

Run the command npm start—this will start the lite-server and fire up your default browser to load the index.html file. You should then see something like:

Drawing into HTML 5 Canvas using Kotlin

This figure shows the Chrome browser displaying the index.html file with the canvas, which has the check mark that was drawn by our Kotlin code, running within the WASM virtual machine.

Bibliography

[AS96]   Harold Abelson and Gerald Jay Sussman. *Structure and Interpretation of Computer Programs*. MIT Press, Cambridge, MA, 2nd, 1996.

[Blo18]   Joshua Bloch. *Effective Java, Third Edition*. Addison-Wesley, Boston, MA, 2018.

[Fow10]   Martin Fowler. *Domain-Specific Languages*. Addison-Wesley Longman, Boston, MA, 2010.

[GHJV95]   Erich Gamma, Richard Helm, Ralph Johnson, and John Vlissides. *Design Patterns: Elements of Reusable Object-Oriented Software*. Addison-Wesley, Boston, MA, 1995.

[HT00]   Andrew Hunt and David Thomas. *The Pragmatic Programmer: From Journeyman to Master*. Addison-Wesley, Boston, MA, 2000.

[Mar02]   Robert C. Martin. *Agile Software Development, Principles, Patterns, and Practices*. Prentice Hall, Englewood Cliffs, NJ, 2002.

[SH06]   Venkat Subramaniam and Andy Hunt. *Practices of an Agile Developer*. The Pragmatic Bookshelf, Raleigh, NC, 2006.

[Sub14]   Venkat Subramaniam. *Functional Programming in Java*. The Pragmatic Bookshelf, Raleigh, NC, 2014.

[Sub18]   Venkat Subramaniam. *Rediscovering JavaScript*. The Pragmatic Bookshelf, Raleigh, NC, 2018.

Index

SYMBOLS

!! (not-null assertion operator), 83, 86

"""

    handling raw strings with, 30

    for multiline strings, 31

#! (shebang), 12, 14

$ (dollar sign) for string templates, 29

${} for string templates, 29

%= operator, 224

&& operator, 90

() (parenthesis)

    anonymous functions, 187

    lambdas, 180, 182, 187, 213, 252

    as optional, 5, 235, 252, 254, 256–260

* operator, overloading, 222–224

*= operator, 224

+ operator

    iteration with extension functions, 230

    Java interop example, 337

    lists, 71

    maps, 74

    overloading, 222, 337

    sets, 73

+= operator, 224

, (comma), separating parameters, 41

- operator

    lists, 71

    maps, 74

    overloading, 222

-- operator, 224

-= operator, 224

->, lambdas, 179

. (dot), as optional, 5, 235, 252, 254, 256–260

.. operator, 54, 56

/= operator, 224

: (colon)

    constraints, 100, 128

    generics, 128

    inheritance, 142

    prefix for return type, 39

    specifying parameter type, 41

    Spring applications interfaces, 381

:: for function references, 183

::class, 21

; (semicolon)

    enum classes, 146

    as optional, 5, 20, 251

    separating paths in classpath, 333

    Spring applications, 377

<*> star projection, 101

<> (angle brackets) for constraints, 128

= operator

    for default arguments, 44

    single-expression functions, 38, 42

== operator

    Java, 28

    Kotlin, 28, 88

=== operator, 28

>= operator, 128, 230

? (question mark), nullable type suffix, 82

?. (safe-call operator), 83–86

?: (Elvis operator), 84, 86, 92

[] (index operator)

    arrays, 68

    key-value pairs, 74

    lists, 70

\ (backslash), escaping symbols with, 29

_ (underscore), skipping properties while destructuring, 50

` (backtick) symbol, escaping method or property names, 335

{} (braces)

    function block syntax, 38, 42

    lambdas, 179

| for multiline strings, 32

|| operator, 90

~ (tilde) for multiline strings, 33

A

abstract classes

    about, 134

    creating, 136–138

    vs. interfaces, 137

abstract keyword, 136

abstract methods
    creating, 136
    interfaces, 134
    overriding, 135, 137
access modifiers, 119, 122, 143
activity_main.xml file, 389, 391–395
adapters, RecyclerView, 399–401
add()
    Java interop example, 343
    lists, 70, 72
addTextChangedListener(), 396
Advanced REST Client extension for Chrome, 379
afterTest(), 359
afterTextChanged(), 397
agile, 25, 87, 95, 150, 154
Agile Software Development, Principles, Patterns, and Practices, 87, 95, 150, 154
airport weather examples
    Android application, 387–403
    programming asynchronously example, 310–317
    source code, 349, 352, 373
    testing, canary, 352
    testing, code coverage, 371
    testing, coroutines, 366–373
    testing, data parsing, 361–363
    testing, data-driven, 356
    testing, empirical, 353–356
    testing, integration, 363, 370
    testing, interaction, 359–361
    testing, setup, 349–352
    testing, top-level functions, 363–366
    testing, with mocks, 357–363, 365, 368–370
    using Pair, 67
algebraic data types, 133
aliases, singletons, 112
also(), 79, 236–239, 243, 254
andThen(), 234

Android applications
    compiling on virtual machines, 5
    Dispatchers.Main context, 293
    emulators, 388, 401
    Kotlin as official language for, 1, 6, 13, 387, 402
    programming, 387–403
Android Studio IDE, 387–403
AndroidManifest.xml file, 388–389
angle brackets (<>) for constraints, 128
annotations
    default, 345
    DSLs, 265–267
    Java interop, 345
    JSON parser, 361
    meta-annotations, 376
    properties in Spring applications, 380
anonymous functions
    vs. lambdas, 186–188
    return keyword, 190
anonymous inner classes, 109, 140, 148
anonymous objects
    as anonymous inner classes, 109
    creating, 108
    iterators as, 230
    limitations, 109
Any
    DSLs and, 79, 254
    methods, 236–243
    type checking with is, 88
    type safety with, 77–80
    when as an expression, 59
APIs
    documentation, 415
    Minimum API Level, 388
    Spring Kotlin API, 6
application plugin, 350
application {} function, 350
apply(), 79, 236–241, 254, 264
ar command, 410
archive file, Kotlin/Native, 410
arguments
    default, 37, 43–45, 343
    lambdas as last parameter, 44, 48, 182, 213, 252
    matching with when, 54, 58–62
    named, 2, 37, 43, 45

spread operator, 46, 48
    syntax, 2
    using variable number of, 38, 46–48
Array, 64, 68–69
arrayListOf(), 72
arrayOf(), 57, 68
ArrayList, 65
arrays
    about, 64
    converting lists to, 49
    creating, 57, 68
    iteration, 57, 65
    size, 69
    spread operator, 48
    using, 68–69
as, explicit casting with, 91–93
as?, explicit casting with, 91–93
asCoroutineDispatcher(), 294
asSequence(), 215
assigned property, 130
assignment, 34
async()
    about, 300
    exceptions, 316
    testing coroutines, 366, 369
    using, 311–313
asynchronous programming, *see also* coroutines
    exception handling, 314–318, 324
    Kotlin advantages, 3–4, 6, 283
    testing, 347, 366–373
ATOMIC coroutines, 296
average, 69
await(), 300, 313, 316, 366

B

backing fields
    creating, 116
    extension properties, 228
    synthesized, 117
    volatile, 345
backslash (\), escaping symbols with, 29
backtick symbol (`), escaping method or property names, 335
base classes
    accessing from inner classes, 140

explicit permission for, 141

specifying, 4

beforeTest(), 359

bidirectional cancellation, 323

bind(), 401

blocks

assuming block expressions with = operator, 42

DSL builders, 263–267

functions, 38, 42

when as an expression, 60

boilerplate, 5

braces ({})

function block syntax, 38, 42

lambdas, 179

brackets [] index operator, 68, 70, 74

Breslav, Andrey, 1

build.gradle file, 376, 389

builders

HTML, 261

scope, 265–267

type-safe DSL builders, 260–265

XML, 262–267

buttons, airport weather example, 396–397

by keyword, 155

C

C

compiler, 410

Kotlin/Native example, 409–411

caching, see memoization

canary testing, 352

cancel(), 318–320

cancelAndJoin(), 318–320

CancellationException, 318

cancellations

bidirectional, 323

coroutines, 316–326

preventing, 321–323

supervisors, 324

timeouts, 325

canvas WebAssembly example, 413–416

captureCoroutine(), 368

casting

avoiding, 90

explicit, 78, 91–93, 362

smart, 78, 87, 89–91

chaining

assignments, 34

methods with apply(), 239

void functions with also(), 243

characters

creating ranges, 54

iterating over ranges, 55

checked exceptions

Java interop, 341–343

try-catch as optional, 24

Chrome

Advanced REST Client extension, 379

transpiling JavaScript example, 408

WebAssembly example, 416

cinterop, 410

class keyword, 114

classes, see also extension functions; interfaces; overloading operators; properties; singletons

about, 4

abstract, 134, 136–138

access modifiers, 119

anonymous inner, 109, 140, 148

base, 4, 140–141

class members, 124

creating, 9, 67, 113–123

creating instances, 114, 126, 128, 145

creating, automatic, 9

data, 68, 129–132

defining methods, 122

defining properties, 114

delegation, 151–162

derived, 142

entity, 380

enum, 145–148

final, 123, 141, 358

generics, 127–129

hierarchy, 4, 133, 148

inheritance, 140–145, 353

initialization code, 119

injecting from within, 232–234

injecting with extension functions, 226–235, 276

inlining, 122, 199

inner, 138–140, 148, 245

minimum syntax for, 114

open, 133, 141, 376

as optional, 22, 37

outer, 139, 245

overloading operators, 128, 223

overriding, 141, 143, 147

as public by default, 114, 119

range, 54

sealed, 133, 144

type inference, 21

classpath option, 8, 11, 333

close(), 99

closures, 188–189, 303

cloud services, 4

coEvery(), 369

coVerify(), 369

code

boilerplate, 5

executing, 7

code coverage, 347, 350, 371

code for this book

airport weather example, 349, 352, 373

reading, xix

source code, xix, 349, 352, 373

collections, see also arrays; lists; maps; sets

convenience methods, 64

destructuring, 65

getting first in internal iteration, 208, 214

immutable interface, 63–66

iteration, external, 54, 57, 64

iteration, internal, 67, 203–218

Java, 64, 335

mutable interface, 63–66

Pair, 63–64, 66–68, 127

vs. sequences, 213, 215

sequences, wrapping in, 215

sorting during internal iteration, 211

Triple, 49, 63–64, 66–67

using, 63–76

views, 65

colon (:)

constraints, 100, 128

generics, 128

inheritance, 142

prefix for return type, 39

specifying parameter type, 41
Spring applications interfaces, 381
comma (,), separating parameters, 41
command line
compiling from, 7–13, 406
REPL, 10, 14
running from, 7–8
targeting to WASM, 413
using experimental features, 297
.Companion, 125
companion object keyword, 124
companion objects
as factories, 125
mocking dependencies, 359
static methods, 134, 136, 231, 339
using, 124–127
compareTo(), 127, 224, 230
compiling, *see also* transpiling to JavaScript
C compiler, 410
from command line, 7–13, 406
with Gradle, 7, 330
Java interop, 5, 14, 330–333, 337
with Kotlin/Native, 5, 13–14, 409–411, 416
kotlinc-native compiler, 411, 416
with Maven, 7, 330
REPL with kotlinc-jvm, 10
Spring applications, 376
to WebAssembly, 5, 13–14, 413–416
to different targets, 13
warnings, 24–26
when as an expression, 59
componentN() methods, 129
composed functions, 234
concurrency, *see also* coroutines
functional style advantages, 178
JDK and, 4, 294
Kotlin advantages, 4
vs. parallelism, 286
structured, 314
understanding, 285–287
Constants class, 331

constraints
generic classes, 127–129
parametric types, 93, 99–101
constructor keyword, 114, 121
constructors
companion objects as factories, 125
data classes, 129
defining, 114, 116, 119–121
generic classes, 128
initialization code, 119
primary, 119–121
sealed classes, 144
secondary, 120
contains()
key-value pairs, 73
lists, 70
overloading, 224
sets, 73
containsKey(), 73
containsValue(), 73
context, DSLs, 250
context, coroutines
Android applications, 395, 397
changing, 297
Do Not Disturb, 321–323
explicitly setting, 293
testing, 367–370
threads, 293–298, 312, 314
continuations
about, 3, 285
sequence() function, 217
understanding, 301–303
contravariance, 78, 94, 98, 101
controllers, Spring applications, 378–380, 383–386
convertToUpper(), 334
Conway's Game of Life, 58
copy(), 129–132
copyFromTo(), 96
coroutineScope(), 319
CoroutineContext
Android applications, 395, 397
async(), 312
custom pool, 294
passing, 293
switching threads, 296
testing, 368
CoroutineExceptionHandler, 315

CoroutineName(), 299
coroutines, *see also* context, coroutines
about, 3–4, 6, 285
async(), 300, 312
await(), 300
cancellations, 316–326
concurrency, structured, 314
concurrency, understanding, 285–287
continuations, 217, 285, 301–303
debugging, 298–300
delaying execution, 296
exception handling, 314–318, 324
as first-class citizens, 287
hierarchy, 318
identifiers, 299
infinite sequences, 303–306
launching tasks, 290
library, 289
names, 299
programming Android applications, 387, 389, 395–397
programming asynchronously with, 309–313
rules, 318
running in a custom pool, 294–296
scope, 300, 314, 319, 395, 397
vs. subroutines, 286
supervisors, 324
suspendible functions, 285, 291–293, 296, 301–303, 318
testing, 347, 359, 366–373
timeouts, 325
using, 287–293
CoroutineScope, 395, 397
CoroutineStart, 296
costs, fluent code, 221
covariance, 78, 93, 96–98
create(), 126, 339, 385
crossinline, 199–201
CrudRepository, 381
curl, 379, 385

D

data classes, 68, 129–132
debugging
    coroutines, 298–300
    with observable delegate, 170
dec(), 224
declaration-site variance, 93, 97
declarative style
    about, 176–178
    uses, xv
default arguments, 37, 43–45, 343
default methods, annotating, 135, 345
defaultTask, 350
DefaultDispatcher, 293
delay(), 291
delegation
    about, 2, 4
    built-in, 166–170
    with by, 155
    cautions, 160–162
    classes, 151–162
    designing with, 151–156
    vs. inheritance, 148–152, 154–155
    Java, 153–154
    Lazy, 166–169
    maps, 75, 164–166
    with memoization, 277–278
    method collisions, 157–159
    observable, 166, 169
    parameters, 156
    properties, 160, 162, 164–166
    variables, 162–164
    vetoable, 166, 170
DELETE method, 378, 385
delete(), 383–384
dependencies
    mocking, 347, 357–363, 365, 368–370
    Spring applications, 376
description property, Spring applications, 380
design by contract, 77, 133–134
Design Patterns, 107, 149
destructuring
    about, 38
    data classes, 130

maps, 75
    specifying type during, 131
    using, 49–51
    with withIndex(), 58, 65
dispatch receivers, 233
dispatchers
    Android applications, 391, 395, 397
    coroutines, 293–295, 312, 366, 368
Dispatchers.Default, 293
Dispatchers.IO
    about, 293
    Android applications, 391, 397
    async(), 312, 366
    with mocking, 368
Dispatchers.Main, 293, 395
div(), 224
-Dkotlinx.coroutines.debug, 298
dollar sign ($) for string templates, 29
domain objects, Android applications, 390
Domain-Specific Languages, 249
domain-specific languages, see DSLs
Don't Repeat Yourself (DRY) principle, 154
dot (.), as optional, 5, 235, 252, 254, 256–260
downTo, 55
DRY (Don't Repeat Yourself) principle, 154
@DSLMarker, 265–267
DSLs
    annotations, 265–267
    Any and, 79, 254
    builders, type-safe , 260–265
    defined, 249
    extension functions, 252, 254–260
    HTML builder, 261
    infix notation, 236, 252, 254, 256–260
    internal vs. external, 250
    Kofu, 378
    Kotlin advantages, 2, 4, 6, 251, 405
    receivers, 244, 253, 256–260, 263–267
    scope, 265–267

semicolon (;) as optional, 5, 20, 251
    types and characteristics, 250
    XML builder, 262–267
duplication, reducing, 6
dynamic programming, with memoization, 279–281

E

Eclipse, 10
edge cases, 356
EditText, 396
Effective Java, 41, 80, 149
else
    nullable references, 87
    sealed classes, 145
    when as a statement, 61
    when as an expression, 60
Elvis operator (?:), 84, 86, 92
empirical testing, 353–356
emulators, Android applications, 388, 401
endInclusive, 230
endpoints, RESTful, 379
@Entity annotation, 380
entity classes, creating, 380
enum classes, 145–148
equality checks, 28, 88
equality operators, 28, 88
equals()
    about, 28, 40
    data classes, 129, 131
    implementation in Any, 79
    overloading, 224
    overriding, 88
    smart casting, 89–91
    using, 88
errors, see also exceptions
    scripts, 12
    testing, 357, 362
    treating warnings as, 25
escaping
    method or property names, 335
    strings, 30
    symbols with backslash (\), 29
event handlers, Android applications, 396–397
every(), 360, 365
exceptions, see also errors
    cancellations, 318, 324
    collections, 65

coroutines, 314–318, 324
equality checks, 28
exception handlers, setting up, 315
Java interop, 341–343
JSON parser, 362
NullPointerException, 28, 77, 80, 86
try-catch and Java interop, 341–343
try-catch as optional, 24
executors
creating, 294
running coroutines in a custom pool, 294–296
Executors API, 294
experimental features, using, 123, 297
expressions
functions as, 39–41
preferring over statements, 33–35
when as, 58–61, 87
<? extends T> syntax, 93
extension functions
about, 2
Any, 78–80
cautions, 229
DSLs, 252, 254–260
mocking, 359
overloading operators with, 223, 226–235
extension properties, 226, 228
extension receivers, 233
external iteration
arrays, 57, 65
collections, 54, 57, 64
forward, 55
imperative style, 53, 62
vs. internal iteration, 204–206
lists, 57, 72
maps, 75
ranges, 53–57
reverse iteration, 55
using, 53–58

F

factories, companion objects as, 125
factory suffix, 125
FAIR tests, 356–357
features, using experimental, 123, 297

Fibonacci sequence
infinite sequences, 216
Kotlin/Native example, 409–411
memoization example, 274–278
field keyword, 117
fields, see also back fields
creating, 115–116
defining, 114, 117
vs. properties, 115
synthesized, 117
@file:JvmName annotation, 345
files
creating Kotlin, 10
loading with REPL, 11
filter(), 56, 205–209, 214–215
final
as default for classes, 141
inline classes, 123
in Java, 26, 41
mocking final classes, 358
preferring, 41
final override, 141
findById(), 381
first, 233
first + other.first, 223
first(), 208, 214–215
flatMap(), 210
flatten(), 209
fold(), 270
for-each iterator, 64
forEach (Java), 64
forEach(), 205, 317
forall(), 357, 364
for loop, external iteration, 53, 55–57, 64, 75
forward iteration, 55, 230
for (x in ..) syntax, 55, 57
fully qualified names
singletons, 112
top-level functions, 345
fun keyword, 38, 122
function references, 179, 183–184, 214, 242
function signatures
autogenerating, 410
collisions, 345
functional composition, 176
functional interfaces, 109
functional pipeline and internal iteration, 205

Functional Programming in Java, 234
functional style
about, 175–178
internal iteration, 53
Kotlin advantages, 3–4, 6, 173
when to use, 178
functions, see also coroutines; extension functions; lambdas; methods; suspendible functions; testing; top-level functions
about, 37
with block body, 38, 42
composed, 234
creating, 38–43
default arguments, 37, 43–45, 343
defining parameters, 41
destructuring, 38, 49–51
as expressions, 39–41
extending, 2
function references, 179, 183–184, 214, 242
function signatures, autogenerating, 410
function signatures, collisions, 345
importing, 359
infix notation, 235
injecting methods into, 234, 276
inlining, 103, 123, 194–201
invoking as a member function, 245
named arguments, 37, 43, 45
names, 201
as optional, 22
parameter type specification, 22
returning functions, 184
sequential execution, 287
single-expression, 38
spread operator, 46, 48
syntax, 38
try-catch as optional, 24
with variable number of arguments, 38, 46–48

G

garbage collection, delegation, 161
gcc command, 410
GCC GNU compiler, 410
generateSequence(), 216

@GeneratedValue annotation, 380
generics
    classes, 127–129
    contravariance, 78, 94, 98, 101
    covariance, 78, 93, 96–98
    reified type parameters, 78, 101–103
    type safety, 78, 93–103
    variance, 78, 93–99
GET method, 378, 383–386
get()
    Android applications, 395
    arrays, 68
    key-value pairs, 74
    lists, 70
    overloading, 224
getAll(), 384
getOrDefault(), 74
getValue(), 75, 162–166
getters
    access permissions, 119
    backing fields, 117
    creating, 116
    creating properties, 114
    inheritance, 141–144
    Java interop, 331, 334
    names, 345
    synthesized, 114, 118
GNU compiler, 410
Gradle
    Android applications, 389
    code coverage, 371
    compiling with, 7, 330
    installing, 351
    Scripts, 389
    specifying main class, 372
    Spring application setup, 376
    testing, canary, 353
    testing, failure messages, 357
    testing, setup, 349–351
gradlew, 351
gradlew.bat file, 351
Groovy, memoization, 275–277
groupBy(), 212

H
H2 library, 376, 380
hasNext(), 231, 306
hashCode(), 40, 79, 129, 131

hashMapOf(), 73
hashSetOf(), 72
headers property, 410
Hello World example, 8–13
-help option, 406
HTML builder, 261
HTML5 canvas WebAssembly example, 413–416
HTTP methods, 378, 383–386

I
-i option (Gradle), 357
@id annotation, 380
id property, Spring applications, 380, 383
identifiers, coroutines, 299
IDEs
    Android Studio IDE, 387–403
    boilerplate, 5
    included in IntelliJ IDEA, 7
    running in, 10, 14
    versions, 10
if
    as an expression, 34
    smart casting, 90
imperative style
    about, 175–178
    external iteration, 53, 62
    Kotlin advantages, 4, 6
    when to use, xv, 178
implicit receivers, 243–247, 253, 256–260
import, 359
inc(), 224
index
    iterating over collections, 57, 65
    operator ([]), 68, 70, 74
index operator ([])
    arrays, 68
    key-value pairs, 74
    lists, 70
IndexedValue, 65
indices property, 58
infinite sequences, 213, 216, 303–306
infix notation
    about, 5
    DSLs, 236, 252, 254, 256–260
    reverse iteration, 55

testing, 353
using, 235
inheritance
    about, 4
    adapters, 399
    classes, 140–145, 353
    vs. delegation, 148–152, 154–155
    interfaces, 135
    KotlinTest, 353
    type invariance, 95
init blocks
    generic classes, 128
    using, 119
init() method, 353–354
initialization
    code, 119
    generic classes, 128
    late, 276
injecting
    with extension functions, 226–235, 276
    methods into functions, 234, 276
    with properties, 226, 228
    static methods, 227, 231
    third-party classes, 228–231
    from within a class, 232–234
inline, 103, 123, 194–201
inlining
    classes, 122, 199
    functions, 103, 123, 194–201
    methods, 199
    properties, 199
    reified type parameters, 103
in operator
    injecting with extension functions, 226
    lists, 70
    sets, 73
inner classes
    anonymous, 109, 140, 148
    nested lambdas, 245
    objects as anonymous, 109
    using, 138–140
inner keyword, 138–140
installation
    Gradle, 351
    Kotlin, 7
    Kotlin/Native, 409

Maven, 351
WebAssembly, 413
instances
    creating in derived classes, 145
    creating in generic classes, 128
    creating with class name, 114
    creating with create(), 126
Int?, 82
intArrayOf(), 57, 69
integration testing, 363, 370
IntelliJ IDEA, 7, 10, 405
interaction testing, 347, 359–361
interfaces
    vs. abstract classes, 137
    anonymous inner classes, 109
    collections, 63–66
    creating, 134–136
    delegation and method collisions, 158
    inline classes, 123
    singletons, 111
    Spring repository interfaces, 381
internal, 119, 122
internal iteration
    about, 53, 58
    collections, 67, 203–218
    common functions, 206–213
    vs. external iteration, 204–206
    lambdas, 203–218
    lists, 72
    performance, 203, 213
    sequences, 203, 213–218
internationalization, 389
interop, *see also* Java interop
    C, 409–411
    JavaScript, 415
IntProgression, 55–56
IntRange, 54, 56
invariance, type, 93–95
invoke(), 224, 353
is operator, 88–91
isActive, 318, 322
isAssigned, 131
isEnabled, 396
it implicit parameter, 181, 183

iteration, *see also* external iteration; internal iteration
    arrays, 57, 65
    enum classes, 146
    with extension functions, 230
    forward, 55, 230
    infinite sequences, 305–306
    iterators as anonymous object, 230
    key-value pairs, 73
    lambdas, 203–218
    lists, 57, 72
    maps, 75, 317
    performance, 203, 213
    ranges, 53–57
    reverse iteration, 55
    sequences, 203, 213–218, 305–306
    in testing example, 366
iterator(), 231, 305–306

J

Jackson-kotlin library, 376
Jacoco, 347, 350, 371
jacoco plugin, 350
JAR files
    jar option, 9
    Java interop, 330
    xf option, 406
jar option, 9
Java, *see also* Java Development Kit (JDK); Java interop
    collections, 64, 335
    converting for Android applications, 387
    delegation, 153–154
    imperative style, 175
    Kotlin basics for, 19–35
    overloaded operators, 337, 344
    similarities to Kotlin, 2
    versions, xviii, 8
Java Development Kit (JDK)
    collections, 335
    concurrency with, 4, 294
    Executors API, 294
    programming Android applications, 387
    version, 7
Java interop
    about, 3, 329
    annotations, 345
    calling Java from Kotlin, 329, 333–336

    calling Kotlin from Java, 329, 336–346
    compilation, joint, 5, 14, 330–333, 337
    exceptions, 341–343
    functions with default arguments, 343
    java tool, 8, 26, 332
    Kotlin advantages, 5–6, 329, 346
    name conflicts, 334
    overloaded operators, 337, 344
    passing lambdas, 340
    static methods, creating, 339
    top-level functions, 344
java tool
    building Spring applications, 379
    compiler warnings, 26
    interop with, 8, 332
Java Virtual Machine (JVM)
    compiling Kotlin code, 5, 14
    wrapping classes for, 23
.javaClass call, 21
JavaScript
    transpiling to, 2, 5, 13–14, 405–408
    WebAssembly example, 415
jcenter repository, 350–351
JetBrains, 1, 10
joinToString(), 208
JPA library, 376
jsinterop tool, 415
JSON
    Android applications, 389–390
    canned response, 360
    parsing, 310, 350–351, 358, 389–390
    parsing test, 361–363
@json annotation, 361
JUnit, 348, 350
@JvmDefault annotation, 135, 345
@JvmOverloads annotation, 344
@JvmStatic annotation, 127, 332, 339

K

key-value pairs
    about, 64
    creating, 73

destructuring, 51, 75
iteration, 73
using, 73–75
Klaxon library
Android applications,
389–390
JSON parser, 310, 351,
361, 389–390
Kofu DSL, 378
Kotlin
about, xv–xvi, 1
advantages, 1–7, 403
basics, 19–35
executing code, 7
installing, 7
as polyglot language, xv,
1
similarities to Java, 2
styles, xv, 3, 6
transpiling to JavaScript,
2, 5, 13–14, 405–408
versions, xviii, 8, 10
kotlin package, 57
kotlin plugin for Gradle, 350
Kotlin SDK, installing, 7
Kotlin standard library
adding to classpath when
compiling, 9
joint compilation, 337,
341
kotlin tool, 9, 14, 26, 332
kotlin-maven-plugin, 351
kotlin-stdlib.jar file, 9
kotlin.collections package, 64
kotlin.js file, 406
kotlin.jvm package, 345
kotlin.meta.js file, 406
kotlin.ranges package, 54–55
Kotlin/Native
about, 5, 13–14
installing, 409
using, 409–411
WebAssembly, compiling
to, 413–416
$KOTLIN_PATH environment
variable, 9, 406
%KOTLIN_PATH% environment
variable, 9, 333, 406
kotlinc-js, 406
kotlinc-jvm
compiling with, 5, 7, 14,
337
coroutines, 289

running scripts with, 12,
14
warnings, 26
kotlinc-native compiler, 411, 416
KotlinTest, see also testing
about, 347–348
assertion options, 353
data-driven testing, 356
Gradle setup, 350
Maven setup, 351
kotlinx.coroutines package, 289,
367
Kotlinx.html, 262
kotlinx.interop.wasm.dom package,
415
kscript library, 13
.kt extension, 9
Kt suffix, 9

L
-l option, 410
labels, explicit, 192, 201
lambdas, see also coroutines
vs. anonymous functions,
186–188
Any methods, 236–243
assuming block expres-
sions with = operator,
42
closures, 188–189
computing array values
example, 69
crossinline, 199–201
defined, 179
delegation, 168–170
DSL builders, 263–267
filter(), 57
implicit receivers, 243–
247, 253
inlining functions, 103,
194–201
invoking as a member
function, 245
iteration, 203–218
Java interop, 340
as last parameter, 44,
48, 182, 213, 252
memoization with, 275–
277
multiline, 179, 182
nested, 245
noinline parameters, 197
non-local return, 191,
193, 201
passing, 179, 252, 340
receiving, 181–183

return keyword, 190–194,
201
storing for reuse, 186
structure and syntax,
179
using, 179–186
languages, see DSLs
last(), 209
lateinit, 276
launch()
Android applications, 397
asynchronous program-
ming with coroutines,
326
context, 293
coroutines names, 299
exception handling, 314–
316
launching tasks, 290
timeouts, 326
layouts, Android applications,
389, 391–395
LAZY coroutines, 296
Lazy delegate, 166–169
lazy evaluation, sequences,
203, 213–218
lazy function, 168
LazyThreadSafetyMode, 168
let(), 79, 236–239, 241, 254
lexical scoping
continuations, 303
lambdas, 188–189, 238,
244
receivers, 245
linkedMapOf(), 73
LinkedHashSet, 72
linkerOpts property, 410
Liskov's Substitution Principle (LSP), 95, 150, 154
List
about, 64
using, 70–72
views, 66
listOf(), 57, 70–71, 335
listOf<T>(), 103
lists
about, 64
accessing elements, 70
convenience methods, 64
converting to arrays, 49
creating, 57, 70–71
creating mutable, 70–71
flattening, 209
iteration, 57, 72
modifying, 70, 72

nested, 209
spread operator, 48
using, 70–72
views, 65
when as an expression, 60
local variables
delegation, 162–164, 170
destructuring, 131
LSP (Liskov's Substitution
Principle), 95, 150, 154

M

MacOS, Kotlin/Native example, 409–411
main()
joint compilation exam-
ple, 332
parameter as optional, 8
Spring applications, 376
WebAssembly example,
415
Main-Class manifest attribute, 9
manifests folder, 388–389
Map
about, 64
delegation, 164–166
destructuring, 51
using, 73–75
map()
internal iteration with,
206–211, 214, 317
lazy sequences, 215
Pair example, 67
testing example, 366
mapOf(), 73
maps
about, 64
creating, 73
delegation, 75, 164–166
destructuring, 75
flattening, 210
iteration, 75, 206–211,
214, 317
lazy sequences, 215
using, 73–75
views, 65
margins, trimming for multiline strings, 32
Maven
code coverage, 371
compiling with, 7, 330
installing, 351
specifying main class,
372
Spring application setup,
376

testing, canary, 353
testing, setup, 349, 351
maven-compiler-plugin, 351
mavenCentral repository,
350–351, 368
McCarthy, John, 167
measureTimeMillis(), 311
members, class, 124
memoization, 269, 274–281
memoize() function, 276
meta-annotations, 376
methods, see also extension
functions; functions
abstract, 134, 136–137
access modifiers, 119
anonymous inner classes,
creating, 140
calling on singletons, 111
chaining with apply(), 239
companion objects, 126
creating, 38
data classes, 129
default, 135, 345
defined, 37
defining, 122
delegation and method
collisions, 157–159
enum classes, 146
extending, 2
infix notation, 235
injecting into functions,
234, 276
injecting with extension
functions, 226, 234,
276
inline classes, 123
inlining, 199
invoking lambdas as a
member function, 245
names, escaping, 335
open, 141
overriding, 135, 137,
141, 157
parameter type specifica-
tion, 22
as public by default,
119, 122
testing, empirical, 353–
356
Meyer, Bertrand, 154
microservices, 4
Minimum API Level, 388
minus operator (-)
lists, 71
maps, 74
overloading, 222

minus(), 224
Mockito, 358
Mockk, 347, 350–351, 358–
363, 368–370
mockkObject(), 359
mocks
defined, 358
testing with, 357–363,
365, 368–370
tools, 347, 350–351, 358
modulepath option, 333
multiline lambdas, 179, 182
multiline strings, 31–33
mutability
cautions, 27
collection views, 65
collections, 63–66
lists, 70–71
maps, 73
properties, 115–118
sets, 72
variables, 26–28
variables in closures, 189
mutableListOf(), 70–71
mutableListOf<T>(), 103
mutableMapOf(), 73
mutableSetOf(), 72
MutableList, 66, 71
MutableMap, 73, 164–166
MutableSet, 72
mvn package, 351

N

name property, enum classes,
146
named arguments, 2, 37, 43,
45
names
companion objects, 125
conflicts in Java interop,
334
coroutines, 299
enum classes, 146
escaping, 335
extension functions con-
flicts, 227
fully qualified names,
112, 345
functions, 201
functions, top-level, 112,
345
getters, 345
labels, 192, 201
named arguments, 2, 37,
43, 45

parameters, 118
properties, 118, 335
setters, 345
singletons, 112
variables, 22, 26, 222, 225
variables in overloading operators, 222, 225
nativelib library, 416
nested classes, *see* inner classes
NetBeans, 10
NetBeans Kotlin Plugin, 10
newSingleThreadExecutor(), 295
next(), 231, 306
Node.js
transpiling JavaScript, 407
WebAssembly example, 413
noinline, 197
non-local return, 191, 193, 198, 201
none(), 180
not(), 224
not-null assertion operator (!!), 83, 86
Nothing, 78–79
notifyDataSetChanged(), 400
npm init, 413
null
checking for, 83
Elvis operator (?:), 84, 86, 92
equality checks, 28
explicit casting, 92
get() return type, 74
mapping nullable types to bytecode, 82
not-null assertion operator (!!), 83, 86
operators, 77
safe-call operator (.?), 83–85
safe-call operator (?.), 86
smart casting, 90
type inference, 4
type safety, 77, 80–87
using nullable types, 82–86
using when, 86
NullPointerException, 28, 77, 80, 86

O

object keyword, 108, 110
object-oriented programming
hierarchies of abstraction, 134
Kotlin advantages, 3, 105
objects, *see also* companion objects; singletons
anonymous, 108–109, 230
creating, 108, 114
grouping during internal iteration, 212
ordering, 127
passing with let(), 241
using, 107–113
observable delegate, 166, 169
observable() method, 169
OCP (Open-Closed Principle), 87, 154
onCreate(), 395
onCreateViewHolder(), 399
open
annotating classes as, 133
class inheritance, 141
classes in Spring, 376
methods, 141
Open-Closed Principle (OCP), 87, 154
operator keyword, 224, 236
operator overloading, *see* overloading operators
operators, *see also* overloading operators
infix notation, 235
injecting with extension functions, 227
optimization problems, *see* rod-cutting problem
Optional, 80
optionalParameter, 237
order
default arguments, 44
destructuring, 50, 131
init blocks, 119
objects, 127
overloading operators, 223
parameters, 44
properties in data classes, 130–131
sorting collections during internal iteration, 211
when as an expression, 60

ordinal property, enum classes, 146
outer classes
accessing members of, 139
nested lambdas, 245
-output option, 406
overloading operators
about, 2
cautions, 222, 225, 254
DSLs, 254
extension functions, 223, 226–235
generic classes, 128
groupBy(), 212
Java, 337, 344
mapping table, 224
using, 222–226
override keyword, 137, 157
overriding
abstract methods, 135, 137
access restrictions, 143
classes, 141, 143, 147
enum classes, 147
methods, 135, 137, 141, 157
properties, 141

P

Pair
about, 63–64
creating instance of, 66
generic classes example, 127
using, 66–68
parallelism
Android applications, 397
vs. concurrency, 286
parameters, *see also* default arguments
compiler warnings, 24
constraints, 93, 99–101
crossinline, 199–201
defining, 41
delegation, 156
extending functions and methods, 2
implicit, 181, 183
implicit receivers, 244
infix notation, 236
initialization code, 119
iteration with lambdas, 207
lambdas as last, 44, 48, 182, 213, 252

lambdas with multiple, 244
lambdas, passing as, 180
lambdas, receiving, 181–183
main() parameter as optional, 8
names, 118
noinline, 197
order of, 44
reified type, 78, 101–103, 194
star projection, 101
type inference, 41, 180, 186
type specification, 22, 37, 41
val vs. var, 41
variable number of arguments, 46
parenthesis (())
anonymous functions, 187
lambdas, 180, 182, 187, 213, 252
as optional, 5, 235, 252, 254, 256–260
parse(), 362
parse<T>, 103
parsers
Android applications, 389–390
JSON, 310, 350–351, 358, 389–390
JSON, testing, 361–363
performance
internal iteration, 203, 213
lambdas, 194
recursion, 270
sequences, 214–216
permissions
access modifiers, 119, 122, 143
explicit permissions for base classes, 141
plus operator (+)
iteration with extension functions, 230
Java interop example, 337
lists, 71
maps, 74
overloading, 222, 337
sets, 73

plus()
Java interop example, 337
overloading operators, 223–225, 337
plusAssign(), 224
pom.xml file, 351, 376
POST method, 378, 385
Practices of an Agile Developer, 25
The Pragmatic Programmer, 154
println(), 40
private, 119, 122
projects
creating Kotlin, 10
creating for Android applications, 388–390
properties, *see also* destructuring
abstract classes, 137
annotating in Spring applications, 380
data classes, 129–132
defining, 114
delegation, 160, 162, 164–166
enum classes, 146
extension, 226, 228
vs. fields, 115
initialization code, 119
injecting, 226, 228
inlining, 123, 199
interfaces, 137
methods, 122
mutable, 115–118
names, 118
names, escaping, 335
overriding, 141
property collisions and receivers, 247
as public by default, 119
read-only, 114
singletons, 111
skipping while destructuring, 50
val, 115
var, 115
protected, 119, 122
public, as default, 114, 119, 122

Q
question mark (?), nullable type suffix, 82
quotes
double quotes (""") for multiline strings, 31
double quotes for raw strings ("""), 30

R
rangeTo(), 224
ranges
classes, 54
creating, 54
index values, 58
iteration, 53–57, 230
skipping values, 56
when as an expression, 60
read-evaluate-print loop (REPL), 10, 14
readFile(), 342
readability
with Any methods, 236–243
costs, 221
implicit receivers, 243–247
infix notation, 235
injecting, 226–235
Kotlin advantages, 221
named arguments, 37, 45
names, 222, 225
overloading operators, 222–226
when as an expression, 59
ReadOnlyProperty, 163
ReadWriteProperty, 163
receivers
Any methods, 237
dispatch, 233
DSL builders, 263–267
DSLs, 244, 253, 256–260, 263–267
explicitly referring, 247
extension, 233
implicit, 243–247, 253, 256–260
injecting from within classes, 233
passing, 244
property collisions, 247
scope, 245, 265–267
recursion
dynamic programming with memoization, 279–281

tail call optimization, 216, 269, 271–274
using, 269–274
RecyclerView, 392–395, 397–401
RecyclerView.Adapter<T>, 399
RecyclerView.ViewHolder, 399
Rediscovering JavaScript, 405
reduce(), 206–208
referential equality, 28
reified, 103
reified type parameters, 78, 101–103, 194
rem(), 224
REPL, 10, 14
repositories, Spring applications interfaces, 381
@RequestMapping annotation, 379
resources for this book
annotations, 346
APIs, 415
DSLs, 249
Eclipse, 10
Kotlin, 10
Kotlin/Native, 409
source code, xix, 349, 352, 373
@RestController annotation, 379
RESTful web services, Spring Boot, 376–386
result, 238
return keyword
anonymous functions, 190
lambdas, 190–194, 201
non-local return, 191, 193, 198, 201
single-expression functions, 38
specifying in block body, 42
return types
inferring, 38, 41
specifying, 22, 39–40, 42
storing lambdas, 186
reverse iteration, 55
rod-cutting problem, 274, 279–281
root(), 263
row(), 364
run(), 79, 236–240, 254, 263
runApplication(), 377
runBlocking()
context, 293–295, 297

continuations, 302
coroutines names, 299
suspending functions, 292
syntax, 289–292
testing coroutines, 366, 372
timeouts, 326
wrapping main() in, 311
runBlocking<Unit>, 302
running
from command line, 7–8
in IDEs, 10, 14
scripts, 11–14

S

safe-call operator (?.), 83–86
scope
Any methods, 238
continuations, 303
coroutines, 300, 314, 319, 395, 397
DSL builders, 265–267
extension functions, 234
labeled return, 192
lambdas, 188–189, 238, 244
receivers, 245, 265–267
when and variable scope, 61
-script option, 12, 14
scripts
Kotlin advantages, 3, 17
kscript library, 13
running, 11–14
transpiling JavaScript, 407
when to use, 23
sealed classes, 133, 144
secondary constructors, 120
semicolon (;)
enum classes, 146
as optional, 5, 20, 251
separating paths in classpath, 333
Spring applications, 377
sequence() function, 217, 304
sequences
vs. collections, 213, 215
infinite, 213, 216, 303–306
lazy evaluation, 203, 213–218
service, 384
@Service annotation, 383

services, Spring applications, 375–386
Set, 64, 72
set(), 68, 224
setOf(), 72
setValue(), 75, 162–166
sets
about, 64
creating, 72
using, 72
views, 65
setters
access permissions, 119
backing fields, 117
creating, 116
inheritance, 141–144
Java interop, 331
names, 345
synthesized, 118
shebang (#!), 12, 14
short-circuit evaluation, 167
shouldBe, 353
side effects
defined, 33
delegation, 160
statements, 33
single abstract method interfaces, 109
Singleton Design Pattern, 107
singletons, *see also* companion objects
calling methods on, 111
creating, 110
function references, 184
mocking dependencies, 359
names, 112
Singleton Design Pattern, 107
static methods, 339
vs. top-level functions, 112
type inference, 40
size property, arrays, 69
skipping
execution with Lazy delegation, 166–169
to end of lambda, 191
properties in destructuring, 50
values when iterating ranges, 56
sleep(), 24
Sletten, Brian, 77
smart casting, 78, 87, 89–91

sortedBy(), 211
sortedByDescending(), 212
sortedMapOf(), 73
sortedSetOf(), 72
source files, 349, 388
spaces, trimming for multiline
    strings, 32
spread operator, 46, 48
Spring
    about, 4
    Initializer website, 376
    Kotlin API, 6
    Kotlin support, 6
    programming applica-
        tions, 375–386
Spring Boot RESTful web
    service, 376–386
Spring-fu, 378
src attribute, 414
StackOverflowError, 216
star projection <*>, 101
start, 230, 414
start at, 259
start by, 259
state
    enum classes, 146
    inner classes, 140
    interfaces advantages,
        137
    reusing in abstract class-
        es, 137
    singletons, 113
statements
    preferring expressions to,
        33–35
    when as, 61
static methods
    annotating, 127, 332,
        339
    companion objects, 126,
        134, 136, 231, 339
    creating, 339
    injecting with extension
        functions, 227, 231
    interfaces, 134, 136
    joint compilation, 332
step(), 56
string templates, 29, 31
String?, 82
strings
    escaping, 30
    handling raw, 30–33
    multiline, 31–33

ranges, 54
    string templates, 29, 31
StringSpec, 353
structural equality, 28
*Structure and Interpretation of
    Computer Programs*, 271
structured concurrency, 314
subroutines vs. coroutines,
    286
sum(), 208
<? super T> syntax, 94
super@Outer, 140
supervisorScope, 324
supervisors, coroutine cancel-
    lations, 324
suspend keyword
    functions, 291, 302, 335
    programming Android
        applications, 395
    testing coroutines, 366
suspend() method, 100, 335
suspendible functions
    about, 285
    cancellations, 318
    continuations, 301–303
    Java interop, 335
    switching threads, 296
    using, 291–293
Swing, Dispatchers.Main context,
    293
Synchronized annotation, 345

T

tail call optimization
    about, 269
    infinite sequences, 216
    using, 271–274
tailrec, 216, 271–274
take(), 217
-target wasm32, 413
targets, compiling to different
    targets, 13
TaskRepository, 381
tasks
    launching in coroutines,
        290
    Spring applications, 376–
        386
tasks() method, 379, 384
templates
    Android applications lay-
        outs, 393
    string, 29, 31
test files, 349

testing
    about, 347
    calling Kotlin from Java,
        336
    canary testing, 352
    code coverage, 347, 350,
        371
    coroutines, 347, 359,
        366–373
    data-driven tests, 356
    dependencies, 357–363,
        365, 368–370
    design, 354
    edge cases, 356
    empirical, 353–356
    FAIR tests, 356–357
    integration testing, 363,
        370
    interaction testing, 347,
        359–361
    with mocks, 347, 350–
        351, 357–363, 365,
        368–370
    parsing data, 361–363
    setup, 349–352
    test files, 349
    tools, 347–348, 350, 358
    top-level functions, 347,
        363–366
TextView, 391–395, 400
TextWatcher, 397
third-party classes
    injecting, 228–231
    injecting from within
        classes, 232–234
    injecting static methods,
        231
    overloading operators, 2,
        223, 226–235
this expression
    accessing members of
        outer classes, 139
    Any methods, 237
    DSLs, 254, 258
    injecting from within
        classes, 233
    memoization, 276
    nested lambdas, 246
    overloading operators,
        223
this.second, 233
this@Outer, 233
this@Point, 233
this@top, 247
threads
    Android applications,
        391, 397

companion object and
  thread safety, 124
coroutines, 293–298
coroutines, testing, 366
creating single thread executor, 294
printing details, 298
switching after suspen-
  sion points, 296
views and thread safety,
  66
throws, Java interop, 341–343
@Throws annotation, 343
tilde (~) for multiline strings,
  33
TimeoutCancellationException, 325
timeouts, coroutines, 325
times(), 224
to(), 66, 73, 79
to...Array(), 49
toString()
  about, 40
  data classes, 129, 131
  implementation in Any, 79
to parameter, contravariance,
  98
TodoApplication, 377
top-level functions
  Java interop, 344
  names, 112, 345
  vs. singletons, 112
  testing, 347, 363–366
@Transactional annotation, 383
Transient annotation, 345
transpiling to JavaScript, 2,
  5, 13–14, 405–408
TreeSet, 72
trimMargin(), 32
Triple
  about, 63–64
  destructuring example,
    49
  using, 66–67
try-Kotlin, 261
try-catch
  as an expression, 34
  Java interop, 341–343
  as optional, 24
  parsing JSON, 363
tuples
  defined, 66
  Pair, 64, 66–68
  Triple, 64, 66–67

type checking
  DSLs, 2
  with Nothing, 78–79
  using, 87–89
  with when, 90
type inference
  about, 4, 21
  functions, 37–38, 41, 185
  functions that return
    functions, 185
  lambdas, 180, 186
  parameters, 41, 180, 186
  short functions, 38
  Unit type, 40, 79
  variables, 26
type invariance, 93–95
type projection, see use-site
  variance
type safety, see also type
  checking
  with Any, 77–80
  DSL builders, 260–265
  explicit casting, 78, 91–
    93, 362
  generics, 78, 93–103
  Kotlin advantages, 4, 6
  null references, 77, 80–
    87
  reified type parameters,
    78, 101–103
  smart casting, 78, 87,
    89–91
  star projection, 101
type specification
  destructuring, 131
  explicit, 22
  as optional, 21
  parameters, 22, 37, 41
(types list) -> output type syntax,
  181

U
UI
  Android applications,
    396–397
  Swing, 293
unaryMinus(), 224
unaryPlus(), 224
underscore (_), skipping
  properties while destructuring, 50
UNDISPATCHED coroutines, 296
unit testing, see testing
Unit type, 40, 42, 79
UnsupportedOperationException, 65
until(), 56

use(), 295
use-site variance, 93, 97, 99
useAndClose(), 100
useJunitPlatform {}, 350
@UseExperimental, 297

V
val
  abstract classes, 137
  delegation, 160
  destructuring, 131
  iterating over ranges, 55
  parameters and, 41
  preferring over var, 26–
    28, 30, 160
  properties, 115
  properties, overriding,
    141
  when and variable scope,
    62
values, see also key-value
  pairs
  enum classes, 146
  external iteration, 53–58
  skipping when iterating
    ranges, 56
  when as an expression, 60
values(), 146
var
  abstract classes, 137
  delegation, 160
  destructuring, 131
  parameters and, 41
  preferring val over, 26–
    28, 30, 160
  properties, 115
  properties, extension,
    228
  properties, overriding,
    141
vararg, 46–48
variables
  creating as mutable or
    immutable, 26–28
  delegation, 162–164, 170
  destructuring, 49–51,
    131
  mutable variables in clo-
    sures, 189
  names, 22, 26, 222, 225
  names in overloading op-
    erators, 222, 225
  storing lambdas, 186
  type inference, 26
  type specification as op-
    tional, 21
  when as a statement, 61

variance, *see also* contravariance; covariance
  declaration-site, 93, 97
  generics, 78, 93–99
  use-site, 93, 97, 99
verify(), 360
vetoable delegate, 166, 170
vetoable() method, 170
View, 399
views
  Android applications, 397–401
  collections, 65
  lists, 65
  maps, 65
  sets, 65
virtual machines, compiling on, 5, 13–14, 413–416
void, 40, 79, 243
Volatile annotation, 345

W

warnings
  compiler, 24–26
  equality checks, 29
  treating as errors, 25
Wasm, *see* WebAssembly
wasm attribute, 414
wasm directory, 413
web servers, WebAssembly example, 413–416
WebAssembly
  compiling to, 5, 13–14, 413–416
  installing, 413
-Werror option, 25
WET (Write Every Time) anti-pattern, 185
when
  about, 88
  argument matching with, 54, 58–62
  cautions, 60
  as an expression, 58–61, 87
  nullable reference, 86
  sealed classes, 145
  smart casting with, 90
  as a statement, 61
  type checking with, 90
  variable scope, 61
where, parametric type constraints, 99–101
withContext(), 297, 321, 367
withContext(NonCancellable), 321
withIndex(), 58, 65
withTimeout(), 326
Write Every Time (WET) anti-pattern, 185

X

XML, DSL builder, 262–267

Y

yield()
  infinite sequences, 217, 304, 306
  suspendible functions, 291–293, 297

Thank you!

How did you enjoy this book? Please let us know. Take a moment and email us at support@pragprog.com with your feedback. Tell us your story and you could win free ebooks. Please use the subject line "Book Feedback."

Ready for your next great Pragmatic Bookshelf book? Come on over to https://pragprog.com and use the coupon code BUYANOTHER2019 to save 30% on your next ebook.

Void where prohibited, restricted, or otherwise unwelcome. Do not use ebooks near water. If rash persists, see a doctor. Doesn't apply to *The Pragmatic Programmer* ebook because it's older than the Pragmatic Bookshelf itself. Side effects may include increased knowledge and skill, increased marketability, and deep satisfaction. Increase dosage regularly.

And thank you for your continued support,

Andy Hunt, Publisher

Rediscovering JavaScript

JavaScript is no longer to be feared or loathed—the world's most popular and ubiquitous language has evolved into a respectable language. Whether you're writing frontend applications or server-side code, the phenomenal features from ES6 and beyond—like the rest operator, generators, destructuring, object literals, arrow functions, modern classes, promises, async, and metaprogramming capabilities—will get you excited and eager to program with JavaScript. You've found the right book to get started quickly and dive deep into the essence of modern JavaScript. Learn practical tips to apply the elegant parts of the language and the gotchas to avoid.

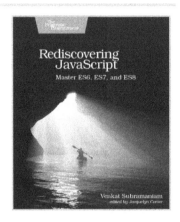

Venkat Subramaniam
(286 pages) ISBN: 9781680505467. $45.95
https://pragprog.com/book/ves6

Test-Driving JavaScript Applications

Debunk the myth that JavaScript is not easily testable. Whether you use Node.js, Express, MongoDB, jQuery, AngularJS, or directly manipulate the DOM, you can test-drive JavaScript. Learn the craft of writing meaningful, deterministic automated tests with Karma, Mocha, and Chai. Test asynchronous JavaScript, decouple and properly mock out dependencies, measure code coverage, and create lightweight modular designs of both server-side and client-side code. Your investment in writing tests will pay high dividends as you create code that's predictable and cost-effective to change.

Venkat Subramaniam
(362 pages) ISBN: 9781680501742. $38
https://pragprog.com/book/vsjavas

Practical Security

Most security professionals don't have the words "security" or "hacker" in their job title. Instead, as a developer or admin you often have to fit in security alongside your official responsibilities — building and maintaining computer systems. Implement the basics of good security now, and you'll have a solid foundation if you bring in a dedicated security staff later. Identify the weaknesses in your system, and defend against the attacks most likely to compromise your organization, without needing to become a trained security professional.

Roman Zabicki
(132 pages) ISBN: 9781680506341. $26.95
https://pragprog.com/book/rzsecur

Small, Sharp Software Tools

The command-line interface is making a comeback. That's because developers know that all the best features of your operating system are hidden behind a user interface designed to help average people use the computer. But you're not the average user, and the CLI is the most efficient way to get work done fast. Turn tedious chores into quick tasks: read and write files, manage complex directory hierarchies, perform network diagnostics, download files, work with APIs, and combine individual programs to create your own workflows. Put down that mouse, open the CLI, and take control of your software development environment.

Brian P. Hogan
(326 pages) ISBN: 9781680502961. $38.95
https://pragprog.com/book/bhcldev

Test-Driven React

You work in a loop: write code, get feedback, iterate. The faster you get feedback, the faster you can learn and become a more effective developer. Test-Driven React helps you refine your React workflow to give you the feedback you need as quickly as possible. Write strong tests and run them continuously as you work, split complex code up into manageable pieces, and stay focused on what's important by automating away mundane, trivial tasks. Adopt these techniques and you'll be able to avoid productivity traps and start building React components at a stunning pace!

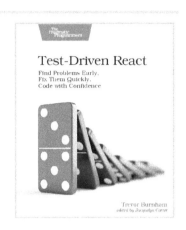

Trevor Burnham

(190 pages) ISBN: 9781680506464. $45.95

https://pragprog.com/book/tbreact

Programming WebAssembly with Rust

WebAssembly fulfills the long-awaited promise of web technologies: fast code, type-safe at compile time, execution in the browser, on embedded devices, or anywhere else. Rust delivers the power of C in a language that strictly enforces type safety. Combine both languages and you can write for the web like never before! Learn how to integrate with JavaScript, run code on platforms other than the browser, and take a step into IoT. Discover the easy way to build cross-platform applications without sacrificing power, and change the way you write code for the web.

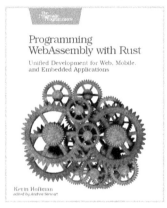

Kevin Hoffman

(238 pages) ISBN: 9781680506365. $45.95

https://pragprog.com/book/khrust

Programming Elm

Elm brings the safety and stability of functional pro-
graming to front-end development, making it one of
the most popular new languages. Elm's functional nature and static typing means that runtime errors are
nearly impossible, and it compiles to JavaScript for
easy web deployment. This book helps you take advantage of this new language in your web site development.
Learn how the Elm Architecture will help you create
fast applications. Discover how to integrate Elm with
JavaScript so you can update legacy applications. See
how Elm tooling makes deployment quicker and easier.

Jeremy Fairbank
(308 pages) ISBN: 9781680502855. $40.95
https://pragprog.com/book/jfelm

Technical Blogging, Second Edition

Successful technical blogging is not easy but it's also
not magic. Use these techniques to attract and keep
an audience of loyal, regular readers. Leverage this
popularity to reach your goals and amplify your influence in your field. Get more users for your startup or
open source project, or simply find an outlet to share
your expertise. This book is your blueprint, with step-
by-step instructions that leave no stone unturned.
Plan, create, maintain, and promote a successful blog
that will have remarkable effects on your career or
business.

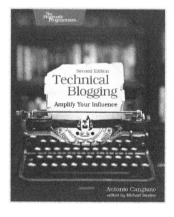

Antonio Cangiano
(336 pages) ISBN: 9781680506471. $47.95
https://pragprog.com/book/actb2

The Pragmatic Bookshelf

The Pragmatic Bookshelf features books written by developers for developers. The titles continue the well-known Pragmatic Programmer style and continue to garner awards and rave reviews. As development gets more and more difficult, the Pragmatic Programmers will be there with more titles and products to help you stay on top of your game.

Visit Us Online

This Book's Home Page
https://pragprog.com/book/vskotlin
Source code from this book, errata, and other resources. Come give us feedback, too!

Keep Up to Date
https://pragprog.com
Join our announcement mailing list (low volume) or follow us on twitter @pragprog for new titles, sales, coupons, hot tips, and more.

New and Noteworthy
https://pragprog.com/news
Check out the latest pragmatic developments, new titles and other offerings.

Save on the eBook

Save on the eBook versions of this title. Owning the paper version of this book entitles you to purchase the electronic versions at a terrific discount.

PDFs are great for carrying around on your laptop—they are hyperlinked, have color, and are fully searchable. Most titles are also available for the iPhone and iPod touch, Amazon Kindle, and other popular e-book readers.

Buy now at *https://pragprog.com/coupon*

Contact Us

Online Orders:	*https://pragprog.com/catalog*
Customer Service:	*support@pragprog.com*
International Rights:	*translations@pragprog.com*
Academic Use:	*academic@pragprog.com*
Write for Us:	*http://write-for-us.pragprog.com*
Or Call:	+1 800-699-7764

Milton Keynes UK
Ingram Content Group UK Ltd.
UKHW031103190724
445808UK00008B/155